Private Security and the Investigative Process

Fourth Edition

Private Security and the Investigative Process

Fourth Edition

by
Charles P. Nemeth

CRC Press
Taylor & Francis Group
Boca Raton London New York

CRC Press is an imprint of the
Taylor & Francis Group, an **informa** business

CRC Press
Taylor & Francis Group
6000 Broken Sound Parkway NW, Suite 300
Boca Raton, FL 33487-2742

First issued in paperback 2021

ISBN 13: 978-0-367-77652-7 (pbk)
ISBN 13: 978-1-138-48964-6 (hbk)

**Visit the Taylor & Francis Web site at
http://www.taylorandfrancis.com**

**and the CRC Press Web site at
http://www.crcpress.com**

To my sons Stephen and Joseph—about to embark on new directions in defense and law—I could not be prouder. Godspeed in these extraordinary changes!

To St. Thomas Aquinas who remarked:

We see and judge of all things in the light of the first truth, forasmuch as the light itself of our mind, whether natural or gratuitous, is nothing else than the impression of the first truth upon it ….

(Summa Theologica, I, Question 88 at Article 2)

Contents

Preface

Composing the fourth edition to any published work says a great deal about the need for a text in the subject matter but also the strength and loyalty of the readers and the publisher who understands the need for this specialized content. For in private security the world has only expanded at every level of our justice model—the investigative realm being no exception. While the fundamental structure of the text remains the same, the content has undergone a vigorous and very aggressive update. The last edition—in 2011— is a long, long time ago in the world of investigative technique and protocol. And in the final analysis, what this edition seeks to do is put the content on the cutting edge of things rather than lagging behind. Hence, there are a few obvious very new threads coursing through this text: first, the rise of the technological influence is clearly stressed; second, the improved techniques of doing things with forensic techniques and digital applications is covered; third, the innovative way in which background information is gathered, and information is stored and catalogued, as well as the collection and preservation techniques—these are part and parcel of the new edition. All content regarding the professional groups like ASIS get some attention and older source materials are buttressed by new authority. The reader will quickly notice the enlivened approach to the internet, web resources, professionals' forms and guides, and will be generally brought up to date on all topics.

Works of this kind serve multiple purposes: education and enhancement of the security profession, as training for field operations, as a research and database, or to disseminate new practices and procedures in a massive industry. I would hope a little of each is accomplished in the authorship of this text, but of primary importance is that the text should remain a product for the practitioner, both entry-level and experienced. At its best, this compilation is a working tool, filled with forms, checklists, guides—documentation that is useful in general and in specific cases. Practitioners will want it as a resource filled with references to other sources, ideas, and suggestions for tactics and security strategy, and as a refresher on methods in a most complex field. Private security is by no means a dull undertaking. The stereotype of the bank guard who sleeps on the job has little or no truth to it. If one disagrees, merely examine the contents of this work.

In Chapter 1, the phenomenon of privatization of once-public law enforcement functions is fully analyzed. The future expansion of private security is inevitable given this tendency. All data from both governmental and private sources confirm this upward direction. Additionally, our world needs an inexhaustible supply of information, especially accurate and verified information, about people, places, and things. The investigative process serves this end.

Chapter 2 highlights the traits, characteristics, professional skills, and personal attributes so essential to the competent investigator. New attention is given to steps in the critical analysis of information, not merely its collection.

How to adeptly conduct an initial interview is the subject matter of Chapter 3. Initial impressions of both clients and their cases and the importance of an objective case evaluation are thoroughly reviewed. This chapter delivers a wide array of new forms and techniques for investigative information gathering.

Witnesses, whether lay or expert, are discussed in Chapter 4. Methods of dealing with testimonial evidence, its content and quality cannot be overemphasized. The chapter also dwells on the role of witnesses in background assessment, character, and their credibility in general.

One of the text's larger chapters is Chapter 5—"Collection of Information," covering what is clearly an *a priori* condition of being a good practitioner in the security industry. Topics include: leads and their development, public and private sources of information—databases and publications, and computer services. Specific practical applications are also included and this is coupled with a new emphasis on the role of technology and the web in the gathering process.

The text's most comprehensive chapter, Chapter 6—"Collection of Evidence and Preservation of the Scene"—continues this direction. Subjects include: investigative kits, physical evidence and its collection, scene sketches, photographic evidence, and documentary applications. All tactics are updated.

In Chapter 7, surveillance techniques, whether singular, on foot, or by patrol car, are examined and graphically reproduced. Special emphasis on tech improvements as to cameras, location, and coverage completes the chapter.

Understanding the dynamics of report writing, with specific forms and documentation, is the prime purpose of Chapter 8. Just as in public law enforcement, security professionals are increasingly burdened by paperwork. Software applications that improve the report writing process receive considerable attention.

Commencing with Chapter 9, the text takes an applied direction. Using the varied skills and competencies discussed in the previous eight chapters, the text sets out to apply these generic principles in specialized case situations. Chapter 9 is dedicated to theft and property offenses. The new "gang" or "organized" retail theft tactic is highlighted.

Covering insurance cases, whether workers' compensation, disability, arson, or personal injury is fully dealt with in Chapter 10. Substantial attention is given to vehicular and accident investigation and reconstruction.

In Chapter 11, the diverse means of investigating personal and professional backgrounds are catalogued; from street interview to web-based databases the techniques are covered in great detail. New checklists and other aids are fully integrated.

Finally, Chapter 12 gives a rudimentary assessment of administrative requirements in the operation of a security office. Topics like billing, letters of introduction, filing, and expense billing are covered. The role of software programs in office maintenance is completely updated.

To my readers; earnest thanks for your patience and trust, and, as always, I look forward to your input and professional insights.

Charles P. Nemeth JD, PhD, LL.M
Chair and Professor
John Jay College of Criminal Justice
Department of Security, Fire and Emergency Management

Acknowledgments

Anytime a work reaches its fourth edition, the history of people and publishers is quite significant. All along the way, the special place of CRC Press, Taylor & Francis—in the world of private security as both an industry and academic endeavor—cannot be overpraised. In a more particular sense, CRC's senior editor, Mark Listewnik, continues to show his dedication to CRC advancing the industry and to be the lead academic center for publications for it. I am always grateful for his loyalty to these products and projects.

As has been the case for so many years, my editor, Hope Coddington, makes all texts and books a living reality. For nearly three decades she has organized our many, many books and done so with exceptional ability. I never take it for granted.

In this edition, a special contribution to Chapter 9 was made possible by my colleague, Dr. Susan Pickman, whose expertise in background analysis is pretty much unrivaled. It was my honor to have her involved in a critique of that chapter. In addition, Background Investigation Authorization and Release Form, Figure 11.2, was provided by Donald Ackerman.

Finally, this text is only as good as the many industry providers have allowed it to be. Company after company have given permission for us to reprint or reference their spectacular array of products and services. I am deeply grateful to John DelVecchio, CEO, Delvepoint and Jay Heath, Creative Director, at IRBsearch and to the following companies Sirchie, St. Louis Tag, LexisNexis, Lawgical-PInow, All State Legal Supply, G. A. Thomson, ASIS International, Securitas, and many, many more.

Author Bio

Dr Charles P. Nemeth has spent the vast majority of his professional life in the study and practice of law and justice. He is a recognized expert on professional ethics and the justice system, private-sector justice and private security systems. Presently he is Chair and Professor of Security, Fire and Emergency Management and Director of the Center of Private Security and Safety at John Jay College in New York City. He is a prolific writer, having published numerous texts and articles on law and justice throughout his impressive career. His text, Private Security and the Law 4th edition (Elsevier, 2012) is considered the foremost treatise on the subject matter. A 5th edition has been published by Taylor & Francis, 2018. His private security expertise is further buttressed by: Private Security and Investigative Process 4th edition (CRC Press, 2019), Criminal Law 2nd edition (CRC Press, 2012), and Law and Evidence 2nd edition (Jones and Bartlett, 2010). In the area of Homeland Security, he has published Introduction to Homeland Security: Practices and Principles 3rd edition (CRC Press, 2010, 2014, 2017). He has also authored a series of philosophical works on Thomas Aquinas including: Aquinas on Crime (St. Augustine's Press, 2010), Aquinas in the Courtroom (Praeger/Greenwood Press, 2001), Aquinas and King: A Discourse on Civil Disobedience (Carolina Academic Press, 2011), and Cicero and Aquinas: A Comparative Study of Nature and the Natural Law (Bloomsbury Publishing, 2018). He has also served as Chief Editor to a peer reviewed journal—*The Homeland Security Review* since 2005 and currently serves as Chief Editor for the *Law, Ethics and Jurisprudence* series to be published by Anthem Press. He has been an educator for more than 40 years. He holds memberships in the New York, North Carolina, and Pennsylvania Bars. Dr Nemeth was previously a Chair at the State University of New York at Brockport and California University of Pennsylvania—one of Pennsylvania's 14 State Universities. He is a much-sought-after legal consultant for security companies and a recognized scholar on issues involving law, professional ethics, and morality and the impact of privatization on public justice models. Dr Nemeth resides in Pittsburgh, Pennsylvania with his spouse, Jean Marie, together for 48 years and blessed with seven children all of whom are accomplished personally and professionally.

1 Introduction to the Private Security Industry and the Investigative Process

1.1 THE PRIVATE SECURITY INDUSTRY: OVERVIEW AND CONTEXT

Any reasonable person has likely already encountered the endless tentacles and reach of the private security industry. The industry weaves its way into every facet of modern life and continually concerns itself with the safety and security of assets and persons across dozens of sectors in an expanding marketplace.

1.1.1 THE CONTEMPORARY STATE OF PRIVATE SECURITY

Since World War II and the Cold War the private security industry has experienced steady growth. "Private security personnel also significantly outnumber sworn law enforcement personnel and nonmilitary government guards by nearly 2 to 1."[1] Today, the public interacts with and depends upon a private-sector model whose tentacles reach into every aspect of communal living. ASIS International, in 2002, saw the opportunities present in the field now and in the future, and stated that the:

> ... demand for heightened security is being increased by theft of information, workplace violence, terrorism and white collar crime. The security industry in the US is a $100 billion a year business and growing. Opportunities exist at all levels within the security industry. All businesses, no matter how small, have security concerns such as fraud, theft, computer hacking, economic espionage or workplace violence.[2]

The developing complexity of the world marketplace, the technological evolution of goods, services, and the transference of money and other negotiable instruments, served as a catalyst to private security growth. By way of example, consider the cyclonic revolution in the banking industry, from ATM machines to paperless checks, from wire transactions to credit card issuances. All of these practices are essentially novel, and at the same time, the subject of some inventive criminality. Here is where the future resides—in a system rooted in private prevention and protection, aligned with the public police model.[3] In the future more collaboration will be witnessed in the crime scene, terrorist investigation, or the public facility. At present, the list of security functions assumed by the private sector continues its unabated growth. No longer will the public and community merely look only to the FBI, the ATF, or state and local police to carry out myriad tasks.

The private security industry possesses an unflappable inertia that will increasingly weave its way into areas of public safety and security.[4] Public policing and safety entities will welcome the assistance. In housing and apartment complexes, in state and federal installations, at military facilities and correctional locales, at traffic intersections and public transportation settings, in executive-protection details and arson/explosives assessments, this is an industry that scoffs at caricatures in the mold of rent-a-cops or retired, unenergetic police, donut in hand. Frank MacHovec calls all security services police functions that are not performed by police.[5] This is an industry on the cutting edge of technology and operational policy. This is an industry public law enforcement now often envies.[6] Less burdened with regulation and free from excessive constitutional oversight and political interference witnessed in public law enforcement, and driven by efficiencies and corporate creativity, the security industry can only march forward.

Private security engages citizens even more than its public counterpart. And it has done so without the fanfare to match its astonishing rise. David Sklansky's *The Private Police* targets the central implications.

> For most lawyers and scholars, private security is terra incognita—wild, unmapped, and largely unexplored … Increasingly, though, government agencies are hiring private security personnel to guard and patrol government buildings, housing projects, and public parks and facilities, and a small but growing number of local governments have begun to experiment with broader use of private police.[7]

The Quiet Revolution[8] of private security could not have greater impact.[9] More than ever, the enormous public demands piled upon the private security industry call for professional planning and policy making, and a renewed dedication to the advancement of this dynamic industry. Combine technology with a rampant wave of economic crime and the climate of accommodation to the private security industry could not be better.

Private sector police come into the equation with far less baggage and a willingness to respond rapidly. Herein is the genius of cooperation, the shared and mutually learned experience. Underlying this text's entire approach is the heartfelt belief that private security should be rooted firmly in the American system of law and order, not be treated as an afterthought where the bones and scraps of undesirable public police functions are tossed out. This enterprise ennobles both its members and constituents. The private sector allows an entire nation to exist and operate by fulfilling its public responsibility through private means.

Indeed, the private sector philosophy is part and parcel of the American tradition. Self-help, self-reliance, and self-protection are not mere slogans but a way of life in the American experience.[10] Self-help and self-protection signify the essence of a free people that does not await public law enforcement's reaction to crime, but displays the moral courage and will to protect its own. The greatness of a nation directly correlates to the willingness of its citizenry to stand up and resist the way of life that crime brings. This is true in the state, the nation, the neighborhood, and the business district.[11]

In business and industry, the private security industry shines since it operates from the same vantage point. Firms that specialize in protection services can visualize how and why communities live and die, thrive or disintegrate. By providing preventative and protective services to private interests, the private practitioner is ultimately securing the stability of the community. Few would argue this is not a primordial public responsibility. On top of this, there is an emerging preference for private sector involvement in American foreign policy. Throughout the Middle East, in Iraq and Afghanistan, the footprint of the private security industry could not be more apparent.[12] Labeling them either as private military specialists or as "dogs of war" mercenaries will say much about the tension this new dimension causes. For those in favor, the private sector soldier provides "great flexibility, with an ability to create unique solutions for each case, knowledge about the problem area and operational expertise, business integrity, secure confidentiality, and a generally apolitical nature."[13] Critics charge that the privatized military operations "exploit violence for personal gain, serve as agents for unsavory power, or happily promote repression, turmoil, and human rights violations."[14] Neither of these cases is fully accurate, and the caricature that the Blackwater firm has turned into provides a poor illustration of this new and emerging dynamic.[15] The role that private security firms play in armed conflicts is a natural progression of mission and privatization.[16]

Whole-scale security systems in the war on terror have come to depend on the private sector system. The fit of private sector justice in the world of military action seems at first glance rather odd, yet the deeper the correlation is considered, the more sense it makes. Private security companies now "possess great flexibility, with an ability to create unique solutions for each case, knowledge about the problem area and operational expertise, business integrity, secure confidentiality and a general apolitical nature."[17] Put another way, the private security industry can provide a mercenary force that sees the problem dispassionately and as a result is an agency more reasonable and rational in outlook.

This turning over of the guard, whether it be executive protection, private prison processing, community and neighborhood intelligence, diplomatic protection, to name just a few functions, manifests a change in the overall paradigm.[18] In both war and peace one witnesses the staggering interlocking of a private justice model in public functions.

Privatization is now predictable nomenclature in the world of public policy and the delivery of governmental services. Coming full circle, legislators and policymakers now evaluate programs and their delivery in light of outsourcing, private contracts, delegable services, and partnerships with the private sector. No longer is this sort of thinking on the fringe. Although the shift has now become self-evident, the transition troubles many.[19] The National Institute of Justice has insightfully discerned the shift back to privatized justice in the form of nonpublic law enforcement:

> Such expanded use of private security and increased citizen involvement signals an increasing return to the private sector for protection against crime. The growth and expansion of modern police reflected a shift from private policing and security initiatives of the early nineteenth century. Now the pendulum appears to be swinging back. Despite the expanded role of the police in crime prevention in recent years, it appears that the private sector will bear an increased prevention role while law enforcement concentrates more heavily on violent crimes and crime response. Economic realities are forcing law enforcement to seek ways to reduce workloads.[20]

In the final analysis, there is something empowering about this reality, and as some have described, a "participatory democratic self-government."[21] In what greater sense does the citizen bear responsibility for the world around them than when that citizen assumes the responsibility of self-help and self-protection?

It appears private security's role in the administration of American justice is both multifaceted and entrenched. Its areas of service not only entail private, individual, or property security, but loss prevention, insurance, military intelligence, and related functions, as well as computer security. Security as a practice, process, and system is embedded in the nation's tradition and is an essential contributor to justice in modern America.

1.1.2 CLASSIFICATIONS AND FUNCTIONS OF THE PRIVATE SECURITY INDUSTRY

The private security industry weaves its threads into every corner of the American experience. Whether by individual delivery, proprietary service, or under a contractual agreement for services, private security touches every aspect of economic life. Contractual services, whereby money is paid for specific security services, promotes safety and security in a host of locales and settings.

> The "private contractual security services" industry encompasses guards, private investigative services, central-station alarm monitoring, armored transport and ATM servicing, security consulting and data security and private correctional facility management services. Niche markets also exist for a wide range of specialized security services, including: bomb sweeps and metal detection; drug testing; pre-employment screening; renting of site secure vaults; radon and hazardous gas testing; and guard dog services.[22]

Proprietary security services deliver similar results. The proprietary sector offers services directly to the public from property protection to private background checks, from fraud prevention systems to banking security controls. Proprietary security reflects the ingenuity and brilliance of its inventors[23] with a surge of private investigators, computer and tech crime specialists, anti-terrorism practitioners, and executive protection specialists. The security industry, according to its premier professional association, ASIS International, breaks down the private security industry into four major disciplines.

Physical security focuses on the protection of people, property, and facilities through the use of security forces, security systems, and security procedures. Physical security personnel oversee proprietary or contract uniformed security operations, identify security system requirements, assess internal and external threats to assets, and develop policies, plans, procedures, and physical safeguards to counter those threats. Physical security can include the use of barriers, alarms, locks, access control systems, protective lighting, closed-circuit television, and other state-of-the-art security technology.

Information security involves safeguarding sensitive information. Although information security has traditionally been associated with protection of US Government classified information, it can also include privacy data, proprietary information, contractual information, and intellectual property. Information security deals with issues such as who should access the data and how the data is stored, controlled, marked, disseminated, and disposed of.

Personnel security deals with ensuring the integrity and reliability of an organization's workforce. Personnel security encompasses background investigations, drug testing, and other pre-employment screening techniques, as well as adjudication of results and granting security clearances and other information access privileges.

Information systems security involves maintaining the confidentiality, reliability, and availability of data created, stored, processed, and/or transmitted via automated information systems. Information systems security personnel develop procedures and safeguards to protect against hackers and other unauthorized efforts to access data, viruses, and a number of other threats to information systems.

Within the major areas, security breaks down into specialties and an endless array of subfields including but not limited to:

- Educational institution security
- Financial services security
- Gaming/wagering security
- Government industrial security
- Healthcare security
- Information systems security
- Lodging security
- Manufacturing security
- Retail security
- Security sales, equipment, and services
- Transportation security
- Utilities security[24]

1.2   THE PRIVATE SECURITY INDUSTRY AND PRIVATIZATION

While public perceptions tend to see the justice model as a public function, there is a long history and tradition involving private operatives providing justice services. In fact, most of our national history displays a preference for private justice and police services.

Primarily, the early colonial need for security did not center on proprietary or commercial interests, but on the fear of fire, vagrants, and Indian attacks. As urban populations grew, the system of sheriffs, constables, and the watch proved inadequate in meeting law enforcement needs. The diversity of the original colonies did not promote any concept of uniform law enforcement practices or a national police. Even with increasing urban congestion and a rising crime rate, little would change in American law enforcement. "Watchmen remained familiar figures and constituted the primary security measures until the establishment of full-time police forces in the mid-1800s."[25]

The seemingly unchanging organization of colonial American law enforcement was not so much a sign of social stability, but more likely a wariness of any public or national force controlled by a federal government. "The principle of states' rights had a profound and continuing impact upon law enforcement."[26] Americans, especially right after the American Revolution, were leery of any federal entity that sought to control and administrate over state and local matters. Law enforcement and security, like other facets of life, were to be controlled by state and local government, which reflected the "states' rights" mentality of the age and the supremacy of a decentralized federalism. Although local and state jurisdictions might have felt politically comfortable with the watch system of security, other factors necessitated a change in American security practices. As in England, the old systems of law enforcement became outdated and inadequate in facing the security problems of the growing nation. "The basic deficiencies of the watch and constable systems rendered them ill-prepared to deal with the unrest that occurred in many American cities during the first half of the nineteenth century."[27] New methods of organizing and defining public and private law enforcement were needed to combat urban problems.

The first half of the nineteenth century saw a rise in urbanization, crime, and the need for better law enforcement.[28] Private security existed, but only on a small scale for business and merchant protection. Although private police greatly contributed to keeping the peace, it became obvious, particularly in the cities, that a centralized public police department was a necessity.

The early 1800s witnessed the birth of American policing as a viable peacekeeping force. New York City had started the rudiments of a police department in 1783, and by 1800 had established the first paid daytime police force. Daytime police forces were also started in Philadelphia (1833) and Boston (1838).[29] These early departments did not supplant the system of the watch but worked as the daytime counterpart. Since the day and night watches would prove inadequate in fighting crime, New York City became the first city to combine its day and night watches into a unified police force in 1844.[30] "Other large cities began to follow the lead—Chicago in 1851, New Orleans and Cincinnati in 1852, and Providence in 1864. The snowballing effect stimulated the modernization of American policing."[31]

At the end of the nineteenth century, the use of state, federal, or local officials to provide protection services was clearly a novel paradigm at this time. With the rise of the railroad industry, the expansion into the Western states, and the full bore of the Industrial Revolution, life became more complicated and shifted law enforcement to the public visage we witness today.

Even with this public sector recognition, life has come full circle.[32]

These once entrenched public services are being returned to private control. In courts, parking authorities, public housing projects, federal installations, detective services, and traffic control, private sector justice has reemerged. The growth, rejuvenation, and return of private sector justice amount to a phenomenon that manifests unlimited growth. See Table 1.1.

Part of this growth can also be attributed to economic forces—the distinction and difference between a public, governmental model and a capitalist system that finds opportunity in any void.

TABLE 1.1

Various Private Sector Justice and Security and the Various Roles and Functions It Can Serve

Community protection and services	Public housing protection
Parking authority control and security	Enforcement of motor vehicle laws
Natural resource activities	Waterways and port services
Air and rail protection	Animal control
Court security	Governmental office security
Private prisons	Code violation inspectors
Special event security	Governmental investigations

Surely, private operatives have stepped up and into a host of functions that the public system simply cannot cover and, just as compellingly, find new sources where income and revenue can be generated. This economic push arises from a system that sees economic growth as its chief reason for existence, and capitalism, in its own way, has generated a private security industry that would not be imaginable in a socialist system.[33]

The *Hallcrest Report II*, the well regarded qualitative and quantitative study of private security, computes this staggering trend at Figure 1.1.[34]

The BLS confirms and corroborates this trend at Figure 1.2.[35]

At every level, one witnesses this orientation towards the private. Even criminal investigative practice is not immune to this change. In 2015 the industry at large expended nearly $377 billion dollars[36] and "plays a major protective role in the Nation's life."[37] The industry's robust economic growth is also well documented by the US Census Bureau as outlined at Figure 1.3.[38]

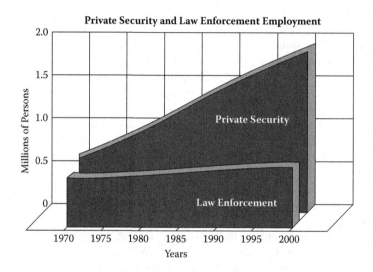

FIGURE 1.1 Hallcrest Report II's assessment of trends in private security jobs versus traditional law enforcement.

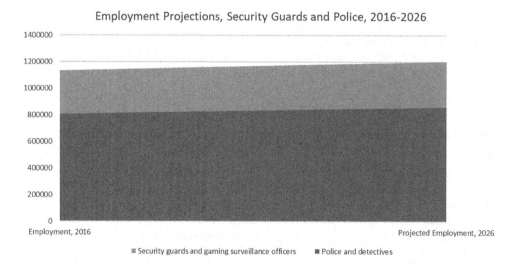

FIGURE 1.2 Employment projections of security guards and police through the year 2026.

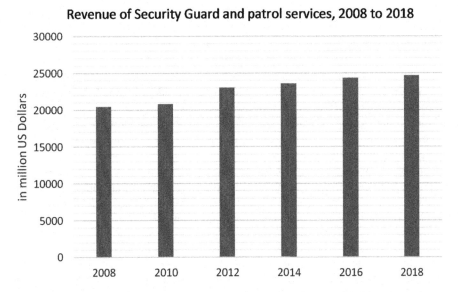

FIGURE 1.3 The revenue figures of security guard and patrol services through 2018. (Source: US Census Bureau.)

The National Center for Policy Analysis (NCPA) foretold of nothing but a further expansion of the private justice function when it concluded:

- There are nearly three times as many private security guards as public law enforcement officers, 1.5 million in 1990, and the private sector spends almost twice as much on private security as we pay in taxes to support the public police.
- Private bounty hunters, or bail enforcement agents, make the private bail bonding system work for persons accused of crimes by tracking down and apprehending those who try to flee.
- And the private sector on occasion has been used innovatively in other ways to prepare cases for district attorneys, to prosecute criminal cases and to employ prisoners behind bars.[39]

The picture for private sector justice is exceptionally bright when it comes to the occupational role known as private investigator. In every sector of the industry, there will be a natural need for investigators. The Bureau of Labor statistics make this clear in Table 1.2.[40]

TABLE 1.2

Statistics Indicating Projected Growth of 11% for Private Detectives and Investigators through 2026

Occupational Title	Employment, 2016	Projected Employment, 2026	Change, 2016–26	
			Percent	Numeric
Private detectives and investigators	41,400	45,800	11	4,400

Source: Bureau of Labor.

This shift from public service to private delivery is properly labeled "privatization"—the transference of public functions to privatized delivery. And while many law enforcement services seem to fit the private security industry perfectly, such as entertainment venue security, executive protective services, retail, corporate, and industrial to name a few, the shift has now even been witnessed in traditional law enforcement and policing functions. This transference was once considered inconceivable, for public law enforcement is and has always been saddled with attending to the needs of the public good.[41]

Few private security companies are concerned with domestic disputes, the transportation of the deceased, stray animals, or protection of the homeless,[42] nor does the industry dwell as heavily on major felonies as the public sector does.

Yet, the linkages between private sector justice operatives and public policing appear to be on the fast track. Aside from occupational demands, the efficiency factor—that capacity to deliver similar services at a lower price, seems another undeniable impetus for the shift. Raymond Bechler's thoughtful piece on the rise of private police makes this point:

> Privatized police ownership can become a reality. Economically, private policing makes sense and could be a financial victory for local governments. As with most budgets, personnel costs generally consume more than half of the entire general fund. Private ownership allows for a different retirement system altogether, thwarting the high cost per employee. The benefits to local government, communities, and to the law enforcement profession can be greatly enhanced by the competition of private police ownership.[43]

Private security companies now engage in community policing, internal investigations, drug and alcohol controls, traffic and public venue controls, to name just a few. No one, less than a decade ago, would ever have envisioned whole communities hiring private security forces to deliver policing services.[44]

The Private Security Advisory Council characterized police work as a public interest function. Public police have "a wide range of responsibilities to protect essentially public concerns, and their efforts are closely tied to statutorily mandated duties and the criminal justice system."[45] However, this range of duties does not preclude the private sector from delivering similar or even identical services.[46]

If anything, the press of increased duties and the rising legal liability for public policing have furthered the paradigm shift to privatized services.

Web Exercise: The trend towards privatization has been unmistakable in all corners of government, from water to airports, and most other governmental functions. Visit www.governing.com/topics/mgmt/pros-cons-privatizing-government-functions.html.

It is utterly undeniable that the public policing system labors under an oppressive oversight regimen when compared to the private police model.[47] At the other end of the spectrum, the legal oversight of the private security operative, while growing, still remains minimalist in comparison. Stephen Rushin argues that private "police assume many of the same roles as traditional law enforcement. But courts and legislatures regulate public and private police very differently."[48] This status is especially true in matters of constitutionalism and its remedies and strictures as applied in public policing.[49]

The Advisory Council relates that police are burdened with constitutional limitations and must interpret and implement certain guidelines in the performance of their law enforcement duties causing natural inefficiencies not experienced by private sector operatives. Public policing is further restrained by public budgeting and financing processes that are inevitably tied to political influence. Police administrators must evaluate and allocate resources according to the needs and demands presently operating within their community structure.[50] Norman Spain and Gary Elkin, in an article titled "Private and Public Security: There is a Difference," note that even despite the differences, the approaches can be totally complementary.

One of the traditional functions of the public police is to deter crime. In reality, their ability to do this is drastically limited. The primary reasons are that the police have little authority to change the conditions that foster crime. They have no authority to decide who will reside in their jurisdiction, whom they will police. Private security forces, on the other hand, may alter—at times drastically—the environment in which they operate.[51]

This evolution in privatized policing is not universally supported and the critics are highly caustic in their assessment of these parallel capacities in the private and public realm. One critic claims that private security has "fallen short of the elite level of security previously provided by the highly trained federal police officers."[52]

Unions and civil service systems are equally critical. Despite this, the movement seems unstoppable. As private security takes on more and more of the once sacrosanct public policing function, the lines blur, the differences melt away, and the mutual need for each system becomes clearer.[53] Private security is not an either/or option or choice but an aligned level of protection, or even a replacement or substitute for a public system that cannot do all the public demands.[54]

The privatization paradigm shift has not arisen by necessity alone or a creeping occupationalism without aim or purpose. What other forces have prompted this shift to the private?[55] First, there exists a growing perception, whether actual or perceived, about rising crime rates in America; second, the cost/benefit analysis generally places private policing in a more efficient position than its public counterpart.

As to the matter of crime, data paint a mixed picture—although most studies reviewed in this text on how the American citizenry feels about issues regarding safety and security show a decrease of those that feel "safe." Even though selected studies may indicate drops in certain felonious categories, the reality of crime spreading is in just about every sector of American life, from the corporate boardroom to the local grocery store. Both qualitatively and quantitatively, crime has a tendency to trend upward, though this picture is skewed due to decriminalization efforts as well as diversion to informal adjudication. No matter how the data unravel and are reported, Americans are nervous about the quality of life in general, the unrest and civil turbulence increasingly witnessed, albeit with a full understanding that criminality is a cyclical phenomena.[56] The FBI's recent Uniform Crime Reporting (UCR) data, at Table 1.3, confirms this.

TABLE 1.3

FBI's Uniform Crime Reporting Data (Percentage Change over 2 Years, 5 Years, and 10 Years)

	Years		
	2016/2015	**2016/2012**	**2016/2007**
Violent crime rate	+3.4	−0.4	−18.1
Murder and non-negligent manslaughter rate	+7.9	+12.8	−6
Forcible rape rate	+4.2	+9.2	−3
Robbery rate	+0.5	−9.1	−30.7
Aggravated assault rate	+4.4	+2.4	−13.5
Property crime rate	−2	−14.5	
Burglary rate	−5.2	−30.2	
Larceny-theft rate	−2.2	−11.2	
Motor vehicle theft rate	+6.6	+2.8	

Source: U.S. Department of Justice, "Crime in the United States, 2016" (Washington, DC: US Government Printing Office), Table 1A. (https://ucr.fbi.gov/crime-in-the-u.s/2016/crime-in-the-u.s.-2016/topic-pages).

Aside from this victimization perspective, the economic aspects of crime also drive the movement to privatization. Business, industry, and the corporate world measure crime in dollar terms and evaluate how the bottom line responds to a crime-ridden world. The effects of crime upon business are many and varied:

- Increased cost of insurance and security protection
- Cost of internal audit activities to detect crime
- Cost of investigation and prosecution of suspects measured in terms of lost time of security and management personnel
- Reduced profits
- Increased selling prices and weakened competitive standing
- Loss of productivity
- Loss of business reputation
- Deterioration in quality of service
- Threats to the survival of small business
- Cost of crime prevention programs
- Cost of crime reporting and mandated security programs
- Loss of tax revenue
- Increased cost of consumer goods and services to offset crime losses
- Loss of investor equity
- Increased taxes
- Reduced employment due to business failures
- Increased cost for technological equipment[57]

The coupling of economic influences with the tidal wave of criminal victimization gives the private security industry legitimacy and poignancy that it would not have otherwise. Not everyone is pleased. Howard Rice critiques not only the growth of private security, but also the striking entanglement resulting from the private employment of public police as both entities carry out their responsibilities:

> In recent trends, private security has outstripped the growth of the public police; more people are now working in private security than in public policing. Yet this numerical comparison fails to reflect another recent trend: the substantial growth in off-duty employment of uniformed police officers by private employers.[58]

It can also be safely argued that the post 9/11 world of terrorism has directly driven growth in the private sector. The task of homeland security is rightly construed in the context of a public-private partnership with the Department of Homeland Security fully advancing cooperation.[59] Since 9/11, the role of private security has been slowly but steadily increasing—and this transference from DHS function to the private sector further corroborates the privatization theory. In fact, the influence of a post-9/11 world has accelerated the private security industry at a pace it could never have foretold. Security Management's Diane Ritchey asserts that the industry has grown 100 years in terms of operational and technological sophistication in a span of ten years on account of the attacks of September 11, 2001—an observation difficult to disagree with.[60]

In the area of critical infrastructure, private security and the DHS work hand in hand. The National Infrastructure Advisory Council, in its report on public-private sector intelligence coordination, identified seventeen business and commercial sectors that need to step up in the fight against terrorism:

- Communications
- Chemical and hazardous materials
- Commercial facilities
- Dams

- Defense industrial base
- Energy
- Emergency services
- Financial services
- Food and agriculture
- Government facilities
- Information technology
- National monuments and icons
- Nuclear power plants
- Post and shipping
- Public health and healthcare
- Transportation
- Water[61]

On a second front, the role of private sector security firms and personnel can only be described as central and integral in the defense of the nation. In the 2014 Quadrennial Homeland Security Review, DHS unreservedly elevates the importance of the private sector in its "Strengthening the Execution of Our Missions through Public-Private Partnerships." Private security is touted as a "partner" in this mission, as DHS declares:

Homeland Security is achieved through a shared effort among all partners, from corporations to non-profits and American families. Together, we can harness common interests to achieve solutions beyond what any of us could do alone. At a time when we must do more with less, two guiding principles help public-private partnerships maximize the investment by each partner and the success of the partnership: (1) aligning interests and (2) identifying shared outcomes.[62]

Overall, the role of private security interests can never be underestimated or underutilized, for as a partner in homeland security the government can:

- Share information and data
- Coordinate with partners on targeted activities
- Link with diverse partners to achieve a stated goal
- Share the expenses of the operations while economically benefiting the providers
- Innovate and produce new strategies, products, methods and means to security[63]

Such partnerships assure the ability to meet the many complex security challenges caused and fomented by the terrorist class.

Web Exercise: See the DHS Critical Infrastructures Sector Partnerships webpage at www.dhs.gov/critical-infrastructure-sector-partnerships.

Given the dual forces of crime and a post-9/11 world, the ripples towards privatization cannot be reversed or ended.[64] Across so many of our cultural and institutional sectors, the private security industry has implanted its skill and competency in either an exclusive mode or by partnership or other cooperative arrangement with the public sector. Table 1.4 captures the sheer scope of the industry's influence.

In each of these sectors, a need for investigative acumen will course its way through the daily grind of protecting assets, people, and the nation-state.

1.3   THE ROLE OF PRIVATE SECURITY AND THE INVESTIGATIVE PROCESS

As the private security industry continues its unabated growth, the opportunity for private investigators will surely follow that lead. As already covered, the range and scope of functions and duties tackled by private security will necessitate investigators to assure integrity in those operations.

TABLE 1.4

Areas in Which Security Serves an Integral Role

Banking and Financial Institutions	**Computer Security**
General Banking Institutions	Banks
Bankcard centers	Telephone Companies
Savings &Loan Companies	Insurance Companies
Financial Centers	Credit Card Companies
	Crime Prevention
Credit Card Security	**Restaurant and Lodging**
Banks	
Retail Stores	
Gasoline Companies	
Educational Institutions	**Establishments**
Universities	Large Restaurant Chains
Junior/Community Colleges	Hotel and Motel Chains
Major School Districts	
Fire Resources and Management	**Retail Stores**
Small Communities	Department Stores
Major, Firms, Aerospace	Grocery Stores
	General Merchandise Stores
Health Care Institutions	**Transportation and Cargo**
Hospitals	Airlines
Convalescent Homes	Trucking Firms
Retirement Communities	Special Couriers
Pharmaceutical Firms	Railroads
	Ports/Maritime Security
Nuclear Security	**Executive Protection**
Production Facilities	VIPs
Power Plants	Diplomats
Transportation Facilities	Celebrities
Public Utilities	**Community**
Departments of Water and Power	Apartment Complexes
Telephone Companies	Afterschool Programs
Major Power Generating Facilities	Neighborhood Patrols

Both externally and internally, the industry will rely on investigative reviews to detect crime and harm, to ferret out harassment and workplace violence, to counter and deter loss to an asset base, or to protect facilities, from colleges to hospitals. In each location, the skills of the competent investigator will always be in demand. On top of this reality will be an ever changing technological landscape where security threats will evolve and emerge in ways once thought mere science fiction. In this virtual, technological plane, investigators will need to hone new and innovative skills to find the facts.[65] A small example of how private industry and its technological inventiveness make new and improved methods of law enforcement possible is the installation of community CCTV systems— none of which was invented by the public domain—all of them created, installed, and monitored by private enterprise. CCTV systems now play a major role in public law enforcement, which relies on its capacity to identify perpetrators and thus be just one example of how the interplay between private and public systems operates and how investigators in both worlds use the same information.[66]

In a general sense, every investigator engages in the process of factual assimilation and the systematic collection of evidence. Investigation calls for intense observation, inspection, evidentiary analysis, and the connectivity to tie a theory to a particular circumstance. Investigation requires the balance of theory with "street smarts." Investigative practice depends on facts and hard information.

A successful private investigator must provide the information necessary to support or refute a claim, cause of action, or criminal prosecution. Every investigator worth his or her salt needs certain essential characteristics, including but not limited to:

- Energy and alertness
- Knowledge of the law
- Ability to set realistic objectives
- Methodical approach
- Knowledge of human nature
- Observation and deduction abilities
- Ability to maintain meaningful notes

Solid investigative practice operates under an investigative plan, creates a theoretical framework that underlines the investigative process, and proposes a cause or case in law that relates to the investigative regimen. The investigative process must reconstruct events, conditions, or (as is often stated) the "truth" itself. Finding the truth can be a challenge for even the most seasoned investigator. Objective and fully reliable information is hard to come by. To reconstruct events and circumstances, the investigator will engage many parties and practices including witnesses, physical and real evidence, documents, forensic science, demonstrative evidence, and the sophistication of expert opinion. In a sense, the investigator reconstructs history for the present. James Davidson and Mark Lytle's *After the Fact* suggests that the investigative process is really a journey into the historical past:

> "History is what happened in the past." That statement is the everyday view of the matter ... The everyday view recognizes that this task is often difficult. But historians are said to succeed if they bring back the facts without distorting them or forcing a new perspective on them. In effect, historians are seen as couriers between the past and present. Like all good messengers, they are expected simply to deliver their information without adding to it.[67]

In sum, the process of investigation requires the conversion of alleged acts into real and useful evidence.[68]

The functions of investigation are many and multifaceted. From its Latin derivative, *vestigare*, investigation implies a tracking, a search, an assimilation, or collection of information and facts. Russell Colling, in his work *Hospital Security*, concludes that the differences between the investigative protocol of the public officer from the private officer are really those of form and mission, and the missions are, in truth, very complementary.

> It is techniques and varying purposes that differentiate the security investigation from that of a law enforcement agency. This is not to say that the security investigation always has a different focus. A police investigation is conducted basically for the purpose of apprehending the perpetrator of a crime and locating evidence for the successful prosecution of a case. Security investigations, on the other hand, may involve, in addition to crimes, the gathering of information in regards to the violation of organizational rules and regulations; a job applicant's background, for conditions that may lead to criminal violations; the need for new security controls and procedures; liability claims or potential claims; unsafe conditions; or evidence needed to prove or disprove certain allegations.[69]

ASIS International has long appreciated the crucial and expanding investigative role that private security is playing:

> Along with this burgeoning of the prevention role, investigative responsibilities have grown as well, calling for more expert investigators using more sophisticated techniques.
> Today, many business firms and other organizations employ investigators directly as part of their in-house security programs. Others retain outside investigators for temporary assignments or on a more permanent basis through contractual arrangements. Some organizations delegate security and investigative duties to employees having assignments in other fields, for

example, personnel, safety, or insurance. Others call on persons with law enforcement experience but little or no exposure to private security to perform these tasks. Private investigative agencies and in-house security departments must sometimes employ persons with limited background in the private investigatory arena to meet the demand for security services.[70]

ASIS International also administers a professional certification for an investigator known as the PCI. See Figure 1.4.[71]

These investigative services and potential clients include a broad spectrum of individuals and entities always in need of these competencies. In many places and contexts, the private security investigator is employed for a host of purposes. A summary list of potential investigative clients is at Table 1.5.[72]

1.3.1 INVESTIGATIVE ACTIVITIES COMMONLY ENCOUNTERED BY PRIVATE SECURITY

The role of private security in the investigative process directly correlates to the subject matter of the investigation. Professor Thomas Eimermann affirms how the nature of an investigation, and its corresponding methodology, will depend upon the subject matter of that investigation.

> The nature of the investigation will, of course, vary considerably with the area of law involved, as well as with the particular facts of the case at hand. Negligence cases require a great deal of investigative work. Damaged cars, broken machines, and injured persons all have to be examined. Witnesses have to be interviewed at length in order to determine the existence of negligence on the part of one or more parties to the accident. In work[ers'] compensation cases, negligence is not an issue, but the extent of damage is. Likewise, the extent to which an injury was work-related becomes an important aspect of the investigation. In probate, an investigation could involve either locating missing heirs or attempting to determine what the mental state of the deceased was at the time the will was written. The underlying skills in all areas are basically the same.[73]

| ASIS | GSX | COMMUNITY | CAREER HQ | STORE | | JOIN | CREATE ACCOUNT | LOGIN | | Q |
| MEMBERSHIP ▼ | CERTIFICATION ▼ | PROFESSIONAL DEVELOPMENT ▼ | PUBLICATIONS & RESOURCES ▼ | GET INVOLVED ▼ | SECURITY MANAGEMENT ▼ |

BECOMING A PROFESSIONAL CERTIFIED INVESTIGATOR (PCI®)

Why Apply for the PCI?

Earning a Professional Certified Investigator (PCI®) designation provides independent confirmation of your specialized skills in security investigations, including case evaluation and review of options for case management strategies. It validates your ability to collect information through the effective use of surveillance, interviews, and interrogations.

What's on the Exam?

The PCI examination consists of 125 scored multiple-choice questions and may also contain 15 randomly distributed pre-test (unscored) questions for a total of up to 140 questions. The 2.5 hours allowed takes into consideration the review of pre-test items.

The exam covers tasks, knowledge, and skills in three primary domains that have been identified by professional investigators as required areas of competency in this field.

Price

- $300 ASIS members
- $450 nonmembers
- Retake fee: $200

Eligibility

Five years of investigations experience, including at least two years in case management*

AND

A high school diploma or GED equivalent

AND

- Be employed full-time in a security-related role
- Not have been convicted of any criminal offense that would reflect negatively on the security profession, ASIS, or the certification program
- Sign and agree to abide by the ASIS Certification Code of Conduct
- Agree to abide by the policies of the ASIS Certification programs as outlined in the Certification Handbook.

*Definitions for this term can be found in the Certification Handbook.

FIGURE 1.4 ASIS International has a recognized industry certification in the Professional Certified Investigator (PCI) program. (Reprinted with permission of ASIS International © 2018.)

TABLE 1.5

Any Number of Industry Organizations Would Need to Enlist Investigative Professionals and Services

Public prosecutors and law enforcement agencies
- Investigation of crimes.
- Locating fugitives and witnesses.
- Securing evidence and surveillance.
- Public/Private Coordination and Planning for Homeland Security.

Patent attorneys
- Investigation of infringements.
- Establishing facts in respect of adoption, use and abandonment.

Banks
- Investigation of crimes.
- Investigation of applicants and employees considered for advancement to positions of trust and responsibility.
- Protection of transportation of valuable property.
- Surveillance of employees and others suspected of improprieties.
- Verification of reported assets.
- Checking the operation of business enterprises.
- Investigation of credit applicants.
- Investigation of computer and e-transaction fraud.

Railway, bus and airline companies
- Honesty and service inspections.
- Investigation of claims.
- Terrorist threats.

Stores
- Store detectives.
- Investigation of thefts, etc.
- Locating credit skips and frauds.

Hotels
- Hotel detectives; investigations of thefts, etc.
- Inspection of service in various departments for honesty, efficiency, waste and violation of regulations.

Surveillance
- Establishing movements, associates, attention to duty during business hours and mode of living, etc.
- Video recording service to document activities of personal injury claimants.

Undercover investigations
- Investigation of employees to expose dishonesty, waste, carelessness, inefficiency, willful neglect, violation of safety rules, favoritism, employee discrimination, lowered morale, sabotage, and other irregularities.

Lawyers
- Investigation of cases in preparation of trial or adjudication.
- Locating witnesses and missing heirs, etc.
- Locating concealed assets and serving papers.

Publishers
- Investigation to defend libel actions.
- Investigation of unfair competition.
- Investigation of copyright infringement.

Insurance companies and self-insurers
- Investigation of defalcations [embezzlement], robberies, burglaries, thefts, losses, fires and other casualty claims.
- Investigation of life, accident, malpractice, compensation and other claims.
- Shadowing claimants to establish extent of their disabilities.

Motor freight, warehouse and freight terminal companies
- Investigation of thefts, etc.
- Investigation of claims.

Manufacturing and wholesale distributing companies
- Investigation of product liability claims.
- Investigation of unfair competition, willful attempts to damage products' reputation, fraudulent disclosure of trade secrets and violation of trade agreements.
- Homeland defense plans.

Character investigations
- Investigations to establish reputation, confirm residence address, present and/or prior employment or business, marital status, habits, mode of living, income, financial and credit responsibility, social and business connections, police record and other details as desired.

Plant and store surveillance
- Over weekends, on holidays, and during night hours, keeping premises under surveillance to detect removal of property, attempted depredations, admittance of unauthorized persons and other improper acts.

The types of investigative practices encountered by the security professional will vary depending upon not only the subject matter but also the expertise of the investigator. So a security firm specializing in worker compensation or disability fraud would target selected investigative practices that zero in on these claims such as interviewing and surveillance as well as medical analysis. The investigative skill set may include the following subject matter:

- Claims investigation
- Divorce investigation
- Location of missing persons
- Location of heirs and assigns
- Civil investigation
- Criminal investigation
- Credit investigation
- Background investigation
- Undercover investigation
- Insurance investigation
- Personal injury investigation
- Traffic accident investigation
- Property loss investigation
- Medical malpractice investigation
- Government agency investigation
- Fire, safety, and OSHA investigations
- Domestic relations investigation
- Patent and trademark investigations
- Organized crime investigation
- Fraud and white-collar crime investigations
- Employee investigation
- Polygraph investigation
- Housing code investigation
- Building trades investigation
- Surveillance activities
- Witness location
- Workers' compensation cases
- Corporate investigation
- Judgment investigation
- Product liability and consumer claims
- Public record searches
- Title searches
- Marine investigation
- Construction accident investigation
- Toxic tort investigation
- Psychological and psychiatric investigation
- Questioned document investigation

As technological, scientific, and other advances occur, for example in the areas of forensic science, DNA, or computer forensics, or the rapid growth of cyber challenges, the need for skilled investigators will mirror the emerging fields. Both the investigative method and the investigators that carry out said investigation will come to depend on not only an expertise but also a recognizable field. In this sense, investigative practice is forever changing. For an outline of the various functions of private security investigators see Box 1.1.[74]

BOX 1.1   AN OVERVIEW OF THE VARIOUS ROLES THAT PRIVATE SECURITY INVESTIGATIONS AND INVESTIGATORS CAN SERVE

Private detectives and investigators typically do the following:

- Interview people to gather information
- Search online, public, and court records to uncover clues
- Conduct surveillance
- Collect evidence for clients
- Check for civil judgments and criminal history

Private detectives and investigators offer many services for individuals, attorneys, and businesses. Examples include performing background checks, investigating employees for possible theft from a company, proving or disproving infidelity in a divorce case, and helping to locate a missing person.

Private detectives and investigators use a variety of tools when researching the facts in a case. Much of their work is done with a computer, allowing them to obtain information such as telephone numbers, details about social networks, descriptions of online activities, and records of a person's prior arrests. They make phone calls to verify facts and interview people when conducting a background investigation.

Detectives also conduct surveillance when investigating a case. They may watch locations, such as a person's home or office, often from a hidden position. Using cameras and binoculars, detectives gather information on people of interest.

Detectives and investigators must be mindful of the law when conducting investigations. Because they lack police authority, their work must be done with the same authority as a private citizen. As a result, detectives and investigators must have a good understanding of federal, state, and local laws, such as privacy laws, and other legal issues affecting their work. Otherwise, evidence they collect may not be useable in court and they could face prosecution.

Skip tracers specialize in locating people whose whereabouts are unknown. For example, debt collectors may employ them to locate people who have unpaid bills.

Security firms reflect this multifaceted approach to investigating and seek out employees who are capable of this sort of multitasking. See Figure 1.5.[75]

1.4   CONCLUSION AND FINAL THOUGHTS

No matter what the case or subject matter, the private security industry desperately needs to produce a regular cadre of seasoned investigators. Business, industry, attorneys, agencies at the federal, state, and local levels, and other employers look to the security investigator to collect information, to resolve factual disputes, and reconcile confusing data and information.

In addition, these same constituencies rely on professional investigators for reports and analysis, case reviews and findings, and status reports on events and conditions that might prompt legal liability. Solidly trained investigators keep the people, places, and institutions out of trouble.

In a general sense, the security investigator lays a foundation, a conceptual framework, upon which cases can be evaluated, decisions can be made, or eventual action and policy making can be formulated. Investigation is the process of fact assimilation. Investigation is the systematic collection of evidence necessary to support or refute a claim, whether civil or criminal in nature. Investigation is the process of observation, close inspection and analysis, and continuous and regular inquiry

Chicago Private Investigation Services

USIA offers **private investigation** services to businesses and individuals all throughout **Chicago** and the **Chicagoland (suburbs)**. When you need to know the truth, look no further than our licensed, professional team of private investigators. Throughout our years of dedicated experience, we have assisted individuals, businesses and legal teams with a wide variety of investigations. Call 1-800-783-9297 or email us to get started today.

Private investigation services offered:

▸ Infidelity investigations

▸ Background checks

▸ Computer and data forensics

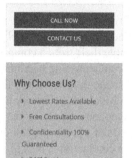

Why Choose Us?

▸ Lowest Rates Available

▸ Free Consultations

▸ Confidentiality 100% Guaranteed

▸ 24/7 Services

FIGURE 1.5 Private Investigative Services provided through USIA. (Used with permission, Ultimate Security and Investigations of America.)

into a specific subject matter. Investigation is the search and journey towards the reconstruction of events and conditions pertinent to a client's needs and interests:

> Successful investigation involves a balance between the scientific knowledge of the investigative process acquired by study and experience and the skills acquired by the artful application of learned techniques.[76]

Therefore, astute investigative practice must include these uniform practices:

1. A logical sequence must be followed
2. Real, physical evidence must be legally obtained
3. Real, physical evidence must be properly stored and preserved
4. Witnesses must be identified, interviewed, and prepared for any potential or actual litigation
5. Leads must be developed
6. Reports and documentation must be collected
7. Information must be accurately and completely recorded
8. Evidence collected must correlate to the claim, cause of action, or offense charged[77]

The investigative process must comprehensively reconstruct events, conditions, or, as is often stated, the truth itself. Finding the truth is often an elusive undertaking. In the process of finding truth, investigators must evaluate, gauge, and assess witnesses, physical and real evidence, documents, testimony, and the entire array of evidentiary considerations in the formulation of a case. *Simply put, the process of investigation requires the conversion of alleged acts into real and useful evidence.*[78]

And that is what the chief aim of this text encapsulates—a manual that lays out the basics for investigative practice but more narrowly tunes its content to the world of private security. As the pages unfold, the reader will be exposed to both general and specific skills and traits that fashion a professional investigator as well as expose the particular protocols for the many types of investigations undertaken by this industry. On top of this the reader will encounter forms, checklists, and a host of useful tools for the practitioner, and be made aware of the professional best practices in the industry, the professional groups and associations relevant to investigations, and the standards by which the investigative process should be judged. What is certain is that no security professional can escape this content in their careers since it is essential to what makes private security so central to our way of life.

NOTES

1. Total private security employment in 1982 is conservatively estimated at 1.1 million persons (excluding federal, civil, and military security workers), 449,000 in proprietary security, and 641,000 in contract security. These rises continue unabated throughout the Western world. Our neighbors to the north have seen a shrinking to a stagnant public police model replaced by a vibrant private policing system. See: "Statistics Canada Website," Table 1: Police officers, private investigators and security guards Canada 1991, 1996, 2001, and 2006, Government of Canada, last accessed August 26, 2018, available at www. statcan.gc.ca/pub/85-002-x/2008010/article/10730/tbl/tbl1-eng.htm.
2. "Professional Development—What is Security?" ASIS International, at www.asisonline.org/career-what.html, last visited October 10, 2002; see also J. Scott Harr and Kären M. Hess, *Careers in Criminal Justice and Related Fields: From Internship to Promotion* (Boston: Cengage Learning, 2009).
3. The growth, internationally, has been equally dramatic. See Jaap De Waard, "The Private Security Industry in International Perspective," *European Journal on Criminal Policy and Research* 7 (1999): 143.
4. Charles P. Nemeth and K. C. Poulin, *The Prevention Agency: A Public Safety Model for High Crime Communities in the 21st Century* (California, PA: California University of PA, 2004); Charles P. Nemeth and K. C. Poulin, *Private Security and Public Safety: A Community-Based Approach* (Upper Saddle River, NJ: Prentice Hall, 2004).
5. Frank Machovec, *Security Services, Security Science* (Springfield, IL: Charles C. Thomas, 1992): 11.
6. Despite the envy from afar, status perceptions are often vastly different. Deborah Michael's study of security officers shows a negative self-image as "junior partners" when compared to public police officers. Deborah Michael, "The Levels of Orientation Security Officers Have towards a Public Policing Function," *Security Journal* (1999): 33.
7. David A. Sklansky, "The Private Police," *UCLA Law Review* 46 (1998): 1177.
8. Sklansky, "Police": 1171.
9. "Groundbreaking Study Finds U.S. Security Industry to be $350 Billion Market," ASIS International, August 12, 2013, www.asisonline.org/News/Press-Room/Press-Releases/2013/Pages/Groundbreaking-Study-Finds-U.S.-Security-Industry-to-be-$350-Billion-Market.aspx.
10. Charles P. Nemeth, *Private Security and the Law*, 5th ed. (Boca Raton, FL: CRC Press, 2018): 1.
11. Carl F. Horowitz highlights the power of the private sector on business and community and establishes the fundamental reason why the private sector is so vital to the control of crime: "Local residents, fearing crime, are unwilling to patronize neighborhood businesses during evening hours. Business owners may be willing to bear the risk of crime in order to attract evening customers, but if residents are too frightened to shop, many of the businesses will not survive. As a result, many inner city residents no longer enjoy the convenience of having neighborhood stores. A lengthy trip thus may be required for groceries, clothing, and other household goods." "An Empowerment Strategy for Eliminating Neighborhood Crime," The Heritage Foundation, March 25, 1991, available at www.heritage.org/crime-and-justice/report/empowerment-strategy-eliminating-neighborhood-crime.
12. E. L. Gaston, "Mercenarism 2.0? The Rise of the Modern Private Security Industry and Its Implications for International Humanitarian Law Enforcement," *Harvard International Law Journal* 49 (2008): 221, www.harvardilj.org/2008/01/issue_49-1_gatson.
13. Robert Mandel, "The Privatization of Security," *Armed Forces &Society* 28 (2001): 129, 132; see also Joshua S. Press, "Crying Havoc Over the Outsourcing of Soldier and Democracy's Slipping Grip on the Dogs of War," *Northwestern University Law Review Colloquy* 103 (2008): 109.
14. Mandel, "Privatization": 129.
15. Mark Calaguas, "Military Privatization: Efficiency or Anarch?" *Chicago-Kent Journal of International &Comparative Law* 6 (2006): 58.

16. Jon Cadieux, "Regulating the United States Private Army: Militarizing Security Contractors," *California Western International Law Journal* 39 (2008): 197.

17. Mandel, "Privatization": 132.

18. Christopher Kinsey, *Corporate Soldiers and International Security: The Rise of Private Military Companies* (New York: Routledge, 2006); Thomas Jäger and Gerhard Kümmel, *Private Military and Security: Companies' Chances, Problems, Pitfalls and Prospects* (Heidelberg, Germany: Springer VS, 2007).

19. Scott M. Sullivan, "Private Force/Public Goods," *Connecticut Law Review* 42 (2010): 857–858; see also Ellen Dannin, "Red Tape or Accountability: Privatization, Public-ization, and Public Values," *Cornell Journal of Law and Public Policy* 15 (2005): 113; Jody Freeman, "The Contracting State," *Florida State University Law Review* 28 (2000): 170; Clayton P. Gillette and Paul B. Stephan III, "Constitutional Limitations on Privatization," *American Journal of Comparative Law* 46 (Supp. 1998): 490; David A. Super, "Privatization, Policy Paralysis, and the Poor," *California Law Review* 96 (2008): 409–410.

20. William C. Cunningham and Todd H. Taylor, *The Hallcrest Report: Private Security and Police in America* (Boston: Butterworth, 1991): 3.

21. David A. Sklansky, "Private Police and Democracy," *American Criminal Law Review* 43 (2006): 89.

22. Paul S. Bailin and Stanton G. Cort, "Industry Corner: Private Contractual Security Services: The U.S. Market and Industry," *Business Economics* 31 (April 1996): 57.

23. See Pinkerton Security Services USA, at www.securitasinc.com/who-we-are/about-securitas-usa/our-history/, last visited September 3, 2018, for information on the merger of Pinkerton, Securitas, and Burns Security.

24. See the ASIS International website at www.asisonline.org for more information.

25. National Advisory Commission on Criminal Justice Standards and Goals, *Report of the Task Force on Private Security* 30 (Washington, DC: US Department of Justice, 1976).

26. Gion Green, *Introduction to Security* (Boston: Butterworth, 1981): 9.

27. Gloria G. Dralla et al., "Who's Watching the Watchmen? The Regulation, or Non-Regulation, of America's Largest Law Enforcement Institution, The Private Police," *Golden Gate Law Review* 5 (1975): 443.

28. For a fascinating look at entirely Western law enforcement see *Lawman* by John Boessenecker (Norman, OK: University of Oklahoma Press, 1998).

29. Erik Beckman, *Law Enforcement in a Democratic Society: An Introduction* (Chicago: Burnham Inc, 1980): 34.

30. Milton Lipson, *On Guard: The Business of Private Security* (New York: Quadrangle, 1975): 21.

31. Beckman, "Enforcement": 34.

32. For an interesting analysis on this private to public—public to private genealogy, see: Karena Rahall, "The Siren Is Calling: Economic and Ideological Trends toward Privatization of Public Police Forces," *University of Miami Law Review* 68 (Spring 2014): 633.

33. See: Stephen Rushin, "Transcripts from the C. Edwin Baker Lecture on Liberty, Equality, and Democracy: Article: The Regulation of Private Police," *West Virginia Law Review* 15 (Fall 2012): 159.

34. William C. Cunningham, John J. Strauchs, and Clifford W. Van Meter, *Private Security Trends 1970–2000: The Hallcrest Report II* (Woburn, MA: Butterworth-Heinemann, 1990), Figure 7.2 at 237.

35. "Employment Projections," Bureau of Labor Statistics, accessed September 3, 2018, at https://data.bls.gov/projections/occupationProj.

36. Michael Moran, "Security Market Growth Continues," *Security Management*, May 5, 2015, https://sm.asisonline.org/Pages/Security-Market-Growth-Continues.aspx; "High Growth Reported for the US Private Security Services Market," *Reuters*, August 5, 2008, last accessed January 2, 2009, at www.reuters.com/article/pressrelease/idus168856+05-Aug-2008+MW20080805.

37. U.S. Department of Justice, National Institute of Justice, *The Growing Role of Private Security* (Washington, DC: U.S. Government Printing Office, 1984): 1; Miroslav Baljak, Ph.D., Ministry of Defence bih (AF bih), *The Role of Private Security Agency in the 21st Century*, accessed September 3, 2018, http://doisrpska.nub.rs/index.php/DEF/article/download/1987/1912; Diane Richey, "Proud To Be Security: How Roles Changed After 9/11," *Security Magazine*, September 1, 2011, accessed September 3, 2018, available at www.securitymagazine.com/articles/82306-proud-to-be-security-how-roles-changed-after-911.

38. "2012 Economic Census. Core Business Statistics Series: Comparative Statistics for the U.S. and the States (2007 NAICS Basis): 2012 and 2007, 2012 Economic Census of the United States," U.S. Census Bureau, accessed September 3, 2018, www.census.gov/data/data-tools.html.

39. Morgan O. Reynolds, *Using the Private Sector to Deter Crime—NCPA Policy Report No. 181*, (Dallas, TX: National Center for Policy Analysis, 1994): 1, accessed September 3, 2018, www.ncjrs.gov/pdf-files1/Photocopy/148741NCJRS.pdf.
40. Bureau of Labor Statistics, United States Department of Labor, *Occupational Outlook Handbook*, Private Detectives and Investigators, visited July 7, 2018, www.bls.gov/ooh/protective-service/private-detectives-and-investigators.htm.
41. The movement of traditional law enforcement functions to the private realm is not merely a national phenomena, but a global, worldwide reality. See Baljak, "21st Century."
42. Richard W. Lukins, "Training for the Security Guard," *Security Management* 20 (1976): 32.
43. Raymond E. Bechler, "Private Police Ownership: Can it Possibly Happen?" *Journal of California Law Enforcement* 45 (2011): 20.
44. See: Charles P. Nemeth, *Private Security: An Introduction to Principles and Practice* (Boca Raton, FL: CRC Press, 2018): 181–183 for an examination of how legal arguments use "public function" to prove the transference.
45. Advisory Committee, "Report Private Security": 5.
46. At the same time, these increased services demand higher levels of training and professionalism for security investigators—see John Manzo, "On the Practices of Private Security Officers: Canadian Security Officers' Reflections on Training and Legitimacy," *Social Justice* 38 (2011): 107.
47. See Nemeth, "Law 5th."
48. See Rushin, "Regulation."
49. See Nemeth, "Law 5th."
50. Ibid.
51. Norman Spain and Gary Elkin, "Private and Public Security: There Is a Difference," *Security World* 16 (1979): 32.
52. Areto A. Imoukhuede, "The Real Homeland Security Gaps," *Ohio Northern University Law Review* 42 (2016): 396.
53. The blurring lines have existed for quite a long time since police "moonlighting" in the world of private security is commonplace even today. See Seth W. Stoughton, "Moonlighting: The Private Employment of Off-Duty Officers," *University of Illinois Law Review* 2017, no. 5 (2017).
54. Advisory Committee, "Report Private Security."
55. See Nemeth, "Private Security": 75.
56. Federal Bureau of Investigation, *Crime in the United States, Uniform Crime Reports* (Washington, DC: U.S. Government Printing Office, 2016), Table 1A, https://ucr.fbi.gov/crime-in-the-u.s/2016/crime-in-the-u.s.-2016/topic-pages/tables/table-1a.
57. Advisory Committee, "Report Private Security": 19.
58. U.S. Department of Justice, National Institute of Justice, *Private Employment of Public Police* (Washington, DC: U.S. Government Printing Office, 1988): 1.
59. The federal government, at both the executive and legislative level, have made support for public-private cooperation a key policy goal. Public-private partnerships have been recognized by several Presidential Directives and national strategies as a necessary element of preparedness: Homeland Security Presidential Directive (HSPD) 7 (LLIS.gov ID# 9937), issued by President Bush on December 17, 2003, tasks the Department of Homeland Security (DHS) and various federal agencies with coordinating information sharing and other protective measures with the private sector; Homeland Security Presidential Directive 9 (LLIS.gov ID# 9938), also issued by President Bush on January 30, 2004, establishes public-private information sharing as part of a national policy to protect the nation's agriculture and food systems; The National Preparedness Standard on Disaster/Emergency Management and Business Continuity (National Fire Protection Association 1600) (www.nfpa.org/PDF/nfpa1600.pdf?Src=nfpa), 2004 edition, recommends cross-sector cooperation on a number of issues; The National Response Plan (LLIS.gov ID# 11904), released December 1, 2004, outlines the roles and responsibilities of the private sector in emergency response, including coordination with public sector responders; The National Strategy for Homeland Security (LLIS.gov ID# 138), released on July 1, 2002, states that "government at the federal, state, and local level must actively collaborate and partner with the private sector"; The National Strategy for the Physical Protection of Critical Infrastructure and Key Assets (LLIS.gov ID# 11888), released in February 2003, states that "local communities play critical roles in ... engaging their public and private leadership in the development of coordinated local and regional plans to assure the protection of residents and businesses."
60. Richey, "Security After 9/11."

61. National Infrastructure Advisory Council, *Public-Private Sector Intelligence Coordination: Final Report and Recommendations by the Council* (July 2006): 67.
62. US Department of Homeland Security, *The 2014 Quadrennial Homeland Security Review* (2014): 58.
63. Ibid.
64. J. R. Greene, T. M. Seamon, and P. R. Levy, "Merging Public and Private Security for Collective Benefit: Philadelphia's Center City District," *American Journal of Police* 14 (1995): 3–20.
65. See "2017 Security Industry Outlook," Pinkerton, accessed September 3, 2018, www.pinkerton.com/our-thoughts/blog/1382/2017-security-industry-outlook.
66. See: Hyungjin Lim and Pamela Wilcox, "Crime-Reduction Effects of Open-street CCTV: Conditionality Considerations," *Justice Quarterly* 34, no. 4 (2017): 597–626, https://doi-org.ez.lib.jjay.cuny.edu/10.1080/07418825.2016.1194449.
67. James Davidson and Mark Lytle, *After the Fact: The Art of Historical Detection*, 5th ed. (Boston: McGraw Hill, 2005): XV.
68. Ronald Mendell, *How to Do Financial Asset Investigations*, 4th ed. (Springfield, IL: Charles C. Thomas, 2012); Cynthia Hetherington, *The Guide to Online Due Diligence Investigations* (Facts on Demand Press, 2015); Cynthia Magno, "Where Crimes Converge Investigations Merge," *Security Management*, March 1, 2005; Patricia W. Kittredge, "Guideposts for the Investigation of a Negligence Case," *Practical Lawyer* 90 (1973): 55; J. Stannar Baker, "Reconstruction of Accidents," *Traffic Digest and Review* 17 (1969): 9; P. Magarick, "Investigating the Civil Case: General Principals," *American Jurisprudence Trials* 1 (1987): 361.
69. Russell Colling, *Hospital Security* (Boston: Butterworth Publishers, 1982): 211; Jos Maas, "Hospital Security: Protecting the Business," *Journal of Healthcare Protection Management*, January 1, 2013.
70. American Society for Industrial Security, *Basic Guidelines for Security Investigation* (1981): 1; see also the ASIS Certification Handbook which highlights the necessary competencies of a variety of positions including the investigator at www.asisonline.org/globalassets/certification/documents/certification-handbook_final.pdf.
71. "Professional Certified Investigator," ASIS International, accessed September 3, 2018, www.asisonline.org/certification/professional-certified-investigator-pci.
72. Pinkerton's, Inc., *Investigations Department Training Manual* (1990): 30–31.
73. Thomas Eimermann, *Fundamentals of Paralegalism* (Little, Brown &Co., 1980): 102–103.
74. Bureau of Labor Statistics, U.S. Department of Labor, *Occupational Outlook Handbook*, Private Detectives and Investigators, accessed August 4, 2018, www.bls.gov/ooh/protective-service/private-detectives-and-investigators.htm.
75. Ultimate Security Investigations of America, 3333 Warrenville Road suite 200, Lisle, IL 60532, https://usaprivatesecurity.com/investigative-services/private-investigation.
76. W. Bennett and K. Hess, *Criminal Investigation* (Eagan, MN: West Publishing Co., 1981): 9; Kären M. Hess, Christine Hess Orthmann, and Henry Lim Cho, *Criminal Investigation*, 11th ed. (Boston: Cengage, 2017).
77. Ibid.
78. Patricia W. Kittredge, "Guideposts for the Investigation of a Negligence Case," *Practical Lawyer* 90 (1973): 55; J. Stannar Baker, "Reconstruction of Accidents," *Traffic Digest and Review* 17 (1969): 9; *American Jurisprudence Trials* 1 (1987): 357.

2 General Characteristics of a Competent Investigator

2.1 INTRODUCTION

In the investigative realm, as in any other occupation, certain skills, qualities, and competencies are essential to success. While differing personalities, styles of operation, and skill levels exist, there are traits that are common in all professional investigators. Although there is variation in how to accomplish the investigative task, there is a sort of "investigative DNA." Russell Colling, in his text, *Hospital Security*, portrays the solid investigator as a "natural."

> The really good investigator has a natural aptitude and is intrigued by the investigative process coupled with the human relations involved. An investigation offers a challenge and will often succeed or fail in direct relation to the degree of competence and enthusiasm displayed.[1]

Adept investigators must possess these attributes:

- Energy and alertness
- Knowledge of the law
- Ability to set realistic objectives
- Methodical approach
- Knowledge of human nature
- Observation and deduction abilities
- Ability to maintain meaningful notes[2]

Undoubtedly, the competent investigator, whether public or private, encompasses all these traits and more. This chapter highlights the types of traits and skill levels needed to succeed in the world of investigative practice.

2.2 A PRIVATE VERSUS PUBLIC MENTALITY

While the crossover between how private security personnel conduct investigations and how public police carry out the same function is undeniable, there are differing visions and ends in mind. Surely the qualities of a competent investigator apply equally in both settings. And that the subject matter of investigations may mirror one another is equally concluded. Indeed, the level of partnership between the public and private systems is exponentially increasing at every level of the investigative process—a reality made even clearer as the privatization transference continues without much restriction. Private police are increasingly carrying out once entrenched public functions. Russell Colling, in his work *Hospital Security*, concludes that the differences between the investigative protocol of the public officer from the private officer are really those of form and mission, and indeed the missions are very complementary.

It is techniques and varying purposes that differentiate the security investigation from that of a law enforcement agency. This is not to say that the security investigation always has a different focus. A police investigation is conducted basically for the purpose of apprehending the perpetrator of a crime and locating evidence for the successful prosecution of a case. Security investigations, on the other hand, may involve, in addition to crimes, the gathering of information in regards to the violation of organizational rules and regulations; a job applicant's background for conditions that may lead to criminal violations; the need for new security controls and procedures; liability claims or potential claims; unsafe conditions; or evidence needed to prove or disprove certain allegations.[3]

The investigative process itself inherently serves the justice system—both the criminal and civil systems that depend upon hard facts and evidentiary quality to prove the case at hand.[4] Whether conducted by private or public police, the criminal and civil systems depend upon an investigative process that is able:

1. To determine if there is sufficient factual evidence to support or defeat each element of a cause of action
2. To accumulate the necessary factual evidence to prove or defeat a case at trial or to form the basis for a settlement
3. To locate leads to additional evidence
4. To locate persons or property
5. To find evidence that might be used to discredit (impeach) a witness or the opponent[5]

The question of what to investigate largely correlates to the mission and goals of the entity undertaking the investigation.[6] While similarities abound between the public and private systems, the difference and distinction between these systems is undeniable. Public policing must, by nature, be more concerned about criminal felonies than any private security firm. Homicide is not as critical a concern for private security forces as it is for the investigator laboring in Chicago or New York City. Other felonies may be better suited to shared practice such as burglary, grand theft and other forms of larceny, fraud and corrupt practice, assault and battery, all of which touch upon the day-to-day grind common to both systems.[7] The Hallcrest Report II surveyed both public and private security professionals as to their overall impressions of what the ultimate goals of these systems are. Both agree that "security services" are part of the overall mission. See Figure 2.1.[8]

The differences are quite obvious with the private model that is more concerned with profit, asset protection, and more targeted activities. The public system, comparatively, displays a broader vision with little if any entrepreneurial spirit since it is governmentally housed. Hallcrest II also assessed how security administrators, the higher echelon of the industry, in proprietary and contractual settings, rank ordered their proper ends and goals. The comparison between these two security sectors is pretty uniform. However, the similarities dissipate a bit when public law enforcement executives prioritize functions.

Public officers are clearly more concerned with arrest and prosecution than their private counterparts. This conclusion is further buttressed by the "general public" concerns within the same list of priorities. This prioritization, in and of itself, is a telling distinction, though it should not be viewed as justification for a sharp division. If anything, both public and private law enforcement share a

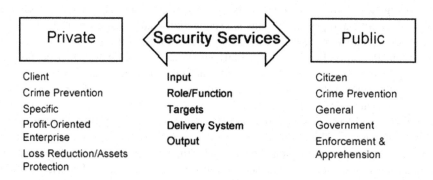

FIGURE 2.1   Comparison between public and private police functions.

generic goal—namely, the general enforcement of laws. As Bill Strudal points out in his article, "Giving the Police a Sense of Security,"

> Our goal, usually not shared by police and security is law enforcement ... if we accept the premise that police and security have the same goals, then why don't we work together on a regular basis? There are differences; nobody can deny that ... there are many other gaps between the two forces, but none is insurmountable with good training and dialogue.[9]

The similarities between function, duty, and obligation are very apparent when the tasks of investigation are considered. The skills of the private sector are essentially identical to the public. Review Box 2.1 to see the diverse opportunities shared and borne by both the private and public sectors.

BOX 2.1   PRIVATE AND PUBLIC SECTOR OPPORTUNITIES

- Public Prosecutors and Law Enforcement Agencies
- Tort Investigation
- Publisher Actions
- Bank Investigations and Security
- Insurance Companies and Self-Insurer Investigations
- Railway, Bus and Airlines Companies Security
- Motor Freight, Warehouse and Freight Terminal Security
- Manufacturing, Wholesale Distributing and Retail Security
- Hotel Security
- Character Investigations
- Surveillance
- Plant and Store Surveillance
- Undercover Investigations

Web Exercise: As more and more public law enforcement services are taken up by private security, the investigative differences melt away. See the content of the sexual offense investigation for campus police sponsored by the State of Virginia at: https://www.dcjs.virginia.gov/training-events/responding-sexual-assault-trauma-informed-approach-sexual-assault-investigations.

Private Security's investigators differ in other ways because of its clientele. For instance, the importance of locating people, conducting accurate and dependable background information and vital records, and conducting due diligence for corporate and business purposes takes on far greater importance than the public police model. Lexis/Nexis, among a growing number of consulting and subscription services, provides state-of-the-art data services, information publicly available on individuals for background checks and investigative purposes.[10]

Despite the differences, the private–public alignment continues to be tighter, so much so that state regulators are now attempting to set up more dependable and uniform standards for the designation of a "private investigator." The International Association of Security and Investigative Regulators was founded in 2001 for this very purpose. See Figure 2.2.[11]

FIGURE 2.2 International Association of Security and Investigative Regulators logo (used with permission, IASIR, www.iasir.org).

The IASIR mission includes:

- Enhancing applicant processing and records management
- Advocating for expedient background investigation and fingerprint processing
- Disseminating information on insurance/bonds
- Keeping abreast of and sharing information about new licensing technology
- Promoting effective state regulation and enforcement
- Assisting in education and training standards
- Eliminating unlicensed activity
- Developing harmony between law enforcement and the regulated industries
- Influencing federal legislation
- Formulating model laws and regulations
- Assisting states in developing and enforcing laws and regulations
- Encouraging reciprocity between states
- Providing training and education opportunities for state regulators

Web Exercise: For an excellent overview of the world of private investigation, visit the Detective Training Institute's Summary at: www.detectivetraining.com/lesson1html/.

2.2.1 OBJECTIVITY AND INVESTIGATIVE PRACTICE

Good investigators are driven by facts rather than by emotions, preconceptions, biases, or opinions that lack a factual basis. "Once an investigator loses sight of the facts and commences to be led by opinions, he no longer maintains the necessary objectivity."[12] Investigators who commence the process of fact gathering and assimilation with preconceived notions and conclusions are destined to produce a faulty result. Therefore, the investigator's strongest suit is an open-minded, hypothesis-driven, scientific approach to the case. Only when an investigator purges personal feelings and preconceptions will the investigative process have integrity, for facts are what drive the investigator and comprise the subject matter of the investigation itself.

Fact gathering must become the hallmark of the security operative's investigative process. If so, the investigator's actions inspire others to believe in the integrity of the process and that judgments are reliable and credible. A recent job description for an investigator stresses these capacities:

- Analyze problems to identify significant factors, gather pertinent data, and recognize solutions
- Plan and organize work, and
- Communicate effectively orally and in writing

These skills develop a professional approach in the investigator and assure a "confident, business-like"[13] investigator working in the field. This allegiance to objective fact gathering is not always easy. Security investigators are often placed in situations that are emotional by design. Domestic disputes, labor unrest, public protest, to name a few settings, represent the types of cases involving heightened emotions.[14] Keeping your head in these scenarios is professionally demanding. Adhering to objective method, remaining emotionally detached, and carrying out the assigned task without animus is a tall order. Indeed, investigative work carries its own series of demands, both physically and emotionally—a reality often forgotten by both practitioners and researchers.[15]

Overcoming the many stresses inherent in the criminal investigation process is essential to any objective analysis of the facts and circumstances of every investigative setting. Sollie, Kop, and Euwema call for what they term an "emotional distancing" from the various stresses that naturally emerge in investigative scenarios, the work demands, the multitasking and pressing problems that often accompany the regimen encountered by investigators.[16]

In addition, training plays a key role in assuring the necessary confidence to stay focused and on track since the "repetition of simple steps … can help keep a sequence of events foremost in an officer's mind even under stress."[17] In the final analysis, the effective investigator searches for objective reality and records it.[18]

Web Exercise: Visit ASIS International's web page on its Professional Certified Investigator (PCI®) Program at www.asisonline.org/certification/professional-certified-investigator-pci and review the skills and knowledge necessary to become a certified investigator by clicking on the "three primary domains" link.

2.2.2 Logic and Investigative Practice

Aside from the emotional control just discussed, the competent investigator must depend upon a logical method and protocol. Fact gathering and deductive reasoning about the facts, conditions and circumstances of a given case demand a logical mind. Logic can best be described as the orderly and sensible review of facts, conditions, and events in a consistent and sequential order. To do so the investigator must devise appropriate inquiry techniques. Simply, ask the right questions in the right order! Since logic is an exercise of pure reason, facts can be evaluated by direct, deductive, inferential, or reverse forms of reasoning. Queries in a general sense will be:

- *Who* was responsible for this information?
- *What* does the information mean?
- *Where* was this information gathered?
- *When* was this information collected?
- *How* was this information acquired?
- *What* other parties or individuals might be responsible for this information?
- *Why* was this information found in this location?

In this way, the investigator looks for correlations. "All possible cause and effect relations must be examined, links found, and conclusions drawn, but only after thoroughly exploring all alternatives."[19] As an illustration, consider a claim of food poisoning alleged against a restaurant and hotel establishment. Assume that you are a security officer assigned to investigate the claim. What types of logical inquiries should be made? Walter J. Buzby and David Paine, in *Hotel and Motel Security Management*, suggest these various lines of inquiry:

1. When did the victim become ill? (date and hour)
2. What was the nature of the illness? (pains, vomiting, dizziness, etc.)
3. How long did the illness continue?
4. Was a doctor consulted or any medicine taken? If a doctor was consulted, a copy of his findings should be secured.
5. What food or foods does the victim claim caused his illness?
6. Why does the victim feel that these foods caused the illness? Did they have a particular odor, taste, or appearance that caused suspicion?
7. What activities did the victim engage in prior to eating the suspected foods? Had the victim been to any parties, consumed any alcohol, medicine? Had they been in the company of any other persons?
8. Had the victim sustained any traumatic experience prior to eating? If so, get full details.
9. If the victim is unable to pinpoint any particular item of food that is suspicious, secure a complete list of all food eaten.
10. Check hotel records (restaurant records) as to number of servings of each item consumed by the victim that were served that day.
11. Check records for any other reports of illnesses on that particular day.[20]

This type of logical processing is often described as the "who, what, where, when, how, and why" questioning sequence. Adept investigators, who ask the right questions, in the right order, will find the facts that are essential to successful case resolution. In a criminal or civil context, the standard 5W and H lines of questioning look like this:

Who Questions
- Who discovered the incident or crime?
- Who reported the incident or crime?
- Who saw or heard anything of importance?
- Who had a motive or other reason for participation?
- Who was responsible for the incident or crime?
- Who can be considered an aider, abetter, co-conspirator, co-defendant, or co-plaintiff?
- With whom did the defendant associate?
- Who are the witnesses?

What Questions
- What occurred during this incident or crime?
- What are the incidents or crimes in question?
- What are the elements of these causes of action or crimes?
- What are the facts and actions committed by the defendant or suspect?
- What do the witnesses know?
- What evidence has been obtained?
- What was done with the evidence?
- What tools and other instruments were employed?
- What weapons or other real evidence exists?
- What means of transportation was used in the incident or commission of the crime?
- What was the modus operandi (method of operation)?

Where Questions
- Where was the incident or crime discovered?
- Where was the incident or crime committed?
- Where were the suspects or defendants seen?
- Where were the witnesses during the event?
- Where was the victim found?
- Where were the tools and other instruments obtained?
- Where does the suspect or defendant live?
- Where does/did the victim live?
- Where is the suspect or defendant now?
- Where is the suspect or defendant likely to frequent?
- Where was the suspect or defendant tracked down?

When Questions
- When did the incident or crime take place?
- When was the incident or crime discovered?
- When were appropriate parties notified of the incident or crime?
- When did the police arrive at the scene?
- When was the victim last seen?
- When was the suspect apprehended?

How Questions
- How did the incident or crime take place?
- How did the suspect or defendant get to the scene?

- How did the suspect or defendant depart from the scene?
- How did the suspect or defendant get the necessary information to commit the wrongful act?
- How much damage was done?
- How much property was stolen?
- How much skill, knowledge, and personal expertise were necessary for this incident or crime to take place?

Why Questions
- Why did the incident or crime take place?
- Why were particular tools or instruments utilized?
- Why was there a particular method employed?
- Why did the witnesses talk?
- Why did the witnesses show reluctance in talking?

Investigative documentation like the *Security Incident Report* at Figure 2.3[21] mirrors this logical progression necessary for effective investigation.

Any investigative report should be objective and logical—in most cases a standardized report form will aid the investigator in collecting the "who, what, where, when, how, and why." In investigative practice, the search for truth, through the reconstruction of events and conditions, requires that the facts be carefully collected and studied.

Investigative logic is an exercise of both the intellect and the imagination. However, it is not fabrication or some type of delusion. Instead, it is the capacity and ability to draw natural inferences based on logic and reality from well-grounded facts. The investigator must be able to distinguish, compare, and contrast the reliable from the conjectural, and just as importantly, be willing to change, modify, adjust a basic theory as the facts emerge, and therefore as the case evolves. E. Smith, in his book, *A Practical Guide for Investigators*, concurs with the view of logical flexibility.

> The theory must be abandoned as soon as proof shows it is inconsistent with facts uncovered. Every theory should be investigated to an end. Nothing should be taken for granted. When discarding a theory, it should not be entirely eliminated from the mind. The ability to judge when a theory should be abandoned is a valuable asset to the investigator.[22]

Throughout the investigative process, a competent investigator can detect or see through the questionable, the dubitable, and the unreliable—whether it be physical or testimonial evidence. And in the case of investigative interviewing, the practitioner must be skilled in detecting deception—knowing when a story simply does not gel or being able to discern the "liar from the truth teller" and "discriminate between true and false intentions."[23]

Web Exercise: Take the sample FBI logical reasoning test at www.fbijobs.gov/sites/default/files/Logical_Reasoning.pdf

2.2.3 Perseverance, Diligence, and Investigative Practice

"Stick-to-itiveness," a professional and personal obsession with getting the facts right, and a corresponding desire to discern the proper resolution of a case, are mandatory attributes of a good investigator. Cases are rarely resolved by chance, but rather by hard work and an equally strong dose of "anticipatory thinking,"[24] which never rules out a theory and always thinks ahead of any explanation. The investigator must be not only a collector and assimilator of information and facts, who subjects those facts to deductive and inferential analysis, but also a person of enormous perseverance. Since most investigations do not move forward in a straight line and are very likely to have impediments placed in the path of resolution, an intense desire to reach proper conclusions can only aid the investigator. The security specialist must be able to handle adversity, dead ends,

SECURITY OPERATIONS

SECURITY INCIDENT REPORT

INCIDENT CODE:

(Refer to Code Sheet)

INSTRUCTIONS: This report shall be completed by the person reporting or involved in the incident or their manager/supervisor (or designee). The completed Report shall be delivered or sent electronically <u>no later</u> than the end of the business day following the date of the incident.

Please refer to the accompanying *Incident Code Reference Sheet* for determining the proper incident code. Use a separate form(s) to report multiple individual incidents. Call the Security Operations Unit for additional information.

A *SECURITY INCIDENT* **IS DEFINED AS:**
- An incident placing a person or property at risk that requires action by law enforcement authorities or security personnel at a County facility whether they were summoned or not; or
- An incident placing a person at risk involving an on-duty County employee during the performance of their official duties. This classification includes while walking to or from an off-site parking facility at the start or end of the workday; or
- An incident of a suspicious or unusual nature on County Property that place people or property at risk; or
- An incident that occurred during non-business hours that impacts or affects the County workplace.

I. DATE OCCURRED: **TIME OCCURRED:**   **DATE COMPLETED:**

COUNTY DEPARTMENT REPORTING:

ADDRESS OF FACILITY:

☐ *On-site security services contracted with Sheriff's Department*

ADDRESS OF INCIDENT: *(If different)*

SUMMARY OF INCIDENT: (*BRIEFLY*** describe the incident here, include full names (first and last), use separate sheet to document details, if necessary.)**

☐ *Continued on a separate sheet(s)*

OTHER PARTIES INVOLVED NOT LISTED IN SUMMARY: *(List any additional parties on a separate sheet)*

1) Name: ☐ Employee Gender: Emp#/DOB/Age:

2) Name: ☐ Employee Gender: Emp#/DOB/Age:

3) Name: ☐ Employee Gender: Emp#/DOB/Age:

II. WORKPLACE VIOLENCE CHECKLIST:

☐ The VICTIM is a County employee?   ☐ The SUSPECT is a County employee.

☐ There was a physical ACT OF VIOLENCE?   ☐ There was a verbal/written THREAT OF VIOLENCE

☐ FIREARM (gun) used   ☐ Other WEAPON used, non-firearm. Type:

☐ HATE CRIME   ☐ RECURRENT ISSUE: Previous incident(s) ☐ Reported ☐ Not Reported

☐ Law Enforcement RESPONDED-Agency: ☐ Complaint/Crime REPORT Taken-Report #:

III. SAFETY PLAN: *The actions below should be considered when dealing with an act or threat of violence if necessary, check ALL that apply:*

☐ 1) On-site security notified.   ☐ 2) Parties involved were separated.

☐ 3) Offer/obtain medical treatment for affected employee(s).   ☐ 4) Offer Security escort to their vehicle/modify parking assignment.

☐ 5) Offer employee reassignment/alternate workplace   ☐ 6) Offer County Employee Assistance Program (EAP) services

☐ 7) Law enforcement patrol check requested for workplace/home.   ☐ 8) Obtain and attach copies of written witness affidavits/statements.

☐ 9) Emergency Protective Order obtained from law enforcement.   ☐ 10) Consult with Security Operations Unit (SOU) personnel.

☐ 11) Seek/request assistance in obtaining a Restraining Order from the Office of County Counsel

☐ 12) Initiate an Incident Event Log and maintained by:

☐ 13) Other action(s) taken:

REPORTED BY: **TELEPHONE:**   **EMAIL:**

MANAGER: **TELEPHONE:**   **EMAIL:**

SIR Form *(Revised 2017)*   Submit By Email

FIGURE 2.3 A standard Security Incident Report.

frustrations, and setbacks, and a wide array of unexpected and even surprising contingencies. Perseverance can be described as a deliberateness that withstands excuse or mitigating factors. Perseverance can also take the form of mental and physical endurance that is not readily swayed. These qualities are particularly essential when the private security operative is involved in cases of terrorism, hostage negotiation, and the design, and implementation of, executive-protection systems.

Perseverance generates a steady stream of leads during the investigative process, such as witnesses. "Occasionally, the investigator may be able to produce an unknown or unsuspected witness, but the discovery of such a witness cannot usually be credited to chance."[25] Instead, the witness will be discovered because the investigator has followed a lead with persistence. In every aspect of the investigative process, this dedication to task and result reaps fruit in the long run. Despite the tediousness of much investigative work, the security specialist must stay resolved and attuned to the overarching goal. The practices of surveillance, inventory, and warehouse searches, auditing techniques, records analysis, and title, tax, and record abstraction are hardly exciting activities, yet each one of these practices may yield remarkable results. The investigator must remain steadfast in the mission and fully recognize that while the investigative process is slow and deliberate, in time it will generate laudable leads.

For example, in building a case for divorce based upon infidelity, adultery, cruelty, or abuse, the investigator must find and evaluate the circumstances, events, and conditions supporting the client's position. The investigator must also accord the opposing party an objective view and not simply believe the allegations and affirmations of any client but confirm the claims. In short, the investigative perspective requires looking at the whole picture—all parties and evidence that bear upon a case. To do so requires a persevering and diligent personality. "Investigation often involves hours, or even days, of waiting and watching, of performing tedious, boring assignments that may or may not yield information or evidence helpful to the case. Nonetheless, patience and perseverance are often the key to successful investigation."[26] Be mindful, however, that perseverance and diligence are not equated with stubbornness and intractability. Perseverance must be tempered with and complemented by an intellectual and personal flexibility. And this sort of tenacity goes a long way to impressing the clientele the security investigator serves—a doggedness that impresses and a demonstration that the needs of the client matter throughout the case.[27]

2.3 HUMAN RELATIONS SKILLS AND INVESTIGATIVE PRACTICE

Because so much of an investigator's success depends upon the ability to collect information, one's capacity for human interaction adds to this competency. Investigators who cannot relate to clients, witnesses, agency heads, government employees, police system and social service personnel, and insurance and claims adjusters, will be less than proficient.[28]

Interpersonal skills promote the acquisition of information and provide a steady stream of intelligence worthy of collection. The importance of human relations cannot be overemphasized since fact gathering and human intelligence keenly depend upon it. Effective human relations assures that the investigator creates a "culture of collaboration" and promotes the "common goals of safety and communication."[29]

Web Exercise: Read the short article on "Communication Skills for Security Personnel" on the International Foundation for Protection Officers website at www.ifpo.org/wp-content/uploads/2013/08/Zumbrum_Effective_Communication_Skills.pdf.

An investigator that alienates a witness loses valuable information. If an investigator cannot express or communicate in clear, understandable terms, questions will not be answered. In this sense being an educated person is crucial to the operation—having the capacity to express ideas and doing so while engendering ease in the party interviewed.[30] If an investigator makes people feel ill at ease, offended, or defensive, the ability to collect information will be substantially impaired. Ideally, private investigators must have personal characteristics that attract and motivate the opposition. "The investigator's career is totally people oriented. Investigation is concerned, directly and indirectly, with and about people. Thus, private investigators need to feel at home with them, understand, motivate, and communicate with them."[31] Without sufficient human relations skills, security specialists operate at a continuous disadvantage. At a minimum, an investigator must be able to accomplish the following:

1. To express positive attitudes towards others
2. To be able to manifest interest in others
3. To be able to build a good human relations
4. To be able to express empathy and concern for others

5. To be able to establish a good rapport with others
6. To be able to adapt to different personalities and circumstances
7. To be able to communicate effectively with others
8. To be a believable personality
9. To be clear and accurate in communications with others
10. To be able to persuade and motivate other people
11. To be able to effectively manage conversations and to elicit information
12. To understand the emotional strengths and weaknesses of others
13. To exercise control of one's emotions
14. To be able to make friends rather than enemies[32]

Web Exercise: Read the article "How to Conduct a Workplace Investigation" on SHRM's website at www.shrm.org/hr-today/news/hr-magazine/pages/1214-workplace-investigations.aspx.

Another measure of human relations skills is the art of communication itself. Most people think of communication as verbal or written; however, nonverbal communication plays a role in investigative practice. Nonverbal communication includes body language and an awareness of sensory perceptions, such as sight, smell, taste, hearing, and touch. Investigators must be attuned to human and environmental conditions.

> *Why* people instinctively like or dislike others; trust or fear them; are attracted to or repelled by others is too complex for us to study definitively. [Investigators] must be aware that their total communication effort is affected by the impression they give others, whether in the form of body odors (good or bad), facial expressions, body language, voice tone, phrasing, and vocabulary, or writing style and technique.[33]

Common sense dictates that information gathering and fact assimilation and collection will be easier for those who can skillfully interact with others. From another perspective, certain personality traits plainly benefit an investigator. Art Buckwalter posed a partial listing of the traits and characteristics necessary in a solid investigator, in his very worthy work, *Investigative Methods*:

- *Alert*—ready and quick to understand or act; aware
- *Believable*—one whom other persons can believe and trust
- *Calm*—able to control emotions; free from agitation and excitement
- *Common sense*—down-to-earth, good judgment
- *Dependable*—worthy of being depended on; reliable and trustworthy
- *Determined*—resolute; able to see an investigation through to its finish
- *Honest*—truthful, frank, honorable, and straightforward in conduct or speech
- *Impartial*—unbiased, equitable, free from favoritism, fair
- *Ingenious*—possessed of inventive ingenuity, shrewd, capable of creating a clever and effective solution to an investigative problem
- *Law-abiding*—conforms to or lives in accordance with the law
- *Level-headed*—has sound judgment, balanced reasoning
- *Objective*—able to concentrate on facts and external aspects of investigation without focusing on subjective feelings
- *Observant*—takes careful notice; with keen powers of observation
- *Patient*—capable of calm waiting and forbearance under provocation; undaunted by obstacles and delays
- *Perceptive*—discerning, aware; has alert senses
- *Persistent*—tenacious, dogged, able to see the problem through
- *Prudent*—capable of directing and conducting oneself wisely and judiciously; discreet, sensible, reasonable, and skillful in the application of capabilities

- *Remembers well*—capable of recollection and recall
- *Responsible*—accountable, reliable; able to answer for own conduct and obligations and to assume trust
- *Resourceful*—able to fall back on other sources or strategies when the usual means are not effective; has reserve abilities and alternative resources
- *Thorough*—able to carry things through to completion; painstaking, exact, and careful about details
- *Versatile*—has many aptitudes, can adapt to circumstances, and situations that require change in tactics or positions[34]

See Figure 2.4,[35] which emphasizes some of these traits.

2.4 ETHICS AND THE INVESTIGATIVE PROCESS

The qualities of objectivity, logic, perseverance, and diligence, and formidable interpersonal skills, represent mandatory attributes of the competent investigator. However, these traits need to be coupled with an ethical and professional philosophy. In short, the security specialist must have an

FORLETTA

Private Eye Blog   Services   Forensics   Missing Persons   Who We Serve   Locations

Our Greatest Strengths

We are experts in complex criminal and civil litigation. We are some of the best private investigation detectives in Pittsburgh and Cleveland. One of our strongest attributes is proven expertise in conducting a "professional interview." We obtain the details rather than give them to the witness. Professional interviewing skills are not learned from a "textbook," they are developed over years of dealing with some of the most sophisticated criminals in the world. We also provide instruction in interviewing techniques to foreign government officials, as well to many local, state and federal law enforcement officials and the U.S. military.

Our Values

Ethics: We will make all reporting based upon truth and facts. No personal feelings or prejudices will interfere with factual and truthful disclosures of the results obtained from investigative assignments for clients.

Service: FORLETTA tailors our services to the needs of our clients. We understand that each client is dealing with unique issues. We focus on those issues and resolve them to the best of our ability.

Professionalism: We pride ourselves on our efficient investigative methods and techniques. We provide our clients detail-oriented reports which have been reviewed and tested by lawyers, judges and other professional experts.

Courage: We will challenge what appears to be undisputed facts and stand by the results we provide our clients with.

Persistency: We will never quit an investigation. We will continue to strive for positive results and the best outcomes of our investigations.

Dependability: We are always available to our clients. We provide our clients regular updates of our investigative efforts. We respond immediately to all inquiries made by our clients.

Respect: We treat our clients like they are a member of our family and treat them with the utmost respect.

FIGURE 2.4   Forletta website screen capture (used courtesy Forletta, www.fcisllc.com/about-us).

ethical compass that guides these practices. Ethics are the stuff of good and moral conduct. In most cases, the security professional inherently knows what correct conduct is. Even so, this same specialist must learn to weigh and evaluate the ethical parameters of each action chosen during the investigative operation. Ethics must always be in the forefront of security practice.[36] Without ethical parameters, investigative practice may lose its legal and moral legitimacy. Those who disregard principles of civilized conduct, who fail to adhere to moral and legal values, and disregard professional behavior that is consistent with democratic notions, cause both individual and collective harm.

Aside from abridging a particular legal or human right, a lack of ethics undermines the legitimacy of an investigation and calls into question its legality. The security industry fully recognizes the correlation between ethics and acceptable investigative practice. Vance Security USA, a division of Andrews International, publishes rules of conduct for all employees. See Box 2.2.[37]

BOX 2.2   TYPICAL RULES OF CONDUCT (COURTESY VANCE SECURITY)

Prohibited Conduct

The following conduct is prohibited and will not be tolerated by the Company. This list of prohibited conduct is illustrative only; other types of conduct that threaten security, personal safety, employee welfare and the Company's operations also may be prohibited.

- Falsifying employment records, employment information, or other Company records
- Recording the work time of another employee or allowing any other employee to record your work time, or falsifying any time card, either your own or another employee's
- Theft, deliberate or careless damage or destruction of any Company property, or the property of any employee or customer
- Removing or borrowing Company or client property without prior authorization;
- Unauthorized use of Company or client equipment, time, materials, copying, phone services, television services to include pay per-view, computers or facilities
- Provoking a fight or fighting during working hours or on Company property
- Participating in horseplay or practical jokes on Company time or on Company premises
- Carrying firearms or any other dangerous weapons on Company premises at any time unless approved in writing by the President of Vance Security
- Engaging in criminal conduct whether or not related to job performance
- Causing, creating, or participating in a disruption of any kind during working hours on Company property
- Insubordination, including but not limited to failure or refusal to obey the orders or instructions of a supervisor or member of management, or the use of abusive or threatening language toward a supervisor or member of management
- Using abusive language at any time on Company premises
- Failing to notify a supervisor four (4) hours or more when unable to report to work;
- Unreported absence of three (3) consecutive scheduled workdays
- Failing to obtain permission to leave work for any reason during normal working hours;
- Failing to observe working schedules, including rest and lunch periods
- Failing to provide a sufficiently specific physician's certificate within 48 hours of request;
- Sleeping or malingering on the job
- Making or accepting personal telephone calls except in cases of emergency
- Working overtime without authorization or refusing to work assigned overtime
- Wearing disturbing, unprofessional or inappropriate styles of dress or hair while working
- Violating any safety, health, security or Company policy, rule, or procedure
- Committing a fraudulent act or a breach of trust under any circumstances

- Committing of or involvement with any act of unlawful harassment of another individual
- Reporting to work while under the influence of a controlled substance; being intoxicated or under the influence of a controlled substance while at work; use, possession or sale of a controlled substance in any quantity while on Company premises, except personal medications prescribed by a physician which do not impair work performance
- Failure to comply with any grooming standard, as described in this Handbook or the hiring package
- Violating the non-disclosure agreement; giving confidential or proprietary information to competitors or other organizations or to unauthorized Vance Security employees; working for a competing business while Vance Security employee; breach of confidentiality of personnel information including personal wage information to other employees
- Spreading malicious gossip and/or rumors; engaging in behavior which creates discord and lack of harmony among employees; interfering with another employee on the job; restricting work output or encouraging others to do the same
- Immoral conduct or indecency on Company property
- Conducting a lottery or gambling on Company premises
- Use of Company or client's telephones for personal calls
- Smoking in restricted areas or at non-designated times, as specified by Company rules. No uniformed officer is permitted to smoke while in the public or clients view
- Creating or contributing to unsanitary conditions
- Buying Company merchandise for resale
- Speeding or careless driving of Company vehicles or of personal vehicles on Company or client property
- Failure to immediately report damage to, or an accident involving, Company or client equipment or property
- Soliciting during working hours and/or in working areas for any reason, including seeking financial gain for yourself, friends, relatives or acquaintances; selling merchandise or collecting funds of any kind for charities or others without authorization during business hours, or at a time or place that interferes with the work of another employee on Company premises
- Not maintaining a telephone at residence and to keep Vance Security informed of any changes in address or telephone numbers to a supervisor and the corporate office
- Failure to immediately depart off the work premises after the completion of a shift
- Discussing Vance Security or client business with the media, insurance companies, attorneys etc., without prior permission from the Chief Financial Officer or President of Vance Security
- Parking in areas not designated parking areas for employees
- Unbecoming conduct of an employee, officer, supervisor or manager of Vance Security
- Violation of posted client policies or procedures
- Violations of any public laws while on duty
- Bringing TV's, video games or other non-approved reading material to their assigned post
- Failure to notify Company of any arrest on or off duty
- Failure to notify Company of suspension or revocation of driving privileges

This statement of prohibited conduct does not alter the Company's policy of at-will employment. Either you or the Company remain free to terminate the employment relationship at any time, with or without reason or advance notice. Violations can result in civil and or criminal prosecution.

Security firms are highly concerned with the ethical dimensions of their employees and hope to hire individuals of good character who possess the attributes of truthfulness, honesty, and loyalty. This honesty in the employee must also extend to the performance reviews and self-evaluation of the investigative protocol. Dave Walsh, Mick King, and Andy Griffiths, in their recent study, "Evaluating interviews which search for the truth with suspects: but are investigators' self-assessments of their own skills truthful ones?" remind the investigative professional that ethics starts with an honest assessment and evaluation of present and past practices.[38]

Their findings conclude that a sector of the investigative community tends to "self-enhance" its investigative practices and, as a result, not fully comprehend the effectiveness of its methods.[39]

Given the contemporary decline of universal perceptions of what is moral, good, and true, and the emergence of conflicting ethical schemes, it has become a more complex task to assure ethical individual and institutional conduct. Attempts have been made, at the legislative level, to promulgate minimum ethical standards. Governmental authorities are increasingly involved in delineating acceptable practices in the security industry. The State of Illinois defines good character and professionalism by defining various types of unprofessional conduct. See Box 2.3.[40]

BOX 2.3   THE STATE OF ILLINOIS OUTLINES SPECIFICS OF WHAT IT DEEMS UNPROFESSIONAL CONDUCT

Sec. 40-10. Disciplinary sanctions.

(a) The Department may deny issuance, refuse to renew, or restore or may reprimand, place on probation, suspend, revoke, or take other disciplinary or non-disciplinary action against any license, registration, permanent employee registration card, canine handler authorization card, canine trainer authorization card, or firearm control card, may impose a fine not to exceed $10,000 for each violation, and may assess costs as provided for under Section 45-60, for any of the following:

  (1) Fraud, deception, or misrepresentation in obtaining or renewing of a license or registration.

  (2) Professional incompetence as manifested by poor standards of service.

  (3) Engaging in dishonorable, unethical, or unprofessional conduct of a character likely to deceive, defraud, or harm the public.

  (4) Conviction of or plea of guilty or plea of nolo contendere to a felony or misdemeanor in this State or any other jurisdiction or the entry of an administrative sanction by a government agency in this State or any other jurisdiction; action taken under this paragraph (4) for a misdemeanor or an administrative sanction is limited to a misdemeanor or administrative sanction that has as an essential element of dishonesty or fraud or involves larceny, embezzlement, or obtaining money, property, or credit by false pretenses or by means of a confidence game.

  (5) Performing any services in a grossly negligent manner or permitting any of a licensee's employees to perform services in a grossly negligent manner, regardless of whether actual damage to the public is established.

  (6) Continued practice, although the person has become unfit to practice due to any of the following:

    (A) Physical illness, mental illness, or other impairment, including, but not limited to, deterioration through the aging process or loss of motor skills that results in the inability to serve the public with reasonable judgment, skill, or safety.

    (B) (Blank).

    (C)   Habitual or excessive use or abuse of drugs defined in law as controlled substances, alcohol, or any other substance that results in the inability to practice with reasonable judgment, skill, or safety.

(7) Receiving, directly or indirectly, compensation for any services not rendered.

(8) Willfully deceiving or defrauding the public on a material matter.

(9) Failing to account for or remit any moneys or documents coming into the licensee's possession that belong to another person or entity.

(10) Discipline by another United States jurisdiction, foreign nation, or governmental agency, if at least one of the grounds for the discipline is the same or substantially equivalent to those set forth in this Act.

(11) Giving differential treatment to a person that is to that person's detriment because of race, color, creed, sex, religion, or national origin.

(12) Engaging in false or misleading advertising.

(13) Aiding, assisting, or willingly permitting another person to violate this Act or rules promulgated under it.

(14) Performing and charging for services without authorization to do so from the person or entity serviced.

(15) Directly or indirectly offering or accepting any benefit to or from any employee, agent, or fiduciary without the consent of the latter's employer or principal with intent to or the understanding that this action will influence his or her conduct in relation to his or her employer's or principal's affairs.

(16) Violation of any disciplinary order imposed on a licensee by the Department.

(17) Performing any act or practice that is a violation of this Act or the rules for the administration of this Act, or having a conviction or administrative finding of guilty as a result of violating any federal or State laws, rules, or regulations that apply exclusively to the practices of private detectives, private alarm contractors, private security contractors, fingerprint vendors, or locksmiths.

(18) Conducting an agency without a valid license.

(19) Revealing confidential information, except as required by law, including but not limited to information available under Section 2-123 of the Illinois Vehicle Code.

(20) Failing to make available to the Department, upon request, any books, records, or forms required by this Act.

(21) Failing, within 30 days, to respond to a written request for information from the Department.

(22) Failing to provide employment information or experience information required by the Department regarding an applicant for licensure.

(23) Failing to make available to the Department at the time of the request any indicia of licensure or registration issued under this Act.

(24) Purporting to be a licensee-in-charge of an agency without active participation in the agency.

(25) A finding by the Department that the licensee, after having his or her license placed on probationary status, has violated the terms of probation.

(26) Violating subsection (f) of Section 30-30.

(27) A firearm control card holder having more firearms in his or her immediate possession than he or she can reasonably exercise control over.

(28) Failure to report in writing to the Department, within 60 days of an entry of a settlement or a verdict in excess of $10,000, any legal action in which the quality of the licensee's or registrant's professional services was the subject of the legal action.

(b) All fines imposed under this Section shall be paid within 60 days after the effective date of the order imposing the fine.

(c) The Department shall adopt rules that set forth standards of service for the following: (i) acceptable error rate in the transmission of fingerprint images and other data to the Department of State Police; (ii) acceptable error rate in the collection and documentation of information used to generate fingerprint work orders; and (iii) any other standard of service that affects fingerprinting services as determined by the Department.

The determination by a circuit court that a licensee is subject to involuntary admission or judicial admission, as provided in the Mental Health and Developmental Disabilities Code, operates as an automatic suspension. The suspension will end only upon a finding by a court that the patient is no longer subject to involuntary admission or judicial admission and the issuance of an order so finding and discharging the patient.

(Source: P.A. 98-253, eff. 8-9-13; 99-174, eff. 7-29-15.)

The State of Virginia calls upon all of its security professionals to pledge ethical conduct in their professional code.[41] Similarly, the National Advisory Committee on Criminal Justice Standards and Goals, in its report, *The Task Force on Private Security*,[42] put forth a code of ethics for security firm managers (Box 2.4).

BOX 2.4   THE CODE OF ETHICS FOR SECURITY FIRM MANAGERS PER THE NATIONAL ADVISORY COMMITTEE ON CRIMINAL JUSTICE STANDARDS AND GOALS

Code of Ethics for Private Security Management

As managers of private security functions and employees, we pledge:

I. To recognize that our principal responsibilities are, in the service of our organizations and clients, to protect life and property as well as to prevent and reduce crime against our business, industry, or other organizations and institutions; and in the public interest, to uphold the law and to respect the constitutional rights of all persons.

II. To be guided by a sense of integrity, honor, justice and morality in the conduct of business; in all personnel matters; in relationships with government agencies, clients, and employers; and in responsibilities to the general public.

III. To strive faithfully to render security services of the highest quality and to work continuously to improve our knowledge and skills and thereby improve the overall effectiveness of private security.

IV. To uphold the trust of our employers, our clients, and the public by performing our functions within the law, not ordering or condoning violations of the law, and ensuring that our security personnel conduct their assigned duties lawfully and with proper regard for the rights of others.

V. To respect the reputation and practice of others in private security, but to expose to the proper authorities any conduct that is unethical or unlawful.

VI. To apply uniform and equitable standards of employment in recruiting and selecting personnel regardless of race, creed, color, sex, or age, and in providing salaries commensurate with job responsibilities and with training, education, and experience.

VII. To cooperate with recognized and responsible law enforcement and other criminal justice agencies; to comply with security licensing and registration laws and other statutory requirements that pertain to our business.

VIII. To respect and protect the confidential and privileged information of employers and clients beyond the term of our employment, except where their interests are contrary to law or to this Code of Ethics.

IX. To maintain a professional posture in all business relationships with employers and clients, with others in the private security field, and with members of other professions; and to insist that our personnel adhere to the highest standards of professional conduct.

X. To encourage the professional advancement of our personnel by assisting them to acquire appropriate security knowledge, education, and training.

ASIS International, the premier professional association of the security industry, promulgates a code of ethics that guides the industry and the particulars of investigative practice that is worth reviewing on their website (www.asisonline.org).[43] (Figure 2.5)

The IAPSC, a professional association of security consultants, delineates ethical and professional parameters in specific detail. For example, its "general" provisions for security consultants specifically outline behavioral and professional guidelines.

- *Certified Security Consultant* will view and handle as confidential all information concerning the affairs of the client.
- *Certified Security Consultant* will not take personal, financial, or any other advantage of inside information gained by virtue of the consulting relationship.
- *Certified Security Consultant* will inform clients and prospective clients of any special relationship or circumstances that could be considered a conflict of interest.
- *Certified Security Consultant* will never charge more than a reasonable fee; and, whenever possible, the consultant will agree with the client in advance on the fee or basis for the fee.
- *Certified Security Consultant* will neither accept nor pay fees or commissions for client referrals.
- *Certified Security Consultant* will not accept fees, commissions or other valuable considerations from any individual or organization whose equipment, supplies or services they might or do recommend in the course of his or her services to a client.
- *Certified Security Consultant* will only accept assignments for and render expert opinions on matters they are eminently qualified in and for.[44]

Parker Security & Investigative Services has composed an all-encompassing code of ethics for its employees. See Figure 2.6.[45]

The question of ethics is both a moral and a practical one.[46] Some have even argued that the increase in privatized services, at every level, and when correlated to the decline of the public sector exclusivity in policing and related services, has been a net cost to our ethical barometer. Allison Stanger remarks, "The gains in agility, efficiency, and innovative problem-solving that appropriate outsourcing can facilitate are not insignificant, but they have come with an ethical cost."[47]

While there is merit to the nervousness in this transference of authority and delegation of traditional public duties, this conclusion is highly debatable, for privatized services can be and often are first-rate operations with first-rate personnel. Concluding that public, governmental oversight produces better personnel belies the continued stream of public corruption cases across the fifty states.

What is not arguable is that the security industry has had chronic difficulties with the high attrition rates of personnel and the low quality of both applicants and currently employed personnel. This revolving door of personnel is a vicious circle, usually triggered by low salaries and little or no training, which in turn translates into the hiring of marginal personnel. With substandard employees comes substandard investigative practice. The industry is fully aware of its compelling need

Code Of Ethics

Aware that the quality of professional security activity ultimately depends upon the willingness of practitioners to observe special standards of conduct and to manifest good faith in professional relationships, ASIS International (ASIS) adopts the following Code of Ethics and mandates its conscientious observance as a binding condition of membership in or affiliation with the organization:

ARTICLE I
A member shall perform professional duties in accordance with the law and the highest moral principles.

ARTICLE II
A member shall observe the precepts of truthfulness, honesty, and integrity.

ARTICLE III
A member shall be faithful and diligent in discharging professional responsibilities.

ARTICLE IV
A member shall be competent in discharging professional responsibilities.

ARTICLE V
A member shall safeguard confidential information and exercise due care to prevent its improper disclosure.

ARTICLE VI
A member shall not maliciously injure the professional reputation or practice of colleagues, clients, or employers.

NOTE: Reference Policy 1080 from Policy & Procedures Manual

FIGURE 2.5 ASIS International code of ethics. (Reprinted with permission of ASIS International © 2018.)

to increase the ethical and professional demands on its personnel. So pressing is this issue that the United States Department of Justice formulated a National Task Force and Advisory Committee on the status of private security, focusing on both the industry and its employees, that set forth some minimal standards of qualification, conduct, and goals. Standard 1.8, reprinted in Box 2.5,[48] outlines the pre-employment screening qualifications.

Toll-Free (866) 888-2153 | Security (229) 888-2153 | Investigations (229) 435-9059

PARKER SECURITY & INVESTIGATIVE SERVICES INC

Home   **Security Guards   Security Cameras   Investigations**

CODE OF ETHICS FOR SECURITY OFFICERS

In recognition of the significant contribution of private security to loss and crime prevention, as a Security Officer I pledge:

1. To accept the responsibilities and fulfill the obligations of my role: protecting life and property; and reducing losses and crimes against my employer's business, or other organizations and institutions to which I am assigned; upholding the law; and respecting the constitutional rights of all persons.

2. To conduct myself with honesty and to adhere to the highest moral principles in the performance of my security duties.

3. To be diligent and dependable in discharging my duties and to uphold at all times the laws, policies, and procedures that protect the rights of others.

4. To observe the precepts of truth, accuracy and discretion without allowing personal feelings, prejudices, and animosities or friendships to influence my judgements.

5. To report to my supervisor, without hesitation, any violation of the law or of my employer or client's regulations.

6. To respect and protect the confidential and privileged information of my employer or client beyond the term of my employment, except where their interests are contrary to law or to this Code of Ethics.

7. To cooperate with all recognized and responsible law enforcement and government agencies in matters within their jurisdiction.

8. To accept no compensation, commission, gratuity, or other advantage without the knowledge and consent of my employer.

9. To conduct myself professionally at all times and to perform m duties in a manner that reflects credit upon my employer, the security profession, and myself.

10. To strive continually to improve my performance by seeking training and educational opportunities that will better prepare me for my security duties.

FIGURE 2.6 Parker Security &Investigative Services Code of Ethics for Security Officer (used with permission of Parker Security &Investigative Services, https://parkerpsai.com).

BOX 2.5   STANDARDS OF QUALIFICATION, CONDUCT, AND GOALS PER THE NATIONAL TASK FORCE AND ADVISORY COMMITTEE

Standard 1.8

Minimum Pre-employment Screening Qualifications

The following minimum pre-employment screening qualifications should be established for private security personnel:

1. Minimum age of 18
2. High school diploma or equivalent written examination
3. Written examination to determine ability to understand and perform duties assigned
4. No record of conviction, as stated in Standard 1.7
5. Minimum physical standards
   a. Armed personnel—vision correctable to 20/20 (Snellen) in each eye and capable of hearing ordinary conversation at a distance of 10 feet with each ear without benefit of a hearing aid
   b. Others—no physical defects that would hinder job performance

---

Securitas publishes minimum qualifications for any position on its website, which are shown at Figure 2.7.[49]

The relationship between professional preparation, qualification standards and ongoing elevation of security personnel, and any notion of ethics, is simply undeniable. Professional standards assume and equate to an ethical expectation of performance. Add to this the inconsistent and almost impossible to determine regulatory state as to investigative licensure—where most states regulating

Job Qualifications, Eligibility, and Expectations

What are the responsibilities of a security officer at Securitas?
Our security officers are employed at client sites throughout the country to help protect our clients' property, their valuables and their employees. This is achieved through patrolling, monitoring and reporting techniques by exercising vigilance, integrity and helpfulness (our core company values).

Our security officers are first class customer service experts; better known in Securitas USA as Service Excellence! As the nature of our business changes, security officer job responsibilities also change to include video, computer and communication technology responsibilities.

As you browse the various open positions you'll notice how diverse security officer job duties are based on individual client needs.

Do I need previous security experience?
No. Anyone who meets our basic application requirements is encouraged to apply. Security officer training is delivered through effective on-the-job-training and mentoring.

What are the qualifications needed to work at Securitas USA?
Our basic employment requirements for security officers include:

- Minimum age of 18 (21 years of age if applying for an armed position)
- Proof of eligibility to work in the United States
- High school diploma/GED (or agreement to complete a GED program within six months of hire)
- A reliable means of transportation and communication (i.e., phone or pager)
- Ability to read, write and speak English
- Willingness to participate in our pre-employment screening process (drug screen and background checks)

FIGURE 2.7   Job qualifications, eligibility, and expectations at Securitas (used with permission of Securitas Inc., www.securitasinc.com/).

security officers have not fully endorsed a similar series of standards for the private detective or private investigator. This lack of unified expectation on qualification adds to the hodgepodge of professional expectations.[50]

J. Gallati attacks the issue of personnel qualification head-on:

> Personnel issues are raised, relative to the selection of qualified personnel in both the proprietary and contract security area. Inadequate salaries and the lack of career-development emphasis create high attrition rates, with the consequent need to hire more and more persons …
>
> Due to the highly competitive nature of contract security, plus the high turnover rates, the cost of adequate training becomes a factor in the bidding process …
>
> Should there be mandatory qualifications for every security employee? Should these qualifications apply to both the selection and training? Should there be federal minimum standards, or state or local regulations? How would such regulations be enforced?[51]

The questions and problems posed by Gallati, as well as numerous other experts in the field of private security, are becoming commonplace critiques. It is a fact that the industry suffers from internal turnover and early career plateaus.[52] It is a fact that pay scales are low, even though improving. It is a fact that investigators who have the perseverance, diligence, logic, objectivity, and enhanced skills of human relations will not fully develop these attributes if they are not well-trained, well-compensated, and guided on a path of high ethical expectations. "The industry itself should zealously rectify any deficiencies in the matter of regulation. Its credibility depends upon enactment."[53] Bottom and Kostanoski concur:

Ethical problems give security and loss control an image problem. Often, it is the employer who needs an ethical overhaul. Business, in general, has an image problem …

Security and loss control is responsive to the demands of the employer. If the employer lacks ethics, it cannot be surprising that the security department has ethical shortcomings. Even if the security department has no part in the unethical conduct, the public is likely to tar all employees with the same brush.[54]

Web Exercise: Watch the videos on personality traits and ethics that make a good private investigator at https://youtu.be/70tDjjAagy8 and https://youtu.be/q-HBSt7iTC8 from ShadowAnyone.com.

No investigative process can reach its full potential if its operatives are viewed as downtrodden or second-rate professionals. Public respect plays an integral role in the investigator's ability to function. If private security operatives are continually under suspicion, both occupationally and personally, their access to facilities and information will be substantially restricted. This image problem must be cleared up if public respect is to be gained. The challenge is to improve the image of this industry and convince the public that security and loss control is more than a uniformed guard leaning against a mall interior.

The joint study entitled *Security Industry Survey of Risks and Professional Competencies* by the ASIS Foundation Apollo Education Group, Inc. and the University of Phoenix is worth looking up as it lays out the essential characteristics of the competent security professional—and talented specialists.[55]

The National Task Force and Advisory Committee, at Goal 2.1, holds:

The responsibilities assumed by private security personnel in the protection of persons and property require training. Training should be instituted at all levels to insure that personnel are fully prepared to exercise the responsibilities effectively and efficiently.[56]

Goal 3.1 of the same Advisory Committee calls for a code of ethics to be adopted and enforced by all private security personnel and their employers. Finally, Standard 3.2 holds that private security personnel should perform their security functions within the generally recognized guidelines for the protection of individual rights.[57]

In sum, the private security industry needs to address both the ethical and professional dimensions of its undertaking. Practitioners, academicians, management, and legislators all concur on these and other challenges in the industry's future.

NOTES

1. Russell Colling, *Hospital Security* (Boston: Butterworth Publishers, 1982): 221; Jos Maas, "Hospital Security: Protecting the Business," *Journal of Healthcare Protection Management* (January 1, 2013).
2. Ibid.; see also the historic role investigative services have played in the world of private security and private protection at Charles P. Nemeth and K. C. Poulin, *Private Security and Public Safety: A Community Based Approach* (Upper Saddle River, NJ: Pearson–Prentice Hall, 2005): 22; Charles P. Nemeth, *Private Security: An Introduction to Principles and Practice* (Boca Raton, FL: CRC Press, 2018); Daniel J. Benny, *Private Investigation and Homeland Security* (Boca Raton, FL: CRC Press, 2016); Robert J. Fischer et al., *Introduction to Security* (New York: Elsevier, 2103).
3. Colling, "Hospital": 211.
4. International Association of Chiefs of Police, *National Policy Summit: Building Private Security/Public Policing Partnerships to Prevent and Respond to Terrorism and Public Disorder* (2004), accessed September 4, 2018, www.theiacp.org/Portals/0/pdfs/Publications/ACFAB5D.pdf.
5. James McCord, *The Litigation Paralegal* (Eagan, MN: West Publishing Co., 1988): 69.
6. See Louis Perry, "How Private Security Can Help Law Enforcement" (May 31, 2012), accessed September 4, 2018, www.policemag.com/blog/patrol-tactics/story/2012/05/how-private-security-can-help-law-enforcement.aspx.
7. See COPS Website, accessed September 4, 2018, www.cops.usdoj.gov/.
8. William C. Cunningham, John J. Strauchs, and Clifford W. VanMeter, *Private Security Trends 1970 to 2000: The Hallcrest Report II* (Woburn, MA: Butterworth Heinemann, 1990): 116.

9. Bill Strudel, "The Private Security Connection: Giving the Police a Sense of Security," *Police Chief* (February 1982): 28–29; Law Commission of Canada, *In Search of Security: The Roles of Public Police and Private Agencies* (2002); George S. Rigakos, *The New Parapolice* (Toronto: University of Toronto Press, 2002).

10. LexisNexis, "Accurint for Private Investigations," www.lexisnexis.com/risk/downloads/literature/accurint-private-investigations.pdf.

11. IASIR, P.O. Box 93, Waterloo, IA, 50704, www.iasir.org.

12. Arnold Markle, *Criminal Investigation and Presentation of Evidence* (Eagan, MN: West Publishing Co., 1976): 1.

13. Art Buckwalter, *Investigative Methods* (Woburn, MA: Butterworth, 1984): 36.

14. Karl Ask and Pär Anders Granhag, "Hot Cognition in Investigative Judgments: The Differential Influence of Anger and Sadness," *Law and Human Behavior* 31 (2007): 537–551.

15. Henk Sollie, Nicolien Kop, and Martin C. Euwema, "Mental Resilience of Crime Scene Investigators: How Police Officers Perceive and Cope with the Impact of Demanding Work Situations," *Criminal Justice and Behavior* 44, no. 12 (2017): 1580–1603, https://doi.org/10.1177/0093854817716959.

16. Ibid.

17. R. A. "Rick" Stern, "Training That's on Target," *Security Management*, April 2012, https://sm.asisonline.org/Pages/Training-Thats-on-Target.aspx; see also: Darius H. Bone, Anthony H. Normore, and Mitch Javidi, "Human Factors in Law Enforcement Leadership," *Law Enforcement Bulletin*, December 9, 2015, https://leb.fbi.gov/articles/featured-articles/human-factors-in-law-enforcement-leadership.

18. Rick Sarre, "Book Review," review of *Private Investigation And Security Science: A Scientific Approach*, 3rd ed., by Frank Machovec, *Criminal Justice Review* 34 (2009): 142.

19. Wayne W. Bennett and Kären M. Hess, *Criminal Investigation* (Eagan, MN: West Publishing Co., 1976): 11; Kären M. Hess, Christine Hess Orthmann, and Henry Lim Cho, *Criminal Investigation*, 11th ed. (Boston: Cengage, 2017).

20. Walter J. Buzby and David Paine, *Hotel &Motel Security Management* (Woburn, MA: Butterworth Publishers, 1976): 122–123.

21. County of Los Angeles Board of Supervisors, Executive Office, Security Operations Unit, 500 West Temple Street, Room #B-98, Los Angeles, California 90012, *Security Incident Report, SIR Form 2017.*

22. Edward Smith, *Practical Guide For Investigators* (Boulder, CO: Paladin Press, 1982): 34; Dean A. Beers, *Practical Methods for Legal Investigations: Concepts and Protocols in Civil and Criminal Cases* (Boca Raton, FL: CRC Press, 2011); Robert J. Fischer et al., *Introduction to Security* (New York: Elsevier, 2103).

23. See Tuule Sooniste, Pär Anders Granhag, and Leif A. Strömwall, "Training Police Investigators to Interview to Detect False Intentions," *Journal of Police Criminal Psychology* 32 (2017): 152–162, doi:10.1007/s11896-016-9206-9.

24. Ann Longmore-Etheridge, "Survey of Risks and Competencies Released," *Security Management*, November 2014, https://sm.asisonline.org/Pages/Survey-of-Risks-and-Competencies-Released.aspx.

25. *American Jurisprudence Trials* 1 (1987): 357, 365.

26. Bennett and Hess, "Investigation": 13; Hess, Orthmann, and Cho, "Investigation 11th"; Charles P. Nemeth, "Private Security."

27. For an excellent article on how performance and persistence pays off in customer service, see James Stewart, "A Plan for Polite Protection," *Security Management*, November 2015, https://sm.asisonline.org/Pages/A-Plan-for-Polite-Protection.aspx.

28. See Jonathan Lafontaine and Cyr Mireille, "A Study of the Relationship between Investigators' Personal Characteristics and Adherence to Interview Best Practices in Training," *Psychiatry, Psychology &Law* 23, no. 5: 782–797, doi:10.1080/13218719.2016.1152925.

29. See Darius H. Bone, Anthony H. Normore, and Mitch Javidi, "Human Factors in Law Enforcement Leadership," *Law Enforcement Bulletin*, December 9, 2015, https://leb.fbi.gov/articles/featured-articles/human-factors-in-law-enforcement-leadership.

30. Questions regarding the value of education in human interaction have been long analyzed in the criminal justice sector—in both public and private setting. See Philip Carlan, "Do Officers Value Their Degrees?" *Law &Order* (December 2006): 59; Dave Walsh, Mick King, and Andy Griffiths, "Evaluating Interviews Which Search for the Truth with Suspects: But Are Investigators' Self-Assessments of Their Own Skills Truthful Ones?" *Psychology, Crime &Law* 23, no. 7 (2017): 647–665.

31. Buckwalter, supra note 4, at 36; Tuule Sooniste, Pär Anders Granhag, and Leif A. Strömwall, "Training Police Investigators to Interview to Detect False Intentions," *Journal of Police and Criminal Psychology* 32 (2017): 152–162.

32. Id. at 35–47; Kären M. Hess, Christine Hess Orthmann, and Henry Lim Cho, *Criminal Investigation* (Cengage, 2017); Charles P. Nemeth, *Private Security: An Introduction to Principles and Practice* (CRC Press, 2017).

33. National Association of Legal Assistants, *Manual for Legal Assistants 10* (West Publishing Co., 1979); Tuule Sooniste, Pär Anders Granhag, and Leif A. Strömwall, "Training Police Investigators to Interview to Detect False Intentions," *Journal of Police and Criminal Psychology* 32 (2017): 152–162.

34. Buckwalter, "Methods": 47–49.

35. "About Us," Forletta Investigative/Security Consultant, 301 Grant Street, Suite 4300, Pittsburgh, PA 15219, accessed September 7, 2018, www.fcisllc.com/about-us.

36. Robert D. McCrie, ASIS Intl. Takes Risks with Guidelines Commission Strategy, *Security Letter*, November 15, 2003; "ASIS Publishes Standards for Professionals," *Corporate Security*, January 31, 2003; Mary Lynn Garcia, "Personal Opinion: Raising the Bar for Security Professionals," *Security Journal* 13 (2000): 79.

37. "Employee Handbook," Vance Security US—Andrews International, Inc., 455 N. Moss Street, Burbank, CA 91502 (2009): 20–22, accessed September 7, 2018, www.andrewsinternational.com/hr/1541/Download/NewHirePacket/VANCE/VANCE%20EMPLOYEE%20HANDBOOK/VANCE%20EMPLOYEE%20HANDBOOK.pdf.

38. Dave Walsh, Mick King, and Andy Griffiths, "Evaluating Interviews Which Search for the Truth with Suspects: But Are Investigators' Self-Assessments of Their Own Skills Truthful Ones?" *Psychology, Crime &Law* 23, no. 7 (2017): 647–665, doi:10.1080/1068316X.2017.1296149.

39. Ibid.: 657.

40. 225 Ill. Comp. Stat. 447/40-10 (2018).

41. See Virginia Private Security Services Advisory Board, *Private Security Code of Ethics*, accessed September 7, 2018, www.dcjs.virginia.gov/sites/dcjs.virginia.gov/files/publications/private-security/private-security-code-ethics.pdf.

42. U.S. Department of Justice, LEAA, National Advisory Committee on Criminal Justice Standards and Goals, *Report of the Task Force on Private Security* (1976).

43. See ASIS International, Code of Ethics.

44. "Certified Security Consultant^SM Code of Ethics," International Association of Professional Security Consultants, accessed September 7, 2018, https://iapsc.org/about-us/certification/code-ethics/.

45. Parker Security &Investigative Services, Inc., P. O. Box 70127, Albany, GA 31708, accessed September 7, 2018, https://parkerpsai.com/code-of-ethics-for-security-officers/.

46. The question of ethics has both national and international implications, especially in light of the industry's increasing role on the world stage—even in the military conflicts in war zones. Marcus Hedahl, "Unaccountable: The Current State of Private Military and Security Companies," *Criminal Justice Ethics* 31, no. 3 (December 2012): 175–192.

47. Allison Stanger, "Transparency as a Core Public Value and Mechanism of Compliance," *Criminal Justice Ethics* 31, no. 3 (December 2012): 288.

48. National Advisory Committee on Criminal Justice Standards and Goals, *Private Security: Report of the Task Force on Private Security* (Washington, DC: US Department of Justice, LEAA, 1976): 82.

49. "FAQS," Securitas USA, accessed September 7, 2018, www.securitasinc.com/join-us/faqs/job-requirements/.

50. See Charles P. Nemeth, *Private Security and the Law*, 5th ed. (Boca Raton, FL: CRC Press, 2018); Thomas Lonardo, Alan Rea, and Doug White, "To License or Not to License Reexamined: An Updated Report on State Statutes Regarding Private Investigators and Digital Examiners," *The Journal of Digital Forensics, Security and Law* 10, no. 1 (2015): 45–56.

51. Robert R. Gallati, *Introduction To Private Security* (Upper Saddle River, NJ: Prentice-Hall, 1983): 269; Lonardo, Alan, and White, "License Reexamined."

52. "Executive Security Focus of New Course," *Forensic Examiner* 17 (2008): 64; Dennis W. Bowman, "Comparing Law Enforcement Accreditation and Private Security Standards," *Journal of Security* 26 (2003): 17; Bruce Mandelblit, "A Sorry State of Security?" *Security* (April 2003): 54.

53. Nemeth and Poulin, "Public Safety": 308.

54. Norman R. Bottom and John Kostanoski, *Introduction to Security and Loss Control* (Upper Saddle River, NJ: Prentice Hall, 1990): 37–38; Marcus Hedahl, "Unaccountable: The Current State of Private Military and Security Companies," *Criminal Justice Ethics* 31, no. 3 (December 2012): 175–192; Stanger, "Transparency."

55. ASIS International, "Security Industry Survey of Risks and Professional Competencies": 11, accessed September 7, 2018, www.apollo.edu/content/dam/apolloedu/microsite/security_industry/AEG-PS-264513-CJS-STEM-SECURITY-SURVEY.pdf.
56. National Advisory Committee, "Private Security Report": 89.
57. Ibid.: 123, 126.

3 Interview and Case Evaluation

3.1 INTRODUCTION: THE INTERVIEW AND THE INVESTIGATOR

Every competent investigator knows the importance of communication skills, especially during interviews with a prospective or existing client, witness, suspect, or other party. This is a core competency for the investigator and the skill of questioning and information gathering should never be presumed to exist in the security operative. The art of investigative interview and questioning takes years to perfect. To be a skilled and proficient investigator will demand interrogation and questioning techniques that lead to the truth of both client and cause. These techniques have a cumulative impact on any given case for one source generally leads to another while one lead builds upon another. Nothing in the investigative process is static. As Tom Shamshank observes:

> Interview subjects may give a private investigator information that leads to a new interview subject that was not initially included in the investigative plan. Whenever an investigator receives a new lead on a possible interview subject they should always follow up on the lead by conducting background research, contacting the new subject and scheduling and completing an interview. Private investigators should follow the same steps when preparing for, conducting and finalizing a follow-up interview as they would for the initial interview.[1]

In essence, the interview process builds tier to tier, person to person avoiding the dead-end street or false lead.

An interview can encompass many purposes including: an initial visitation with a prospective client; an ongoing dialogue with a long-term client; an observational review and analysis of a witness or suspect statement; an interrogation of a suspected wrongdoer; a character assessment by a suspect's neighbor; internal investigation of workplace violence or sexual harassment, internal theft assessment, or a background information check.[2] In any of these scenarios, the private investigator must gauge his time and energies wisely and discern the difference between idle chitchat and productive discussion.

At a minimum, an interview is a conversation designed to garner facts and clarify issues, promote the interchange of ideas and information and develop a positive relationship between the interrogator and the interviewee. "Properly handled, an interview is an accurate communication of information; improperly handled, it can become a serious source of bias restricting or distorting the communication flow."[3] Given how closely our public and private justice systems work together, the investigative process must be assured of integrity and professionalism especially when the public police system relies so heavily on private expertise—in areas where only the private sector appears to have the expertise upper hand such as in bank fraud, cyber analysis, securities violations, and computer and digital forensics. Private security has far more personnel than the public system and this entanglement and reliance further stresses the need for strong interchange and the free flow of information.[4]

Whatever the circumstances and conditions surrounding the interview process, certain practices are universal.

1. Select a time and a place mutually convenient
2. Prepare in advance for an interview
3. Begin the interview on a cooperative and pleasant note
4. Establish a rapport with the respondent or interviewee

Without proper preparation, an interview will be a flawed exercise from the outset. Knowing what to ask, identifying how issues correlate to selected questions, and being flexible in question sequencing and follow up, as well as being able to conduct a meaningful post assessment of the interview constitute the interview protocol. "The issues to be discussed and the questions to be asked must be clear before the interview. In complicated discussions, the investigator may decide to list objectives and questions in advance, but the list should not be used during the actual interview."[5]

Web Exercise: Visit PI Now.com's Investigator Center and read "10 Interview Techniques for Private Investigators that Quickly Build Rapport" at www.pinow.com/articles/353/10-interview-techniques-for-private-investigators-that-quickly-build-rapport.

Aside from these suggestions, professional interviews must foster a climate where information is more readily acquired rather than a tight-lipped, stonewalled reaction. Data also suggests a real need for both genders assuming the role as private investigators, for in some cases the female investigator may be more effective eliciting information than the male counterpart especially in more sensitive cases such as harassment, sexual crime, or stalking.[6]

When the investigator acts professionally, courteously, and respectfully, respondents are more willing to answer in full. See Figure 3.1.[7]

3.2 INITIAL INTERVIEW

The earliest encounter that many security professionals have with a client may be at initial interview. Whether meeting client, suspect, victim, witness, plaintiff, or defendant, the initial interview

FIGURE 3.1 Private investigators and investigation companies should conduct investigations thoroughly, professionally, and discreetly (used with permission, Cape Fear Investigative Services, Inc.).

generally forges early impressions of case and participants. At the initial interview, the security investigator's human, interactive talents are put to the test and the tone set for the upcoming investigative process. Success in the initial interview depends on a host of variables including:

1. That a client's confidences are respected
2. That a client's cooperation is secured
3. That the investigator is friendly, courteous, and polite at all times
4. That the investigator practices the art of conversation
5. That the investigator exudes confidence and reassures the client
6. That the investigator promotes a good, positive attitude on behalf of the law firm he or she represents
7. That all information collected is an accurate presentation of the client's representations
8. That regular and constant communication is necessary to insure subsequent releases of information called for in the initial interview[8]

From the outset, the interviewee must feel welcome and respected: this assures a positive interview environment. Setting the appropriate tone between the investigator and the interviewee is a crucial first step in this important information gathering process.[9] "An attitude of superiority on the part of the investigator should be avoided. Many people may not have had the educational opportunities that may have been offered to the investigator and nothing antagonizes these people more quickly than a patronizing attitude. Therefore, the investigator should try to meet everyone on as close to an equal level as possible and should show friendship toward those whom he intends to interview."[10]

Whether or not information is free-flowing and naturally forthcoming largely depends on the investigator's capacity to create an environment conducive to discussion.[11] While an oral exchange can be both pleasant and easy to manage, it is an inadequate way of obtaining formal information and creating the foundational support necessary for case development. Because of this, the best practice is that security investigators memorialize the interview content by form, checklists, fact-gathering sheets, and other written instruments.

Web Exercise: Visit PI Now.com's Investigator Center and read "Private Investigator Basics Part 2: Interviewing" at www.pinow.com/articles/1182/private-investigator-basics-interviewing for some salient information on interview prep and follow-up.

Aligned with the interview protocol will be the varied tasks of information gathering, and while the oral exchange unfolds, the non-testimonial sorts of evidence peek through—the documents, the files, the medical reports or police reports display their relevancy. Private investigators are quite adept at tracking down these files in the usual and many alternate ways due to a preferential constitutional oversight. "Although private investigators don't have access … to classified government documents, they can nevertheless obtain hard-to-get information"[12] that the client might require.

This creative approach must never lose sight, however, of privacy dimensions and potential civil liability for breaching the space of an investigative target or suspect. Invasion of privacy tort claims are not imaginary and the investigator must bear in mind that their method can become a legal liability.[13]

Most contract or proprietary security firms have implemented uniform, standardized procedures. In The PI Agency's Request for Investigation at Figure 3.2,[14] preliminary investigation information is collected. This document is a critical component of the initial interview for prospective or existing clients.

3.2.1 Initial Interview: Administrative Requirements

Before the initial interview commences, the interviewer need to compile and collect certain documentation to assure the integrity and effectiveness of the interview. In other words, the "talking" must be useable, accessible, and formalized to later usage. Nothing here need be too complicated but all of these recommendations are necessary.

www.ThePIAgency.com   **Request For Investigation**
Probity Investigations, Inc.   678.316.9374 office
sales@ThePIAgency.com   770.234.5111 fax

Date: _____   Budget Amount _____   _____
                                              (Dollar Amount or # Days)   (Our File Number)

☐ Domestic   ☐ Infidelity   ☐ Child Welfare   ☐ Check a Mate   ☐ Background Service

Additional Instructions: _____

CLIENT INFORMATION

Name _____   Home Phone _____
Home Address _____   Cell Phone _____
_____   Email Address _____
_____   Occupation _____
Contact Method _____   Work Schedule _____

Describe your situation: _____
_____

Relationship with Subject: ☐ Spouse   ☐ Divorced   ☐ Boy/Girlfriend   ☐ Engaged   Living -   ☐ Together   ☐ Separate

SUBJECT INFORMATION

Name/Alias _____   Cell Phone _____
Address _____   S.S.N. _____
City/State/Zip _____   D.O.B. _____

Sex   ☐ Male ☐ Female   Race _____   Height _____   Weight _____
Hair _____   Eyes _____   Glasses ☐ Yes ☐ No   Married ☐ Yes ☐ No

Describe subject: _____
Vehicle Make _____   Model _____   Color _____   Tag# _____
Vehicle decals/markings: _____
How many children: _____   Ages _____   How many stepchildren: _____   Ages _____
History of Violence? ☐ Yes ☐ No
If yes, describe: _____

Describe criminal history, if any: _____

Are there any legal proceedings, divorce actions, temporary restraining orders, injunctions, peace bonds, etc. on file that effect either you, the suspect, the children, or the other person you suspect is involved? ☐ Yes ☐ No.
If yes, please explain:
_____
_____

Employer _____   Phone _____
Address _____   Occupation _____
_____   Work Schedule _____

Who do you expect involved? Provide address, phone, vehicle and description. _____

FIGURE 3.2   An example of a preliminary investigation form (used with permission, Probity Investigations, Inc.).

3.2.1.1   Authorization and Release

Information gathering reflects the subsequent content but to have full and unbridled access to it, the party must permit or authorize its access. In anticipation of the initial interview stage, complete an "Authority to Release Information" form which grants the authorized party access to every record listed at Box 3.1.

BOX 3.1 A SAMPLE AUTHORITY TO RELEASE INFORMATION FORM

Authority to Release Information

To Whom It May Concern:

I hereby authorize any investigator or other authorized representative of _____ _____ bearing this release or copy thereof within one year of its date, to obtain any information in your files pertaining to my employment, military, educational records (including, but not limited to, academic achievement, attendance, athletic, personal history, and disciplinary records), medical records, credit records (including credit card and payment device numbers), and law enforcement records (including, but not limited to, any record of charge, prosecution or conviction for criminal or civil offenses). Thereby direct you to release such information upon request to the bearer. This release is executed with full knowledge and understanding that the information is for the official use of _____. Consent is granted for _____ to furnish such information, as is described above, to third parties, in the course of fulfilling its official responsibilities. I hereby release you as the custodian of such records, and any school, college, university, or other educational institution, hospital or other repository of medical records, credit bureau, lending institution, consumer reporting agency, retail business establishment, law enforcement agency, or criminal justice agency, including its officers, employees, or related personnel, both individually and collectively, from any and all liability for damages of whatever kind, which may at any time result to me, my heirs, family or associates because of compliance with this authorization and request to release information, or any attempt to comply with it. I am furnishing my Social Security Account Number on a voluntary basis with the understanding such is not required by Federal statute or regulation. I have been advised that _____ _____ will utilize this number only to facilitate the location of employment, military, credit, and educational records concerning me, in connection with this application. Should there be any question as to the validity of this release, you may contact me as indicated below.

Full Name: _____
(Signature) include maiden &any other previously used name

Full Name: _____
(Typed or printed) include maiden &any other previously used name

Social Security #: _____

Parent or Guardian: _____
(if under 18 years of age)

Date: _____

Current Address: _____

_____

_____

Telephone Number: _____

Cellular: _____

Witness: _____

3.2.1.2 Interview Information or Fact Sheets

Before conducting the interview, the investigator wisely should lay out the purpose or objectives of the process. If hired by another, evaluate the request closely and accurately and tailor the interview protocol to the aim of the client. As an example, the insurance industry contracts with proprietary security firms for claim investigations and as part of the agreement between the investigator and the insurance client, the company delineates, in detail, the information sought or desired. A requisition document, general to the industry, defines the parameters of information to be gathered in the initial interview. See Figure 3.3.[15]

---

www.ThePIAgency.com   **Request For Investigation**
Probity Investigations, Inc.   678.316.9374 office
sales@ThePIAgency.com   678.828.5750 fax

Date: ___/___/___   Budget Amount _____   _____
                            (Dollar Amount or # Days)   (Our File Number)

☐ Workers' Comp   ☐ Undercover   ☐ Data Mining   ☐ Welfare Check   ☐ Corporate Service

Additional Instructions:_____ _____

CLIENT INFORMATION

Requestor   _____   Phone (___) _____ Ext _____

Client   _____   Type of Claim: ☐ W/C ☐ A/L ☐ _____

Address   Claim# _____

           _____   D.O.I. _____

Client Attorney _____   Phone (___) _____ Ext _____

CLAIMANT INFORMATION

Name/Alias   _____   Phone (___) _____   ☐ Published

Address   _____   S.S.N. _____-_____-_____   ☐ Non-Published

           _____   D.O.B. _____/_____/_____

Sex ____   Race ____   Ht ____   Wt ____   Hair ____   Eyes ____   Glasses ____   Married ____

Vehicle Make _____   Model _____   Color _____   Tag# _____

Spouse Name _____   Children _____

Other Info (cell phone#, hats, tattoos, appearance type) _____

INSURED / EMPLOYER INFORMATION

Name   _____   Phone (___) _____ ☐ cell ☐ home

Address   _____   Employer _____

           _____   Okay to Contact? ☐ Yes   ☐ No

Other Info   _____   _____

CLAIMANT's MEDICAL & LEGAL INFORMATION

Doctor   _____   Phone (___) _____ Ext _____

Address   _____   Next Appointment _____/_____/_____

           _____   Okay to Contact? ☐ Yes   ☐ No

Primary Injury _____   Occup. _____

Receiving Benefits? ☐ Yes ☐ No   Limitations _____

Attorney   _____   Phone (___) _____ Ext _____

Address   _____   Litigation Date _____/_____/_____

           _____   Previously Investigated? ☐ Yes   ☐ No

FIGURE 3.3 A sample investigative form for an insurance claim (used with permission, Probity Investigations, Inc.).

The initial interview may focus more narrowly on the specific action or investigative purpose. Investigators laboring in the negligence field need to compile, early on, the full picture and portrayal of the client. The "Personal Injury Questionnaire" at Box 3.2, used for the compilation of background information, pertinent data on the client's legal representation, economic and personal injury losses, as well as insurance policy information, is a common initial interview form.

BOX 3.2   A SAMPLE PERSONAL INJURY QUESTIONNAIRE

Personal Injury Questionnaire

Please tell us how you preferred to be contacted:

Name
Address 1
Address 2
City
State
Zip Code
Home Phone
Work Phone
Cell Number
Special Contact Information

Incident Information:

Date and Time of
  Incident:
Location of Incident:
Did the incident occur within the   ☐ Yes ☐ No
  scope of your employment?
If yes, describe:
Did the incident occur within the scope of the responsible   ☐ Yes ☐ No
  party's employment?
If yes, describe:
  Tell us what you believe happened:

Are there any photographs or video of the   ☐ Yes ☐ No
  scene, people, vehicles or anything else?
If yes, describe:

Immediate Injury Information

Please list all of your injuries from the incident and describe in detail:

Describe all medical treatment you have had as a result your injury:

Are you still treating? With who?

NOTE: Skip to <u>ONE</u> of the four categories in red below that best describes the incident: (1) Motor vehicle accident (injured in a car accident); (2) Product Liability (injured by a product); (3) Premises Liability (injured on someone's property); or (4) Malpractice (injured by a medical provider).
(Motor Vehicle Case)

Where were you in vehicle?

Name and address of investigating authority (Police Dept., Sheriff, Highway Patrol, etc.):

Did you or the other driver(s) receive any citation?   ☐ Yes ☐ No

If yes, explain what (you) (other driver) were cited for:

What were the weather and road conditions like?

Provide accident report if you have it: ☐ Yes ☐ No

Had you or anyone else been drinking or taking drugs to your knowledge?   ☐ Yes ☐ No

  If yes, describe:

  How did you leave the scene?

(Product Liability Cases)

Describe in detail the product that you believe injured you:

Who owns the product?

Where is the product?

Do you have access to the product?

How old is the product?

Do you or does anyone else to your knowledge have any photographs of the product taken   ☐ Yes ☐ No

  shortly after the incident?

If yes, where are the photographs?

(Premises Liability Cases)

To whom was the incident reported?

Were any photographs taken of the scene or the cause of the incident shortly afterwards? ☐ Yes ☐ No

If yes, where are the photographs?

What were you wearing, including your shoes?

Do you still have your clothing and shoes? ☐ Yes ☐ No

Did the incident occur outside or inside? ☐ Yes ☐ No

(Medical Negligence Cases)

Name, address and telephone number of every person or entity who you believe was the cause of your
  injuries or illness and why you believe that.

GENERAL INFORMATION – please fill out all questions below, regardless of case type.
Employment History &Lost wages

Current Employer's Name:

Were you employed here at time of accident?

Address:

Title:

Job Duties:

Wages/Earnings:

Dates of employment:

Did you lose any time from work as a result of the injury you sustained from the incident? ☐ Yes ☐ No

If yes, give the dates you were unable to work:

Did you lose earnings or have any other losses as a result of being unable to work? ☐ Yes ☐ No

If yes, state the amount of earnings lost: $

Past Claims History:

Have you ever been involved in any lawsuits? ☐ Yes ☐ No

If yes, please provide the following information:

Nature and reason for case:

Outcome:

Have you ever filed a Workers' Compensation claim? ☐ Yes ☐ No

If yes, please provide the following information:

For what type of injury:

Date of claim:

Outcome:

Past Medical History

Please provide the following information:
1. Your prior health status (circle one):   ☐ Excellent ☐ Good ☐ Fair ☐ Poor
2. Prior health history, including any prior hospitalizations or
   injuries, including approximate dates:

During this early phase of the initial interview, the investigator compiles the very basics on the parties and underlying theories of the negligence or other case being examined. Investigators are frequently asked to identify, list, and discover parties in a personal injury lawsuit. What types of parties, that is, plaintiffs and defendants, are possible? In a property, vehicular, or related claim, the defendant's insurance policies are reviewed for policy limits.

Investigators often use both an abridged version of an accident fact sheet, as well as a comprehensive form. For the former, see Figure 3.4. This type of document should be placed in the beginning of the file or permanently affixed to the inside cover of the file for easy access for other parties who need to examine the file.

Auto accidents generate an early need for reliable information. Information gathering at the initial interview sets the stage for all subsequent investigative activities. Figure 3.5 calculates the extent and severity of personal injuries resulting from an auto accident.

Critical Questions:
Review Figure 3.5 and answer the following questions.

1. Why does the form distinguish between immediate injuries and permanent ones?
2. Why are questions 4 and 5 important?
3. Which questions on the form are geared to a common insurer's defense, namely, a preexisting condition?
4. Which questions attempt to quantify the economic cost of this physical injury?

Each initial interview will vary by the subject matter and content of the investigation.[16] If not an auto accident, what of product defect and personal injury?[17]

Each form should properly lay out a sequence of questions that prove or disprove an argument or theory; that memorialize initial impressions of the interviewed party and demonstrate an evidentiary proof of, say, product defect and a plan of corresponding liability or defense. Insurance companies hire private investigators to determine the authenticity of claims under product liability actions. Is the injury feigned? Is the product actually defective or was the product being misused? Was the user following or disregarding the express directions and instructions for product usage? See Figure 3.6.

Critical Questions:
Review Figure 3.6 and answer the following:

1. Question 16 solicits information regarding how a product was being used. Why is that important?
2. At Question 21, the client's awareness of danger in relation to the product is examined. Do you know why?
3. Why are Questions 29 and 30 important in a product liability case?

Investigators encounter the intensity of domestic disputes, including abuse and violence, in divorce and separation cases. In these sorts of cases, objective fact gathering takes on heightened importance

Accident Fact Sheet

Client Personal Information

Client Name	Date of Birth
Address	Home Phone
City, State, Zip code	Social Security No.

Client Accident Information

Date/Time of Accident

Location of Accident

Description of Accident

Medical Information

Bodily Injuries

Name of Ambulance Company	Cost
Name and Address of Hospital	
Name of Treating Physician(s)	

Client Insurance Information

Insurance Company	Phone Number
Address	Contact Person
Vehicle Owner	Claim Number
Name of Insured	

Defendant Insurance Information

Insurance Company	Phone Number
Address	Contact Person
Vehicle Owner	Claim Number
Name of Insured	

FIGURE 3.4 A sample accident fact sheet.

since emotions tend to distort reality. The reliability, credibility, and veracity of any party's claim must be critically examined. Hence, the investigator gauges and assesses witnesses by a deep and intense evaluation of their representations—looking for holes in the story or confirmation that the story, as told, be true. Figure 3.7, or a similar form, should be inserted at the beginning of the divorce, custody, or protection from abuse case file. Essential background information is collected, such as petitioner's name, address, and phone numbers, and the names of the children. A small space for notes is provided.

Personal Injury Case –
Medical and Consequential Loss

INTERVIEW GUIDE

Use with 475 M.V. (Motor Vehicle), 485 A.C. (Accident Case) or with 490 P.L. (Products Liability)

File No. _____

Client _____   Date _____ Time _____ To _____

Interviewed by _____   Fee Arrangement _____

Referred by _____   Date of Accident _____

Statute of Limitations expires _____

(Where space is found insufficient use blank sheet and refer to question number)

PERSONAL INJURIES

1. Nature and extent of injuries _____
    _____
    _____
    _____
    _____
    _____
    _____

2. Immediate effect of injuries (unconsciousness, pain, inability to move or walk, cuts, abrasions, lacerations, bleeding, fractures and other physical discomforts) _____
    _____
    _____
    _____
    _____

3. Permanent injuries: list all permanent injuries, including scars, disfigurements, possibility of plastic or remedial surgery _____
    _____
    _____
    _____

4. Identify ambulances or other emergency vehicles _____
    _____
    _____

5. First aid or other medical treatment at scene, nature of assistance and names and addresses of those rendering assistance _____
    _____
    _____
    _____
    _____

480S - Personal Injury Initial Interview Guide
Rev. 9/97   P12/99

FIGURE 3.5 Personal injury initial interview guide. (Permission granted by ALL-STATE LEGAL, 800.222.0510, www.aslegal.com.)

6. If taken to hospital: (a) by what means and by whom (b) name and address of hospital (c) date of admission (d) date of discharge (e) treatment received and from whom _____

_____

_____

_____

7. If taken elsewhere than to hospital, where, by what means and by whom_____

_____

_____

8. X-rays, EEG, EKG and other tests: (a) by whom and where _____

_____

(b) parts of body x-rayed and what x-rays disclosed_____

_____

(c) results of EEG, EKG and other tests _____

_____

9. Treatment by doctors and paramedical personnel: (a) name and address of each and nature of specialty (orthopedic, therapeutic, surgical, psychiatric, general medical, dental, etc.) (b) nature and extent of treatments and where given _____

_____

_____

_____

_____

10. Outpatient treatment: name and address of hospital, date and nature of each treatment, name and address of each doctor, nurse or paramedical personnel _____

_____

_____

_____

_____

11. Medical expenses: where and by whom, dates, total charges, amounts paid to date and by whom paid (hospital, treating and consulting doctors, nurses, paramedics, laboratories, x-rays, appliances, special clothing, etc.)_____

_____

_____

_____

_____

_____

480S - Personal Injury Initial Interview Guide
Rev. 9/97   P12/99

©1998 by ALL-STATE LEGAL®
A Division of ALL-STATE International, Inc.
www.aslegal.com   800.222.0510   Page 2

FIGURE 3.5 (CONTINUED)

12. Future or anticipated medical treatments: nature, for how long and estimate of cost _____

_____

_____

_____

13. Dates of home confinement _____

_____

14. Home nursing care: name, address, phone of each person, nature of services, dates performed and amount

   paid _____

_____

_____

15. Household help: name, address, phone of each person, nature of services, dates performed and amount paid

_____

_____

_____

16. Present complaints_____

_____

_____

_____

17. Activities limited by injury (hobbies, chores, day-to-day activities, walking, etc.) _____

_____

_____

18. If client refused to accept any medical care or treatment recommended by doctors, show the care or

   treatment refused, doctor involved, date of each refusal and reasons for refusal _____

_____

_____

_____

PREVIOUS MEDICAL HISTORY

19. General condition of health in last 10 years_____

_____

_____

20. Nature, dates, extent of injuries from prior accidents, diseases or other disabling illnesses (heart, lung, brain,

   kidney, blood, vascular, sight, hearing, speech, dental, surgery, etc.) _____

_____

_____

_____

_____

480S - Personal Injury Initial Interview Guide
Rev. 9/97   P12/99

©1998 by ALL-STATE LEGAL®
A Division of ALL-STATE International, Inc.
www.aslegal.com   800.222.0510   Page 3

FIGURE 3.5 (CONTINUED)

21. Names and addresses of doctors involved (include x-rays, EEG, EKG and other tests) _____

_____

_____

_____

22. If hospitalized, names and locations of hospitals, duration and dates of hospitalization _____

_____

_____

_____

23. Aggravation or effect of present injuries on any existing or prior physical or mental condition _____

_____

_____

24. Physical examinations: for insurance, military employment or for other purposes, results and whether

insurance, employment or military service denied _____

_____

_____

_____

25. Previous accident or injury claims: names and addresses of attorneys, insurance companies, disposition of

each claim (including Workers' Comp.) _____

_____

_____

_____

EMPLOYMENT AND INCOME PRIOR TO ACCIDENT

26. Name, address and phone of employer _____

_____

27. Employer's business _____

28. Positions held and duties _____

_____

_____

29. Hours worked: per day _____ per week _____ hourly pay $ _____

30. Average weekly earnings for preceding 12 months $ _____

31. Earnings reported on income tax returns for past 2 years (show breakdown if more than one employer or

business) _____

_____

EMPLOYMENT AND INCOME FOLLOWING ACCIDENT

32. Time lost from work (itemize) _____

_____

_____

FIGURE 3.5 (CONTINUED)

33. If client returned to work after accident, for each employment show: (a) name, address, phone and business of employer _____

_____

(b) positions held and duties _____

(c) hours worked: per day _____ per week _____ hourly rate $_____

(d) average weekly earnings $ _____

34. Date of return to full employment _____

35. If client did not return to work, explain _____

_____

_____

36. If injuries impaired or in any manner restricted ability to perform duties of employment or business, explain

_____

_____

_____

_____

37. Lost time since returning to work (dates, periods, reason, income lost, sick leave used) _____

_____

_____

_____

38. If a promotion or increase in salary was expected at the time of the accident but did not materialize, give details _____

_____

_____

39. If injuries resulted in loss of business income, explain_____

_____

_____

_____

40. If substitute help was required in client's business to perform all or part of client's duties, give names, addresses and phone numbers of each person, nature of services, dates performed and amount paid

_____

_____

_____

41. List fellow employees, supervisors or business associates who have knowledge regarding client's employment and what each knows _____

_____

480S - Personal Injury Initial Interview Guide
Rev. 9/97   P12/99

©1998 by ALL-STATE LEGAL®
A Division of ALL-STATE International, Inc.
www.aslegal.com   800.222.0510   Page 5

FIGURE 3.5 (CONTINUED)

_____

_____

42. If client lost any rights or benefits related to employment (such as seniority or pension rights), explain

_____

_____

_____

43. Nature, extent and source of any other income or pecuniary loss _____

_____

_____

RÉSUMÉ OF EMPLOYMENT HISTORY FOR 5 YEARS PRECEDING THIS ACCIDENT

44. Employer, position or nature of employment, period, average earnings _____

_____

_____

_____

EDUCATION AND TRAINING

45. Educational background (schools attended, major subjects, degrees)_____

_____

46. Special skills or licenses_____

_____

47. If client's plans or prospects for further education or employment changed as a result of this accident, explain

_____

_____

48. If nature of employment at time of accident was different, inferior to or in a field other than that for which client had been previously engaged in or trained for (a) explain (lessening of demand for specific professional personnel etc.) (b) show resulting reduction in earnings _____

_____

_____

SUBSEQUENT INJURIES

49. If client has been injured since the date of the injury in question, indicate what the injury was, how it was received and the hospitals and treating physicians involved _____

_____

_____

_____

_____

480S - Personal Injury Initial Interview Guide
Rev. 9/97   P12/99

©1998 by ALL-STATE LEGAL®
A Division of ALL-STATE International, Inc.
www.aslegal.com   800.222.0510   Page 6

FIGURE 3.5 (CONTINUED)

𝔓𝔯𝔬𝔡𝔲𝔠𝔱 𝔏𝔦𝔞𝔟𝔦𝔩𝔦𝔱𝔶 -
𝔉𝔞𝔠𝔱𝔲𝔞𝔩 𝔍𝔫𝔣𝔬𝔯𝔪𝔞𝔱𝔦𝔬𝔫 (𝔍𝔫𝔠𝔩𝔲𝔡𝔦𝔫𝔤 𝔓𝔯𝔬𝔭𝔢𝔯𝔱𝔶 𝔇𝔞𝔪𝔞𝔤𝔢)

INTERVIEW GUIDE
(For personal injuries and related damages use with form 480S)

File No. _____

Interviewed by _____   Date _____ Time _____ To _____

Referred by _____   Fee Arrangement _____

Date of Accident _____

Statute of Limitations expires _____

CLIENT - SPOUSE - CHILDREN

1. Full name _____   SSN _____

2. Other names used _____   Birthdate _____

3. Residence _____

   Municipality _____ County _____ State _____ Zip _____

4. Telephone: Home _____ Business _____ Fax No. _____

5. If a minor or incompetent: names, addresses, and phone of parents and name, address, relationship and

   phone of guardian _____

   _____

   _____

   _____

SPOUSE

6. Full name _____   SSN _____

7. Other names used _____   Birthdate _____

8. Residence if different _____

   Municipality _____ County _____ State/Zip _____

   Telephone No. _____ Fax No. _____

CHILDREN

9. Name, sex, age and residence of minor children _____

   _____

   _____

DESCRIPTION OF PRODUCT

10. Name of product _____

11. Trade name and/or manufacturer _____

    _____

12. Model number and other identification _____

    _____

490 P.L. - Product Liability
Initial Interview Guide
Rev. 9/97

©1998 by ALL-STATE LEGAL®
A Division of ALL-STATE International, Inc.
www.aslegal.com   800.222.0510   Page 1

FIGURE 3.6 Product liability interview guide. (Permission granted by ALL-STATE LEGAL, 800.222.0510, www.aslegal.com.)

13. Description of product and use for which intended _____

_____

_____

_____

14. Availability of copies of advertisements_____

_____

_____

PRODUCT FAILURE

15. Date and place of accident or period of exposure to product_____

_____

_____

16. How product was being used_____

_____

_____

_____

17. Describe what happened _____

_____

_____

_____

18. What did product do or fail to do that caused injury or damage_____

_____

_____

_____

19. Cause of the product failure or malfunction (indicate presence or absence of any safety devices)_____

_____

_____

_____

_____

20. If instructions and warnings were not fully followed, explain any deviations _____

_____

_____

_____

_____

21. Client's awareness of danger in use of or exposure to product _____

_____

_____

490 P.L. - Product Liability
Initial Interview Guide
Rev. 9/97

©1998 by ALL-STATE LEGAL®
A Division of ALL-STATE International, Inc.
www.aslegal.com   800.222.0510   Page 2

FIGURE 3.6 (CONTINUED)

22. Is the product or similar products made with safety devices? If so, were they available and in use? Explain

_____

_____

_____

WITNESSES

23. Name, address, and phone number of each. Indicate family or other relationship to anyone involved in

accident

_____

_____

_____

24. Location of witnesses in proximity to scene of accident_____

_____

_____

25. Conversations, remarks and oral statements made at scene of accident, by and to whom, and in whose

presence _____

_____

_____

_____

_____

_____

_____

_____

26. Statements made to police: identify officer, date, time, in whose presence and details _____

_____

_____

_____

_____

27. Statements made at hospital, by and to whom, date, time, in whose presence and details _____

_____

_____

28. Location and availability of copies of all written statements (identify) _____

_____

_____

PURCHASE OF PRODUCT

29. Product was purchased on_____ for $ _____ new ☐   used ☐

30. Name, address and phone number of seller _____

_____

_____

490 P.L. - Product Liability
Initial Interview Guide
Rev. 9/97

©1998 by ALL-STATE LEGAL®
A Division of ALL-STATE International, Inc.
www.aslegal.com   800.222.0510   Page 3

FIGURE 3.6 (CONTINUED)

31. Name and address of salesperson _____

_____

32. If not purchased by client, then by whom and relationship to client _____

_____

_____

33. If not purchased, how acquired by client (rented, borrowed) explain _____

_____

_____

34. Describe containers, instructions, warnings and manufacturer's warranty which came with product _____

_____

_____

_____

35. Availability of above _____

_____

36. Verbal representations made at time of purchase, by and to whom, in whose presence and details _____

_____

_____

_____

PRODUCT HISTORY

37. Ownership and control from original purchase to time of accident _____

_____

_____

_____

38. Trace usage from original purchase to time of accident _____

_____

_____

_____

39. Care and maintenance of and repairs to the product from original purchase to time of accident_____

_____

_____

_____

40. Describe any trouble or difficulty with prior use of product _____

_____

_____

490 P.L. - Product Liability
Initial Interview Guide
Rev. 9/97

FIGURE 3.6 (CONTINUED)

LOCATION OF PRODUCT

41. Present location of product and person in control _____

_____

_____

42. Present condition of product _____

_____

_____

43. Availability of same or similar products for inspection and testing _____

_____

_____

INVESTIGATION

44. Full details of any investigation of the incident, by whom and for whom. Availability of reports of

investigation _____

_____

_____

_____

45. If a report or complaint was made, give full details (to whom, by whom, dates, obtain copy and indicate

response) _____

_____

_____

_____

_____

_____

_____

46. Details of experiences of others with this or similar products _____

_____

_____

_____

PROPERTY DAMAGE

(If personal injuries are involved use form 480S for medical and related damages, lost wages, future earnings, etc.)

47. Describe in detail what property was damaged _____

_____

_____

_____

_____

_____

_____

490 P.L. - Product Liability
Initial Interview Guide
Rev. 9/97

©1998 by ALL-STATE LEGAL®
A Division of ALL-STATE International, Inc.
www.aslegal.com   800.222.0510   Page 5

FIGURE 3.6 (CONTINUED)

48. Name and address of party making repairs. Attach copy of repair bills or estimates if no repairs made (indicate which were paid)_____

_____

_____

49. If any damaged items were sold or otherwise disposed of, enter name and address of person to whom sold or transferred, date and consideration received _____

_____

_____

_____

_____

50. Market value of damaged items prior to accident $_____ before repairs $_____

after repairs $_____

51. Itemize and explain additional expenses incurred, such as costs of replacement, storage charges, additional living expenses, etc. _____

_____

_____

_____

_____

_____

INSURANCE

52. If there is insurance covering any of the damages, provide full details (i.e., homeowners, accident, medical insurance) _____

_____

_____

_____

_____

_____

FOR OFFICE USE ONLY
Received

☐ Retainer Agreement   ☐ Hospital and Medical Reports

☐ Police Report Authorization ☐ Medical and related bills

☐ Police Report   ☐ Rental of appliances, etc.

☐ Photographs

☐ Other

490 P.L. - Product Liability
Initial Interview Guide
Rev. 9/97

©1998 by ALL-STATE LEGAL®
A Division of ALL-STATE International, Inc.
www.aslegal.com   800.222.0510   Page 6

FIGURE 3.6 (CONTINUED)

DIVORCE QUESTIONNAIRE

Your Full Name	Today's Date:
Your Current Address	Number of Marriages:
	County/State of Marriage:
Home Number	County where you reside:
Cell Number	Email Address:
Work Number	Date of Birth:
Spouse's (Ex-Spouse) Full Name	Number of Marriages
Current Address	County of residence
Home Number	Work Number
Cell Number	Other Number
	Date of Birth
Marital Residence Address	County
Date of Marriage	Date of Separation

ALIMONY

$_____ Per Month to: ( ) HUSBAND ( ) WIFE ( ) NO ALIMONY	
Wife wants her name to be	Maiden Name of Wife
( ) Maiden Name OR ( ) Previous Name Restored	Name to be Restored

EMPLOYMENT

Your Employer's Name	Address of Employer
Position	Monthly Gross Income $
Spouse's Employer	Address of Employer
Position	Monthly Gross Income $

ADDITIONAL INFORMATION

FIGURE 3.7 Matrimonial interview questionnaire.

Domestic disputes and litigation have seen widespread technology uses as the parties track one another. While there are implications relating to lawfulness and privacy, the private security investigator has far more latitude than his or her public counterpart.[18] Some examples include using tracing devices on vehicles, surveillance equipment to track and follow adulterous spouses, and the digital imaging of a hard drive on a home computer to assure preservation. While these tactics are far from the once romantic norm experienced by these couples, the battle landscape of divorce, custody disputes, and false allegations makes the investigator's services a must. A seasoned family law and domestic dispute investigator summarizes the skills needed to be effective in this often brutal environment.

There are two sides to the investigative business. One would be what I call the gumshoe side, where you're conducting surveillance, locating witnesses, interviewing them who may have knowledge of whatever it is you're trying to prove. In surveillance, the best way to have that evidence admissible in court is detailed reports, photographic evidence to prove you were out there and to document what you've done. The other side is the technology side, which is the computer forensics work. Texts, e-mails, and voicemails can be the deal-killer or the deal-maker in these cases because it's very difficult to argue with that kind of evidence. If you get a hold of somebody's smartphone it can just be a wealth of evidence and really make the difference.[19]

A more comprehensive example which deals with grounds for divorce is reproduced at Figure 3.8.

Critical Questions:
Review Figure 3.8 and answer the following questions.

1. Question 12 requests a marriage certificate. Why?
2. What other domestic relations cause of action within the present marriage could possibly be pending before a court of local jurisdiction?
3. This form does not assume a no-fault situation. Where are grounds of fault discussed?
4. Question 50 deals with the question of reconciliation. Do you think this is an important point in the initial interview process? Explain.

Web Exercise: Read the *Family Lawyer Magazine* article "Private Investigators Share Some Tricks of the Trade," at https://familylawyermagazine.com/articles/private-investigators-tricks-trade.

3.2.1.3 Follow-Up Letter

It is sound practice to follow up any witness, client, or other party interviewed with a letter that recites the scope and content of the interview. See Box 3.3.

**BOX 3.3   SAMPLE LETTER TO FOLLOW UP ON
A WITNESS OR CLIENT INTERVIEW**

[Date]
[Name of Client]
[Address]
Dear [client]:

When we discussed your claim the other day, I am sure that much of the information was new and unfamiliar to you. I am writing at this time to go over some of the items we discussed and the way we handle the investigation of injury claims. This also can serve as a reference for you in the future if a question arises as to how an investigation proceeds.

Preparation and Investigation

We already have begun the information-acquisition procedure. In the future, if you receive any calls from another party or any insurance company, you should refer the call directly to us. Do not answer any of their questions or provide any information. Members of your family or others who are likely to answer your phone should be given the same instruction.

I will attempt to acquire witness statements from individuals who have information about how the injury occurred. If you learn of any additional names of witnesses, please contact us immediately. If anyone calls you with information, please make sure to get the party's name, telephone number, and address before giving him or her our number to call.

I have written for medical information concerning the injuries involved. It will be important for you to keep me advised of any new doctor that you see. Please be sure to keep all receipts for drugs or any type of medical apparatus that you purchase. It would be quite helpful if you could send to us copies of all medical bills that you receive. This information is very important as it advises use of your medical expenses and the dates of treatment and the type of services that have been rendered. If a hospital admission is anticipated for any procedure of any nature, call to let us know in advance. If the hospital does not give you a copy of a bill, attempt to retain your patient number which can be found on your identification bracelet. This helps us locate your medical records.

If there is any significant change in your medical condition, please let us know. If you are going to be out of town for any length of time, please give us a call with a forwarding number in case it becomes necessary to contact you.

Sincerely,

[Name of Investigator]

Matrimonial Interview Information Record

(To be completed in conjunction with Form No. 830S)

File No. _____ Case No. _____

Interviewed by _____ Date _____ Time: _____ To _____

Referred by _____ Fee Arrangement _____
(Where space is found insufficient use blank sheet and refer to question number.)

CLIENT

1. Full Name _____

2. Maiden name _____

3. Other names used _____

4. (a) Res. Phone _____ (b) Bus. Phone _____

   Fax Number _____ Eye Color _____

SPOUSE

5. (a) Full Name _____ (b) S.S. # _____

6. Maiden name _____

7. Other names used _____

8. Physical Description: Height _____   Weight _____   Color eyes _____   Color hair _____

   Glasses _____   Scars or Marks _____   Other _____

PRESENT MARRIAGE

9. Date _____ Place _____

10. Availability of marriage certificate _____

11. Residences since marriage (show dates) _____

   _____

   _____

CHILDREN OF PRESENT MARRIAGE

12. (a) Minor Child _____

   (b) School _____

829S - Matrimonial Interview Information Record
Rev. 3/98   P3/98

©1998 by ALL-STATE LEGAL®
A Division of ALL-STATE International, Inc.
www.aslegal.com   800.222.0510   Page 1

FIGURE 3.8   Sample matrimonial interview information record. (Permission granted by ALL-STATE LEGAL, 800.222.0510, www.aslegal.com.)

13. Names, birth dates and residence of adult children and school currently attending _____

_____

14. Which children are adopted (a) _____ Date _____

    (b) _____ Date _____

15. Health status and nature of physical or other disability of each child _____

_____

16. Monthly (4.3 weeks) support received or paid for any children (a) _____

                                                                    (b) _____

17. Voluntary ☐   or by Court Order ☐   (if by Court Order give details) _____

_____

PRIOR MARRIAGE (answer on a separate page if more than one)

18. Party involved: Client ☐   Spouse ☐   Date _____   Place _____

19. Prior marriage name_____   Name of prior spouse _____

20. Cause of dissolution_____

21. Court and date of dissolution _____

22. Copy of judgment attached ☐ _____

OTHER CHILDREN OF CLIENT OR SPOUSE

23. Names and birth dates of minor or handicapped children (and name of parent) _____

_____

24. Residence and Custody_____

25. Names, birth dates and residence of adult children and school currently being attended (name parent) _____

_____

26. Health status and nature of physical or other disability_____

_____

27. Support received or paid for any children _____

_____

28. Voluntary ☐   or by Court Order ☐   (if by Court Order, give details) _____

_____

829S - Matrimonial Interview Information Record
Rev. 3/98   P3/98

FIGURE 3.8 (CONTINUED)

One's skill and expertise in eliciting information from witnesses and clients depends upon numerous factors. Remember that you, as an investigator, are conducting and controlling the interview, setting the tone and pace of informational response. Therefore, the burden rests upon the interviewer. The process of collecting information often involves the art of compromise and conciliation. "To minimize the stress, avoid conduct that can be interpreted by the witness as creating a 'pressure situation.' Give an impression of relaxed efficiency, not nervous haste. Smile and demonstrate real interest; not gloom, worry or distraction. Be thoughtful, courteous, and responsive; not inconsiderate, rude, or remote."[20]

EMPLOYMENT - CLIENT

29. Occupation _____ Job title _____ How long employed _____

30. Tel. No. _____ Fax No. _____

31. Work days and hours _____

32. Union ☐ Non-Union ☐ Union Name _____ Union Card No. _____

EMPLOYMENT - SPOUSE

33. Occupation _____ Job title _____ How long employed _____

34. Employer's name, address & phone # _____

_____

35. Work days and hours _____

36. Union ☐ Non-Union ☐ Union Name _____ Union Card No. _____

OTHER FAMILY ACTIONS–PRESENT MARRIAGE

37. List Court, docket number, nature of proceedings, dates, by whom instituted, disposition, and names of attorneys involved. Include all family actions involving support, custody or domestic violence (pending and closed)

_____

_____

_____

CAUSE OF ACTION

38. Desertion ☐   Separation ☐   Extreme Cruelty ☐   Adultery or Deviant Sexual Conduct ☐

Drug Addiction or Drunkenness ☐   Imprisonment ☐   Institutionalization for Mental Illness ☐

Other ☐

FACTS AND CIRCUMSTANCES

39. Provide, on separate sheets, a chronological statement detailing all events, reasons and causes for divorce or dissolution of marriage. Include names and addresses of witnesses and each person who participated in the incidents or acts.

40. Likelihood of reconciliation _____

_____

_____

829S - Matrimonial Interview Information Record
Rev. 3/98   P3/98

FIGURE 3.8 (CONTINUED)

With new clients, the investigator must create a positive first impression and recognize that the initial interview is, hopefully, the gateway to a long-term relationship. Correspondence and other explanatory documentation teach the new client about investigative dynamics.

3.2.2 RECORDING INTERVIEW IMPRESSIONS

The success of the initial interview process and subsequent interaction between the client and the investigator is a recurring concern of security management and administrative personnel. Most well-managed security firms contact clients directly regarding the type of treatment they receive by using a "Client Contact Report" (see Figure 3.9) or similar form.

CUSTODY

41. Reasons for custody of minor children as expressed by client: _____

_____

_____

    (a) Type of custody _____

    ☐ Joint legal custody with _____ parent having primary residential care

    ☐ Joint physical custody

    ☐ Sole custody to one parent, visitation by the other

42. Reasons why a party should or should not have custody of children _____

_____

_____

VISITATION   **M = Mother**   **F = Father** (Note by "M" or "F" for each category)

    a. Holidays/School Break

	CURRENT	PROPOSED		CURRENT	PROPOSED		CURRENT	PROPOSED		CURRENT	PROPOSED
New Year's Day	___	___	2nd Night Passover	___	___	1st Evening	___	___	Mother's Day	___	___
Martin Luther King Day	___	___	Memorial Day	___	___	Hanukkah	___	___	Father's Day	___	___
President's Day	___	___	July 4th	___	___	Christmas Eve	___	___	Summer	___	___
President's Week	___	___	Labor Day	___	___	Christmas Day	___	___	Vacation	___	___
Good Friday	___	___	Rosh Hashanah	___	___	Christmas Week	___	___	Other	___	___
Easter Sunday	___	___	Yom Kupper	___	___	New Year's Day	___	___			
1st Night Passover	___	___	Thanksgiving Day	___	___						

829S - Matrimonial Interview Information Record
Rev. 3/98   P3/98

©1998 by ALL-STATE LEGAL®
A Division of ALL-STATE International, Inc.
www.aslegal.com   800.222.0510   Page 4

FIGURE 3.8 (CONTINUED)

3.3 CASE EVALUATION AND SUBSEQUENT INTERVIEWS

After the information is gathered, it should be assessed for quality and reliability, and this evaluation will lead to the conclusion about the merits of a particular case or claim. The merit of an underlying claim, allegation, or assertion can often be gleaned from the initial interchange between investigator and client. Over time, the investigator develops a sixth sense about the merits of a client's claim and either comes to accept the general assertions of the interviewed party or discount the worth of the statements. Scott Fulmer, an experienced private investigator with a firm in Dallas has posted ten investigative rules to live by. By design these rules are imbued with common sense and humor but each of these suggestions goes a long way on our journey to investigative professionalism. See Box 3.4.[21]

Client Contact Report

| Office _____ | Operation _____ |
| Client _____ | Date Commenced _____ |

| Date | contacted | | | Initiated by | | Briefly describe discussion |
	In person	phone	email	client	Invest.	

FIGURE 3.9   Sample client contact report.

BOX 3.4   10 INTERVIEW TECHNIQUES FOR PRIVATE INVESTIGATORS THAT QUICKLY BUILD RAPPORT (USED WITH PERMISSION, SCOTT B. FULMER, UTAH PRIVATE INVESTIGATOR, PRINCIPAL AT INTERMOUNTAIN PI, AUTHOR, *CONFESSIONS OF A PRIVATE EYE*)

1. **Be Prepared:** It's the motto of the Boy Scouts but it will serve you well in all endeavors; especially in building rapport. I cannot stress this enough: Do your homework! Just as a good lawyer never asks a question in court that he doesn't already know the answer to, likewise, a good investigator is prepared ahead of time. This is especially important if the interview becomes confrontational. Gather as much information as you can before the interview. The more information you have about the subject the easier it will be to build rapport.
2. **Take your seat (in the position of power):** To build rapport and preserve the upper hand in an interview you will want to sit in the position of power. You should arrive early to all interviews. If you are conducting the interview at someones home or in a conference room, make sure to position yourself so that you sit at the head of the table (the position usually reserved for the head of the household or head of the company). Point to the chair to your right and suggest that the person you are interviewing sit there. They will then view you as an authority figure and see themselves as your assistant.

3. **Body Mirroring:** One of the most powerful, non-verbal methods of building rapport is by mirroring someones body language. To the uninitiated this sounds ridiculous. Trust me. It is an excellent way to build rapport. When you mirror the subjects body movements, as well as the speed and timbre of their speech patterns, you become like them. But dont be too obvious. Your movements must be fluid and natural. untrustworthy.Remember: We are most comfortable around people who are like us.

4. **Whats in a Name?** As Juliet stated in Shakespeare's immortal play Romeo and Juliet, *That which we call a rose, by any other name would smell as sweet.* Basically Juliet is stating that a name is an artificial contrivance. She would love Romeo regardless of what his name was. That may have worked for the Bard, but in real life a person's name is very important. We all like to hear the sound of our name. When conducting an interview use the person's name at least a couple of times. This builds trust and encourages them to listen to you. But do not use their name more than a couple of times during an interview. While using their name creates rapport, overuse of their name has the opposite effect. Overuse of their name will make you sound like a slick huckster and the subject will feel like they are being taken advantage of.

5. **Psychological Pause:** When questioning a subject throw in a psychological pause. This is simply a two- or three-second pause (or longer) taken during questioning. It is used for effect and should be inserted in areas of the interview where you normally wouldn't pause. For example: I want you to know that I've spoken with everyone about the incident and I feel that (insert psychological pause here) maybe you're not telling me everything you know?

   This unnatural pause creates a mild level of tension in the interview.

6. **Re-Direct the Question (Put touchy subjects on the backburner):** Rapport must be built up at the beginning of the interview. Do not make the mistake of tackling serious or confrontational issues before you have had a chance to build rapport. For example if you suspect a witness of knowing something about missing inventory or embezzlement in the workplace, build the rapport before asking direct questions. If you broach a subject and the subject clams up, gently back off. Show you understand how difficult this interview must be for them. Simply stated, I can see that question made you uncomfortable. That's not my intention. I can't imagine how difficult this must be for you. I'll tell you what: let's not worry about this right now. Why don't you tell me how you started working at ABC Packaging?

   By redirecting the questioning you are showing trust and concern for the witness. You are relieving the tension caused by your question. You're showing the subject you care and, yes, you are building rapport. You have just scored a point with them. Later on in the interview as rapport has been established you can sneak in the question, Everyone knows you had nothing to do with the missing inventory. But you know who is involved. I know you want to do the right thing. You have a family to support. That's much more important than your relationship with a few people at work.

7. **Family and Children First:** The very first thing I do before an interview is quickly scan the room for photographs of the subjects family or childrens coloring book drawings. People love to talk about their families. Look for pictures that include babies or recent weddings. You may spend the first 10 minutes of the interview talking to the subject about their children or grandchildren. Ask them an open-ended question such as, What do you like best about being a grandma? But remember the sole reason for all of this is to build rapport with your subject.

8. **Wave the flag:** Look for military mementos, plaques or pictures of people in uniform. Did both you and the subject serve in the military? If so, any discussion of your service will definitely will build rapport. Be sure to ask them where they served. You may have more in common than you know.

9. **Sports!** Seize upon any type of sports memorabilia in your subjects office. Look for golf knickknacks or signs of the subject's favorite sports teams. If you happen to be a Cowboys fan and their office is plastered with Steelers memorabilia this still allows you an opening such as: Oh no! You're one of them! If you do not care for sports at least check the Internet or local newspaper for the latest scores or big events so you can carry on a decent conversation. You must do everything you can to find common ground.

10. **Use the Mystique:** Finally, use what I like to call the PI mystique. You are a private investigator and most people find that fascinating. You see it every time someone asks you what you do for a living. Their reply: Wow. That must be exciting! Images of Jim Rockford, Thomas Magnum and Sam Spade are conjured up in their minds. The follow-up question is always: What's it like? Share some war stories with them. Tell them about some of your most exciting cases or describe some of the gadgets you use. They will hang on every word.

Web Exercise: Visit the PrivateInvestigatorEDU.org website and read the article on investigative process or PIs at https://privateinvestigatoredu.org/private-investigations-process.

The interview process may, and often does, assist the investigator in dealing with individuals and cases that are suspect. Examples of cases and clients you want to avoid are:

1. Clients who are trying to make a change in society
2. Clients who are crusaders
3. Clients who simply want revenge
4. Clients who have a "pot-of-gold-at-the-end-of-the-rainbow" mentality
5. Clients who are mentally or emotionally disturbed
6. Clients who proclaim too much the merits of their case
7. Clients who are shoppers for professional services
8. Clients who have other underlying and unknown motivations[22]

Experience teaches investigators that certain cases are naturally suspect and dubious. However, each case should be judged individually; the investigator must "listen and observe how the client tells the story. Proving the case may require that this person be a witness."[23] Determining whether or not the case is worthy of engagement largely depends on the client's sincerity and authenticity. "Clients may be abrasive, dull, neurotic, alcoholic, nervous, argumentative, or entirely inarticulate, yet still be able to testify effectively about potentially winning claims that the attorney can accept."[24] The investigator who conducts a professional initial interview will filter out the troublesome client.

Finally, the investigator must take his or her interviewees as he or she finds them. One cannot assume that a client will necessarily be cooperative, friendly, or generally receptive to any type of questions. Witnesses, clients, suspects, or other parties will all exhibit personal traits and characteristics that are unique to that individual and nearly impossible to predict. "When witnesses appear to be reluctant to cooperate, the investigator should attempt to determine the cause for this reluctance: Are they friends of the other party or the victim? Do they fear some sort of retaliation? Are they simply afraid of being called to testify at the trial stage?"[25]

The investigator will also be dealing with individuals who may be characterized as hostile, adverse, friendly, or expert in nature. These types of witnesses are covered in detail in Chapter 4.

Remember these general suggestions:

1. Interview witnesses in a timely fashion
2. Solicit as much factual information from witnesses as is possible
3. Utilize witnesses as leads to other potential sources of information
4. Convert all witnesses' statements to writing

5. Befriend witnesses and avoid antagonism at all costs
6. Keep in touch with witnesses as the case progresses[26]

Be especially attentive to legal and ethical issues that can arise during the interview process. Privacy statutes or civil rights violations, sexual harassment, or misrepresentation or other falsehood should perpetually guide the suitability of questions and interrogation tactic chosen. In most cases, pretext interviews are entirely improper. "Outright misrepresentation should be avoided and impersonation of law enforcement or other government officials should never take place."[27]

Use common sense and adhere to professional standards of investigative practice, and both case and client will be rewarded.

NOTES

1. Tom Shamshak, "Private Investigator Basics Part 2: Interviewing," PInow.com, May 7, 2012, accessed September 7, 2018, www.pinow.com/articles/1182/private-investigator-basics-interviewing.
2. John G. Igwebuike and Kendall D. Isaac, "Employer Implications of Conducting Background Checks in the Post-911 Environment," *American University Labor &Employment Law Forum* 4, no. 1 (Winter 2014): 46–65, https://digitalcommons-wcl-american-edu.ez.lib.jjay.cuny.edu/lelb/vol4/iss1/2/.
3. American Society for Industrial Security, *Basic Guidelines for Security Investigations* (1981): 45; E. Smith, *Practical Guide For Investigators* (Paladin Press, 1982): 34; Dean A. Beers, *Practical Methods for Legal Investigations: Concepts and Protocols in Civil and Criminal Cases* (Boca Raton: CRC Press, 2011); Robert J. Fischer et al., *Introduction to Security* (New York: Elsevier, 2103).
4. See Petter Gottschalk, "Dependency of Police Prosecution on Private Examinations of Financial Crime Suspicion: The Case of Langemyhr Investigation in Norway," *International Journal of Criminal Justice Sciences* 10, no. 1 (January–June 2015): 102–114.
5. ASIS, "Basic Guidelines": 46; Shamshak, "Basics Part 2."
6. See Corina Schulze, "P.I. Jane: Predictors of Women's Representation in Private Investigations," *Security Journal* 27, no. 4 (October 2014): 361–373, doi:10.1057/sj.2012.34; see also Kelly Armstrong and Larry Organ, "Sexual Harassment in the Workplace," *Trial* 50, no. 4 (April 2014): 42, www.justice.org/cps/rde/xchg/justice/hs.xsl/4938.htm.
7. Cape Fear Investigative Services, 401 N. Chestnut St., Suite D, Wilmington, NC 28401, accessed September 7, 2018, http://capefearinvestigative.com.
8. Carol Bruno, *Paralegal's Litigation Handbook* (Eagan, MN: West Group, 1980): 68–83; Tuule Sooniste, Pär Anders Granhag, and Leif A. Strömwall, "Training Police Investigators to Interview to Detect False Intentions," *Journal of Police and Criminal Psychology* 32 (2017): 152–162; Scott Fulmer, "10 Interview Techniques for Private Investigators that Quickly Build Rapport," October 13, 2010, accessed September 7, 2018, www.pinow.com/articles/353/10-interview-techniques-for-private-investigators-that-quickly-build-rapport.
9. Assuring good people in the investigative function is a critically important step for those entrusted with their hire. Bad decisions on personnel cause bad investigative results. When hiring investigative personnel be sure to hire those that can develop a good rapport at the beginning of the investigative interview. See Philip Segal, "Five Questions Litigators Should Ask Before Hiring an Investigator (and Five Tips to Investigate It Yourself)," Litigation 43, no. 3 (Spring 2017): 52–56; Douglas R. Richmond, "Watching Over, Watching Out: Lawyers' Responsibilities for Nonlawyer Assistants," *The University of Kansas Law Review* 61, no. 441 (December 2012): 441–493.
10. *American Jurisprudence Trials* 1 (1987): 357, 374; Fulmer, "10 Interview Techniques."
11. An illustrative example of how these skills play out concerns the investigation of potential jury for a selected jury pool. Here the investigator must get a host of constituencies to relay information about a potential juror. Katherine Allen, "The Jury: Modern Day Investigation and Consultation," *The Review of Litigation* 34, no. 3 (Summer 2015): 529–562.
12. Marc Davis, "Detective Work," *ABA Journal* 102, no. 3 (March 2016): 33.
13. See Richmond, "Watching Over."
14. Probity Investigations Inc., The PI Agency, North Georgia Office, 2095 Highway 211 NW, Suite 2F-131, Braselton, GA 30517.
15. Ibid.

16. For a close scrutiny of what to look for in a bank fraud investigation, see "Ten Steps for Conducting Fraud Investigations," *Bank Security Report* 44, no. 3 (March 2015): 4.

17. Experienced investigators in the private sector encounter all sorts of case types, but it is fair to say they see these types of cases with regularity: child custody and visitation investigations, serving papers, internal investigations, interviewing and questioning techniques, stakeouts and surveillance, tailing a target. See "The Investigative Process for PIs: From Taking a Case to Bringing It to a Close," PrivateInvestigatorEDU.org, accessed September 7, 2018, https://privateinvestigatoredu.org/private-investigations-process.

18. See "Private Investigators Share Some Tricks of the Trade," *Family Lawyer Magazine*, July 12, 2013, https://familylawyermagazine.com/articles/private-investigators-tricks-trade/.

19. Ibid.

20. National Association of Legal Assistants, *Manual for Legal Assistants* (Boston: Cengage, 1979): 246; "The Investigative Process for Pis"; Davis, "Detective Work."

21. Fulmer, "10 Interview Techniques."

22. Lawrence Charfoos and David Christensen, *Personal Injury Practice: Technique and Technology* (Rochester, NY: Lawyers Cooperative Publishing, 1986): 428; Davis, "Detective Work."

23. Charfoos and Christensen, "Personal Injury": 433; see also Julius Glickman, "Persuasion in Litigation," *Litigation* 8 (1982): 30; David Horowitz, "How to Handle a New Client," *Practical Lawyer* 21 (1975): 11–12.

24. Charfoos and Christensen, "Personal Injury": 433; Philip Segal, "Questions Litigators Should Ask before Hiring an Investigator," *GP Solo* 34, no. 6 (November–December 2017): 66; Richmond, "Watching Over."

25. Thomas Eimermann, *Fundamentals of Paralegalism* (Aspen Publishers, 1980): 117; Fulmer, "10 Interview Techniques."

26. Mark Weinstein, *Introduction to Civil Litigation* (Eagan MN: West Publishing, 1986): 54–55; "The Investigative Process for PIs"; Davis, "Detective Work."

27. ASIS, "Basic Guidelines": 52; Davis, "Detective Work."

4 Witness Testimony and Evidence in the Private Security Industry

4.1 THE PURPOSE OF WITNESSES

The value of any case, claim, or legal action depends on many factors although the quality and accuracy of evidence is chief among many choices. Testimony, whether formal or informal, under oath or unsworn, responsive to court demand or cordial request, is a primary form of evidence and one that carries extraordinary weight. In the world of security investigation, the job could not be done without testimony from witnesses. Investigators collect statements, record confessions or admissions of guilt or liability, memorialize expert findings in reports and documents, and amass documentary files that mirror the spoken testimony of a witness, such as in deposition or interrogatory form or the filing of a claim by an affirmative statement. Without witnesses, the task of the investigator would be an impossible duty.

All witnesses provide information, leads, and other insights for the case or claim and deliver testimony for a host of reasons including but not limited to:

- Identification of suspects
- Narration of facts and conditions surrounding the case
- Discussion of motive and modus operandi
- A tool of quality control by eliminating remote suspects
- Proof of a hunch, guess, or professional conjecture
- Direct eyewitness information[1]

This testimonial journey begins at the beginning of every case the investigator is assigned to. Ralph F. Brislin's remarkable manual, *The Effective Security Officer's Training Manual*, relays intelligently:

> Upon arrival at the scene and once you have determined who requires first aid, attempt to identify anyone and everyone who may have knowledge of what occurred. Ask witnesses to remain in the area until you have had a chance to talk to them. It is critical in this situation that you have a notebook and pen at your disposal. Attempt to interview those persons who were actually involved, whether they are the alleged victims or perpetrators.[2]

In the same way as an investigator looks for physical evidence at the scene, he or she identifies people who can provide actual testimonial knowledge of the event.[3] The array of potential witnesses will depend on the facts, the location, and the participants. Witnesses can and do vary in capacity and age, with increasing numbers of lay witnesses reaching into upper age which has its own set of challenges.[4] The importance of this evidentiary form cannot be discounted for it is as valuable as the forensic techniques we have become obsessively reliant upon. Sometimes a witness can deliver the clearest proof sought.[5]

4.2 TYPES OF WITNESSES

Witnesses generally fall into two categories: lay and expert. An expert witness has a specialized knowledge upon which his or her testimony rests, such as a chemist, a DNA specialist, a ballistics examiner, etc. All other witnesses are labeled lay witnesses, those who testify to objective reality without a scientific vein or purpose.[6] To illustrate, in a speeding case, the lay witness relays, "He was going fast." While the expert, holding radar results, states, "The radar reading was 101 mph." Each contributes important evidence although their approaches are quite distinct. How lay witnesses are utilized in a case depends on many factors but what is undeniable is their range of potential uses. Here are a few examples of lay witness activity:

- The actual victim of an intentional deed
- A victim of a crime
- A personally injured party in a negligence or medical malpractice case or similar tort
- An eyewitness, that is, an individual who personally witnessed the event and can testify to the facts and conditions
- Described as a character witness—he or she is capable of attesting to the good, bad, or indifferent nature of an individual's character or, at least, the community's perception of that character
- Expert in nature, having the capacity to testify as to certain fields of expertise that are beyond the scope of the normal layperson
- Lay witnesses, who give factual recitations and, in some cases, opinions
- Further described as friendly to one's case or viewed as being adverse, unfriendly, or hostile

Web Exercise: Read the legal guide "Types of Witnesses in a criminal case" at www.avvo.com/legal-guides/ugc/witnesses-in-criminal-cases.

4.2.1 MISSING OR UNKNOWN WITNESSES

Investigators often operate under the false assumption that witnesses are available and accessible. "Missing witnesses or parties (sometimes referred to as skips) are generally divided into two categories. The first and most common type is the unintentional skip, whose whereabouts are unknown because he has moved without leaving a forwarding address, and the passage of time has left his trail cold. The second type is the intentional skip, who leaves no forwarding address when he moves in order to avoid contact with his past. Often, the intentional skip may be seeking escape from an unpleasant situation, such as a domestic or creditor problem."[7]

Finding an unknown or missing witness can be difficult, particularly in criminal matters. Missing witnesses can submerge into a sort of underworld, particularly in major metropolitan areas where they are hard to track down. In domestic relations cases, especially in the prosecution of individuals who neglect support or alimony obligations, investigators encounter individuals who move from jurisdiction to jurisdiction and often create new and illegal identities. Despite the difficulties, witnesses can and usually are found. Some suggested steps to tracking missing witnesses include:

Client interview: Often forgotten is the client himself. He will often have secondary addresses, hiding places, or insights into customs and habits regarding travel and location of a given individual.

Telephone books: Scan all available telephone books for names or aliases that might match the individual in question. Also, look in earlier phone books, since it is common for names that were once listed to become unlisted pending or during certain legal difficulties. Also, if a number is secured, try to call and use fictitious, though not illegal, circumstances to introduce oneself to determine the location of a specific person.

Mail and telegrams: The use of certified mail, Western Union, or other electronic means can be a practical and useful way of tracking a witness. Although Western Union no longer sends telegrams, companies such as American Telegram and the International Telegram Service are available. If a last known address is found, a subpoena or summons to serve on a witness will satisfy most jurisdictional requirements.

Police reports or other documents: The investigator can assume that other parties who were in attendance at a crime or accident scene may have taken down the names of other witnesses in some type of report or documentation.

Canvass community: With a picture or other identification aid in hand, investigators can often spend productive time canvassing businesses, shops, restaurants, and people of the community. This is a typical and long-standing investigative technique.

Newspaper and other media sources: At scenes of crimes or personal injury litigation, a newspaper reporter may have taken pictures or made some record of the case. Even more frequent is the possibility of a photo or video record on various social media formats.

Public transportation carriers: Checking with bus, taxi, train, and trolley drivers and other individuals who provide regular service to the public may lead to identification of a specific witness.

City address directories: If a name is not available, a street address can sometimes be cross-referenced with a specific name if a telephone company provides such information. City directories also can provide information and are available at most public libraries.

Postal Service: Registered or certified mail or other means of address authentication are useful ways of verifying the location of a specific witness. While postal regulations do not provide for the direct disclosure of forwarding addresses, there are indirect methods of finding the location of a specific witness. In criminal actions, and under the authority of postal inspector activities, access to this traditionally confidential information is made available to public law enforcement representatives.

Other leads: Check any of the following: social clubs, union halls, professional organizations, schools and educational institutions, utility companies, veterans' offices, government agencies, welfare offices, recreational organizations, public record depositories, department of motor vehicles, voter registration records, marriage, birth, and death records, police records, NCIC records.

It is also essential that investigators develop relationships with firms that locate missing heirs, witnesses, and judgment debtors, particularly companies that specialize in the areas of estates and trusts, criminal law and litigation, and debtor, creditor, and collection practices. See Figure 4.1[8] for one of these firms.

4.2.2 LAY WITNESSES

A lay witness, simply defined, is any witness who is not an expert. A lay witness must have the general capacity to testify, record, recollect, narrate, attest to, and affirm certain conditions and facts. In this way, the witness is construed as competent enough to testify. Federal Rule of Evidence 601 outlines the theme of competence:

> Every person is competent to be a witness except as otherwise provided in these rules. However, in civil actions and proceedings, with respect to an element of a claim or defense as to which State law supplies the rule of decision, the competency of a witness shall be determined in accordance with State law.[9]

Additionally, he or she must have the requisite level of mental capacity and emotional competency to outline in some logical and sensible sequence the facts, conditions, and events. In formal litigation, a lay witness's testimony "is limited to those opinions or inferences that are (a) rationally based

FIGURE 4.1 Investigative services can help with a variety of services, including missing persons (used with permission, Martin Investigative Services).

on the perception of the witness and (b) helpful to a clear understanding of the witness' testimony or the determination of a fact in issue."[10] Generally, lay opinions unrelated to personal experience are not probative although opinions based on personal observation and perception (such as those related to alcohol intoxication, speed at which a vehicle was moving, height, distance, etc.) are readily accepted.[11] To say that lay witnesses may or may not have perceptual flaws is imminently fair for the assertion itself should never go unchallenged. Lay witnesses like all witnesses need to get their facts straight. For example, a recent study challenged the reliability of witnesses picking suspects from lineups or showups with results that demonstrated striking inaccuracies.[12] "Minimally, witnesses can testify to facts or truths personally experienced. Lay witnesses can and do go beyond mechanical recitation of data and expand the scope of testimony by giving opinions on actually observed events."[13]

The *Federal Rules of Evidence*, at 701, clearly delineates the lay witness's testimonial capacity:

> If the witness is not testifying as an expert, the witness' testimony in the form of opinions or inferences is limited to those opinions or inferences which are (a) rationally based on the perception of the witness and (b) helpful to a clear understanding of the witness' testimony or the determination of a fact in issue, and (c) not based on scientific, technical, or other specialized knowledge within the scope of Rule 702.[14]

Despite these limitations, the role of lay witnesses' testimony should never be minimized in the litigation sphere.[15] "A popular notion among most lay people is that expert testimony is the only form of evidence admissible in a criminal or civil action. This perception is a result of many factors, such as media coverage of flamboyant witnesses and other fringe litigation. However, the bulk of testimony given in any criminal or civil action is fundamentally 'lay' in nature."[16] Just as in expert testimony, the lay witness needs to meet certain criteria for testimonial admissibility.

In any investigative process, the investigator should corroborate the reliability of the testimony. A lay witness may testify about what he or she has perceived, understood, or experienced, but said testimony should be confirmed and corroborated. While the testimony of lay witnesses is unacceptable in matters requiring expert opinion, the statements of lay witnesses serve a variety of purposes during investigation, from corroboration of facts to the elimination of a suspected party.[17] Finally, lay witnesses should be employed as lead providers, becoming even more significant as a case unfolds.

4.2.3 Expert Witnesses

The role of expert witnesses in the investigative process is unquestionably significant. Experts scrutinize evidence, perform a quality control function at initial case review, and provide insights into cases being investigated. Just as the courts have increasingly relied on expert testimony as a form of explanation and illumination, so too the security industry relies heavily on expertise in the assessment of cases. "If scientific, technical, or other specialized knowledge will assist the trier of fact to understand the evidence or to determine a fact in issue, a witness qualified as an expert may testify thereto in the form of an opinion or otherwise."[18] "An expert witness is considered to be one who is qualified to speak with authority by reason of his or her special or unique training, skills or familiarity with a particular subject. An expert witness is allowed to render opinions and draw conclusions (in contrast, witnesses not qualified as experts are generally not allowed such latitude)."[19]

In the most general sense, experts, according to Doni Ryskamp fall into three main avenues of choice:

Practitioners whose expertise comes from hands-on work in a particular industry. Physicians, auditors, and engineers often fall into this category. Some of these experts operate their own consulting firms, with expert testimony making up some or all of their workload.

Academics whose field of study encompasses the questions or facts at issue in the case. Academics with experience in specific methodological approaches, such as statistical analysis or assessment, may also fall into this category.

"Professional experts" who work with expert consulting firms. These individuals often start their careers as academics, practitioners, or both, then transition into providing expert testimony in their field as a part- or full-time career. They are often well versed in the applicable courtroom and deposition rules but may be negatively received by the court due to their cessation of "hands-on" work in their field.[20]

Web Exercise: Visit Expert Witness Exchange at www.expertwitnessexchange.com and explore the various categories of expert witnesses in their catalog.

It is generally accepted that an expert has a certain level of knowledge, understanding, and experience which exceeds that of the ordinary layperson. Standards of education, personal qualification, experiential activities, scholarly publication and production provide the foundational basis for expert qualification.

4.2.3.1 Qualifications of the Expert

To achieve expert status, a formal evaluation of certain characteristics must be done. The claim of expertise must be backed up by the following variables.

4.2.3.1.1 Experience

Once the determination has been made that the subject matter of the witness's testimony has "crossed the barrier of judicial acceptability" and is a discipline which passes credible review with respected scientific researchers and that it assists the tribunal, the next issue is the qualification and character of the proposed expert witness. Under FRE Rule 702, an expert should be "qualified as an expert by knowledge, skill, and experience."[21] A finding of suitable qualification can depend on the following criteria.

- The witness has specialized training in the field of his expertise
- The witness has acquired advanced degrees from educational institutions
- The witness has practiced in the field for a substantial period of time
- The witness taught courses in the particular field
- The witness has published books or articles in the particular field
- The witness belongs to professional societies or organizations in a particular field
- The witness has previously testified and has been qualified as an expert before a court or administrative body on the particular subject to which he has been asked to render an opinion[22]

Degreed and intellectually advanced persons do not automatically qualify as experts. Qualifications bear a foundational relationship to the evidence being proffered. For example, in *Will v. Richardson-Merrell, Inc.*,[23] a plastic surgeon's testimony regarding the influence and effects of a drug called Benidictin was declared improper since the expertise of the plastic surgeon was pharmacological. While knowledge is an *a priori* expert qualification, the extent of an expert's knowledge is demonstrated under these lines of inquiry:

- How many times has the expert acted as a consultant?
- In how many cases has the expert actually testified?
- Were the issues in previous cases similar to the issues in the case before the bar?
- Has the expert ever been employed by the opposing counsel?
- What percentage of the expert's previous trial work was done on behalf of plaintiffs' cases and what percentage was on behalf of defendants' cases?
- What record-keeping method does the expert use to insure against conflict of interest problems?
- Has the expert written or published any articles, papers, or treatises concerning the subject matter involved in your case?[24]

Witnesses without a remarkable experiential history lack the mettle to withstand challenge by the opposing side hoping and wishing to undermine that testimony.[25] Weight given to the expert evidence largely depends on the credibility, the experiential history, and the resume of the expert.

4.2.3.1.2 Education and Training

Experience is merely one aspect of qualification. Another facet is the academic background of the proposed expert. Does the proposed expert have advanced degrees from a college or university? Aside from a baccalaureate degree, most experts possess a minimum of a master's degree. In many scientific fields, a doctorate is required. Psychiatric evaluations call for an M.D. with postdoctoral training in psychiatry. Certain other fields such as ballistics and fingerprint analysis do not necessarily call for postbaccalaureate study and are usually manned by law enforcement forensic experts. Plainly though, more degrees lead to the proposition, rightly or wrongly, that the witness's education makes their testimony more credible. Degrees are in some ways merely pieces of paper. Look to the grantor of the degree since some institutions are suspect. Less-than-honorable degree-granting institutions of higher learning that commonly advertise in periodicals, magazines, and newspapers need to be avoided.

Unfortunately, a negative stereotype is often applied to certain degree-granting state and religiously affiliated schools. This author has been a long-term critic of the legal profession's heavy and unwarranted emphasis on Ivy League degrees. Being a graduate of an Ivy League institution is no assurance of expertise or superior intelligence. In selecting experts, extreme positions at either end of the educational spectrum are to be shunned. An expert whose educational preparedness is based on a "matchbook" university or other "diploma mill" will be given very little weight if admitted at all. On the other hand, a jury and the court alike should resist dogmatic acceptance of the testimony of expert witnesses from historically prestigious institutions. There is an amazing diversity of expertise in the modern world based on both experience and academic training, from graduates of the smallest of religiously affiliated institutions to the largest of state universities to the ivy-covered halls.

4.2.3.1.3 Professional Associations and Other Memberships

Membership in professional groups or organizations is a supposed sign that the expert is currently maintaining the expertise espoused. Membership in professional organizations and scientific groups keeps the expert on the cutting edge of his or her developing discipline. In discerning the utility of an expert witness, consideration is carefully given to memberships. An impressive membership history will shape jurors' perceptions. "[T]he jurors will form their initial impressions regarding the expert's demeanor and credibility, and those impressions will determine their overall empathy and identification with the expert then testifying."[26]

Pay significant attention to whether or not the proposed expert has all required licensure and certifications in a proclaimed specialization, and is in receipt of a certificate of training or other documentation, or has been admitted to any professional associations or groups which attest to the specialized nature of the expertise.

4.2.3.1.4 Publications, Conferences, and Presentations

Expert witnesses become even more compelling when publications—whether books, studies, or periodical articles—are highlighted during qualification questioning. Whether misplaced or not, the lay person perceives a publication record as evidence of an enlightened professional. Publications, especially those that are found in refereed or edited journals, manifest the general academic community's acceptance of the expert's theoretical posturing. Practice, in and of itself, is less persuasive than the expert who frames theoretical problems in publicly published forums. The true expert, the more believable one, is that witness who has written and researched in his field as a complement to pure experience. Not to be forgotten are textbook publications, authored participation in legal materials, or editorial contributions to legal advisory committee reports and documents. The formality and permanency of writing indelibly impresses the fact finder.

Indicative of expertise is the expert's record of attendance at continuing education seminars, conferences, and conventions. These actions impress upon the jury the expert's commitment to excellence; the expert's willingness to be in the scientific forefront, and the expert's recognition that his or her field of study is constantly changing, maturing, and intellectually developing. In medical and scientific fields, this approach is mandatory.

What the investigator wants in all cases is the most technically competent expert, with the most exemplary credentials obtainable in the field. In general, credentials should show that the expert has devoted a substantial part of his or her professional experiences to his or her fields of specialization. Among the matters to investigate are education, licensure, or board certification, if acceptable, and practical experience. Experience should be evaluated in terms of quality as well as quantity. Factors affecting quality include exposure to authorities in the field or recognition by peers through awards, honors, or membership in professional societies. Authorship of articles in applicable trade or professional publications is also impressive and any articles should be reviewed for content to determine what positions the expert has gone on record as taking. The more education or practical experience the better the expert is, both from the standpoint of evaluating the case, and the ultimate testimony at trial.[27]

Undoubtedly, certain experts will be stronger in some of these criteria than others. In a perfect world, all of these qualifications would be met. Generally, keep in mind the following suggestions as to whether or not an expert is worthy of hire:

1. Previous experience with the witness, if any
2. Reputation amongst other experts
3. Degree of specialization and technical areas
4. Publications
5. Previous testimony recorded in transcripts, newspaper articles, or other information about the witness
6. Catalogs or other types of university or college literature where the witness is on the faculty
7. Professional advertising literature that is published by the expert
8. The expert's resume
9. Previous depositions of the expert[28]

Employ the checklist at Box 4.1 as a screening and qualification device.

BOX 4.1   SAMPLE EXPERT WITNESS QUESTIONNAIRE

Expert Witness Questionnaire

Name: _____

Address: _____

_____

Home Phone: _____ Work Phone: _____

Fax Number: _____ E-mail address: _____

Business or Occupation: _____

Name of Organization: _____

Length of Time in Business: _____

Position Held in Organization: _____

Prior Positions: _____

Education: _____

Under Graduate Degree: _____ Institution: _____

Graduate Degree: _____ Institution: _____

Post Graduate: _____ Institution: _____

Specialized Training: _____

Courses: _____

Licenses and Certifications: _____

Professional Associations and Organizations: _____

_____

Academic Background: _____

_____

Expert Witness Experience: _____

_____

Specializations: _____

_____

The areas of expertise are only limited by a judicial decision as to what is scientifically acceptable and what is not.[29] Courts have long construed certain disciplines as having "crossed the barrier of judicial acceptability"[30] while barring the admissibility of those fields deemed untried or untrue. For example, the fields of astrology or para-sensory perception still have not developed sufficient scientific support, nor is it likely to occur, to be viewed as legitimate scientific endeavors.[31]

But this mentality has been under siege since the 1990s. Instead of scientific rigor, the United States Supreme Court has issued two rulings, *Daubert*[32] and *Kumho*[33], both of which effectively end the reign of *Frye* in the federal system.

The federal courts, by and through a pivotal ruling, *Daubert v. Merrell Dow Pharmaceuticals*,[34] have effectively made the *Frye* rule moot in their jurisdiction. *Daubert* has been the primary support of those hoping to achieve the admissibility of "sciences" once scorned. Strict reliance on the general consensus test of *Frye (the technique is generally accepted as reliable in the relevant scientific community)* is being replaced with a "more searching and flexible inquiry about the reliability and relevance of the offered evidence."[35] Under *Daubert*, judges are "gatekeepers" now performing dual functions; screening "expert scientific testimony not merely to assure that the expert is qualified, but also to assure that the expert methodology is 'reliable.'"[36] Judges were to determine whether "the scientific evidence had sufficient testing, peer review and publication."[37] *Daubert*'s suggestions were toothless and as a result unpredictability at the lower courts became normal. It is questionable whether judges are even capable of performing the latter function.[38] Like it or not, until and when *Daubert* is modified, judges have taken on an increasing screening role in scientific evidence.[39]

Daubert's lenient and inconsistent results have generated enormous criticism.[40]

The U.S. Supreme Court's 1999 ruling, in *Kumho Tire Co. v. Carmichael*,[41] accelerated the gatekeeping role of the judge when it comes to the quality and content of expert evidence. Not only are the questions of qualification and field pertinent, but also the methodology behind the results testified to.[42] *Kumho* is a valiant attempt to banish a burgeoning "junk science" industry from the courtroom. Expert evidence should be primarily rooted in a "real science"[43] that only arises from "careful and controlled experimentation."[44]

For private security operatives, the liberalization of the scientific rules, replaced with the vagaries of *helpfulness* and the like, were once thought friendly to some industry practices. For example, in the investigative realm, polygraphs and other truth-measuring devices have never crossed the barrier of judicial acceptability and federal legislation restricts their use. Traditional *Frye* rules shut that door.[45] But many argue that *Daubert* opens up the new vista of admissibility making it more likely than not, at least over time, that the polygraph may encounter no judicial resistance.[46] On the other hand, psychiatry and psychology, although imprecise disciplines, are liberally accepted as areas of expert testimony by our courts and legislatures—and this easy access, with new and novel theories, is bound to grow in the years to come. So the elasticity of the *Daubert* principles have advanced "junk science" in most quarters and made once implausible arguments into acceptable advocacy. In this way, the investigator can take more chances on an argument than was possible under *Frye*.

As in other evidentiary forms, the proponent needs to demonstrate the expert's evidence, for potential usage or admissibility, following specified rules and steps—whether outlines in codifications or customary advice from a particular jurisdiction. The National Center on Domestic and Sexual Violence, which advances a myriad of theories as to victimization, uses a *Daubert* template to scrutinize case, expert witness, and client.[47] See Box 4.2.

BOX 4.2   SAMPLE DAUBERT QUESTIONS FOR EXPERT WITNESSES

Daubert Questions for Expert Witness

1. EXPERT QUALIFICATIONS:

Name?	Field of expertise?
Address?	Purpose and nature of consultation?
Occupation?	Research?
Present employment?	What scientific testing did you undertake?
Past employment?	
Educational background?	Findings and opinions?
Current professional involvement?	Definitions?
Membership in professional societies?	

2. PROPOSED TESTIMONY IS SUFFICIENTLY TIED TO FACTS OF CASE SO THAT IT WILL AID THE FINDER OF FACT IN RESOLVING A FACTUAL DISPUTE:
   - What does your testimony concern?
   - In your opinion, how does that testimony relate to the nature of this suit (or it's underlying issues)?
   - Do you believe the research you have done could have been done by the average lay-person (without your type of education or experience)?
   - Do you consider the research you have done to be decipherable by the average lay-person?
   - Do you feel your testimony will better aid the finder of fact to understanding the work you will present?

3. TESTING OF THE THEORY OR TECHNIQUE (FALSIFIABILITY):
   - What theory/technique did you use in your research?
   - How often do you use this theory/technique?
   - Do you use this theory/technique in other subject areas, or is it unique to the subject matter addressed in this case?
   - How did you test this theory/technique?
   - Did you use the same testing method every time to test for accuracy?
   - Did anyone, other than you, test your theory/technique for accuracy?
   - What test did that person use?
   - When did that person do his/her testing?
   - What were the results?

4. EXTENT TO WHICH THE TECHNIQUE RELIES UPON THE SUBJECTIVE INTERPRETATION OF THE EXPERT:
   - Does the technique you used generally require subjective or objective interpretation among others in the field?
   - Was the technique used in your research interpreted subjectively or objectively?
   - Do you feel another person in your field would have interpreted your technique in the same you have?
   - Is there a way to cross-check the subjective interpretation for accuracy?
   - Did such cross-checking take place?
   - What were the results?

5. WHETHER THE THEORY/TECHNIQUE HAS BEEN SUBJECTED TO PEER REVIEW OR PUBLICATION:
   - Has your theory/technique been published?
   - Where was it published?
   - When was it published?
   - Were there any criticisms?
   - What were the nature of the criticisms?
   - Has your theory/technique been reviewed by your peers?
   - By whom was it reviewed?
   - When was it reviewed?
   - What was their opinion of your technique after having reviewed it?

6. THE THEORY/TECHNIQUE'S KNOWN OR POTENTIAL RATE OF ERROR:
   - Does your theory/technique have a known or potential rate of error?
   - What is that rate of error?
   - How did you arrive at that rate of error?
   - Is that rate of error common for the theory/technique you used?
   - Did you carefully consider alternative causes or theories?
   - What makes yours the best to use or most reliable?

7. GENERAL ACCEPTANCE OF THE THEORY/TECHNIQUE BY THE RELEVANT SCIENTIFIC COMMUNITY:
   - Have you used this theory/technique outside the purposes of litigation?
   - In what instances?
   - When?
   - Where?
   - Was the theory/technique used, consistent from those instances until now?
   - Was the theory/technique altered this time because of the litigation?

Questions of admissibility and formal courtroom use may not even be the investigator's end or aim, for in many cases the expert witness may serve as screener, evaluator, and recommender on the client and its corresponding facts. The expert may simply aid the investigator in determining the substantiality, credibility, veracity, and scientific plausibility of a claim or defense or underscore the value and merit of an argument.

And in other cases, the parties know the evidence posed by the expert will never see admission in any judicial framework, yet the evidence usage, informally, may still be worth the evaluation. Polygraphs are a solid example of a useful, yet nonjudicially recognized form of expert evidence.

From another slant, the expert witness should be relaying testimonial findings on a field that has crossed some threshold of judicial and scientific acceptability. Astrology should not cut it, nor fortune-telling. Investigators should screen the expert's capacity by making sure the field upon which their expertise is based has scientific and factual recognition. Legitimate fields cover a great deal of territory and include:

- Actuaries
- Agriculturalists
- Anthropologists
- Appraisers
- Archaeologists
- Aviation safety experts

- Biologists
- Botanists
- Chemists
- Criminalists
- Electrical contractors
- Engineers
- Environmentalists
- Foresters
- Geologists
- Meteorologists
- Metallurgists
- Microscopic specialists
- Nuclear scientists
- Physicists
- Psychiatrists
- Psychologists
- Radiologists
- Security analysts
- Surveyors

In medical claims, the investigator could correctly depend upon any expert from these fields and subfields.

- Allergy
- Anesthesiology
- Cardiology
- Chest surgery
- Chiropractic
- Dentistry
- Dermatology
- Endocrinology
- Gastroenterology
- Geriatrics
- Gerontology
- Gynecology
- Hematology
- Hospital administration
- Immunology
- Industrial medicine
- Internal medicine
- Medical laboratory technology
- Medical photography
- Neurology and neurosurgery
- Nuclear medicine nursing
- Obstetrics
- Occupational therapy
- Ophthalmology and optometry
- Orthopedics
- Osteopathy

- Otolaryngology
- Pathology
- Pediatrics
- Pharmacy
- Physical medicine/physical therapy
- Plastic surgery
- Preventive medicine
- Proctology
- Psychiatry and psychoanalysis
- Psychology
- Radiology
- Surgery
- Urology
- Veterinary medicine[48]

4.2.3.2 Sources of Expert Witnesses

Expert witnesses come from many quarters. Paul Kirk's *Locating Scientific and Technical Experts* assembles expertise through many avenues including educational groups, associations, scientific bodies, and boards that are sure to have members with the needed backgrounds.[49] *The Lawyer's Desk Reference Manual* also contains pertinent information on expert groups and associations. There are a host of possible avenues for locating expert witnesses.

Seen regularly in the legal community are published directories which compile listings of experts and their intellectual endeavor. Some examples are:

- American Medical Forensic Specialists, 6425 Christie Ave., Suite 260, Emeryville, CA 94608. Toll free (800) 275-8903. Phone (510) 985-8333. Fax (510) 985-7383. Email info@ amfs.com. Web www.amfs.com/
- *Consultants and Consulting Organizations Directory*, 41st Edition, Gale, a Cengage Company, ISBN: 9781410317230. Web www.gale.com/
- Locating Scientific and Technical Experts in 2 AM. JUR. TRIALS, 302-356 (1987)
- Locating Medical Experts in 2 AMERICAN JURISPRUDENCE TRIALS, 112-133 (1987)
- TASAmed, 1166 DeKalb Pike, Blue Bell, PA 19422-1853. Phone (800) 659-8464. Fax (800) 850-8272. Email tasamed@tasanet.com. Web www.tasamed.com/.

Consult *Who's Who Directories* for specific fields: law, engineering, biochemistry, geology, mathematics, psychology, psychiatry, and related fields. Most reference librarians will be happy to assist in sorting out and discovering these rich forms of source material.

4.2.3.2.1 Private Consulting Services

No area of expert consulting services is more dynamic than that provided by private entities. Expert consulting services are structured for two major rationales: first, to act as a resource directory, a referral fee-for-service network for attorneys, investigators, and aligned firms searching for a specific expert and a corresponding topic; and second, to provide evaluative and research services. Two of the most often seen and well known of these private consulting services are:

- Technical Advisory Service for Attorneys (TASA), 1166 DeCalb Pike, Blue Bell, PA. Phone (800) 523-2319. Web www.tasanet.com/
- Professional Expert Consulting Services, LLC, 14507 Lemoyne Blvd., Suite 8, Biloxi, MS 39532. Phone (228) 669-4004. Web www.thepcs.org/

Another influential player which catalogs by expertise and provides contact information is the American Association for Justice (AAJ), 777 6th Street, NW, Suite 200, Washington, DC 20001. Phone (800) 424-2725. Web www.justice.org/.

Experts also play a major role in case evaluation and screening for government agencies, attorneys, and investigators. A variety of private companies, both for profit and not for profit, whose purpose is the evaluation and assessment of cases and claims, provide a resource to investigators. For example, in medical cases, such expert service companies with special skills in malpractice review medical records and histories followed by giving an expert opinion on the validity of a present or future condition. Other companies assess products for technical or structural deficiencies or provide insight into the impact of action or inaction by a vendor, dealer, or manufacturer.

An investigator looking for expertise need not rely on private, for-profit firms. Experts can be located in other areas, including:

- Colleges and universities
- Professional associations
- Scholarly literature and reviews
- Trade schools
- Telephone books
- Who's Who books

Though the field of expert service companies is wide, investigators should not overlook local authorities, such as the family physician, an auto mechanic in a product liability case, the osteopathic specialist in rehabilitative back and neck medicine, and so forth.

Whether the investigator utilizes the expert witness in a testimonial fashion or as a quality control assessor, the expert must meet certain minimum criteria. "In general, credentials should show that the expert has devoted a substantial part of his or her professional life to the applicable subject area. Among the matters to investigate are education, licensure or board certification, if applicable, and practical experience. Experience should be evaluated in terms of quality as well as quantity. Factors affecting quality include exposure to authorities in the field or recognition by peers through awards or honors or membership in professional societies."[50] In addition, the fuller the record of scholarly production in peer reviewed publications and texts, the more persuasive the expert becomes. Investigators will want to highlight the expert's pedigree by reference to academic degrees, institutions attended, and the amount of practical experience amassed over the career.[51]

Finally, investigators must not be duped or overly impressed with expert credentials; for one expert who attests that a certain condition is causally tied or correlated to given circumstances, another will evaluate the same facts and correlations and reach the opposite conclusion. For example, a psychiatrist who asserts that the legal measure of insanity has been proven will be likely countered by another psychiatric expert alleging the defendant is lucid and free from the legal state of insanity. The testimony of experts cannot be viewed as infallible. Treat testimonial and evidentiary results of experts sensibly,[52] and remember that an expert, when paid for his or her consultation, will favor the payor, and in this sense, given this contractual relationship, no one is free from economic bias.

4.2.3.3 Expert Service Contracts

Expert consulting service companies provide expert witnesses to firms and investigative units in need of the specialized review. These consulting firms are not charities and charge clients in various ways, including set fee, hourly rate, or in some circles, a fee based upon a settlement or judgment in a legal case. Expert service contracts are standard documents employed in this arrangement. See Box 4.3.

BOX 4.3 SAMPLES OF EXPERT WITNESS AND CONSULTANT RETAINER FORMS

Expert Witness / Consultant Retainer Agreement

Retaining	
Attorney: _____	Examinee: _____
Law Firm: _____	Examinee's
Address: _____	Address: _____
_____	_____
_____	_____
Phone No: _____	Examinee's
Fax No: _____	Phone No: _____

Thank you for referring your questions regarding the above-named case to me for forensic psychiatric evaluation. I am pleased to provide professional services regarding this case upon receipt of an executed copy of this Expert Witness Retainer Agreement in addition to the agreed upon retainer fee of $_____.

My current billing rate is $____ per hour. I bill my rate in quarter-hour increments for all time devoted to the case, including phone calls, consultations, research and preparing reports, as needed. I will refund any unused portion from the retainer fee once it is clear that my services will no longer be required. However, my minimum charge for agreeing to be retained as an expert or consultant in this case is 4 hours of my time, or $_____.

In the event that work in the case exceeds the initial retainer fee, no report will be released nor testimony scheduled (in court or by deposition) until the entire balance is paid. Testimony in court or by deposition is billed in half-day (4-hour) blocks. Payment for my time involved in such testimony must be pre-paid. In the event there are travel expenses, these must be paid by the retaining attorney. Fees for travel-time may vary but I will provide a good-faith estimate depending on the situation. If an examinee fails to show up for the evaluation, I still must charge for the time I had blocked out for the case. A rescheduled date and time can be arranged. If the attorney decides not to reschedule, the minimum charge for the 4-hour block of time will still apply.

I strongly recommend that the retaining attorney forward for my review all relevant medical records, mental health records, investigation reports, witness statements, depositions and other case information prior to my evaluation of the subject to be evaluated. I recommend these materials be sent as far in advance of my scheduled examination of the subject as possible so that I might be as efficient as possible in evaluating the case.

Once it is decided that I will no longer be involved in the case, either because the case has resolved or my services are no longer required the retaining attorney, I may return all documents and notes to the retaining attorney. There may be a charge for large volumes of materials returned to cover excessive postage.

By signing below, the retaining attorney indicates acceptance of this service agreement and the contractual provisions contained herein. Please return this form along with the agreed upon retainer fee noted above. In return, I will countersign and send a completed contract back to the retaining attorney. If this signed service contract and retainer are not received within 7 business days of our initial communication about the case, then my name shall not be listed by the retaining attorney or retaining firm as a witness and I will be free to be retained by other parties, including opposing counsel.

Upon being retained by an attorney, company or firm I am retained for that specific case only and may be retained by any other attorney, including opposing counsel for other cases so long as there is not a direct conflict-of-interest. I am available for retainer on an ongoing basis for a negotiated fee, which must be specified in writing. This method of retainer may be useful for corporations or firms dealing with mental health related legal issues on a regular basis.

Contract accepted by:

_____ Date:_____

_____ Date:_____

Be certain that the contract covers accurately the costs and fees of usage and disputes and squabbles avoided. Otherwise, expert testimony may evolve into an extraordinary liability.[53]

4.2.4 CHARACTER WITNESSES

Investigators must commence an inquiry with an open mind but also a very healthy doubt about the credibility of the claim and the claimant. Investigators cannot assume that any allegation be true.[54] Every investigative assignment should be adjudged as to its credibility and authenticity. Investigators must be wary of those making claims to outlandish victimization or who engage in excessive hyperbole. A story may or may not be true and whether the story be reliable or not often depends on the character and reputation of the story's source. All facts, every allegation and assertion, need to be checked for their fundamental credibility. The validity of any case or claim depends on the veracity of the witness and his or her testimony. In criminal cases, before sentencing, defendants generally march in a parade of witnesses attesting to character, from the defendant's mother to the pastor down at the local church. How reliable is such testimony? And should it be viewed with a jaundiced eye. From another vantage point, will this evidence be beneficial or, as some critics of its use argue, even become a negative since a jury may question the credibility of the character witness and "thus see defendants more negatively than if they never heard supporting testimony at all."[55]

That same inquiry should be applied to ambulance chasers, excessive litigators, and those seeking a fortune from car crashes or medical malpractice. Precisely what the character of these cases consists of is inexorably interlinked with the character of the person alleging those facts. Investigators need to become competent in vetting both the claim and the claimant.

Other factors related to bias or prejudice are worthy of consideration when determining the veracity of every witness. The investigator needs to be wary of intimate witnesses, those too close to the party for any testimony be objective. When finance or money is involved, reputational evidence given by someone who stands to benefit economically is not reliable either. In sum, character witnesses can be as flawed or righteous as those on whose behalf they speak. Finally, be skeptical of those who speak for a larger community when giving reputational evidence. It is difficult enough to know one's own view let alone the entire community. In the final analysis, character testimony is a blend of both worlds—the character witness giving his own impression in light of those in the community, and at the same time portraying, in lay form, the community's perception and belief about the defendant's reputation.[56]

Web Exercise: Read the web article on defendants and character witnesses at www.nolo.com/legal-encyclopedia/as-defendant-can-i-offer-evidence-good-character.html.

Character witnesses relay circumstantial insight and evidence about a particular party. The chief rationale for the character witness is not that he or she is an expert in a psychological or psychiatric sense, but instead is qualified to give a judgment of a community's perception of an individual's reputation.[57]

4.3 PROCESSING WITNESSES

As indicated in Chapter 3, the techniques of interviewing a witness call for effective human interaction that produces results.[58] "Interviewing witnesses is an art. Usually, if the witness is a friend or relative of the client, he or she will readily speak to the attorney or the investigator. When the witness is not such a person, the job of the interviewer will be not only to get a statement but to get the witness to speak at all."[59]

Web Exercise: Read the article on how to interview different types of witnesses at PoliceOne.com's website at www.policeone.com/investigations/articles/7787318-7-types-of-witnesses-and-how-to-interview-them/.

Sample letters advising witnesses of your desire for them to cooperate and provide you with information as a witness appear in Box 4.4 and 4.5. Notice that the letters are neither antagonistic nor overly formal or legalistic in approach or design. Instead, they convey the intention to work amicably with the witness and show that his or her testimony is sufficiently urgent.

BOX 4.4   SAMPLE LETTER SEEKING INFORMATION FROM WITNESSES

NAME/ADDRESS
IN RE: Witness Statement
Our Client:
Date of Accident:

Dear:

I am an investigator for the above-named client who has granted me full power of attorney to collect information regarding the above-reference accident. A copy of that power of attorney is enclosed. I am writing about my client whom I represent for recovery of economic loss and damages that resulted from an incident seen by you.

Would you please call me at your convenience to advise me of the facts you saw relative to this matter. I must stress that this matter may be unjustly resolved without your assistance. If you have any questions, Please feel free to call.

Sincerely,

(Investigator)
Enclosure

**BOX 4.5   SAMPLE LETTER SEEKING INFORMATION
FROM WITNESSES IN REGARD TO AN ACCIDENT**

IN RE: Witness Statement
Our Client:
Date of Accident:

Dear:

I am an investigator for the above-named client who has granted me full power of attorney to collect information regarding the above-referenced accident. A copy of that power of attorney is enclosed. I am writing to request your assistance in representing my client who was injured in an accident that you witnessed. I am attempting to recovery my client's economic losses and damages as a result of this incident.

I have enclosed a form for information concerning the facts you observed on the day of the accident. I also have enclosed a self-addressed envelope for your use. If, for any reason, filling out this form will be difficult or inconvenient, please feel free to call me, and my office will be glad to take your statement over the phone.

Thank you for taking the time to tell us the facts of this incident. Without your information, this matter may not be resolved justly. If I can be of any assistance, please feel free to call.

Sincerely,

(Investigator)
Enclosure

Figure 4.2 is the enclosure referenced in the letter above. Investigators should evaluate the quality of the witness by the statement he or she offers.

Request For Witness Statement

Your
Name: _____

Date of
Birth: _____

Where were you when you saw the facts concerning this incident?
_____
_____
_____
_____

What did you see?
_____
_____
_____

Did you hear anyone, including the people involved in the incident, say anything?
_____
_____
_____
_____
_____
_____

Do you know of any other witnesses?   ( ) YES   ( ) NO

If yes, do you know the names of the witnesses or can you describe them?
_____
_____
_____
_____
_____
_____

Additional comments:
_____
_____

FIGURE 4.2   A sample Request for a Witness Statement form.

4.4 CONCLUSION

The chapter provides a thumbnail sketch of witnesses—those parties that will deliver testimonial proof of a claim or assertion; corroborate a claim or fact; or aid and assist the investigator by confirming events and conditions, relaying reputational character, or expertly assessing the validity of a case. Special emphasis on the evidentiary case law relating to expert witnesses and the scope of expert testimony was provided. Types of witness, from lay to expert, missing to character were analyzed as well as practical suggestions given in the processing of same. A host of practice tools, such as forms, checklists, and step-by-step guidance for the busy practitioner were also included.

NOTES

1. Bennett L. Gershman, "The Eyewitness Conundrum," *New York State Bar Journal* 81 (2009): 24. Law witnesses cannot always be trusted or be deemed reliable. See "Police, Prosecutors Still Rely on Unreliable Eyewitness Accounts," *Courts Today* (October–November 2008): 12; Francesca T. Palmer, Heather D. Flowe, Melanie K. T. Takarangi, and Joyce E. Humphries, "Intoxicated Witnesses and Suspects: An Archival Analysis of Their Involvement in Criminal Case Processing," *Law and Human Behavior* 37, no. 1 (February 2013): 54–59, www.jstor-org.ez.lib.jjay.cuny.edu/stable/43586894; Anne Bowen Poulin, "The Investigation Narrative: An Argument for Limiting Prosecution Evidence," *Iowa Law Review* 101, no. 2 (January 2016): 683, http://law.uiowa.edu/journals/ilr; Helene Love, "Aging Witnesses: Exploring Difference, Inspiring Change," *International Journal of Evidence &Proof* 19, no. 4 (2015): 210–227, https://doi-org.ez.lib.jjay.cuny.edu/10.1177/1365712715591462.
2. Ralph F. Brislin, *The Effective Security Officer's Training Manual* (Oxford: Butterworth-Heinemann, 1995): 89; "The Investigative Process for PIs: From Taking a Case to Bringing It to a Close," PrivateInvestigatorEDU.org, accessed September 8, 2018, https://privateinvestigatoredu.org/private-investigations-process; "Investigating Crime Scenes: Police vs. Private Investigators," *Guns, Gams &Gumshoes*, September 27, 2015, https://writingpis.wordpress.com/2015/09/27/investigating-crimes-scenes-shaun-kaufman-colleen-collins/.
3. Witnesses come in a variety of states—including the intoxicated. For this special challenge see Palmer et al., "Intoxicated Witnesses."
4. See Love, "Aging Witnesses."
5. Lisa P. O'Donnell, "Empower your witness: Experts and lay witnesses are crucial to any case, so they need to be well prepared for what they're likely to face at trial," *Trial*, July 2011: 40.
6. See Charles P. Nemeth, *Law and Evidence*, 2nd ed. (Burlington, MA: Jones &Bartlett, 2011).
7. *American Jurisprudence Trials* 2 (1987): 229, 235; Alexandra Wells, "Ping! The Admissibility of Cellular Records to Track Criminal Defendants," *Saint Louis University Public Law Review* 33 (2014): 487; Peggy Shapiro and Perry Myers, "Locating Elusive Witnesses: An Introduction," *Illinois Bar Journal* (July 2003): 357; "How Is Skip Tracing Performed?," BountyHunterEDU.org, accessed September 8, 2018, www.bountyhunteredu.org/what-is-skip-tracing/.
8. "Find Missing Persons," Martin Investigative Services, Newport Beach Headquarters, 620 Newport Center Drive, Suite 1400, Newport Beach, CA 92660, accessed September 8, 2018, www.martinpi.com/locate-people/find-missing-persons/.
9. *Fed. R. Evid.*: 601.
10. *Fed. R. Evid.*: 701.
11. "Evidence: Lay Opinion Testimony—Sound of Car Running Over Body," *Criminal Law Reporter*, January 7, 2009: 353.
12. Susan M. Campers, "Time to Blow up the Showup: Who Are Witnesses Really Identifying?," *Suffolk University Law Review* 48 (2015): 845.
13. Nemeth, "Evidence": 151 et seq.; O'Donnell, "Empower your witness."
14. *Fed. R. Evid.*: 701.
15. Timothy J. Perfect et al., "How Can We Help Witnesses to Remember More? It's an (Eyes) Open and Shut Case," *Law &Human Behavior* 32 (2008): 314; Deborah M. Nelson, "Use Lay Witnesses to Prove Mild Traumatic Brain Injury," *Trial*, May 2008: 70.
16. Charles P. Nemeth, *Litigation, Pleadings, and Arbitration*, 2nd ed. (Cincinnati, OH: Anderson Publishing Co., 1990): 421; for an excellent analysis of historic distrust of lay opinion, see D. Garrison Hill, "Lay Witness Opinions," *South Carolina Lawyer*, September 2007: 34.

17. For an interesting case of how a lay witness was permitted to give testimony on perceived mental state, see Nelson, "Traumatic Brain Injury."

18. *Fed. R. Evid.*: 702.

19. Chris Vail, "Presenting Winning Testimony in Court," in *The Security Supervisor Training Manual*, eds. Sandi J. Davies &Ronald R. Minion (Oxford: Butterworth-Heinemann, 1995); Gary L. Birnbaum and Vail Cloar, "Surviving on cross-exam: tips for expert witnesses," *Journal of Accountancy* 218, no. 4 (October 2014): 18, www.journalofaccountancy.com.ez.lib.jjay.cuny.edu/.

20. Dani Alexis Ryskamp, "Selecting an Expert Witness: Pitfalls and Best Practices," The Expert Institute, September 19, 2017, www.theexpertinstitute.com/selecting-an-expert-witness-pitfalls-and-best-practice.

21. *Fed. R. Evid.*: 702.

22. See Nemeth, "Litigation": 421; see also John Tarantino, *Trial Evidence Foundations* (Costa Mesa, CA: James Publishing, 1987): 4–5; Peter M. Durney and Julianne C. Fitzpatrick, "Retaining and Disclosing Expert Witnesses: A Global Perspective," *Defense Counsel Journal* 83, no. 1 (January 2016): 17; Ryskamp, "Expert Witness."

23. 647 *F. Supp.* (S. D. Ga., 1986): 544, 547.

24. Beverly Hutson, *Paralegal Trial Handbook* (Hoboken, NJ: Wiley, 1991): 3–15; Birnbaum and Cloar, "Surviving on cross-exam."; Christian C. Mester, "Expert preparation: Even experienced litigators can miss key steps when preparing an expert for deposition—and even the best witness can make mistakes that trip up your case. Use this step-by-step plan to show your witnesses the way," *Trial*, May 2010: 16, www.justice.org/cps/rde/xchg/justice/hs.xsl/4938.htm.

25. See Birnbaum and Cloar, "Surviving on cross-exam."

26. Mark Dombroff, *Dombroff on Unfair Tactics* (Hoboken, NJ: Wiley, 1988): 415; Mester, "Expert preparation."

27. Lawrence S. Charfoos and David W. Christensen, *Personal Injury Practice: Technique and Technology* (Rochester, NY: Lawyers Cooperative Publishing, 1986); Durney and Fitzpatrick, "Global Perspective"; Ryskamp, "Expert Witness"; Gil I. Sapir, "Qualifying the Expert Witness: A Practical Voir Dire," *Forensic Magazine*, February–March 2007: 1–5, www.chm.uri.edu/forensics/courses/Appendix%20 -%20forensic%20science%20&%20expert%20witness/Voir%20Dire.pdf.

28. Dombroff, "Unfair Tactics": 417; Lyle Griffin Warshauer and Michael J. Warshauer, "Prepping your expert: expert witnesses can be blindsided when their opinions are attacked in court. Advising them about the rigors of litigation is essential—it can be the difference between winning and losing your case," *Trial*, September 2012: 14.

29. For more complete coverage of the use of experts, see Andre Moenssens, "The Impartial Medical Expert: A New Look at an Old Issue," *Medical Trial Technique Quarterly* 25 (1978): 63; Robert Porro, "Expert Witnesses: Crossroads of Law, Science and Technology," *American Trial Advocacy* 2 (1979): 291; Michael T. Smith and Walter R. Lancaster, "Impeaching a 'National Expert' in a Catastrophic Collision Case," *For The Defense* 23 (1981): 8; David E. Bernstein, "The Misbegotten Judicial Resistance to the Daubert Revolution," *Notre Dame Law Review* 89, no. 1 (2014): 27; Sandra Guerra Thompson, "Daubert Gatekeeping for Eyewitness Identifications," *Southern Methodist University Law Review* 65 (Summer 2012): 593.

30. Frye v. United States, 293 F. 1013 (1923).

31. Fritz Jekel, "When an Expert Isn't an Expert," *Trial*, July 2008: 50.

32. Daubert v. Merrell Dow Pharmaceuticals, 509 U.S. 579 (1993).

33. Kumho Tire v. Carmichael, 526 U.S. 137 (1999).

34. 509 US 579 (1993).

35. Ellen Moskowitz, "Junk Science," *Hastings Center Reporter* (1996): 48; see also Lewis H. LaRue and David S. Caudill, "A Non-Romantic View of Expert Testimony," *Seton Hall Law Review* 35 (2004): 1; Gary Edmond, "Expertise in the Courtroom: Scientists and Wizards: Panel Three: Science, Scientists and Ethics: Article: Supersizing Daubert Science for Litigation and Its Implications for Legal Practice and Scientific Research," *Villanova Law Review* 52 (2007): 857; Thompson, "Daubert Gatekeeping."

36. Michael H. Gottesman, "Should State Courts Impose a 'Reliability' Threshold?," *Trial*, September 1997: 20–23; Bernstein, "Judicial Resistance."

37. Edward R. Cavanagh, "Decision Extends Daubert Approach to All Expert Testimony," *New York State Bar Journal* (July/August 1999): 9; see also Edward J. Imwinkelried, "The Next Step after Daubert: Developing a Similarly Epistemological Approach to Ensuring the Reliability of Nonscientific Expert Testimony," *Cardozo Law Review* 15 (1994): 2271; Thompson, "Daubert Gatekeeping."

38. Paul Reidinger, "They Blinded Me with Science," *ABA Journal* (September 1996): 58–62; Thompson, "Daubert Gatekeeping."

39. In fact, the Federal Judicial Center has formally recognized the need for judicial involvement by increasing science training for district court judges and by publishing a handbook on scientific evidence, which includes detailed "reference guides" on scientific and technical specialties frequently encountered in the courtroom. Paul S. Miller and Bert W. Rein, "Whither Daubert? Reliable Resolution of Scientifically-based Causality Issues in Toxic Tort Cases," *Rutgers Law Review* 50 (1998): 563; see also Victor E. Schwartz and Cary Silverman, "The Draining of Daubert and the Recidivism of Junk Science in Federal and State Courts," *Hofstra Law Review* 35 (2006): 217; Thompson, "Daubert Gatekeeping."

40. Bernstein, "Judicial Resistance."

41. 119 S. Ct. 1167 (1999).

42. Robert W. Littleton, "Supreme Court Dramatically Changes the Rules on Experts," *New York State Bar Journal* (July/August 1999): 8, 12.

43. Ibid.

44. Ibid.

45. For example, it is very unlikely that Frye would have permitted Palm Crease evidence as recently occurred. See "Palm Crease Expert Was Properly Allowed to Identify Sex Abuser's Hand in Photograph," *Criminal Law Reporter*, February 11, 2009: 525.

46. Paul C. Giannelli, "Daubert 'Factors,'" *Criminal Justice* (Winter 2009): 42; Mara L. Merlino et al., "Judicial Gatekeeping and the Social Construction of the Admissibility of Expert Testimony," *Behavioral Science &Law* 26 (2008): 187; Edward J. Imwinkelried, "Law for the Expert Witness," *Jurimetrics* (Winter 2008): 241; Thompson, "Daubert Gatekeeping."

47. See also Sapir, "Practical Voir Dire."

48. See D. Rubsamen, "Locating Medical Experts," *American Jurisprudence Trials* 2 (1987): 112–133.

49. I. Gross, "Locating Scientific and Technical Experts," *American Jurisprudence Trials* 2 (1987): 293, 302–356.

50. Charfoos and Christensen, "Personal Injury Practice": 493; Ryskamp, "Expert Witness."

51. Charfoos and Christensen, "Personal Injury Practice": 493; Ryskamp, "Expert Witness."

52. Charfoos and Christensen, "Personal Injury Practice": 502.

53. Michael Wagner in his keenly authored work, *Expert Problems*, manifests a brilliant recognition of expert fees out of control. "Perhaps no more than any other professionals, lawyers know what hourly rate billing can mean. Hours are deposited on billing sheets, bit by bit, day by day. They do not look like much while they accrete, but before long the bill is a mountain. The gradual deposits of time are continuous; with hourly billing there is less incentive not to do something. If you are paid for every hour, you think less about the need for what fills up that hour's time. If you want to be stuck by your expert like some clients are stuck by their attorneys, insist on an hourly billing." Michael J. Wagner, "Expert Problems," *Litigation* 15 (1989): 35, 36; see also Durney and Fitzpatrick, "Global Perspective."

54. "Asking Character Witnesses Hypotheticals That Assume Guilt Generally Is Permissible," *Criminal Law Reporter*, December 19, 2007: 320; Barrett J. Anderson, "Recognizing Character: A New Perspective on Character Evidence," *The Yale Law Journal* 121, no. 7 (May 2012): 1912–1968, www-jstor-org.ez.lib.jjay.cuny.edu/stable/41510461.

55. M. Greer, "Cross-examined character witnesses may hurt defendants on trial." *Monitor on Psychology*, May 2004, Vol 35, No. 5, print version: 22.

56. Evidence–Character Witnesses–Impeachment with Evidence of Defendant's Prior Convictions–Preservation of Issue, *Crim. L. Rep.*, March 4, 2009: 609; M. Greer, "Cross-examined Character Witnesses May Hurt Defendants on Trial," *Monitor on Psychology* 35, no. 5 (May 2004): 22, www.apa.org/monitor/may04/crossexam.aspx.

57. See J. McCord, *Litigation Paralegal* (Eagan, MN: West Publishing, 1988); Greer, "Character Witnesses."

58. Too many witnesses can muddle the obvious so to speak and when the narrative becomes too confusing, one is trying to do too much with that narrative. See Anne Bowen Poulin, "The Investigation Narrative: An Argument for Limiting Prosecution Evidence," *Iowa Law Review* 101, no. 2 (January 2016): 683.

59. Mark Weinstein, *Introduction to Civil Litigation* (Eagan, MN: Wiley Publishing, 1986): 54.

5 Collection of Information

5.1 THE NATURE OF INFORMATION AND THE RULES OF COLLECTION

Records, files, documentary evidence, and other written and oral forms of information are the "stock in trade" of the good investigator. In order to track clues in a typical investigative pattern, some form of documentary, testimonial, or physical evidence is necessary. The investigator must depend upon more than opinion or rumor. Critical to the success of any investigation is the integrity and substantiality of information gathered. For example, a security firm that is hired to determine the character of a potential employee may attach any or all of the following to its written report:

- Past character references
- Offense reports
- Military reports
- Litigation documents
- Credit history reports
- Deeds, titles, or insurance documents
- Arrest reports

The mere assertion that a person's character is flawed will not cut it. The documents posed here can be drawn on to flesh out the claim of bad character and corroborate the conclusion.[1]

The scope of this chapter involves information and its collection. Professional investigators need to master the art of information gathering as well as its analysis. What to look for and whom to ask are perennial issues for the investigator. Information is everywhere. The trick is how to get it and be assured of its meaningfulness. Acquiring information largely depends upon access to either persons or institutions. In the process of acquiring information, the investigator must respect the law and the fundamental tenets of privacy. As the American Society for Industrial Security remarks:

> Many organizations, notably some credit agencies, operated with little legal restraint. Inaccurate and often irrelevant records were maintained, and flagrant misuse of information was common. Until recent years, investigators—whether public or private, for ill or good—had almost open access to many kinds of data banks. Subsequent laws and regulations have placed restrictions on what information can be gathered, how it can be obtained, and what use can be made of it. To violate these restrictions exposes all parties involved, including the investigator, to certain risks.[2]

Attention to privacy and the constitutional rights of others should be an ongoing ethical and professional concern of the security investigator.

> Under current circumstances the investigator must, by and large, identify for himself what is permissible in the way of gathering information. He must find out what restraints apply to him as well as what rights he is entitled to exercise in the course of an investigation. On occasion, the investigator should re-verify these rights and limitations when a new investigation is undertaken. Every investigator should stay abreast of the changes resulting from legislative or regulatory action, as well as from court decisions, in each jurisdiction where he conducts investigations.[3]

Both federal and state statutes address the issue of information gathering and the perennial issue of individual privacy. A short list of federal legislation includes:

- Privacy Act of 1974[4]
- Financial Privacy Act of 1978[5]
- Privacy Protection Act of 1980[6]
- Fair Financial Information Practices Act of 1981[7]
- Privacy of Electronic Fund Transfers Act of 1981[8]
- Fair Credit Reporting Act of 1970[9]
- Omnibus and Crime Control Bill of 1968[10]
- Freedom of Information Act (FOIA)[11]

At every level of the investigative process, security operatives need to exercise the type of demeanor and professional courtesy consistent with these enactments.[12]

The United States Department of Justice, through its Bureau of Justice Statistics, authored *Privacy and Security of Criminal History Information: An Analysis of Privacy Issues*, stating:

> "Privacy" has gained attention of late in every area of personal affairs. Of singular importance has been the subject of "privacy and security" of criminal justice information. Often the desires for anonymity by those who have confronted the criminal justice system clash with society's inquiries pursuant to a "right to know."[13]

In the same vein, the *National Advisory Commission on Criminal Justice Standards and Goals* calls upon state governments to adopt legislation that provides for:

> ... the protection of security and privacy in criminal justice information systems. The enabling statute should establish the minimum standards for protection of security and privacy and civil and criminal sanctions for violation of the rules and regulations adopted under it.[14]

The Hallcrest Report: Private Security and Police in America issues similar cautions about privacy concerns although its picture manifests the preeminence of the security industry when compared to its public counterpart. Here private sector justice operates without the onerous constitutional restraints so evident in public policing. Hallcrest concludes:

> The information sources used by private investigators are much the same as those used by law enforcement officers. However, the private investigator is not subject to as many limitations as the police officer on collecting information since the admissibility of evidence in court is frequently not a concern. In the private sector, an investigator can pursue a case to the level of detail and expenditure set by the client. On the other hand, the police detective may be hampered by large caseload and internal case management criteria that limit the time and resources which can be devoted to a single case. The main constraint upon private investigators is the Privacy of Information Act, which restricts access to many credit, banking, and government records, and also most police information. Telephone company records, credit information, employer information, and criminal record information are frequently off limits to private investigators.[15]

In the age of virtual access, increasing concerns involving privacy are evident. Various state and federal efforts to protect privacy rights are making progress in protecting privacy and ensuring access to the justice sector.[16]

For example, in the area of criminal histories, much is at stake when requesting a criminal history in various states. Requesters are either criminal justice agencies, individuals, or noncriminal justice agencies. In the instructions which appear on the reverse side of a typical criminal record request form, individuals are advised that a full criminal report will not be made available, only a "rap sheet."

Web Exercise: Read through the methods to request a criminal record and download the various criminal history request forms from www.psp.pa.gov/pages/request-a-criminal-history-record.aspx.

Many of the theoretical restrictions on public record access for private security operatives are alleviated by the interplay between public and private police. With record numbers of public police moonlighting as private security officers, access to records becomes an academic argument.

The Hallcrest Report stresses the profitability of the relationships between private investigators and public law enforcement. "Private security firms trade heavily upon personal relationships; personalities rather than legitimacy or legality of need determine the amount of information and level of cooperation received from law enforcement."[17] In its national survey of private investigative firms, the practice of lending information is pervasive.

> ... private investigative firms reported frequent contact with detectives in law enforcement agencies; in fact, 58% reported daily or weekly contact. Little contact was reported with law enforcement supervisors and managers. Law enforcement administrators in the national survey, however, reported less frequent contact of their detectives with private security personnel; only 44% reported daily or weekly contact with their detectives. Cities above 100,000 population reported twice as much daily contact ...

> Thus, private investigators report frequent contact with law enforcement detectives, but purportedly do not seek law enforcement information or provide information from their investigations on a regular basis ... Four out of ten firms reported that they employ off-duty law enforcement officers. Officers employed in this capacity could be in a position to obtain police information to gain favor with their secondary employer in private security.[18,19]

The underground network of sharing information does not cease here. Private security investigators hone relationships with numerous other parties, including:

- Court clerks
- Correctional personnel
- Deed and title personnel
- Notaries public
- Bankers
- Insurance representatives
- Telephone company employees
- Personnel agencies

By forging complementary and tactful relationships with information sources such as those listed above, the investigator has access to an unlimited supply of information. Despite bureaucratic and regulatory obstructions, an inquisitive person will eventually gain access to the desired information, even though the practice is legally suspect.

In order to assure fairness, government and its guardians of records balance the interests of both the subject of the file or document and the public's need, desire, and right to examine the data and information contained therein.[20] Dual-edged by nature, privacy protects the individual from excessive scrutiny and review, and in doing so, stifles the flow of and access to information, thereby thwarting public understanding. In balancing these competing interests, access and dissemination must adhere to these principles:

1. No personal information systems should be maintained whose very existence is secret.
2. A data subject should have access to information about himself and know the purposes for which it is maintained.
3. A data subject should be permitted to challenge and seek corrections of information about himself.
4. Data should be used only for the purposes for which they were intended, unless the data subject consents.
5. Information used should be accurate, timely, relevant, and complete.
6. Information should be protected against unauthorized access, alteration, or destruction.[21]

5.2   LEADS AND CONTACTS FOR THE PRIVATE INVESTIGATOR

Any good investigator develops contacts and sources for information, and security professionals have come to rely on both public and private sources. The more predictable contacts are:

- Government employees
- Code enforcement officers
- Tow truck operators
- Bank officers and personnel
- Body shop and auto repair specialists
- Department and retail store employees
- Tax agents
- Utility employees
- County clerks
- Private security employees
- Recorders of deeds
- Police officers
- Registers of wills
- Neighborhood snitches
- Insurance company personnel
- Neighborhood busybodies
- School and educational personnel
- Social club heads and board members
- Hospital and medical personnel
- Tag, title, and inspection employees
- Emergency medical services personnel
- Corporation registration and licensing employees[22]

The investigator should maintain a list of information sources, which references information by topical concern, similar to that shown at Box 5.1. The investigator identifies a topic, such as a deed or death certificate, and then refers to the source chart.

BOX 5.1   A LIST OF STANDARD INFORMATION SOURCES

INFORMATION SOURCES

Address	City Directory; Telephone Directory; Voters Registration.
Attorneys	Martindale-Hubble Lawyers Directory; State Lawyers Manual; State Bar Registries.
Automobiles	State Dept. of Motor Vehicles.
Owners	State Dept. of Motor Vehicles.
Liens	State Dept. of Motor Vehicles.
Autopsy Report	County/City Clerk, County/City Court House; Bureau of Vital Statistics; City Health Department.
Business Reputation	Local Better Business Bureau; Trade Associations.
Civil Litigation	U.S. District Court House; Justice of the Peace; (also townships, credit bureaus).
Corporations	Articles of Incorporation; County Court House (home office); Dun &Bradstreet; Poors' Directory of Directors.
Deaths	County/City Clerk, County Court House; City Health Department; Coroner's Office; Bureau of Vital Statistics; Medical Examiner, County.

Deeds	City/County Clerk, County Court House; Recorder of Deeds.
Criminal Records	U.S. District Court, Local/State Police Dept.; Sheriff's or Marshal's Office.
Doctors	American Medical Association Directory; County Medical Association Directory; State Medical Association Directory.
Financial	Mortgages, County Court House; Dun &Bradstreet (credit bureaus).
Fires	Fire Marshal, Fire Department.
Liens	County Court House, Recorder of Deeds.
Location—Persons	Probate Court; Credit Companies (credit card leads); Banks (checks); Dept. of Motor Vehicles (license change).
Maps, Townships	County Surveyor's Office.
Marriage Licenses	County Clerk's Office, County Court House; Vital Statistics, State Board of Health.
	County Judge, Circuit Court, Court of Common Pleas, Municipal Archives &Record Retention Center.
	(Note: County Court House is usual place. Various cities and counties have different locations.)
Military Discharges	If public, County Court House.
Misdemeanor	Municipal Criminal Court; Local Police Department.
Mortgages	County Court House (see excise stamps for real value).
Manufacturers	Thomas Buyers Guide &McRaes' Registry of Manufacturers.
Names—Trade	Thomas Buyers Guide &McRaes' Registry of Manufacturers.
Officers of Corporations	Poors' Directory of Directors.
Co-partnerships &corporations	Moody Directory.
Probation	Municipal [or other] Criminal Court.
Property (Personal)	County Court House.
Real Estate	County Court House; County, City, or State Tax Bureau.
Trademarks	Thomas Buyers Guide &McRaes' Registry of Manufacturers.
Taxes	County or City Clerk.
Personal	City—Treasurer's License Record.
Property	City, County, &State Tax Bureau.

The investigator may wish to expand this database depending on local issues and resources.

Contacts, for the most part, are preexisting sources. There is nothing all that original here in some settings. Institutions of government, by way of example, have always existed and provide information sources. Even so, there are many information sources that need to be developed and honed. The *Security Investigator's Handbook* notes that contacts do not happen overnight. "If the experienced investigator wants to be successful, he would do well to find out where his sources of information are. Developing contacts is a lengthy process, but knowing where to find public information is only a matter of careful preliminary research."[23]

Web Exercise: Visit *How to Investigate.com*. It is a rich web location that instructs on how to gain access to public records: http://howtoinvestigate.com/public_records.htm.

Thus, access to information depends upon creativity and innovation. The investigator needs to push the right buttons, yet do so in an efficient and effective way. Even assuming that information is available for public review and inspection, the task of finding it and knowing the steps and processes to gain access to it are just as critical to a successful investigation.

The well-prepared investigator knows where information in general is kept, and what kinds of information are kept where. If he knows this, he will have a head start on finding something in particular. If he does not, he will be like a man looking for a needle and not even knowing which haystack to search.[24]

Information may be retrievable from either public or private sources—some governmental others private in design.[25] Cultivate relationships with those whose access to information is worth mining. Understand that most occupations are grounded in some sort of information base that is useful to the investigative process. Contacts come in many shapes and sizes:

- Airline clerks, attendants
- Barbers
- Bartenders
- Bell hops
- Building managers
- Bus drivers
- Cab drivers (trip sheets)
- Dentists
- Doormen
- Hairdressers
- Hostesses
- Hotel clerks
- Janitors, maids (bars, hotels, motels)
- Mail carriers
- Neighborhood children
- News vendors
- Night watchmen
- Operators of street businesses
- Parking lot attendants
- Parolees and probationers
- Physicians
- Pool hall operators
- Public utility servicemen
- Railroad agents, conductors
- Shoe-shine operators
- Street vendors (all-night stands)
- Tradesmen (delivery services)
- Waitresses and waiters

Exactly who and what those sources will be depends upon the subject matter of the investigation. For example, the Federal Bureau of Investigation's *Economic and Financial Crimes Training Unit* publishes *Investigators' Guide to Sources of Information*[26]—a reference authority essential to an investigator working in these particular fields. The guide is a fundamental tool for the field investigator and is loaded with practical suggestions pertaining to information access, particularly the importance of developing community contacts, discerning the informal "community power structure." Known in some circles as a "reputational study," what the investigator looks for and identifies are the political players more capable than any other of providing critical information. The reputational study affords the investigator a feel for the power structure, whether economic, judicial, or social in nature. The investigator then concentrates on these players to gain access to information.

5.3 PUBLIC SOURCES OF INFORMATION

Public access to information is partially guaranteed under statutory and common law principles. However, that access is not without restriction, as in the case of privacy, and it is subject to certain regulatory processes. More common public requests include judgments, birth records, marriage

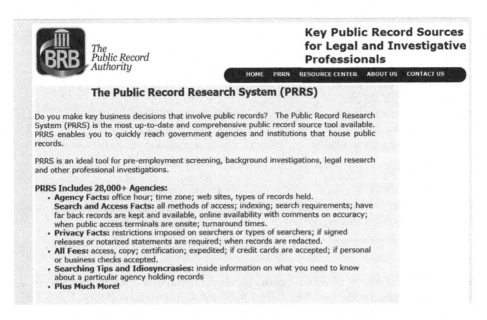

FIGURE 5.1 Key public record sources for legal and investigative professionals. (Used with permission, BRB Publications.)

records, filings for incorporation and other business entities, tax records, voter registrations, and motor vehicle and auto licensing documentation.

BRB Publications provides a public record research service for an annual subscription or on an a la carte basis. Results include information from federal, county, and local courts, recorder and assessor records, state agencies, occupational licensing boards, and accredited colleges and universities. For more information visit its website at www.brbpublications.com/products/Prrs.aspx. See Figure 5.1.

Records involving governmental benefits, such as social security, Medicaid, and disability or veterans' benefits are regular requests for the investigator. To determine previous residence or locality through the use of the social security number, look at the first three digits (see Box 5.2).

BOX 5.2   LISTING OF SOCIAL SECURITY NUMBER CODES BY STATE

SOCIAL SECURITY NUMBERS - STATE CODES

001-003 New Hampshire	429-4432 Arkansas
004-007 Maine	433-439 Louisiana
008-009 Vermont	440-443 Oklahoma
010-034 Massachusetts	449-467 Texas
035-039 Rhode Island	468-477 Minnesota
040-049 Connecticut	478-485 Iowa
050-134 New York	486-500 Missouri
135-158 New Jersey	501-502 North Dakota
159-211 Pennsylvania	503-504 South Dakota
212-220 Maryland	505-508 Nebraska
221-222 Delaware	509-515 Kansas
223-231 Virginia	516-517 Montana
232-236 West Virginia	518-519 Idaho

237-246 North Carolina	520 Wyoming
247-251 South Carolina	521-524 Colorado
252-260 Georgia	525 New Mexico
261-267 Florida	526-527 Arizona
268-302 Ohio	528-529 Utah
303-317 Indiana	530 Nevada
318-361 Illinois	531-539 Washington
362-386 Michigan	540-544 Oregon
387-399 Wisconsin	545-573 California
400-407 Kentucky	574 Alaska
408-415 Tennessee	575-576 Hawaii
416-424 Alabama	577-579 District of Columbia
425-428 Mississippi	716-717 Pennsylvania Railroad

Since 2011, the assignment of social security numbers is primarily done under a random assignment rather than a geographic one. The Social Security Administration (SSA) changed the way social security numbers (SSNs) are issued on June 25, 2011. This change is referred to as "randomization." The SSA developed this new method to help protect the integrity of the SSN. SSN randomization will also extend the longevity of the nine-digit SSN nationwide.

Randomization affected the SSN assignment process in the following ways:

It eliminated the geographical significance of the first three digits of the SSN, referred to as the area number, by no longer allocating the area numbers for assignment to individuals in specific states.It eliminated the significance of the highest group number and, as a result, the High Group List is frozen in time and can only be used to see the area and group numbers SSA issued prior to the randomization implementation date.

Previously unassigned area numbers were introduced for assignment excluding area numbers 000, 666 and 900-999.[27]

5.3.1 Federal Agencies

A wealth of information exists in the public domain; the following agencies can provide valuable data and information:

- Federal Aviation Administration
- Department of Justice
- Department of Transportation
- Civil Rights Commission
- Internal Revenue Service
- Federal Trade Commission
- National Oceanic and Atmospheric Administration
- Census Bureau
- Occupational Safety and Health Administration
- Veterans Administration
- Department of Agriculture
- Transportation Safety Board
- Department of the Interior
- Civil Aeronautics Board

- Department of Commerce
- Department of Energy
- Consumer Product Safety Commission
- Department of Education
- Employment Standards Commission
- Department of Homeland Security

At the federal level, the investigator needs to identify both subject matter and corresponding agency to make an inquiry. Become familiar with the chart at Box 5.3.

BOX 5.3   THE INVESTIGATIVE PRACTICE AND CORRESPONDING FEDERAL AGENCY

INVESTIGATIVE PRACTICE	FEDERAL AGENCY
Banking	Office of the Controller of the Currency, U.S. Treasury Department; Board of Governors of the Federal Reserve System; Federal Deposit Insurance Corporation (FDIC); Federal Home Loan Bank Board; Farm Credit Administration; Resolution Trust Corporation (FTC).
Criminal Matters &Records	Federal Bureau of Investigation; U.S. Department of Justice; National Crime Information Center (NCIC); Department of the Treasury; Department of Drug Enforcement Administration; Central Intelligence Agency; Bureau of Alcohol, Tobacco, and Firearms.
Labor	National Labor Relations Board; Department of Labor; Occupational and Safety Health Administration (OSHA).
Forensic Matters	U.S. Department of Defense; U.S. Army: Pathology; U.S. Air Force: Pathology; Forensic Laboratories of the Federal Bureau of Investigation.
Political Conduct	Congressional Record Index; Congressional Quarterly; Office of Public Records; Code of Federal Regulations; Federal Elections Commission.
Securities	Securities and Exchange Commission; Department of the Treasury; Federal Bureau of Investigation.

Web Exercise: Visit the FBI's web location. It is an excellent research resource for anyone working in the justice system. See: www.fbi.gov/resources/library.

5.3.2   STATE AND LOCAL AGENCIES

While state and local governments amass sweeping levels of information and data, there is no uniform method for accessing such information. There are usually directories that list agencies that can be useful for accessing information (e.g., *National Directory of State Agencies, The Pennsylvania Manual, Illinois Blue Book*). Entries often include phone numbers, addresses, functions, agencies, and major personalities of government, such as the commissioner of state police.

Automobile accident report forms, authored by state police authorities, as well as local and municipal entities, are a staple of private security investigators who work for either a plaintiff or a defendant (see Chapter 3, Figures 3.5–3.7). While the legal admissibility of accident reports is a contested arena, there are few restrictions on access to accident reports as a pure public record.

Every state sets policy on records access and each and every state designates various offices or officers to handle the record processing. Typical agencies that amass source material for the investigator include but are not limited to:

- Department of Motor Vehicles
- Tax Assessors

- Department of Transportation/Streets and Highways
- Voter Registration Offices
- Bureau of Vital Statistics
- Department of Labor and Industry
- State Revenue Commissions
- Department of Corrections
- Department of Insurance
- Department of Corporations and Business
- Department of Business
- Secretary of State
- Professions and Licensing
- Department of Vocational Rehabilitation
- District Attorney's Office
- Medical Examiner's Office
- Office of the County Coroner
- County Recorder of Deeds
- Traffic Department
- Register of Wills
- Department of Public Works
- County Clerks
- County and Local Courthouses

Record availability is increasingly online. Copies of wills, tax records, traffic infractions, and reports of the medical examiner are just a few of the legions of public documents now accessible in the virtual world.[28] See Figure 5.2.[29]

Investigators utilize a wide array of online portals and search engines that give regular access to public records. A representative grouping with links follows:

BeenVerified's background check allows you to search billions of public records online for criminal records, arrest records, bankruptcies, and more. You can find people using address, phone number, and email lookups.www.beenverified.com/.

Intelius is a powerful search tool that allows you to search nationwide public records by maiden/spouse name, age, date of birth, social security number (SSN), unlisted numbers, addresses, roommates, and family members. www.intelius.com/.

LexisNexis® is a leading global provider of content-enabled workflow solutions designed specifically for professionals in the legal, risk management, corporate, government, law enforcement, accounting, and academic markets. LexisNexis provides customers with access to billions of searchable documents and records from more than 45,000 legal, news and business sources. https://risk.lexisnexis.com/.

Spokeo People Search is a search engine that organizes vast quantities of information from a large variety of public sources. The public data is presented in an integrated, coherent, and easy-to-follow format. There is a fee associated with this search. www.spokeo.com/.

The Records Project is an online community dedicated to building the largest, free public records encyclopedia. https://publicrecords.onlinesearches.com/.

Search Systems is a large directory of links to free public record databases on the internet. Use this resource to find business information, corporate filings, property records, unclaimed property, professional licenses, offenders, inmates, criminal and civil court filings, and much more. http://publicrecords.searchsystems.net/.

ZabaSearch is an excellent and powerful public records search engine. It aggregates data and information from a huge number of public records databases and presents the information in an easy to use and coherent fashion. It's a great site for the busy private detective. www.zabasearch.com/.[30]

FIGURE 5.2 Such sites as CourthouseDirect.com help investigators search public records throughout the country virtually. (Used with permission, CourthouseDirect.com.)

Web Exercise: Pick two of the free web search engines above and search your own personal data. Compare the results.

5.4 PRIVATE SOURCES OF INFORMATION

While government agencies at the federal, state, and local levels may provide the bulk of information needed by the investigator, private sources of information should not be neglected. Private firms and entities are now in the information business and security professionals should take full advantage of these services.[31] See Figure 5.3.[32]

5.4.1 DIRECTORIES, DATABASES, AND ATLASES

Directories, atlases, and databases are essential tools when seeking information. While the areas covered by these resources tend to be rather global, more particularized information on trademarks, congressional record announcements, corporate operation and value, affirmative action programs, labor and employment statistics, and other mundane business record keeping are discovered within these sources. With the advent of electronic data transmission and internet capacity, increasing amounts of this type of information can be discovered online.

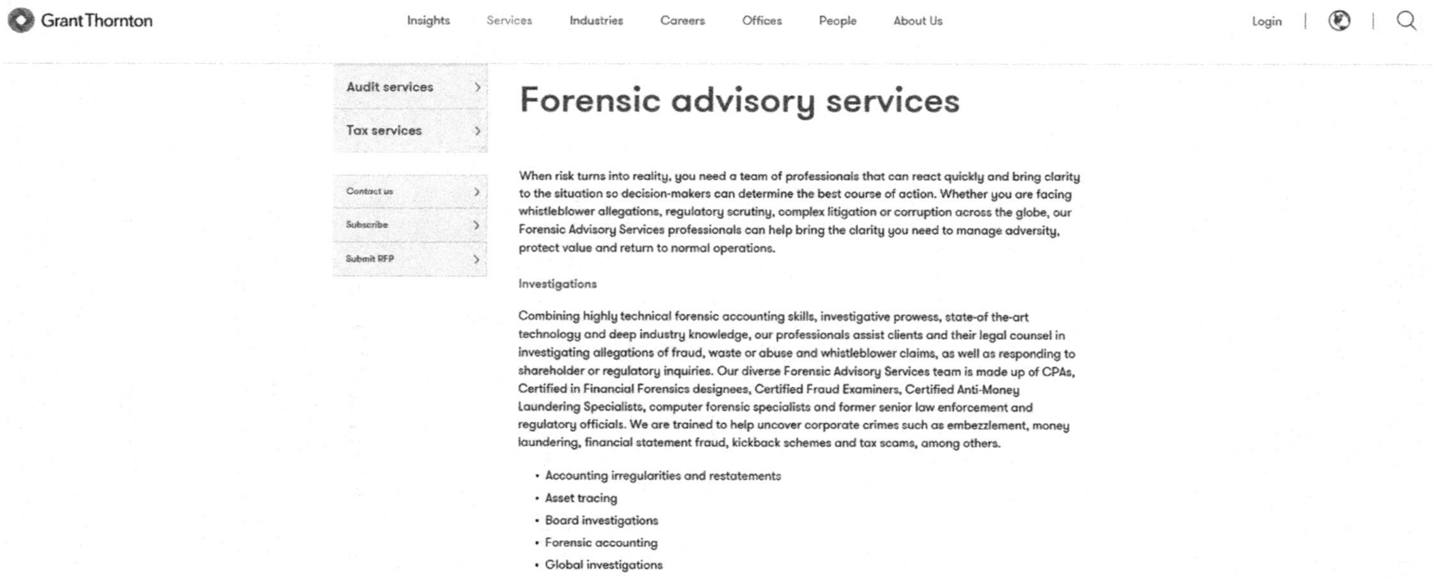

Grant Thornton

Insights Services Industries Careers Offices People About Us

Login

Audit services

Tax services

Contact us

Subscribe

Submit RFP

Forensic advisory services

When risk turns into reality, you need a team of professionals that can react quickly and bring clarity to the situation so decision-makers can determine the best course of action. Whether you are facing whistleblower allegations, regulatory scrutiny, complex litigation or corruption across the globe, our Forensic Advisory Services professionals can help bring the clarity you need to manage adversity, protect value and return to normal operations.

Investigations

Combining highly technical forensic accounting skills, investigative prowess, state-of-the-art technology and deep industry knowledge, our professionals assist clients and their legal counsel in investigating allegations of fraud, waste or abuse and whistleblower claims, as well as responding to shareholder or regulatory inquiries. Our diverse Forensic Advisory Services team is made up of CPAs, Certified in Financial Forensics designees, Certified Fraud Examiners, Certified Anti-Money Laundering Specialists, computer forensic specialists and former senior law enforcement and regulatory officials. We are trained to help uncover corporate crimes such as embezzlement, money laundering, financial statement fraud, kickback schemes and tax scams, among others.

· Accounting irregularities and restatements

· Asset tracing

· Board investigations

· Forensic accounting

· Global investigations

FIGURE 5.3 Instances in which forensic advisory service providers can help. (Used with permission, Grant Thornton.)

Web Exercise: Visit Ebsco, one of the world's largest providers of online databases and research sources at www.ebsco.com.

5.4.1.1 Business Databases

There are a multitude of databases with information regarding business and industry. The leading ones are:

Moody's/Value Line: Corporate schematic of ownership and value. www.moodys.com; www. valueline.com.

Dow Jones: SEC extracts on institutional holdings, tender offers, and insider trading. www. dowjones.com.

Dow Jones News Service: Stock, commodity, futures, and options trading information, and other news services. www.dowjones.com/products/newswires.

The following national business databases are also available:

- Standard &Poor's
- Dunn's Financial Records
- Experian National Business Database
- Census Bureau Business Register
- PTS Annual Reports Abstracts
- Insider Trading Monitor
- Trade and Industry Index
- Business Wire
- Business Dateline
- Trinet Company Database
- Wall Street Journal
- Dunn's Electronic Yellow Pages
- Thomas Register Online
- Dunn's Market Identifiers
- Publishers, Distributors and Wholesalers
- Dunn's Million Dollar Directory

5.4.1.2 Miscellaneous Databases

Other databases covering nonbusiness information include:

Congressional Record Abstracts: Abstracts of the congressional record, congressional information service, abstracts of congressional publications.

LexisNexis and *Westlaw*: Case law, statutory, and administrative decision making through electronic transmission.

Medical Indexes: The indexes and abstracts of articles from major medical journals.

Gale Infotrac: A directory of legal articles and citations.

Congressional Statistics Index: Thorough index of statistical publications of US government agencies.

Federal Register: Publication of notices, rules, and regulations of government offices.

City Directories: Addresses based on name and street number.

Directory Listings of Professions: ATLA, ABA, and state and local bar association lists.

Who's Who Publications: Notably in law, engineering, medicine, and other scientific fields.

Telephone Directories: Available at most local libraries.

These databases may provide both specialized, narrow information necessary for the investigation, or the type of global background needed to fully comprehend the case at hand.

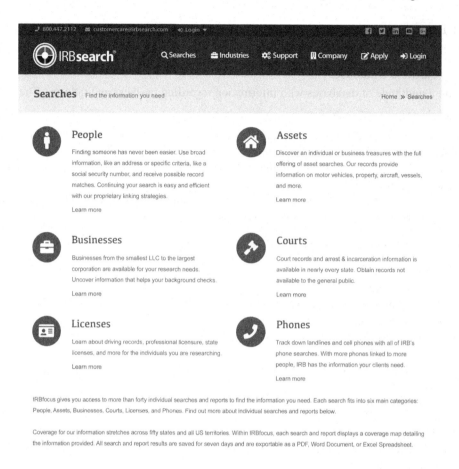

FIGURE 5.4 The various records that can be searched and reports that can be provided by modern research service companies. (Used with permission, IRB Search.)

Web locations now deliver varying sources of information to seasoned investigators. Some of the more common providers are:

TransUnion – www.tlo.com/investigators
IRBsearch – www.irbsearch.com/searches.html
TracersInfo.com – www.tracersinfo.com/

See Figure 5.4.[33]

5.4.2 Libraries

Federal, state, county, and municipal libraries are often forgotten as sources of investigative information. Many local and state libraries have significant law collections, directories of all kinds, telephone books, and other source materials. Research librarians can assist on historical and contemporary questions that may influence law and legislation. University and college libraries are another resource, generally stocked with an array of scholarly journals and periodicals and other information necessary to research any technical or sophisticated question. State college and university libraries are generally participants in interlibrary loan programs, affording access to every major library in the continental United States. University libraries also have access to literally every other library imaginable through their databases systems and electronic software for full text journals.[34]

Web Exercise: Visit https://dc.lib.jjay.cuny.edu which lists the digital collections at John Jay College of Criminal Justice.

5.4.3 NEWSPAPERS

Most major city newspapers have a library or holding acquisition center, usually referred to as a *morgue*, for all previous editions of the newspaper. Stories of topical concern are arranged chronologically or in some other order for appropriate indexing and cataloging.

Access to information in a newspaper is only limited by the scope of the paper's coverage. Box 5.4 lists the possibilities.

BOX 5.4   LIST OF THE VARIOUS DEPARTMENTS IN THE NEWSPAPER AND LEADS THAT CAN BE FOLLOWED

Department	Lead
Obituaries	Family, previous residence, previous occupation, other background information, photograph or likeness.
Advertising	Credit records, business relationships.
Editorial	Major stories, corporate and business activities, urban crime, numerous other leads.
Local Columnist	Personal information, political information.

As a rule, newspapers are placed onto microfilm, microfiche, or other electronic medium for storage or research purposes. When looking for back issues of particular publications, consult the reference librarian, the index to the particular newspaper, or the text newspapers on microfilm. There are also abstract databases now available through online computer systems. They are:

- AP News
- Thompson Reuters
- Newswire ASAP
- Businesswire
- PR Newswire
- Chicago Tribune
- Reuters
- Financial Times Fulltext
- UPI News
- Japan Economic Newswire
- USA Today Decisionline
- McGraw-Hill News
- Washington Presstext

Web Exercise: Access to newspapers will include the virtual world as well since most major metropolitan papers are now published in electronic versions. For a listing of these online editions, visit: www.newspaperarchive.com.

5.4.4 THE INTERNET AND WEB-BASED SEARCHES

A plethora of information is at the investigator's disposal when using the internet, various web locations, and its search engines. The most commonly employed search engines are:

- Google
- Bing
- Yahoo
- Ask.com
- AOL.com
- Internet Archive

All these search engines tend to be general by design and as the investigator looks more closely, the internet capacity to gather specialized information will depend on highly-focused search mediums.[35]

5.4.4.1 Social Media Searches

Social media—in the form of LinkedIn, Facebook, Twitter, Instagram, and other such services—is a rich source of information for the investigator whereby a good deal can be garnered about a subject's overall activities and mindset. A review of media posts, status updates, photos, and electronic conversations will tell you much about that subject. Certain types of cases greatly benefit from this review including actual litigation, domestic relations, and custody battles, or as an overview of character and background.

A private investigator can pull data from social media sites like:

- Facebook
- Twitter
- Instagram
- YouTube
- Tumblr
- Internet Messaging Services[36]

5.4.5 PROFESSIONAL ASSOCIATIONS AND GROUPS

Many quasi-private and not-for-profit associations, groups, and foundations can provide access to relevant information. Consult the *Encyclopedia of Associations*, a reference tool found in most libraries, which comprises more than 12,500 associations and includes the following categories:

1. Trade, business, and commercial organizations
2. Agricultural organizations and commodity exchanges
3. Governmental, public administration, military, and legal organizations
4. Scientific, engineering, and technical organizations
5. Educational and cultural organizations
6. Social welfare organizations
7. Health and medical organizations
8. Public affairs organizations
9. Internal foreign interests, nationality, and ethnic organizations
10. Religious organizations

Some of the more influential bodies and groups the investigator should keep in mind are:

The Better Business Bureau: The Bureau receives hundreds of thousands of complaints nationwide each year. It also maintains extensive files on con artists and other unsavory characters. The main office is: Better Business Bureau, 230 Park Avenue, New York, NY 10017.

United States Department of Commerce: A provider of background information on companies in other countries, financial references, and general reputation in trade and financial circles. The United States Department of Commerce also has regional and district offices throughout the United States. United States Department of Commerce, Washington, DC 20230.

5.4.6 AUTO RECORDS

The investigator will find other sources, whether governmental, quasi-public, or private in nature, whose complete or partial function is to compile information on motor vehicles and their operators. For example, the United States Department of Commerce keeps records on individuals whose driver's licenses or permits have been revoked for driving while intoxicated or for causing a vehicular death in violation of the Highway Safety Code. The American Association of Motor Vehicle Administrators and the American Trucking Association have informational pamphlets and booklets that assist investigators in checking certain motor vehicle records. The National Automobile Dealers Association issues a publication that lists the licensing requirements for motor vehicle dealers, salespeople, and others in related fields.[37]

Web Exercise: Visit www.investiator.com for an excellent resource on auto records. Policies, addresses, and general requirements for all 50 jurisdictions are available at this location.

Of enormous assistance in cases of motor vehicle theft, fraud, and collusive insurance claims, is the work of the National Insurance Crime Bureau (NICB), a not-for-profit organization formed in 1992 from a merger between the National Automobile Theft Bureau (NATB), and the Insurance Crime Prevention Bureau (ICPI). The mission of the NICB is to lead a united effort of insurers, law enforcement agencies, and representatives of the public to prevent and combat insurance fraud and crime through data analytics, investigations, training, legislative advocacy, and public awareness.[38] See Figure 5.5 for a detailed description of its five core functions.

Vehicle identification numbers (VIN) are also held within the data bank of NICB, as well as information relating to salvaged and stolen parts. The private investigator may also wish to purchase commercial manuals that highlight the skills of auto theft prevention and detection.

Whether using public or private sources, the security investigator must collect, collate, and interpret sufficient data to support, refute, or establish his or her investigative direction. The evidentiary sources are only limited by the scope of the facts and the imagination, creativity, perseverance, logic, and deductive reasoning of the investigator.

5.5 THE BACKGROUND INVESTIGATION

Security firms conduct a wide array of background investigations for a host of clientele in domestic, civil, criminal, accident, and other cases.[39] Whether the corporation about to hire an executive wishes to confirm his or her background, or the prospective federal employee is being scrutinized by security independent contractors, background investigation is a staple of the security industry. Background investigations for prospective employees deliver an assurance of hire that would not otherwise exist by addressing these critical concerns:

- Determine whether the candidate is qualified for the position
- Protect the company's reputation and organizational assets
- Safeguard against negligent hiring claims
- Ensure the safety of other employees
- Avoid employee theft[40]

As in other forms of investigation, the information within federal, state, and local agencies is of public record although the access policies are of a dizzying variety.

Our Five Fraud-fighting Core Functions

NICB is guided by an Integrated Business Plan, or IBP, that allows us to adapt to changing market conditions and stay ahead of criminals. Our IBP is based on the following five operational functions:

DATA ANALYTICS

NICB develops, compiles, analyzes and disseminates information to help prevent, detect and deter insurance fraud. We identify and provide data on questionable trends, patterns, entities and organized rings, included NICB's valuable electronic *Fore*WARN℠ and *Med*AWARE® Alerts, which are integrated into ISO ClaimSearch®.

INVESTIGATIONS

NICB conducts multi-claim, multi-carrier investigations of major criminal activity. Much of our success is due to our network of relationships with members and strategic partners, as well as law enforcement agencies, prosecutors and others who are dedicated to uncovering and stopping insurance and vehicle crimes.

TRAINING

NICB delivers customized, face-to-face training and education at member locations to help companies stay current on the latest insurance crime issues and schemes, red flag indicators and fraud-fighting technologies. Additional training is available through various NICB Academies, as well as the online National Insurance Crime Training Academy (NICTA). We also provide in-person and online training for members of law enforcement.

LEGISLATIVE ADVOCACY

NICB's legislative advocacy team leads the property-casualty industry's anti-fraud and vehicle theft legislative and regulatory agenda. We promote statues, regulations and policies at all levels of government to help serve member interests in preventing, detecting and defeating insurance-related crimes.

PUBLIC AWARENESS

NICB creates extensive media campaigns to inform the public, news media, member companies and their policyholders, and the general public about insurance crime issues. We encourage consumers to anonymously report fraud via our website, phone, text message or our fraud tips app. Our consumer services also include our popular VINCheck® service, which helps the car-buying public to determine if a vehicle has been reported as stolen, but not recovered, or as a salvage vehicle.

FIGURE 5.5 Five fraud-fighting core functions of the NICB. (Used with permission, National Insurance Crime Bureau.)

Held at city hall, courthouses, and county offices, this information includes property deeds and titles, records of lawsuits, marriages, births, deaths, probated wills, financial statements, transfers of property, tax liens, mechanic's liens, property taxes, military discharges, divorces, criminal convictions, records of lunacy hearings, and other matters.[41]

While there are certain common characteristics to public records access, the investigator needs to become familiar with the state by state nuances. In most county courthouses, information involving property, voter registration, mortgages and deeds, tax liens and liability, divorce, marriage, adoption, and criminal records are easily accessible. Security firms usually provide the investigator with standardized forms to complete these searches. No other exercises test the investigator's capacity to collect information better than the background investigation.

At the state level, a large portion of records for background review are now online. Precisely what is available will depend on the jurisdiction. A rough sketch of the possibilities includes the following:

Property records
- Land records and deeds
- Foreclosures and tax lien sales
- Assessor and property tax records
- GIS and mapping

Vital records
- Genealogy records
- Birth records
- Death records
- Marriage records
- Divorce records

Community health and safety
- Sustainability and environmental health
- Traffic cameras and reports
- Crimes and crime data

Jobs and employment
- Employee directory
- Government jobs and employment listings

Criminal and court records
- Warrants
- Jail and inmate records
- Sex offender registration
- Court records

Licensing and permits
- Business licenses
- Contractor licenses
- Professional licenses
- Bar associations
- Permits and inspections

Codes, regulations, and other sources
- Laws and codes
- Voter and elections information
- UCC filings
- Unclaimed property[42]

Web Exercise: Discover the public records online access in the state of Delaware at: https://publi-crecords.onlinesearches.com/Delaware.htm.

To conduct this type of investigation properly the investigator must consider and evaluate the following:

- Personal life and information
- Criminal background
- Motor vehicle record
- Educational background
- Employment history
- Reputation and character
- Economic interests (e.g., real property, assets)
- Financial conduct[43]

Background investigations are summarized at Figure 5.6.

Background Check Worksheet

Case name: _____

Case File Number: _____

Investigator: _____

Personal Information: Department of Motor Vehicle Record:

Social Security #: _____   Name: _____

Date of Birth: _____   Address: _____

Height: _____   _____

Weight: _____   Date of Birth: _____

Eye Color: _____   OLN #: _____

Hair: _____   Expiration Date: _____

Sex: _____   Class: _____

Race: _____   Restrictions: _____

Additional Information: _____   Suspension/revocations: _____

_____

_____

_____

_____

_____

Statewide Criminal Check:

_____

_____

_____

_____

_____

Organized Crime Check:

_____

_____

_____

_____

_____

_____

Additional Information:

_____

_____

_____

_____

_____

_____

FIGURE 5.6 Standard background check worksheet.

Some of the information sought may be accessed through databases that are computer ready. See Figure 5.7. Many security firms are now subscribing to databases and online services, examples of which have been referred to in previous sections of this chapter. A Computer Services Request Form organizes and categorizes the many options of database subscription services.

5.6 REAL PROPERTY TITLE SEARCH

The permanency of real estate records provides a dependable data source for investigators. Rich in historical and personal information, title searches display a good deal of information about a specified client. The chain of title lists a great deal of useful information such as:

Computer Services Request Form

Case Name: Subject Name:
Case File Number: Subject Address:
Date:
Requested by: Subject Birthdate:
Search Performed: Subject Social Security #:
Search Retrieved: County:
IRSC Search Case Number: Additional Subject Information:
Cost of Search: Billed:

☐ Credit Check   ☐ Drivers Record
☐ Preliminary Asset Search   ☐ Motor Vehicle Registration
☐ National Locate   ☐ Automated Name Index
☐ Pre-Employment Check   ☐ National Drivers Record
☐ Preliminary Background Search   ☐ National Automated Number Index
☐ National Pre-Employment Check   ☐ National Fictitious Business Filings
☐ Sleuth SID   ☐ Business Public Filings
☐ National Identifier Search   ☐ Business Credit Report
☐ Interstate Public Filings   ☐ National Business Report
☐ National Movers Index   ☐ Business Factual Data Report
☐ On-Line Property Search   ☐ Special Request
☐ National Statewide Property Search   ☐ Newspaper Magazine Index
☐ National Real Property   ☐ National Aircraft Title Search
☐ Statewide UCC   ☐ National UCC
☐ Statewide Marriage & Death   ☐ Criminal Convictions History
☐ Superior & Municipal Criminal Index   ☐ National Civil Court Index
☐ Voter Registration   ☐ Workers Compensation Claim Filings
☐ Federal Court Records   ☐ Multistate Corporate Filings

FIGURE 5.7 A typical computer services request form to allow information to be sought through computer and database records. (Used with permission, Martin Investigative Services.)

- Partners and co-venturers in the transfer of grantor/grantee
- Mortgages
- Credit history
- Relatives and other personal information
- Marriages and divorces
- Previous residences and addresses
- Civil actions
- Level of financial worth
- Building permits
- Tax liens or previous obligations not met
- Satisfaction pieces

- Partnerships and other joint venturers
- Criminal conduct/fraud
- Existence of trusts
- Legal owner versus equitable owner
- Liens and other secured interests

TITLE SEARCH

1. Client: _____ File No.: _____
2. Current Owners (As title is vested): _____
   _____
3. Brief Property Description: _____
4. _____ County taxes paid through: _____
   City or Town of _____ taxes paid through: _____
   See attached tax sheet for listing information.
5. Res. Cov.:   Book _____ Page _____ Date of Recording _____
   Amended.:   Book _____ Page _____ Date of Recording _____
   Amended: Book _____ Page _____ Date of Recording _____
   Set back:
       Front: _____
       Side: _____
       Rear: _____
       Utility Easements: _____
   _____
6. Map Information:
   Book/Cabinet: _____ Page/Slide: _____
   Set Backs: Front: _____ Rear: _____
   Side: _____
   Easements _____
   Does Survey Match Plat? _____
7. Means of Access: _____
8. U.C.C.'s: (only HHG or fixture filings) - None
       File No.: _____
       Grantor: _____
       Grantee: _____
       Date: _____
       Collateral: _____
9. DT's:

	Book/Page	Grantor	Trustee	Beneficiary	Inst. Date	Date Rec.	Face Amt.

10. Judgments: _____
11. Suits Pending: _____
12. Special Proceedings: _____
13. If Corporate Party, Name of Record: _____
14. Home Owner's or Property Owner's Assessments: _____
15. Are there any grantors in chain not joined by spouses?
    Name: _____
    Book/Page: _____
    Marital Status: _____
16. Are there any estates in chain?
    Decedent: _____
    Date of Death: _____
    Administration info.: _____
    Tax Certificate: _____
17. Utility Easements:

	Instrument	Book/Page	Grantor	Grantee	Inst. Date	Date Rec.

18. Are there any other defects or caveats?
    _____
    _____
    _____
19. Search period was from:
    Date and Time of Recording: _____
    of _____ (deed, will, DT)
    from: _____ to: _____
    (Trustee) for: _____ (Beneficiary)
    face amount (if DT): _____
    to: _____, _____ .m., _____ day of _____, 19 _____.
20. SD Memo: _____ attached
    Title Policy: _____ attached
    Title Opinion: _____ attached

    Last out in current Owners Outs: _____
    Have you drawn out metes and bounds calls or have a copy of a survey? _____
Abstractor: _____

FIGURE 5.8 A sample title search form.

While there are diverse ways in which the varied jurisdictions record and catalog real estate transactions, there are some uniform practices.[44] Titles can be searched and analyzed by and through:

- Grantor (seller) index
- Grantee (buyer) index
- Tax parcel numbers
- Plot plans
- Date of transaction
- Street addresses
- Deed numbers
- Deed books

If these standard methods of tracking ownership result in a dead end, the investigator has alternative methods and means by evaluating title abstracts, tax reports and records, UCC lien filings, second and third mortgage filings (look at the mortgage books), judgments, and promissory notes with security. A helpful tool for recording information when searching land records is at Figure 5.8.[45]

5.7 CONCLUSION

Information gathering is a seminal skill for any investigator—it is the lifeblood which undergirds every case whether criminal or civil. Solid investigative technique relies upon effective collection techniques from the outset of every case, from initial interview to post-case evaluation. Aside from knowing what to look for and gather, the investigator needs also to prepare documents to memorialize this information for present and future use. Throughout this chapter, the reader is exposed to a wide array of information gathering tactics, source material, places where information is readily available, as well as the many unique investigative demands in each type of case. Hence, the chapter covers how and where information can be gathered, whether at the local library, the governmental office of vital statistics, or a government agency that serves as a repository. Literally hundreds of suggestions for where to find information are sprinkled throughout the chapter.

Side by side, the reader gets specific suggestions on common investigative case situations such as auto accident and negligence, crimes and misdemeanors, workers comp and disability, insurance cases, real property title chains as well the location of missing person and witnesses. How to organize that information to make an efficient case file is another subject of the chapter. Finally readers learn about how information can be gathered in the virtual world by the use of databases and search services such as Lexis/Nexis and Facebook. In sum, the chapter provides the necessary information gathering steps and techniques to assure sufficient and reliable information for a successful investigation.

NOTES

1. *POST Background Investigation Manual: Guidelines for the Investigator* 2018 (California Commission on Peace Officer Standards and Training, 2018), http://lib.post.ca.gov/Publications/bi.pdf.
2. Ibid.; American Society for Industrial Security, *Basic Guidelines For Security Investigations* (1981): 5.
3. *POST Background Investigation Manual*; ASIS, "Security Investigations": 5, 6.
4. 5 U.S.C. § 552a.
5. 12 U.S.C. § 3401 et seq.
6. 42 U.S.C. § 2000aa-6.
7. See U.S. Code.
8. See U.S. Code.
9. 15 U.S.C. § 1681 et seq.
10. 5 U.S.C. § 5315-5316, 7313.
11. 5 U.S.C. § 552.

12. Anne T. McKenna, "Pass Parallel Privacy Standards or Privacy Perishes," *Rutgers Law Review* 65 (Summer 2013): 1041; Erin Murphy, "The Politics of Privacy in the Criminal Justice System: Information Disclosure, the Fourth Amendment, and Statutory Law Enforcement Exemptions," *Michigan Law Review* 11 (February 2013): 485.

13. *Justice Information Privacy Guideline: Developing, Drafting and Assessing Privacy Policy for Justice Information Systems* (National Criminal Justice Association, 2002), https://it.ojp.gov/documents/ncisp/privacy_guideline.pdf; U.S. Department of Justice, Bureau of Justice Statistics, *Privacy and Security of Criminal History Information: An Analysis of Privacy Issues* (U.S. Government Printing Office, 1980): 1.

14. U.S. Department of Justice, *Report of The National Advisory Commission on Criminal Justice Standards and Goals* (U.S. Government Printing Office, 1973): 9.

15. William C. Cunningham and Todd H. Taylor, *The Hallcrest Report: Private Security and Police in America* (Chancellor Press, 1985): 57; *POST Background Investigation Manual*; *Justice Information Privacy Guideline: Developing, Drafting and Assessing Privacy Policy for Justice Information Systems* (National Criminal Justice Association, 2002), https://it.ojp.gov/documents/ncisp/privacy_guideline.pdf; McKenna, "Privacy Standards"; Erin Murphy, "The Politics of Privacy in the Criminal Justice System: Information Disclosure, the Fourth Amendment, and Statutory Law Enforcement Exemptions," *Michigan Law Review* 11 (February 2013): 485.

16. Laura Spadanuta, "Protecting Personal Information," *Security Management*, October 2008: 24; "Legal Protections for Personal Data," EPIC.org, accessed September 8, 2018, https://epic.org/privacy/consumer/legal.html; McKenna, "Privacy Standards"; Murphy, "Politics of Privacy"; for suggestions on how to fashion a workable privacy policy in the handling of information, see National Criminal Justice Association, *Justice Information Privacy Guideline: Developing, Drafting and Assessing Privacy Policy for Justice Information Systems* (2002): 65 et seq, accessed September 8, 2018, https://it.ojp.gov/documents/ncisp/privacy_guideline.pdf.

17. Cunningham and Taylor, "Hallcrest Report": 57; *POST Background Investigation Manual*; Chang-Hun Lee and Ilhong Yun, "Factors Affecting Police Officers' Tendency to Cooperate with Private Investigators," *Policing* 37, no. 4 (2014): 712–727; Jeremy G. Carter, David L. Carter, Steve Chermak, and Edmund McGarrell, "Law Enforcement Fusion Centers: Cultivating an Information Sharing Environment While Safeguarding Privacy," *Journal of Police and Criminal Psychology* 32, no. 1 (2017): 11–27, doi:http://dx.doi.org.ez.lib.jjay.cuny.edu/10.1007/s11896-016-9199-4.

18. Ibid.; Lee and Yun, "Police Officers"; Carter, Carter, Chermak, and McGarrell, "Law Enforcement Fusion Centers."

19. Cooperation between the public policing system and the private investigator needs to be encouraged, honed, and fostered on both sides of the continuum because each force needs the other. Most analytical studies suggest "that the public police need to utilize private investigators and that cooperation being essential for better public service" (Lee and Yun, "Police Officers": 712).

20. See Douglas H. Frazer, *The Complete Handbook of Investigations &Privacy Rights* (2012), accessed September 8, 2018, www.dewittross.com/docs/doug-frazer-publications/the-complete-handbook-of-investigations---december-2012.pdf.

21. BJS, "Privacy and Security": 9; NCJA, "Justice Information Privacy Guideline"; Murphy, "The Politics of Privacy."

22. P. Fuqua and J. Wilson, *Security Investigator's Handbook* (Gulf Publishing Co., 1979): 21–22; Frazer, "Investigations &Privacy Rights."

23. Fuqua and Wilson, "Handbook": 22; Frazer, "Investigations &Privacy Rights."

24. Fuqua and Wilson, "Handbook": 17; Frazer, "Investigations &Privacy Rights."

25. "4 Reliable Resources Private Investigators Use," North American Investigations, July 25, 2017, https://pvteyes.com/4-reliable-resources-private-investigators-use/.

26. GAO Office of Investigations, Investigators' Guide to Sources of Information (Washington, DC: U.S. Government Printing Office, 1997), www.gao.gov/assets/200/198282.pdf.

27. "Social Security Number Randomization," Social Security Administration, accessed September 8, 2018, www.ssa.gov/employer/randomization.html.

28. Robert McCrie, "Manual to Online Public Records and Public Record Research Tips Book," *Security Letter*, January 2009: 4.

29. CourthouseDirect.com, accessed September 8, 2018, www.courthousedirect.com/.

30. Michael Kissiah, "List of the Top Online Public Records Research Websites," April 5, 2013, www.einvestigator.com/public-records-research/.

31. L. Scott Harrell, "Private Investigation Database Resources," *Pursuit Magazine*, September 1, 2008, http://pursuitmag.com/private-investigation-database-resources/.

32. "Business Risk Services—Forensic Advisory Services," Grant Thornton, accessed September 8, 2018, www.grantthornton.com/services/advisory/business-risk/forensic-advisory.aspx.

33. "Searches," IRBsearch, accessed September 9, 2018, www.irbsearch.com/searches.html.

34. "Keystone Library Network Page," Pennsylvania State System of Higher Education, accessed September 8, 2018, www.passhe.edu/executive/academic/kln/Pages/default.aspx.

35. See Kimberly Faber, "Investigators Share Which Databases They Prefer to Use," PInow.com, April 3, 2017, www.pinow.com/articles/2087/13-investigators-share-what-databases-they-prefer-to-use.

36. "Social Media Investigation," PInow.com, accessed September 8, 2018, www.pinow.com/investigations/social-media-investigations.

37. Federal Bureau of Investigation, Training Division, *Economic and Financial Crimes Training Unit, Guide to Sources of Information* (Washington, DC: U.S. Government Printing Office, 1980): 65–68; Federal Bureau of Investigation, Domestic Investigations and Operations Guide (Washington, DC: U.S. Government Printing Office, 2008), https://fas.org/irp/agency/doj/fbi/diog.pdf.

38. "About NICB," National Insurance Crime Bureau, accessed September 8, 2018, www.nicb.org/about-nicb.

39. Amy Thomson, "Valuable Files to Review in a Background Investigation," PInow.com, August 14, 2013, www.pinow.com/articles/1683/valuable-files-to-review-in-a-background-investigation; subjects can also be tracked by cell phone monitoring. See also Michael Kissiah, "Private Investigator Software," eInvestigator.com, February 7, 2018, www.einvestigator.com/private-investigator-software/.

40. "Background Check: How Do You Conduct a Background Check," PInow.com, accessed September 8, 2018, www.pinow.com/investigations/background#3.

41. Fuqua and Wilson, "Handbook": 18; Frazer, "Investigations &Privacy Rights."

42. "Public Records Search," Online Searches, accessed September 8, 2018, https://publicrecords.online-searches.com/.

43. Scott B. Fulmer, "Conducting Background Checks—10 Tips for Private Investigators," PInow.com, April 12, 2011, www.pinow.com/articles/337/conducting-background-checks-10-tips-for-private-investigators; PInow.com, "Background Check," www.pinow.com/investigations/background.

44. See Charles P. Nemeth, *Reality of Real Estate* (Upper Saddle River, NJ: Prentice Hall, 2007); Michael Sankey, *A Primer on Searching Recorded Documents, Judgments, and Liens*, accessed September 8, 2018, www.prrn.us/documents/Searching.pdf; Public Record Retriever Network, *Tip Sheet for Searching Court Records*, accessed September 8, 2018, www.prrn.us/documents/CourtTipsheet.pdf.

45. North Carolina Bar Foundation, *II Practical Skills Course* (1988): 57–58.

6 Collection of Evidence and Preservation of the Scene

6.1 INVESTIGATIVE TECHNIQUE: INITIAL SCENE VISITATION

Standard investigative practice calls for the security officer to attentively protect the crime scene and preserve the evidence. "Collection, preservation and the assurance of evidentiary integrity"[1] are central to the investigative regimen. This is true in any type of case consisting of criminal conduct or civil injuries; insurance investigations for arson, fraud, and vehicular accidents; terrorist acts; bomb threats; executive protection threats; intrusions into hotels and motels, colleges and universities; violent labor disputes; workers' compensation, as well as suspected retail theft. The skills and competencies required of a public police officer apply equally to the private security officer and investigator. This chapter presents a comprehensive analysis of methods and techniques employed by security investigators that insure the integrity of evidence during the collection process and the continuing preservation of the scene.

From the outset, the security investigator should possess certain "tools" in order to accomplish a thorough and useful collection of evidence at a scene. In some quarters, these materials would be part of an evidence collection "kit." Included in the toolkit would be:

Essential

- Bindle paper
- Biohazard bags
- Body fluid collection kit
- Camera with flash and tripod; extra film, if not digital; extra flash memory cards, if digital
- Casting materials
- Consent/search forms
- Crime scene barricade tape
- Cutting instruments (knives, box cutter, scalpel, scissors, etc.)
- Directional marker/compass
- Disinfectant (such as a 10% bleach solution)
- Evidence collection containers including rigid containers for firearms and ammunition boxes, pie boxes with sheet cotton for document recovery; manila folders
- Evidence identifiers (numbers, placards)
- Evidence seals/tape
- First-aid kit
- Flashlight and extra batteries
- High-intensity lights
- Latent print kit
- Magnifying glass
- Measuring devices
- Permanent markers
- Personal protective equipment (PPE)
- Photographic scale (ruler)
- Presumptive blood test supplies
- Sketch paper

- Tools
- Tweezers/forceps
- Window screen fabric in rolls or sheets

Optional

- Audiotape recorder
- Bloodstain pattern examination kit
- Business cards
- Chalk
- Chemical enhancement supplies
- Compass
- Entomology (insect) collection kit
- Extension cords
- Flares
- Forensic light source (alternate light source, UV lamp/laser, goggles)
- Generator
- Gunshot residue kit
- Laser trajectory kit
- Maps
- Marking paint/snow wax
- Metal detector
- Mirror
- Phone listing (important numbers)
- Privacy screens
- Protrusion rod set
- Reflective vest
- Refrigeration or cooling unit
- Respirators with filters
- Roll of string
- Rubber bands
- Sexual assault evidence collection kit (victim and suspect)
- Shoe print lifting equipment
- Templates (scene and human)
- Thermometer
- Traffic cones
- Trajectory rods
- Video recorder
- Wireless phone

Kits for specific evidence collection applications may include the following:

Blood collection

- Bindle
- Coin envelopes
- Disposable scalpels
- Distilled water or single use sterile water droppers
- Evidence identifiers
- Drying box

- Latex gloves
- Photographic ruler (ABFO scales)
- Presumptive chemicals
- Swabs

Fingerprint

- Adhesive and gelatin lifting materials
- Brushes
- Chemical enhancement supplies
- Cyanoacrylate (super glue) wand/ packets
- Fingerprint ink pads, cards, and card holders for exemplar collection
- Flashlight
- Forensic light source
- Lift cards, including 8.5″ × 11″ inch card stock
- Lift tape
- Measurement scales
- Powders

Bloodstain pattern documentation

- ABFO scales
- Calculator
- Laser pointer
- Permanent markers
- Protractor
- String
- Tape

Electronic and digital evidence recovery

- Anti-static bags
- Bubble-wrap and other packing materials
- Cable tags and ties
- CDs and 3.5 inch diskettes
- Faraday bags
- Hand truck
- Nut drivers, hex and star type
- Pliers: needle-nose and standard
- Rubber bands
- Magnifying glass
- Printer paper
- Secure-bit drivers
- Screwdrivers, nonmagnetic flat-blade and Philips-type
- Tweezers, small nonmagnetic
- Wire cutters

Excavation and evidence recovery

- Cones/markers
- Evidence identifiers

- Hand tools (hammer, chisel/screwdriver, forceps, hand saw, box cutter, drywall saw, etc.)
- Metal detectors
- Paintbrushes
- Shovels/trowels
- Sifting screens
- String
- Weights
- Wooden/metal stakes

Impressions—footwear, tire tracks, and tool mark

- Bowls/mixing containers
- Boxes
- Casting kit (e.g., Duplicast©, Mikrosil©, or polyvinylsiloxane (PVS) materials, silicone-type sealant)
- Dental stone
- Evidence identifiers
- Material for forms
- Measurement scales
- Permanent markers
- Snow print wax
- Stirring sticks
- Water

Pattern print lifter

- Chemical enhancement supplies
- Electrostatic dust lifter
- Gel lifter
- Wide format lift tape

Trace evidence collection

- Acetate sheet protectors or clear secondary liners
- Bindle paper or weigh paper for bindles
- Butcher paper
- Clear packing/sealing tape 2.5 to 4 inches wide
- Cotton-tipped swab
- Flashlight (oblique lighting)
- Forceps/tweezers (disposable or clean smooth tipped)
- Glass jars, bottles, vials with airtight, screw-on lids
- Metal friction lid cans with fitting lids
- Slides and slide mailers
- Trace evidence vacuum with disposable collection filters
- Transfer pipettes (glass or plastic)[2]

The investigator should pay close attention to state and local laws guiding various legal issues including crime scene access, preservation, and chain of custody requirements, and sanctioned laboratory facilities capable of conducting evidentiary analysis.

6.2 INVESTIGATIVE TECHNIQUE: PRELIMINARY EVIDENCE COLLECTION STRATEGIES

If the investigator is fortunate enough to have early access to the civil or criminal scene, securing the scene's physical integrity—the conditions surrounding the occurrence and the preservation of its evidence—whether evidence of personal injury, or damage to property or contraband, is a critical initial step in the evidence process.

This initial scene search should be a planned, coordinated, and competent action that is legally permissible and does not interfere with or obstruct the function of public justice. To illustrate, investigators for insurance companies should be cautious upon scene approach and announce to public law enforcement their status and intentions. Without exception, private investigators must give way to official action, function, or activity. Only persons who have a legitimate investigative interest should be permitted into the scene, and the number of such persons should be minimal. As a rule, the larger the number of persons on the scene, the greater is the potential for scene contamination.

Two fundamental priorities govern investigative conduct upon initial visitation:

1. The acquisition and preservation of physical, real, documentary, and tangible evidence
2. The notation of mental impressions regarding motive and *modus operandi* that arise from the placement and station of the overall scene

Upon entry, the investigator must make every effort to capture events and conditions as presently existing for preservation purposes. The U.S. Department of Justice, through its National Institute of Justice, has published a reference work for private and public law enforcement titled *Crime Scene Search and Physical Evidence Handbook*.[3] It emphasizes the urgency and importance of the preliminary review:

> Aside from any other consideration, the investigator should consider the crime scene as highly dynamic, that is, undergoing change; and fragile, in the sense that the evidence value of items it contains can be easily downgraded. Usually, there is only one opportunity to search the scene properly. Making a good preliminary survey of the layout helps to use that opportunity to best advantage.[4]

The investigator's preservation of the scene is a landmark responsibility because no scene remains fixed for long. Every scene will change by the mere passage of time.[5]

The investigator should first take into account all the information and opinions that have been accumulated by persons preceding him on the scene. The apparent physical focal point or points of the crime are of particular interest in this information exchange, as are the perceptions of other officers as to items or material having potential evidentiary value.[6]

The maintenance of crime scene integrity begins with the observations of the first officer or investigator on the scene, which comprise these steps:

a. Note or log dispatch information (e.g., address/location, time, date, type of call, parties involved).
b. Be aware of any persons or vehicles leaving the crime scene.
c. Approach the scene cautiously, scan the entire area to thoroughly assess the scene, and note any possible secondary crime scenes. Be aware of any persons and vehicles in the vicinity that may be related to the crime.
d. Make initial observations (look, listen, smell) to assess the scene and ensure officer safety before proceeding.
e. Remain alert and attentive. Assume the crime is ongoing until determined to be otherwise.
f. Treat the location as a crime scene until assessed and determined to be otherwise.[7]

The Pennsylvania State Police in its *Crime Laboratory Operations Manual* corroborates the importance of this early stage in the investigative process by noting:

- Form objectives of the search and decide what to look for.
- Take special note of evidence that may be easily destroyed such as shoeprints in dust, footprints, etc.
- Organize the search by making assignments for photographs, fingerprints, and evidence handling.
- Decide on a search pattern and issue instructions to assist personnel.[8]

Web Exercise: Review the recommended procedures for crime scene preservation from *Police: The Law Enforcement Magazine* at: www.policemag.com/channel/patrol/articles/2016/09/how-to-preserve-a-crime-scene.aspx.

The need to preserve physical evidence requires a resolute effort to cordon off and secure the scene and physical conditions at the scene in order to prevent—or at least minimize—any distortions or aberrations of the original scene. A few prototype forms for physical evidence collection are outlined in the Figures that follow.[9] The checklist for physical evidence at Table 6.1 is usable in both criminal and civil litigation.[10]

TABLE 6.1
Sample investigator checklist from a crime scene

Investigator's Checklist at the Crime Scene

Investigator/IOC's Inquiry Checklist

#	INQUIRY	YES	NO
a	**When**, **where** and **why** did it happen?		
b	**Who** is the victim?		
c	Possible **motive/s**?		
d	**How** did the perpetrator gain entry into the crime scene and how did he flee the scene? When?		
e	Is the **perpetrator** to be found among a selected few?		
f	Could **any specific individual** be suspected? Why?		
g	Is there a **description of the perpetrators**? **Accomplices**?		
h	Is there any **information on vehicles used**?		
i	Is there **anything missing from the crime scene** or from the victim?		
j	Did the **perpetrator leave anything behind** through which he could be traced?		
k	Are there any **other incidents**, **occurrences**, circumstances or observations that could **be connected** with the crime?		
l	**Determine if** the particular area is **the primary crime scene** or is it just the **finding place** and the crime happened in some other place? If so, secure the primary crime scene.		

Investigator's Activity Checklist

#	ACTIVITY	YES	NO
1	**Who received the report of the incident?** – How was it received? – When was it received (time)?		
2	**Who reported the incident?** – Name, address – Phone number – Where the concerned could be reached in the near future		

(Continued)

TABLE 6.1 (CONTINUED)
Sample investigator checklist from a crime scene

3	**Factual information.** – What happened? – Time, place? – Circumstances surrounding the incident? – Is the suspect identified? – Weapons?		
4	**Initial measures undertaken:** – Date, time – Responsible officer		
5	**Response time?**		
6	**Logbook?**		
7	**Measures undertaken by the first officer arriving at the scene?**		
	a. Murder: (body still on the scene) – Post-mortem changes – Algor mortis (blood circulation stops) – Livor mortis (body cools down) – Rigor mortis (body becomes rigid) – Life-saving measures? – Is the scene the primary crime scene or finding place?		
	b. Murder: (body brought to hospital) – Officers immediately ordered to proceed to the hospital? – Seizure of the victim's clothes? – Interviews with attending hospital staff – Who brought the body to the hospital? – How has clothing been handled? – Presence of wallet – Mobile phone – ID-card – Other items etc. – If shots have been fired, paraffin casting of the person's hands for extraction of gunpowder residue		
	c. Kidnapping/Abduction: – Accurate description of the kidnapped person? – Accurate description of all circumstances around the abduction? – Collection of dental records, x-ray pictures? – Collection of medical records, x-ray pictures? – Seizure of DNA-carrying items (toothbrush, safety razor, combs)? – Fingerprints? – Comparison samples from relatives (preferably mother)? – Photos? – Flash alarm?		
	d. In all cases: – Cordon off a sufficiently large area around the crime scene, taking into account perpetrator's potential hide-out, ports of entry and departure. – Ensure protection of the cordoned off crime scene and secure evidence that could be destroyed by external factors. – Record or take note of everyone who enters the crime scene. – Notes of bystanders? – Make a documentation of the crime scene (lighting, odor, windows) (photo or sketch).		

(Continued)

TABLE 6.1 (CONTINUED)

Sample investigator checklist from a crime scene

	– Make a description of the surrounding area of the scene (dwellings, shops, bus stops, restaurants etc., security guards, street cleaners, etc.). – Take note of license numbers of parked cars in the vicinity/area (potential witnesses). – Check for presence of CCTV. – Mobile phone?		
8	**Crime scene examination**: – Outcome of proceedings (protocol)? – Documentation (photos, videos, sketches)? – Collected samples? – Further forensic investigations? – Results? – Prudence of early decision to lift cordons?		
9	**Organizational setup**: – Structure – Allocation of resources (reinforcements) – Officer-in-charge – Priorities and directions – Tasking – Documentation – Briefings – Contingency plans – Media relations (monitoring and collection of articles, and other media coverage of the incident)		
10	**Alert** other police stations and units in the adjacent areas? Routines?		
11	Immediate measures to **track down and apprehend** the perpetrator Check-points etc.? Employment of **canine**? Flash alarms?		
12	**Canvassing operation (house-to-house) around the crime scene and the route of escape** – Prepared templates with battery of questions? – Comparison materials (cars, colors, etc.). – Interviews?		
13	**Other initial measures**: – Secured CCTV footages? – Interview of people on the spot? – Treatment of witnesses and family of the victim? – Request of lists of mobile communications in the area during critical time (mobile phone operators)? – Interviews with ambulance staff or other people bringing the body from the scene (if victim was alive did he say something?). – If victim alive at hospital and under treatment, presence of investigator? – Man hotline? – Other incidents connected to the case at hand? – Contact with prosecutor?		
14	**House search at victim's dwelling and other premises, cars, etc?** – Seizure and analysis of: – Computers – Mobile phones – Pagers, diaries – Photos – Letters – Receipts – Balance sheets etc.		

(Continued)

TABLE 6.1 (CONTINUED)

Sample investigator checklist from a crime scene

15	**Identification of suspect?** – Physical evidence? – Eye witnesses (line-up, video, photo identification)? – Composite sketches? – Flash alarm?		
	Remarks/Recommendations:		

In Box 6.1,[11] Physical Scene Investigation Checklist, the investigator is provided with step-by-step instructions on how to perform a preliminary review and examination. Note that the checklist includes reporting weather and lighting conditions; establishing a perimeter to secure the scene by keeping out foreign parties; observations regarding odors and the sensible policy of calling in additional help, if necessary.

BOX 6.1 ORGANIZATION AND PROCEDURES FOR SEARCH OPERATIONS, ADAPTED FROM CALIFORNIA COMMISSION ON PEACE OFFICER STANDARDS AND TRAINING'S WORKBOOK FOR THE "FORENSIC TECHNOLOGY FOR LAW ENFORCEMENT" (USED WITH PERMISSION, CA POST)

Preparation

1. Evaluate the current legal ramifications of crime scene searches (e.g., obtaining of search warrants).
2. Discuss upcoming search with involved personnel before arrival at scene, if possible.
3. Select, when feasible, person-in-charge prior to arrival at scene.
4. Consider the safety and comfort of search personnel—do not be caught unprepared when encountering a potentially dangerous scene or inclement weather—examples are:
   o Clothing
   o Communication
   o Lighting assistance
   o Shelter
   o Transportation
   o Food
   o Medical assistance
   o Scene security
   o Equipment

5. Organize communication with services of an ancillary nature (e.g., medical examiner, prosecuting attorney) in order that questions which surface during crime scene search may be resolved. Take steps to organize a "command post" headquarters for communication, decision making, etc., in major/complicated investigations.

Basic Stages

1. Approach scene, secure and protect scene.
2. Initiate preliminary survey/determine scene boundaries.

3. Evaluate physical evidence possibilities.
4. Prepare narrative description.
5. Depict scene photographically.
6. Prepare diagram/sketch of scene.
7. Conduct detailed search.
8. Record and collect physical evidence.
9. Conduct final survey.
10. Release crime scene.

Approach Scene

1. Be alert for discarded evidence.
2. Make pertinent notes as to possible approach/escape routes.

Secure and Protect Scene

1. Take control of scene on arrival.
2. Determine extent to which scene has thus far been protected.
3. Ensure adequate scene security.
4. Obtain information from personnel who have entered scene and have knowledge relative to its original conditions—document who has been at scene.
5. Take extensive notes—do not rely on memory.
6. Keep out unauthorized personnel—begin recording who enters and leaves.

Initiate Preliminary Survey

1. The survey is an organizational stage to plan for the entire search.
2. A cautious walk-through of the scene is accomplished.
3. Person-in-charge maintains definite administrative and emotional control.
4. Select appropriate narrative description technique.
5. Acquire preliminary photographs.
6. Delineate extent of the search area—usually expand initial perimeter.
7. Organize methods and procedures needed recognize special problem areas.
8. Determine personnel and equipment needs; make specific assignments.
9. Identify and protect transient physical evidence.
10. Develop a general theory of the crime.
11. Make extensive notes to document scene physical and environmental conditions, assignments, movement of personnel, etc.
12. On vehicles get VIN number, license number, position of key, odometer reading, gear shift position, amount of fuel in tank, lights turned on or off.

Evaluate Physical Evidence Possibilities

1. Based upon what is known from the preliminary survey, determine what evidence is likely to be present.
2. Concentrate on the most transient evidence and work to the least transient forms of this material.
3. Focus first on the easily accessible areas in open view and progress eventually to possible out-of-view locations—look for purposely hidden items.

4. Consider whether the evidence appears to have been moved inadvertently.
5. Evaluate whether or not the scene and evidence appears intentionally "contrived."

Prepare Narrative Description

1. The purpose of this step is to provide a running narrative of the conditions at the crime scene. Consider what should be present at a scene (victim's purse or vehicle) and is not observed and what is out of place (ski mask).
2. Represent scene in a "general to specific" scheme. Consider situational factors: lights on/off, heat on/off, newspaper on driveway/in house, drapes pulled, open or shut.
3. Do not permit narrative effort to degenerate into a sporadic and unorganized attempt to recover physical evidence—it is recommended that evidence not be collected at this point, under most circumstances.
4. Methods of narrative—written, audio, video.

Photograph Scene

1. Begin photography as soon as possible—plan before photographing.
2. Document the photographic effort with a photographic log.
3. Ensure that a progression of overall, medium, and close-up views of the scene is established.
4. Use recognized scale device for size determination when applicable.
5. When a scale device is used, first take a photograph without the inclusion of this device.
6. Photograph evidence in place before its collection and packaging.
7. Be observant of and photograph areas adjacent to the crime scene—points of entry, exits, windows, attics, etc.
8. Consider feasibility of aerial photography.
9. Photograph items, places, etc., to corroborate the statements of witnesses, victims, suspects.
10. Take photographs from eye-level, when feasible, to represent scene as it would be observed by normal view.
11. Film is relatively cheap compared to the rewards obtained—do not hesitate to photograph something which has no apparent significance at that time—it may later prove to be a key element in the investigation.
12. Prior to lifting latent fingerprints, photographs should be taken 1:1, or use appropriate scale.

Prepare Diagram/Sketch of Scene

1. The diagram establishes permanent record of items, conditions, and distance/size relationships—diagrams supplement photographs.
2. Rough sketch is drawn at scene (normally not drawn to scale) and is used as a model for finished sketch.
3. Typical material on rough sketch:
   o   Specific location
   o   Date
   o   Time
   o   Case identifier
   o   Preparer
   o   Weather conditions
   o   Lighting conditions

    o   Scale or scale disclaimer
    o   Compass orientation
    o   Evidence
    o   Measurements
    o   Key or legend

4. Number designations on sketch can be coordinated with same number designations on evidence log in many instances.
5. General progression of sketches:
    o   Lay out basic perimeter
    o   Set forth fixed objects, furniture, etc.
    o   Record position of evidence
    o   Record appropriate measurements—double check
    o   Set forth key/legend, compass orientation, etc.

Conduct Detailed Search/Record, and Collect Physical Evidence

1. Accomplish search based on previous evaluation of evidence possibilities.
2. Conduct search in a general manner and work to the specifics regarding evidence items.
3. Use of specialized search patterns (e.g., grid, strip/lane, spiral) are recommended when possible.
4. Photograph all items before collection and enter notations in photographic log (remember—use scale when necessary).
5. Mark evidence locations on diagram/sketch.
6. Complete evidence log with appropriate notations for each item of evidence.
7. Ensure that evidence or the container of evidence is initialed by investigator collecting the evidence.
8. Do not handle evidence excessively after recovery.
9. Seal all evidence containers at the crime scene.
10. Do not guess on packaging requirements; different types of evidence can necessitate different containers.
11. Do not forget entrance and exit areas at scene for potential evidence.
12. Be sure to obtain appropriate "Known" standards (e.g., fiber sample from carpet).
13. Constantly check paperwork, packaging notations, and other pertinent recordings of information for possible errors which may cause confusion or problems at a later time.
14. Four basic premises:
    o   The best search options are typically the most difficult and time consuming.
    o   You cannot "over-document" the physical evidence.
    o   There is only one chance to perform the job properly.
    o   There are two basic search approaches, in this order:
        ■   A "cautious" search of visible areas, taking steps to avoid evidence loss or contamination.
        ■   After the "cautious" search, a vigorous search for hidden/concealed areas.

Conduct Final Survey

1. This survey is a critical review of all aspects of the search.
2. Discuss the search jointly with all personnel for completeness.
3. Double check documentation to detect inadvertent errors.

4. Check to ensure all evidence is accounted for before departing scene.
5. Ensure all equipment used in the search is gathered.
6. Make sure possible hiding places or difficult access areas have not been overlooked in detailed search.
7. Critical issues: have you gone far enough in the search for evidence, documented all essential things, and made no assumptions which may prove to be incorrect in the future?

Release Crime Scene

1. Release is accomplished only after completion of the final survey.
2. At minimum, documentation should be made of :
   o   Time and date of release
   o   To whom released
   o   By whom released

3. Ensure that appropriate inventory has been provided as necessary, considering legal requirements, to person to whom scene is released.
4. Once the scene has been formally released, reentry may require a warrant.
5. Only the person-in-charge should have the authority to release the scene. This precept should be known and adhered to by all personnel.
6. Consider the need to have certain specialists survey the scene before it is released (e.g., blood pattern analysts, medical examiner).

Another important form is the Protection of the Scene Checklist at Box 6.2.[12] By adhering to the standards and policies presented in this document, the private investigator will be assured of evidence integrity. Pay particular attention to the materials and supplies (such as signs, lighting, flags, rope, chalk or crayon, barricades, and other security personnel) needed to prevent intrusion.

BOX 6.2   PROTECTION OF THE CRIME SCENE CHECKLIST (SOURCE: NATIONAL INSTITUTE OF JUSTICE (NIJ))

Secure and Control Persons at the Scene

a. Control all persons at the scene.
   1.   Restrict movement of persons at the scene.
   2.   Prevent persons from altering physical evidence.
   3.   Prevent persons from destroying physical evidence.
   4.   Continue to maintain safety at the scene.
   5.   Restrict areas of movement within the scene.
   6.   Continue to control the scene by maintaining officer presence.

b. Identify all persons at the scene.
   1.   Identify suspects (secure and separate).
   2.   Identify witnesses (secure and separate).
   3.   Identify bystanders (remove from the scene).
   4.   Identify victims/family members/friends (control while showing compassion).
   5.   Identify medical and assisting personnel.

   c. Exclude unauthorized/nonessential personnel from the scene.
     1. Law enforcement officials not working the case.
     2. Politicians.
     3. Media.
     4. Other nonessential personnel (e.g., any persons not performing investigative or safety functions at the scene).

Establish and Preserve Scene Boundaries

   a. Establish scene boundaries by identifying the focal point(s) of the scene and extending outward.
     1. Secure areas where the crime occurred.
     2. Secure areas that are potential points and paths of entry/exit of suspects/witnesses.
     3. Secure areas where victim(s)/evidence may have moved or been moved.
     4. Initially secure a larger area, since it is easier to contract than to expand the boundaries.

   b. Set up physical barrier(s).
     1. Set the physical perimeter for established scene boundaries (with crime scene tape, rope, cones, vehicles, personnel, etc.).
     2. Set the physical perimeter for established scene boundaries by using existing structures (walls, rooms, gated areas, etc.).

   c. Document entry of all people entering and exiting the scene.
     1. Record the names of persons entering the scene.
     2. Record the names of persons exiting the scene.

   d. Maintain integrity of the scene.
     1. Control the flow of personnel and animals entering and exiting the scene.

   e. Attempt to preserve/protect evidence at the scene.
     1. Protect evidence from environmental elements, if possible.
     2. Protect evidence from manmade intrusions (e.g., shoe or tire impressions).
     3. Protect evidence from mechanical devices (e.g., sprinklers, helicopters).
     4. Protect evidence from animals.

   f. Document the original location of the victim(s) or objects at the scene that were observed being moved.
     1. Document point of origin of the victim(s) or items at the scene.
     2. Document alternate location.

   g. Follow jurisdictional laws related to search and seizure.
     1. Determine the need for obtaining consent to search or a search warrant

When examining particular activities, such as bombs and explosives in executive protection situations, the focus on physical evidence becomes more refined. Some clues for the recognition of concealed explosive devices include:

- Recently disturbed ground
- Sawdust

- Brickdust
- Wood chips
- Electrical wire
- String
- Fishing line
- Dirty rope (fuses)
- Tin foil
- Partly opened drawers
- Fresh plaster or cement
- Loose floorboards
- Disturbed carpeting
- Loose electrical fittings
- Out-of-place objects
- Greasy paper wrapping, etc.[13]

If security personnel are conscious of the risks of explosive devices and can recognize their components, camouflage, or disguises, then they will easily detect the clues of placement.[14]

Unfortunately, clues are not always visible, for a neat and tidy bomber will leave no trace of his work unless it is a "lure" to draw personnel into a kill zone. However, an untidy or ill-trained bomber may leave visible clues, which include:

External clues:

- Abandoned vehicles
- Abandoned vehicles on routes
- Accidents/crashes on routes
- Disturbed ground, small hollows after rain
- Military containers of ammunition/explosives
- Footprints or vehicle tracks for no apparent reason
- Vegetation camouflage, cut, bent, or withered
- Cut vegetation
- Heaps of leaves or scrub
- Marks on trees (indicating traps to the enemy)

Internal clues:

- Obviously out of place or "lure" objects
- Explosive wrappings, ammunition, or explosive containers
- Sawdust, brickdust, or metal filings
- Dusty footprints
- Scratched or new paint and timber
- Clothes pegs, nails, electric leads, tin foil, string, wire, mousetraps, watch and clock parts
- Marks on walls (indicating traps to the enemy)
- Loose floorboards or raised carpeting, tiles, etc.
- New brickwork, plastering, or concrete[15]

Private security personnel involved in investigating bomb threats will find the "Bomb Search Report" outlined in Chapter 8 (see Figure 8.10) very useful.

Web Exercise: Crime scenes have come to depend upon a particular job—the crime technician. Read about the usual expectations for this position at: https://study.com/articles/Crime_Scene_Analyst_Job_Description_Duties_and_Requirements.html.

To assure integrity in evidence collection be certain the scene suffers no tampering or contamination—an obligation throughout the entire investigation.

6.3 INVESTIGATIVE TECHNIQUE: SCENE SKETCHES AND OTHER GRAPHIC PORTRAYALS

The investigator should make a representative sketch of the scene as a standard addition to the written report. Scene survey sketches are considered mandatory in most criminal and civil investigations. A scene sketch is a handmade pictorial representation of conditions at a scene. Some typical uses and justifications for scene sketches are:

- To refresh the memory of the investigator
- To record the exact location of evidence found in relationship to pieces of furniture or fixed objects
- To provide a permanent record
- To assist all persons concerned in understanding facts
- To supplement photographs and notes

Web Exercise: New and innovative approaches using cutting-edge technology are now available to justice professionals when sketching the scene. Visit: www.smartdraw.com/crime-scene/crime-scene-investigation-software.htm.

While there is no absolute sketch method to follow, all sketches must be accurate, made to scale, and recorded uniformly.[16]

If one aspect of a sketch is accurate, such as the dimensions of a field in which a body was found, and the position of an object within the field is only roughly estimated, the distortion thus introduced renders the sketch relatively useless. It is important that the coordinate distances of an item in the sketch be measured in the same manner.[17]

Sketching methods fall into these basic categorizations:

1. Triangulation (see Figure 6.1[18])
2. Baseline or coordinate (see Figure 6.2[19])
3. Cross projection (see Figure 6.3[20])
4. Rough and smooth (finished) sketches (see Figures 6.4[21] and 6.5[22])

6.3.1 RULES FOR SKETCHING

Regardless of the sketching method chosen,[23] the following rules apply:

- Decide what is to be sketched—the key features.
- Indicate North on the sketch. (Use a compass if necessary.)
- Control all measurements by using measuring tape or ruler.
- Have someone else verify all measurements. (Do not estimate distance by pacing.)
- Take two separate sets of measurements when noting the position of a body; one set from the head and another from the feet.
- Locate all objects accurately and identify all objects drawn in sketch either by numerals or letters. Draw "stick" figures to represent bodies.
- Include all essential items in the drawing.
- Make all sketch corrections at the scene.
- Record date, time, by whom drawn, case number, and names of persons that assisted with measurements.
- Use legend (drawing and charting symbols).

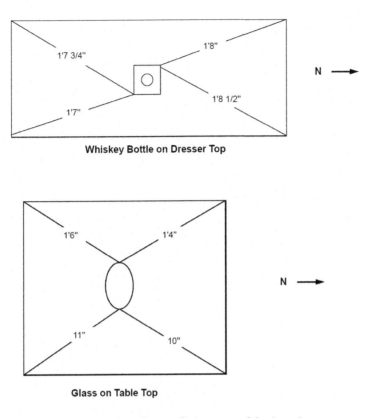

FIGURE 6.1 2-V method of triangulation. (Source: Department of the Army.)

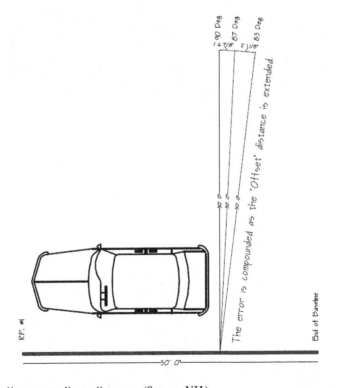

FIGURE 6.2 Baseline or coordinate distances. (Source: NIJ.)

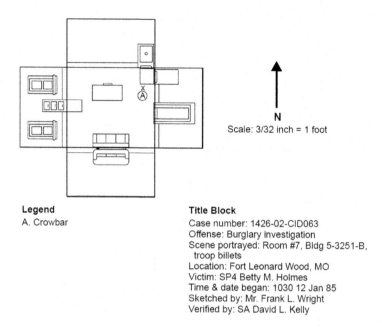

Legend
A. Crowbar

Title Block
Case number: 1426-02-CID063
Offense: Burglary investigation
Scene portrayed: Room #7, Bldg 5-3251-B,
  troop billets
Location: Fort Leonard Wood, MO
Victim: SP4 Betty M. Holmes
Time & date began: 1030 12 Jan 85
Sketched by: Mr. Frank L. Wright
Verified by: SA David L. Kelly

FIGURE 6.3 Example of a cross projection sketch. (Source: Department of the Army.)

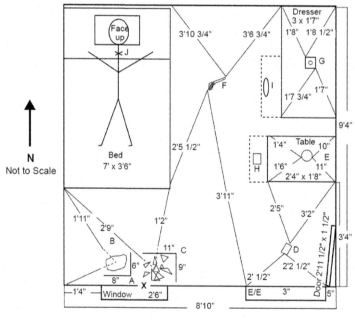

Legend
A. Hole
B. Red stain
C. Glass fragments
D. Shell casing
E. Glass
F. Pistol
G. Bottle
H. Canister
I. Cigarette
J. Neck injury

Title Block
Case number: 0123-02-CID037
Offense: Undetermined death
Scene portrayed: Room #C-33, Bldg #3203,
  troop barracks
Location: Fort Leonard Wood, MO 65473
Victim: SGT Janet Williams
Time & date began: 1115 2 Jan 02
Sketched by: SA William Mac
Verified by: SA John Friend

FIGURE 6.4 Example of a flat projection or overview (rough sketch). (Source: Department of the Army.)

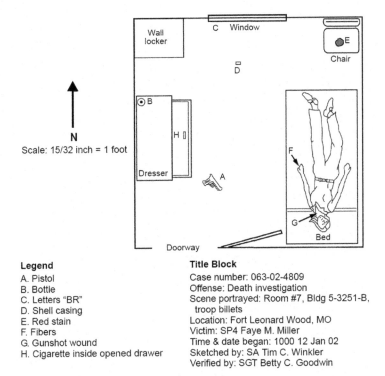

Legend

A. Pistol
B. Bottle
C. Letters "BR"
D. Shell casing
E. Red stain
F. Fibers
G. Gunshot wound
H. Cigarette inside opened drawer

Title Block

Case number: 063-02-4809
Offense: Death investigation
Scene portrayed: Room #7, Bldg 5-3251-B,
   troop billets
Location: Fort Leonard Wood, MO
Victim: SP4 Faye M. Miller
Time & date began: 1000 12 Jan 02
Sketched by: SA Tim C. Winkler
Verified by: SGT Betty C. Goodwin

FIGURE 6.5   Example of a finished sketch drawn to scale. (Source: Department of the Army.)

Web exercise: Read the article on "Crime Scene Diagrams" by *Forensic Magazine* at www.forensicmag.com/article/2014/01/crime-scene-diagramming-back-basics.

6.3.2 RULES FOR MEASURING

All measurements should be taken from fixed objects.[24] Some locations for taking indoor measurements are:

- Walls
- Room corners
- Door and window frames
- Bathroom fixtures

Outdoor measurements should also be taken from fixed objects:

- Corners of buildings (record address).
- Light poles (record pole number).

Graphic portrayals are not limited to scene sketches. External injury and wound charts serve the investigator in cases of workers' compensation, personal injury, and disability cases. See Figure 6.6.

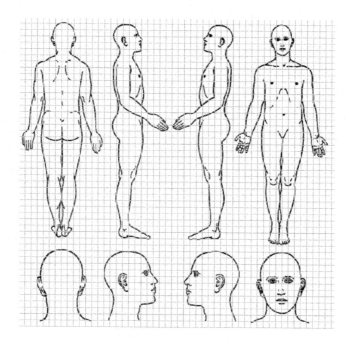

FIGURE 6.6   Human figure and head to illustrate location injury or trauma.

6.4   INVESTIGATIVE TECHNIQUE: PHOTOGRAPHIC EVIDENCE

Photographic evidence, whether by traditional film or digital means, also plays a key role in the development of an investigator's case. The scene shown in Figure 6.7 would be difficult to present accurately with a sketch or description alone. Evidence such as this must be depicted as accurately as possible in photographs since the scene will be altered after objects such as vehicles and bodies are moved.

FIGURE 6.7   Photographic evidence at an accident scene.

Private investigators working in civil or criminal matters usually become adept photographers. However, since they frequently are not on the scene as early as public law enforcement investigators, cooperative arrangements, and relationships with public police are essential.[25]

Probably more pictures for use in court are obtained from police photographers than any other source. Almost every police department is equipped with some photographic equipment, a camera or two at least, and in a city of any size, you will find a police photographic laboratory. Patrol cars are often equipped with cameras. In special accident investigations, cars are more elaborately equipped as are the station wagons or trucks used as field crime investigation laboratories.[26]

Web Exercise: Find out how digital photography is changing the landscape of photography at the crime scene, accident, or other event at: www.fletc.gov/training-program/digital-photography-law-enforcement-level-1.

Photography is also regularly employed by coroners, medical examiners, forensic experts, scientific experts, attorneys, claims adjusters, and government agencies.

Today law enforcement officials and attorneys everywhere realize the importance of photographing the scene of the crime. Good crime scene photographs are useful even though the case never reaches trial. They give police officials and attorneys the best possible pictorial record of the scene of the crime. Pictures also are useful when questioning witnesses and suspects. Often a guilty party will confess when confronted with indisputable photographic evidence ... Throughout the world, the standard police practice is to make photographs of all scenes of serious crimes as soon as possible after discovery before anything is moved or even touched. This rule is so well known now that there is little excuse for anyone ignoring it.[27]

In order for photography to reach its primary evidentiary quality, it must precisely depict the scene, persons, or objects as found. It must also avoid being inflammatory or too gruesome for subsequent admission.[28] Thus, the investigator performing photographic functions is concerned about two fundamental queries:

1. What is the time relationship between the event or condition in question and the photographic action?
2. What photographic perspective, angle, or plan was employed during the photographic action?

A true and reliable representation is a photographer's seminal obligation, since significant distortions reduce or destroy the evidentiary value of the photographs. Taking pictures from various angles and directions aids in the development of a reliable perspective. A professional photographic portfolio accounts for:

- Approaches to the scene
- Surrounding areas
- Close-ups of entrances and exits
- General scenario shots
- Differing angle shots
- Differing height shots
- Shots of location before and after removal of evidence
- Color *and* black-and-white shots taken in cases where defense challenges gruesomeness of photos

6.4.1 LOCATION OF CRIME SCENE

The crime scene photographer should "capture the whole scene first using wide-angle shots covering the entire scene from the approach and through every area."[29]

The following suggestions for recording exterior and interior crime scene locations are from the *Crime Laboratory Operations Manual*:

Exterior locations:

1. Establish the location of the scene by photographs from a distance to include a landmark.
2. Take medium-distance photographs to show the relative position of closely related items of evidence.
3. Take close-up photographs of individual items of evidence.

Interior locations:

1. Establish the location of the building by photograph.
2. Photograph from eye level, rooms and other interior areas from typical observation points to show relative positions of all items within the area.
3. Take medium-distance photographs to show the relative positions of closely related items of evidence.
4. Take close-up photographs of individual items of evidence.[30]

The photographic log at Figure 6.8 aids in recording significant information.

A diversity of photographs gives a permanent, accurate perspective to a case that the limitations of memory do not permit.

> Accurate and complete photographing of the crime scene can mean the difference in a case being properly prosecuted. All forensic photography should include a scale that will provide subsequent viewers with information that will allow the photographs to be seen in perspective.[31]

Pictures taken from various angles and directions assure a comprehensive and trustworthy record.

Look at the photos of an automobile accident (see Figures 6.9 through 6.12) from several different perspectives, including wide-angle, close-up, posterior, anterior, and aerial views. Can you make any conclusions or deductions regarding the condition of the vehicle? Consider why these pictures would be important in an investigation of an auto accident case.

6.4.2 PHOTOGRAPHY AND SPECIAL APPLICATIONS

6.4.2.1 Vehicular Accidents and Related Auto Claims

Timeliness, always a pressing concern of the investigator, takes on added meaning in a case involving autos. Because of the need to get traffic moving again, officials must intrude at the scene and move evidence to prevent further accidents. The scene should be recorded promptly and accurately before removal of evidence. When photographing a vehicular accident scene, standard practice comprises pictures or notations of:

- The overall scene of the accident—from both approaches to the point of impact.
- The exact positions of the vehicles, injured persons, and objects directly connected to the accident.

PHOTOGRAPHIC LOG

Roll #: _____   Date taken: ___/___/___   Photographer: _____
Digital Camera: _____   Film Camera: _____   Color: _____   B&W: _____

Exp. #	Item and Location	Flash	Aperture
1			
2			
3			
4			
5			
6			
7			
8			
9			
10			
11			
12			
13			
14			
15			
16			
17			
18			
19			
20			
21			
22			
23			
24			
25			
26			
27			
28			
29			
30			
31			
32			
33			
34			
35			
36			

FIGURE 6.8   Sample photographic log.

FIGURE 6.9   Wide-angle aerial view.

FIGURE 6.10   Close-up view.

FIGURE 6.11   Posterior view.

FIGURE 6.12   Anterior view.

- All points of impact, marks of impact, and damage to real property.
- All pavement obstructions and defects in the roadways.
- Close-ups of damage to vehicles. One photograph should show the front and one side, and another [photograph] should show the rear and other side of the vehicle.
- Skid marks. If possible, photographs should be taken before the vehicle has been removed and again after it has been moved.
- Tire tracks, glass, and other associated debris.[32]

A visual aid or checklist will assist the investigator who is required to photograph the scene. Pictures should reflect some of the issues included within Box 6.3.[33]

BOX 6.3   GUIDELINE CHECKLIST—AUTO ACCIDENT SCENE (SOURCE: NATIONAL INSTITUTE OF JUSTICE, U.S. DEPARTMENT OF JUSTICE)

Guideline Checklist—Auto Accident Scene

A. Scene
1. Description/State of Repair of Road
2. Road/Weather/Lighting/Visibility, etc.
3. Description of Collision (abutment, other car(s), etc.)

B. Vehicles (Victim's and Others)
1. Make/Model, etc.
2. Speed (comparison with speed limit)
3. Direction Traveling
4. Safety Devices
   a. Lap Belts
   b. Shoulder Belts
   c. Other Restraints
   d. Locked Doors
   e. Cushioned Dash
   f. Pushout Windows

5. Vehicle Defects
6. Evidence of Alcohol/Drugs

C. Other Than Vehicular Collision (single vehicle, explosion, avalanche, etc.)
1. Description of Events
2. Evidence of Alcohol or Drugs

D. Victim
1. Location at Moment of Accident
   a. Driver/Passenger (seat location)
   b. Body Location (post accident)

2. Clothing (description/condition)
3. Alcohol or Drugs Present (where, form)
4. Consistency of Injuries w/Accident

E. Other
1. Possibility of Homicide
2. Possibility of Suicide

Web Exercise: Read the article at www.kansascityaccidentinjuryattorneys.com/library/kansas-city-car-accident-lawyer-tells-how-to-photograph-a-crash-scene.cfm for tips on photographing an accident scene.

An investigator whose practice is geared toward personal injury, insurance defense, or motor vehicle property damage claims, must develop photographic skills. The photographer in this area of expertise should, at a minimum, consider these questions when photographing evidence:

1. What is the extent of damage to the vehicle?
2. What is the extent of personal or bodily injury to the victim, driver, pedestrian, or other interested parties?
3. Have any parts or components of the vehicle been identified as or suspected of being defective and, if so, have they been properly photographed?
4. Has the automobile been photographed from various angles and directions?
5. Has the scene of the accident been photographed and fully identified?
6. Have injuries of victims, passengers, pedestrians, or other parties been photographed at various stages (e.g., at time of incident, during treatment, and at intervals thereafter)?

Various examples of photographic evidence pertaining to auto cases are assembled below. Answer the questions that accompany each photo. (See Figure 6.13 through 6.15.)

6.4.2.2 Bodily Injuries and Photographic Method

Depending on the time at which the pictures of bodily injuries are taken, conditions can either improve or worsen; however, injuries tend to worsen during the first two to three weeks in a bodily injury case. Fresh injuries tend to minimize the range and extent of damages. Take photographs at regular intervals in order to show bruised areas as they become more visible. In the majority of cases, a good investigator should photograph actual injuries and complement the photos with solid demonstrative evidence.

FIGURE 6.13 Overturned vehicle in high-speed collision: Can you pinpoint any evidence, within the confines of this picture, that leads to a conclusion or deduction about how the accident may have occurred?

FIGURE 6.14   Evidence of skid marks: Can deductions be made relative to the speed of the vehicle in question?

FIGURE 6.15   Vehicle from high-speed collision: Can a deduction be made regarding the degree or angle of impact?

6.4.2.3 Arson/Insurance Fraud and Photographic Evidence

Private investigators are often hired to investigate claims of insurance fraud involving the burning of the insured's vehicle or a residential or commercial structure. In the area of fire science investigation, the change is ongoing and swift and necessitates keeping up with the field's evolution. "Fires represent a rich source of material" for every investigative photographer.[34]

> When photographing the arson scene, complete coverage of the damage is important. But perhaps of even greater importance are objects or areas that are suspected to have been the point or points of initiation of fire. Close-up photographs should be made of all such objects or areas.[35]

Chapter 10 provides photographs and checklists pertaining to arson investigation.

6.4.2.4 Burglary/Criminal Trespass/Forcible Theft and Photographic Evidence

In the protection of assets, the security investigator regularly handles cases of larceny, theft, fraud, cybercrime, and burglary. Property offenses cut away at asset control and maintenance—one of the chief missions of the private security industry. In cases of burglary, which occur at corporate and industrial facilities, warehouses, and other facilities, photographic proof of illegal breaking and entering assists the prosecution in meeting this elemental burden. See Figure 6.16 for a representation of photographic proof of forced entry.

When investigating property offenses, the photographer focuses on:

- The interior and exterior of the building.
- Damaged areas, particularly those around the points of entry and exit used by the criminal.
- Close-ups of damaged containers that were the target of the burglar—safes, jewelry boxes, strong boxes, etc.
- Tool marks, both up close and from a perspective that will allow the position of the mark with respect to the general scene to be noted.[36]
- Fingerprints. Although fingerprints are of major interest to all types of investigations, they are of particular value in a burglary investigation. Fingerprints are photographed only when they are visible without development and when they cannot be lifted after they have been developed.[37]

FIGURE 6.16 A case of burglary—points of forced entry: Can you identify points or evidence of forced entry?

6.4.2.5 Drug and Alcohol Abuse and Photographic Evidence

The war against drugs has resulted in a significant increase in the use of security forces and enterprises especially in regard to employees at major companies and industries. The legal, personal, and societal problems created by substance abuse are now mind-boggling and have impacted every corner of the American experience.[38] As the American Society for Industrial Security (ASIS) reminds its membership:

> In today's society, alcohol and drug abuse constitute tremendous threats to the safety and security of any organization. Drug-addicted or alcoholic employees can increase the number of workplace accidents and thefts. Employers should screen applicants to keep individuals with untreated addictive or criminal tendencies from entering the company workforce. Companies can face serious liability if substance-dependent employees are untreated. Severe losses, injuries, or even death can result.[39]

No segment of society is immune to the pressing problems associated with drug and alcohol abuse. These problems cost industry millions of dollars each year in lost work hours, accidents, and theft. For the sake of safety and job performance alone, management must form clear policies stating that no one under the influence of alcohol or illegal drugs will be permitted to work. The company must also decide whether violators will be rehabilitated or discharged. The likely spread of these habits from one employee to another is an insidious side effect.

American corporations are relying heavily upon the expertise of private security, not just from the perspective of identifying prospective employees' habits, but also monitoring their employees using substances in the workplace. Surveillance photography is an effective means of gathering evidence in order to prosecute a drug case. See Box 6.4[40] for an all-encompassing list of the required information.

BOX 6.4 GUIDELINE CHECKLIST—POSSIBLE DRUG OVERDOSE SCENE (SOURCE: NATIONAL INSTITUTE OF JUSTICE, U.S. DEPARTMENT OF JUSTICE)

Guideline Checklist–Drug Overdose

A. Report
1. Date/Time/Reporting Means
2. Who Reported/Relationship to Victim
3. Time Delay between Crime and Report
4. Reported Circumstances of Crime

B. Scene
1. Description/Condition/Relationship to Victim (home, etc.)
2. Location of Medicine, Drugs, Alcohol, and Containers
3. Location of Paint, Glue, Solvents, and Containers
4. Location of Paraphernalia
5. Location of Soot or Pill Residue/Blood Tinged Swabs or Tissue
6. Suicide Note
7. Evidence of Struggle/Illness, etc.

C. Medicine/Drugs/Alcohol (product and container)
1. Medicine Prescribed for Victim
   a. Type/Amount Prescribed/Amount on Hand

       b. Location (table, floor, bathroom, etc.)
       c. Victim's History of Normal Ingestion
       d. Same Medication Prescribed by More Than One M.D.
       e. "Stockpiling"
       f. Recent Use Indicators
       g. Evidence of Accidental Ingestion

  2. Medication Prescribed to Another Person
       a. Type/to Whom Prescribed/Relationship to Victim
       b. Location
       c. Amount Prescribed/Amount on Hand
       d. Same Medication Prescribed by More Than One M.D.
       e. "Stockpiling" Another Person's Medications
       f. Recent Use of Another Person's Medication
       g. Evidence of Accidental Ingestion

  3. Illicit Drugs and Narcotics/Alcohol/Paint, Glue, Solvent
       a. Types/Quantities/Form (powder, pill, etc.)
       b. Evidence of Use or Accidental Ingestion

D. Paraphernalia
1. Smoking
2. Drinking
3. Injecting
4. Ingesting
5. Inhaling

E. Residue (soot, powder, etc.)
1. Types
2. Quantity

F. Victim
1. Clothing Condition/Appropriateness/Contents
2. Tattoos, Rings, Pins, etc. (suggesting drug cult)
3. Needle Injection Sites (old and new)
4. Paraphernalia Still on/in Body
5. Pills and Capsules in Hands or Mouth/on Face
6. Soot or Pill/Capsule Residue on Body
7. Drug History
8. Rigor and Liver Mortis Consistent with Body Location and Position
9. Resuscitation Efforts (when/kind/by whom)
10. Hospital/Emergency Room/M.D. Administered Drugs (when/type/quantity/means)

Web Exercise: Find out about professional photographer organizations that are certified in matters of crime scene and the investigative process. Visit the following websites to explore their certifications:

The International Association for Identification (IAI) has a Certified Forensic Photographer (CFPH) (www.theiai.org/certifications/imaging/index.php). Evidence Photographers International Council (EPIC) (www.evidencephotographers.com/).

6.5 INVESTIGATIVE TECHNIQUE: DOCUMENTARY EVIDENCE

Proficient investigators know the ins and outs of collecting information and documents and reports. Invariably, extensive time is spent collecting documents and creating standard correspondence files. Be creative; think hard about those persons who can provide leads and other matters of evidentiary value.

6.5.1 POLICE RECORDS

Police regularly complain that the majority of the time expended in their job relates primarily to paperwork and secondarily to social work. Investigators will quickly discern the magnitude of documentation. Discovery of police documentation, from field notes to a final report, should be of professional interest to an investigator working on a particular case. Investigators fill out many standardized forms and documents during the typical criminal or civil case. Some more frequently seen examples follow.

6.5.1.1 Alcohol or Chemical Reports

There has been an increased emphasis on the defense and prosecution of driving while intoxicated or driving under the influence cases. Forms or documentation relative to states of intoxication are helpful. One such form, Psycho-Physiological Test Results (see Figure 6.17), measures a person's ability to do specific functions such as walking, placing a finger to the nose, bending, and standing erect. Another is an Alcohol Influence Report at Figure 6.18[41] which reports breathalyzer results measuring alcohol vapor in the respiratory system.

6.5.1.2 Accident Reports

Police accident reports are relied upon heavily because they are fresh impressions of liability. Usually at the scene of an accident before any other party, police will transcribe the facts; however, they also may make judgments regarding conduct probative of either civil or criminal liability. Police reports are thoroughly examined in other portions of this text.

6.5.1.3 Domestic Relations Documentation

In the area of domestic relations, police departments expend considerable resources protecting spouses and children from abuse. More and more police departments are being expected to file and keep paperwork regarding these matters, and public outcry increases when police do not take an activist role in these matters. A Domestic Violence Offense Report typically is filled out by a police agency. This type of document is quite effective in corroborating or supporting any claim for abuse as grounds for divorce or may serve as evidence in custody or visitation contests.

6.5.1.4 Radio Logs

Another example of police documentation is the Radio Log document. Recent 911 controversies alleging a slower than usual response time emphasize the crucial nature of radio logs.

6.5.1.5 Arrest Reports—Narcotics

Another form regularly used is an Arrest Report for a Narcotics Division. With the plague of drugs affecting our entire society, police departments have set up narcotics units whose individuals are solely dedicated to the investigation and prosecution of narcotics matters.

6.5.1.6 Violence in the Workplace

An unfortunate reality for commercial entities is the increase in violence in the workplace. The costs of violence are reason enough to adopt documentation policies. There are various reasons:

Psycho-Physiological Test Results

CD#   Subject
Date

1. Walking Heel-to-Toe
7 steps forward, turn to right/left, 4 steps back

_____ Staggering   _____ Performed correctly
_____ Unable to perform   _____ Falling off balance
_____ Other   _____ Did not follow instructions
                                         _____ Off white line

2. Finger to nose
Right hand _____ times

                                         _____ Missed nose ____ times
                                         _____ Touched nose _____ times
                                         _____ Did not follow instructions
                                         _____ Performed correctly
Left hand _____ times   _____ Missed nose ____ times
                                         _____ Touched nose _____ times
                                         _____ Did not follow instructions
                                         _____ Performed correctly

3. Bending forward
Eyes closed, feet together, tuck in chin, bend for 30 seconds

_____ falling   _____ Swaying side to side
_____ other   _____ Swaying front to back
                                         _____ Little/no motion
                                         _____ Did not follow instructions

4. Standing Erect
Eyes closed, feet together, arms alongside

_____ Falling   _____ Swaying side to side
_____ Other   _____ Swaying front to back
                                         _____ Little/no motion
                                         _____ Did not follow instructions

5. Alphabet
Ask subject to recite the alphabet

_____ Yes   _____ Recited correctly
_____ No   _____ Unable to recite correctly

6. Counting
Ask subject to count to ten

_____ Yes   _____ Forward 1-10
                                         _____ Able to perform correctly
                                         _____ Missed numbers
_____ no   _____ backwards 1-10
                                         _____ Able to perform correctly
                                         _____ Missed numbers

Other optional tests: Explain test and note observations

Officer's Signature   _____

FIGURE 6.17   An example of a Psycho-Physiological Test Results form.

type name of police department here   - ALCOHOL INFLUENCE REPORT FORM

Defendant (First name) (Initial) (Last name)	Case Number	Sequential File No.
Age	Sex	Weight	Eyes	Arrested by	

CHEMICAL BREATH TEST INFORMATION

Instrument: Breathalyzer, Model 900 [ ]   Breathalyzer, Model 900A [ ]   Dominator Albreath [ ]

	Instrument Serial Number	Ampoule Control Lot Number	Purge % Results	Samples Taken Date / Time	Blood Alcohol % Results
Test #1					
Test #2					
Test #3					
Test #4					

BREATHALYZER CHECK LIST - *N.J.A.C.* 13:51-3.6(a)2

Mark all applicable boxes with an "X" or a check mark.

Set Up Phase   [ ]   Verify Power switch is turned "On". If the power switch is in the "Off" position, turn the switch "On".

TESTS
#1   #2   #3   #4   **Preparation Phase**

#1	#2	#3	#4		
[]	[]	[]	[]	1.	Instrument temperature: Verified temperature, thermometer reached 50°C, plus or minus 3°C.
[]	N/A*	N/A*	N/A*	2.	Reference Ampoule: Gauged; Inserted in left hand holder.
[]	[]	[]	[]	3.	Test Ampoule: Gauged; Opened; Verified volume; Inserted in right hand holder.
[]	[]	[]	[]	4.	Bubbler: Inserted into test ampoule; Connected to outlet.
[]	[]	[]	[]	5.	Light turned on; Instrument balanced, Blood Alcohol Pointer set on Start Line.

Purge Phase

[]	[]	[]	[]	6.	Turned control knob to the "Take" position; Flushed; Turned control knob to the "Analyze" position.
[]	[]	[]	[]	7.	Purge: When red empty signal appeared, waited 90 seconds; Light turned on; Instrument balanced.
[]	[]	[]	[]	8.	Purge Result Recorded.
[]	[]	[]	[]	9.	Blood Alcohol Pointer set on Start Line.

Analysis Phase

[]	[]	[]	[]	10.	New mouthpiece inserted in breath tube.
[]	[]	[]	[]	11.	Take Breath Sample: Turned control knob to the "Take" position; Took breath sample from defendant; Turned control knob to the "Analyze" position.
[]	[]	[]	[]	12.	Date & Time Recorded.
[]	[]	[]	[]	13.	When red empty signal appeared, waited 90 seconds; Light turned on; Instrument balanced.
[]	[]	[]	[]	14.	Breath Test Result Recorded.

Second or subsequent breath tests

[]	[]	[]	[]	15.	Test ampoule removed; properly disposed. Power switch remained "On'. Return to Step 1, start next breath test.

*Steps marked with an "N/A" are only performed on the first breath test, and do not have to be repeated on any subsequent breath tests.

Breath Test Operator   Copy Given to Subject

Rank	Signature	Badge #	Date	Time

FIGURE 6.18   An example of an Alcohol Influence Report form.

- Businesses are beginning to realize the high costs of just one violent incident. These costs can include medical and psychiatric care as well as potential liability suits, lost business and productivity, repairs and clean-up, higher insurance rates, consultants' fees, increased security measures and—most important of all—the death or injury of valued employees and coworkers.
- Threats and other violent, abusive behaviors are no longer tolerated in the workplace.

- Executives, professionals, and administrative personnel are no longer immune to acts of violence in the workplace.
- Layoffs, increased workload, having to do more with less, and other unpopular changes in the work environment have been associated with increased risk for violence.
- Recent reports and surveys suggest that workplace violence impacts large numbers of employers and employees.
- It's the right thing to do. Employers have both a moral and a legal obligation to provide a safe workplace for their employees, clients, and visitors.[42]

If violence occurs prepare a threat report like that in Box 6.5.

BOX 6.5   AN EXAMPLE OF A THREAT REPORT

Threat Report

Name of person(s) making threat _____

Relationship to company _____

Relationship to recipient of threat, if any _____

Name(s) of the recipients or victims _____

_____

Date and location of incident _____

What happened immediately prior to the incident _____

_____

_____

_____

The specific language of the threat _____

_____

_____

Any physical conduct that would substantiate an intention to follow through with the threat _____

_____

How the threat-maker appeared, both physically and emotionally _____

_____

_____

Names of others who were directly involved, and any actions they took _____

_____

_____

_____

How the incident ended _____

_____

_____

Names of witnesses _____

_____

_____

What happened to the threat-maker after the incident _____

_____

_____

What happened to other employees directly involved in the incident, if any _____

_____

Names of any supervisory staff involved and how they responded _____

_____

What event(s) triggered the incident _____

Any history leading up to the incident _____

The steps that have been taken to assure the threat will not be carried out _____

_____

Suggestions for preventing this type of incident from occurring again _____

_____

_____

Web Exercise: Read the Guide to Conducting Workplace Investigations at www.corporatecompliance.org/Portals/1/Users/169/29/60329/Workplace_Investigations_Guide.pdf.

6.5.1.7 Missing Person Reports

A "Missing Person" report is useful to investigators working on cases of insurance fraud, escape from prison, violation of probation and parole, change of identity, or other forms of subterfuge.[43]

Web Exercise: For a sample missing person report, look over the Missing Person Report of the State of California's Department of Justice, here: http://lib.post.ca.gov/Publications/Missing_Persons_Forms/mp_report.pdf.

6.5.1.8 Disposition Sheets

In final record keeping, the police department maintains a Disposition Sheet, which confirms the arrest and selected charges.

Web Exercise: Go to this web link for various examples of disposition documents:[44]

www.illinoislegalaid.org/sites/default/files/legal_content/file_form_content/Worksheet%20for%20criminal%20records%20expungement%20and%20sealing.pdf.

6.5.1.9 Suspect Descriptions

Two forms of suspect descriptions are outlined below. Abbreviated suspect descriptions can prove helpful during the initial investigation (see Figure 6.19), but the suspect description form at Box 6.6 is much more comprehensive and will result in more accurate information.

BOX 6.6   AN EXAMPLE OF A COMPREHENSIVE SUSPECT DESCRIPTION FORM

Details Description

1. SEX (Male, Female)
2. RACE (Caucasian, African American, Native American, Pacific Islander, Asian, etc.)
3. AGE _____
4. HEIGHT (Compare with person with whom you work) _____ ft. _____ in.
5. WEIGHT (Compare with person with whom you work)   lbs.
6. PROBABLE NATIONALITY (American, English, Latin, Scandinavian, Japanese, etc.)
7. BUILD (slender, medium, heavy, stocky, athletic, very heavy, very thin, etc.)
8. POSTURE (erect, stooped, slumped, etc.)
9. COMPLEXION (fair, dark, red, tanned, pale, freckly, pimply, rough, smooth, etc.)
10. HEAD (large, medium, small, round, square, oblong, broad, inclined forward, backward, sideways)
11. HAIR (color _____; color at temples _____; baldness: frontal, top, receding at hairline, totally bald; texture: thick, thin, coarse, straight, wavy, kinky, curled, bushy; parted on right, left, middle, no part)
12. EYES (brown, blue, green, grey, hazel; clear, bloodshot; large, small, deep-set, protruding, straight, slanted, cross-eyed, narrow, squinting, close-set, wide apart; eyelashes: long, short; glass eye. If glasses worn: type, color of rims, etc.)
13. FOREHEAD (broad, narrow, high, low, receding, vertical, bulging)
14. EYEBROWS (thin, bushy, penciled, natural, arched, horizontal, slanting up or down, meeting)
15. NOSE (long, medium, short; thin, thick, straight, concave, convex, pointed, flat, turned up, turned down, pointed to right or left; nostrils: large, small, high, low, flared)
16. MUSTACHE OR BEARD (short, medium, long, pointed, ends turned up or down; thick, thin; type of beard or sideburns). Compare with color of hair
17. CHEEKS (full, fleshy, sunken, etc.)
18. CHEEKBONES (high, low, prominent, not prominent)
19. MOUTH (turned up or down at corners, held open or closed, distorted by speech or laughter)
20. LIPS (with reference to either upper or lower: thick, thin, puffy, overhanging, compressed, protruding, retracted over teeth; cracked, scarred; red, pale, blue)
21. TEETH (white, yellow, stained, loose, decayed, broken, filled, braced, capped, receding or projecting, false, prominent bridgework, etc.)
22. CHIN (small, large, normal, square, curved, pointed, flat, double, dimpled, protruding, receding, etc.)
23. JAW (long, short, wide, narrow, thin, fleshy, square, heavy, etc.)
24. EARS (small, medium, large, close to or projecting from head; oval, round, rectangular, triangular; pierced, cauliflowered, hairy; contour of the lobe, lower portion)
25. NECK (small, medium, long, straight, curved, thin, flat, goiterous, crooked; Adams' apple: flat, prominent, medium, absent)

26. SHOULDERS (small, heavy, narrow, broad, square, round, stooped, not equal, etc.)
27. HANDS (long, short, broad, narrow, thin, fleshy, rough, bony, soft, smooth, hairy, square, tapered, etc.)
28. FINGERS (short, long, slim, thick, tapered, square, stained, mutilated, etc.)
29. FINGERNAILS (length, description, foreign matter under nails; painted)
30. VOICE (pleasant, well-modulated, low, high, lisp or other impediment of speech, gruff, polite, regional or foreign accent)
    REMEMBER EXACT LANGUAGE USED _____
    _____
    _____
    _____

31. WALK (long or short stride, energetic, slow, fast, springy step, limp)
32. APPEARANCE (loud, conservative, neat, sloppy)
33. CLOTHING: (list color, pattern, type, material, condition, how worn)
    Hat or cap _____
    Overcoat _____
    Pants
    Suit _____
    Dress _____
    Shirt _____
    Tie _____
    Shoes _____
    Socks _____
    Belt _____
    Mask _____

34. JEWELRY (rings, watches, chains, earrings, tie pins, lapel pins, bracelets, cuff links, etc.)
    Describe _____
    _____

35. PECULIARITIES (most important of all) (scars, marks, tattoos, moles, birthmarks)
    Describe _____
    _____

36. TYPE OF WEAPON USED:

                     Name _____
                     Address _____
                     _____
                     Date _____

Describe the Suspect.

The primary or most useful information to obtain when describing a suspect is:

Sex _____ Race _____ Age _____ Height _____ Weight _____

If a weapon is used it is very helpful to know if the weapon is a:

☐ Revolver

☐ Automatic

Other useful information is:

_____
Hair

_____
Color of eyes

_____
Glasses

_____
Moustache/Beard, Sideburns

_____
Complexion

_____
Tattoos, Amputations, Scars, or Marks

_____
Speech impediments or accents

_____
Distinguishable gait or limp

_____
Hat

_____
Shirt

_____
Coat

_____
Tie

_____
Pants and Shoes

FIGURE 6.19　An example suspect description form.

Vehicle Description.

The primary or most useful information to obtain when identifying a motor vehicle is the *license number*, **with state of issue or identifying colors.** _____
Other useful information is:

_____ _____ _____
What make?   Body Style? (2 dr., 4 dr., conv., etc.)   What year?

_____   _____
What color? Two color (two tone)?   Identifying dents, scratches?

The police can use answers to as many of these questions as possible. Please remember that wrong information is worse than no information at all. Answer only those questions that you're sure of.

1. How many suspects were there? _____
2. What did they do? _____
   _____
   _____
3. What did they say? _____
   _____
   _____
4. What did they take? _____
   _____
   _____

5. Which way did they go?_____
   _____
   _____

6. Were there any other witnesses? _____
   Names and addresses? _____
   _____
   _____
   Phone numbers? _____
   _____

7. Is there any other information you feel is important? _____
   _____
   _____
   _____

FIGURE 6.19 (CONTINUED)

6.6 INVESTIGATIVE TECHNIQUE: MEDICAL RECORDS

Standard medical records are indispensable in the investigation of any medical, personal injury, or related claim. Medical releases authorizing the transferral of information from a hospital, physician, consultant, emergency room, or employer should be signed. A general medical release, granted by the client, is at Box 6.7.

BOX 6.7   AN EXAMPLE OF A MEDICAL RELEASE FORM

MEDICAL RELEASE

You are hereby authorized to release to the investigator any and all information, without limitation, that you possess. This release includes, but is not limited to, billing information, admission records, X-ray reports, lab reports, nurses' notes, progress reports, and discharge summaries.

This authorization shall not expire until expressly canceled. A copy of this release shall be as effective as an original.

NAME OF CLIENT

Name: _____

Dated: _____

Signature: _____

Being attentive to privacy considerations and the emerging or existing legislation that guides the personal integrity of medical records is an ongoing security concern. The Health Insurance Portability and Accountability Act of 1996 (HIPAA), Public Law 104-191, was enacted on August 21, 1996. Sections 261 through 264 of HIPAA require the Secretary of the U.S. Department of Health &Human Services to publicize standards for the electronic exchange, privacy, and security of health information. Collectively these are known as the Administrative Simplification provisions.[45] HIPAA principles surely apply unless consent and waiver is secured.[46] See Box 6.8.

BOX 6.8   SAMPLE HIPAA AUTHORIZATION FORM

SAMPLE HIPAA AUTHORIZATION FORM

I, _____ , give permission to [Name of Institution] to:
☐ use the following protected health information, and/or
☐ disclose the following protected health information to:

_____

_____

[Name(s) of entity to receive information]

Information to be disclosed (check all that apply):
☐ Medical Records
☐ Treatment Records _____
☐ Diagnostic Records
☐ Other: _____

_____

_____

This protected health information is being used or disclosed for the following purposes:

_____

_____

_____

This authorization expires [specify (1) date or (2) event that relates to the purpose of this use or disclosure].

If the person or entity receiving this information is not a health care provider or health plan covered by federal privacy regulations, the information described above may be disclosed to other individuals or institutions and no longer protected by these regulations.

You may refuse to sign this authorization. Your refusal to sign will not affect your ability to obtain treatment or payment or your eligibility for benefits.

You may inspect or copy the protected health information to be used or disclosed under this authorization. For protected health information created as part of a clinical trial, your right to access is suspended until the clinical trial is completed.

Finally, you may revoke this authorization in writing at any time by sending written notification to [Name of Privacy contact] at [office address]. Your notice will not apply to actions taken by the requesting person/entity prior to the date they receive your written request to revoke authorization.

Signature of Participant or Personal Representative

Date

Printed Name of Participant or Personal Representative

Description of Personal Representative's Authority

Medical records prompt a host of ethical and practical dilemmas. The Electronic Privacy Information Center warns not only consumers but the investigators:

Besides information about physical health, these records may include information about family relationships, sexual behavior, substance abuse, and even the private thoughts and feelings that come with psychotherapy. This information is often keyed to a social security number. Because of a lack of consistent privacy protection in the use of Social Security Numbers, the information may be easily accessible.

Information from your medical records may influence your credit, admission to educational institutions, and employment. It may also affect your ability to get health insurance, or the rates you pay for coverage. More importantly, having others know intimate details about your life may mean a loss of dignity and autonomy.[47]

Efforts to federally control access to medical records are often seen as legislative initiatives.

A policy statement or draft laying out the several parameters of information disclosure, release, and protection is an essential security function. Every office entrusted with the protection of records should implement a policy similar to Box 6.9.

BOX 6.9   A STANDARD INFORMATION SECURITY POLICY

INFORMATION SECURITY POLICY

1) Purpose
   To provide guidelines for ensuring that only authorized persons have appropriate access to computerized information, while safeguarding the information's confidentiality, security and integrity.
2) Policy
   a) *Definitions*

i)   Security
Protection of information resources from unauthorized change, destruction, or disclosure, whether intentional or accidental.

ii) Information Resources
These include, but are not limited to: hardware, software, storage media, computer sign-on codes, and information transmitted, stored, printed, and/or processed by a computer system.

iii) Confidential Information
Information that requires special safeguards due to its private nature, including: patient care and treatment information, including patient's identity and diagnosis; and, personnel information regarding salaries, benefits, performance reviews and disciplinary action.

b) *Development and support of information security process*
   1. The Hospital will implement processes to ensure sufficient security and confidentiality for its information.
   2. The Hospital will address security issues during the purchase and implementation of new information systems.
   3. Management staff in each department will develop and maintain information security policies specific to their department, if appropriate, which are consistent with this policy.
   4. The orientation program for new employees will address the Hospital's information security policies. At the time of orientation, each new employee will sign a confidentiality agreement that summarizes the Hospital's information security policies and the individual's responsibilities regarding these policies. This agreement will be filed in the employee's records in the Personnel Department.
   5. Management staff in each department will inform their staff of institutional and departmental information security policies. Management will ensure that these policies are addressed at departmental staff meetings annually.

c) *Authorization to access information resources*
   1. Only persons who have valid business reasons for accessing the Hospital's information resources will be granted access. Individuals will be given access to information resources in keeping with their job requirements.
   2. No one may access the Hospital's information resources or applications without prior written authorization and approval. It is illegal to use a Hospital computer or access information stored or maintained by the Hospital without the Hospital's consent.
   3. All passwords to the Hospital's computer systems are confidential and are the property of the Hospital. These include, but are not limited to, passwords to network systems, mainframe systems, PCs, voice mail, and long distance telephone codes.

d) *Computer equipment security*
   1. Terminals, network devices, and personal computers in unsecured areas will be secured against theft and use by unauthorized persons.
   2. Personal computers in unsecured areas will be set up to use power-on passwords and keyboard passwords, to prevent unauthorized persons from using the device without providing the appropriate password.

3. Anyone who signs on to a computer system must sign off and/or physically secure the terminal or PC when leaving it unattended.
4. Where possible, computer systems will be set up to automatically sign off or password-protect terminals and PCs after a specified period of inactivity.
5. Access to data centers will be secured by means of locked entryways, Only persons authorized to operate or maintain the computer systems will be issued keys, passcards, or other means for unlocking the entryway. Authorized visitors to the Data Center will be escorted by authorized staff.

e) *Security of computer-related media*
1. Printed reports containing confidential or sensitive information will be stored in a secure area, inaccessible to unauthorized persons. Confidential reports will be rendered unreadable before being discarded.
2. CDs, hard drives, flash drives, and other media containing confidential information will be labeled "confidential" and will be protected appropriately.
3. CDs, hard drives, flash drives and other media containing computer files will be stored in areas accessible only to authorized persons.

f) *Protection of computerized files*
1. Departments and individuals must establish regular schedules for making backup copies of data files stored on personal computers, network file servers, and other computer systems.
2. Backup copies will be stored in a safe location (not exposed to heat or magnetic fields). Backup copies for network file servers and mainframe computer systems will not be stored in the same room as the servers or data storage devices.
3. Virus protection programs will be installed and executed regularly on each PC and computer system.
4. Software will not be copied from public access bulletin boards or other non-Hospital computer systems without first being scanned by a virus protection program.

g) *Dial-up access to information sources*
1. Authorized employees, physicians, and other authorized parties will be permitted to use telephone lines to access Hospital information resources, with proper safeguards.
2. All dial-up connections to Hospital computer systems will be routed through devices that provide for password verification, call-back security, or other similar features.
3. Modems or personal computers that do not have dial-up access security features will not be connected to direct-inward-dial telephone lines.

h) *Violations of Information Security Policy*
i) Failure to comply with these information security policies and procedures may result in disciplinary action, termination of access privileges to Hospital information systems, and civil or criminal actions, at the discretion of Hospital management.
ii) Management staff in each department will monitor and counsel their staff in matters of information security.

3. *Procedure*
a) *Security administration*

      i)   A system security administrator will be designated for each network system and each mainframe application.

          (1)   System security administrators will be responsible for issuing sign-on codes for the system(s) for which they are responsible. System security administrators are responsible for ensuring that all persons who receive sign-on codes have proper authorization to access the system.

          (2)   The Information Systems Department will maintain a list of all designated system security administrators and their backups.

b)   *Obtaining authorization to access information resources*

      i)   Requests for access to the Hospital's information resources must be submitted in writing to the appropriate system security administrator.

      ii)   Requests for access to information sources must be approved by the appropriate Hospital management.

      iii)   All persons who request access to computer systems will be required to sign a Confidentiality Agreement that summarizes the Hospital's information security policies and the individual's responsibilities regarding these policies.

c)   *Issuance of computer sign-on codes*

      i)   Each person authorized to access a Hospital computer system will be issued a unique, individual identification code and password. The person must supply this identification immediately after initial contact with the computer, or further access will be denied.

      ii)   Each authorized user is responsible for changing his or her password periodically (at least every 90 days) on systems where this can be done.

Requesting hospital records from emergency rooms, consultants, or other medical professionals working for hospitals is standard investigative practice. See a client authorization request for hospital records at Box 6.10.

**BOX 6.10   A TYPICAL CLIENT AUTHORIZATION
REQUEST FOR HOSPITAL RECORDS**

Date:

To:

RE:

Our File No.:

Dear _____:

I have retained this firm to represent me in injuries sustained as a result of an accident that occurred on _____. Please send to this firm's address the medical records for this accident as well as a complete billing summary for services rendered to date. Please bill _____ for this report.

Sincerely,

_____

Patient Account #: _____

Another example of a medical information request document that complements an investigative file is a request for a copy of an office record. In this case, the correspondence is usually directed to the treating physician's clerk or other paraprofessional who handles records. This should not be confused with a direct request for a medical evaluation or report, which is usually in the form of a standardized document such as a tabulated bill. See Box 6.11.

BOX 6.11 A REQUEST LETTER FOR A COPY OR COPY OF OFFICE MEDICAL RECORDS

Date:

Name:
Address:

IN RE: Request for Copy of Office Record
     Name of Patient:
     Date of Injury:

Dear Dr. _____:

Please be advised that I am an investigator in the above-referenced case and have been given full power of attorney to seek information and records. Attached is a copy of the power of attorney. I am writing at this time to request a copy of the medical record that has been prepared by your office for this patient. Please send me a copy of this record as soon as possible.

I have enclosed a copy of a medical release which authorizes me to acquire this information. If there is any charge for copying or printing the requested material, please send a statement together with the requested information.

Sincerely,

Name of Investigator

Enclosure

Access requests for every type of record, whether admission and discharge records, emergency room records, X-ray reports, medical expense records, billing statements, payroll information, life squad reports, death certificates, etc., follow a similar format.

6.7 INVESTIGATIVE TECHNIQUE: RECORDS INVOLVING ECONOMIC DAMAGES

Customarily, investigators involved in cases of workers; compensation, disability, social security, or personal injury collect not only evidence of actual medical injuries, but also records concerning economic losses. Economic losses can take many forms, from losing the value of certain property to the loss of past, present, and future earnings capacity. Because of these factors, the investigator needs to gain access to employment and payroll records.

An example of an authorization and request for employment records, at Figure 6.20, inquires about the client's payroll history, as well as the period of employment and the extent of weekly and overtime pay.

Often, employers compile and maintain records dealing with medical benefits because of a medical insurance, workers' compensation, or disability plan. A release or authorization for this information directed to the employer is at Box 6.12.

Authorization and Request for Employment Records

To: _____   Re: _____
                                            Name of Employee

_____   _____
                                            Address

_____   _____

_____   _____

                                     S.S#: _____

You are hereby requested and authorized to furnish to my Attorney whose name and address is:

or my attorney's authorized representative, any information you may have regarding my past or present employment. Please provide copies of any records along with any other requested information. I would appreciate your full cooperation.

Dated:_____   _____
                                                          Employee

Additional Remarks: _____

_____

_____

_____

_____

_____

_____

Dated:_____   _____
                                                            Title

FIGURE 6.20   An authorization and request for employment records form.

BOX 6.12   A STANDARD MEDICAL BENEFIT RELEASE FORM

MEDICAL BENEFIT RELEASE FORM

This employee's records release authorizes you to furnish to the investigator named any record, information, or knowledge which is in your possession. This release includes, but is not limited to, information concerning my rates of pay, sick records, overtime records, vacation records, personnel records, injury and health records, tax and social security records, and insurance benefits records. The release shall remain valid until it is expressly canceled. A copy of this release shall be as effective as an original.

Name: NAME-OF-CLIENT

Social Security Number: _____

Date of Birth: _____

Name of Investigator: _____

Dated: _____   Signature _____

A wage release authorization is at Box 6.13

BOX 6.13   A TYPICAL WAGE RELEASE AUTHORIZATION

WAGE RELEASE

This wage release authorizes you to furnish to the investigator named any record or information that you possess concerning my wage and earning records. This release includes, but is not limited to, information concerning my rate of pay, number of hours worked, gross pay, net pay, or weekly check amounts.

This release shall remain valid until it is expressly canceled. A copy of this release shall be as effective as an original.

Name: NAME-OF-CLIENT

Social Security Number: _____

Date of Birth: _____

Name of Investigator: _____

Dated: _____ Signature _____

Information regarding the returns can be secured by IRS Tax Information Authorization Form 8821; an example of this form is at Figure 6.21.

6.8   INVESTIGATIVE TECHNIQUE: PRESERVATION OF EVIDENCE

Preservation of evidence and the assurance of its integrity during the investigative process are undeniable responsibilities of the public and private police system. Investigators are continually concerned with whether or not the chain of custody of the evidence has been distorted, broken, contaminated, abused, reformulated, recast, or changed in any significant way. Competent investigators need to devise a systematic approach—a "quality assurance system"[48] that insures evidentiary integrity. Evidence such as tools, guns, glass fragments, hairs, fibers, body parts—any real, physical evidence—should be stored in an environment that maintains, as scientifically as possible, its original status.[49]

> The investigator himself should bear in mind the possibility that he himself may destroy or contaminate evidence before it is noticed or recognized. Minute spurts of blood, particles of dust, dirt, and debris are not always obvious to the naked eye and can be destroyed or rendered worthless as evidence if the investigator is not sufficiently observant during his investigation. Defense counsel should recognize the possibility or probability of contamination having occurred and conduct his cross-examination accordingly.[50]

The entire concept of chain of custody governs the conduct and tactics of an investigator:

> Chain of custody is the description of the identification and control of evidence from the time it is collected at the scene until it is entered into evidence in court. The legal "chain of custody" must be maintained at all times.[51]

The Pennsylvania State Police, in its *Crime Laboratory Operations Manual*, offers timeless advice on the preservation of evidence.

Form **8821**

(Rev. January 2018)

Department of the Treasury
Internal Revenue Service

Tax Information Authorization

▶ Go to *www.irs.gov/Form8821* for instructions and the latest information.

▶ **Don't sign this form unless all applicable lines have been completed.**

▶ **Don't use Form 8821 to request copies of your tax returns**
or to authorize someone to represent you.

OMB No. 1545-1165

For IRS Use Only

Received by:

Name _____

Telephone _____

Function _____

Date

---

1   Taxpayer information. Taxpayer must sign and date this form on line 7.

Taxpayer name and address	Taxpayer identification number(s)
	Daytime telephone number Plan number (if applicable)

---

2   Appointee. If you wish to name more than one appointee, attach a list to this form. **Check here if a list of additional appointees is attached** ▶ ☐

Name and address	CAF No. _____
	PTIN _____
	Telephone No. _____
	Fax No. _____
	Check if new: Address ☐ Telephone No. ☐ Fax No. ☐

---

3   Tax Information. Appointee is authorized to inspect and/or receive confidential tax information for the type of tax, forms, periods, and specific matters you list below. See the line 3 instructions.

☐ By checking here, I authorize access to my IRS records via an Intermediate Service Provider.

(a) Type of Tax Information (Income, Employment, Payroll, Excise, Estate, Gift, Civil Penalty, Sec. 4980H Payments, etc.)	(b) Tax Form Number (1040, 941, 720, etc.)	(c) Year(s) or Period(s)	(d) Specific Tax Matters

---

4   Specific use not recorded on Centralized Authorization File (CAF). If the tax information authorization is for a specific use not recorded on CAF, check this box. See the instructions. If you check this box, skip lines 5 and 6 . . . . ▶ ☐

5   Disclosure of tax information (you **must** check a box on line 5a or 5b unless the box on line 4 is checked):

a If you want copies of tax information, notices, and other written communications sent to the appointee on an ongoing basis, check this box . . . . ▶ ☐

Note. Appointees will no longer receive forms, publications, and other related materials with the notices.

b If you don't want any copies of notices or communications sent to your appointee, check this box . . . . ▶ ☐

---

6   Retention/revocation of prior tax information authorizations. If the line 4 box is checked, skip this line. If the line 4 box isn't checked, the IRS will automatically revoke all prior Tax Information Authorizations on file unless you check the line 6 box and attach a copy of the Tax Information Authorization(s) that you want to retain. . . . . ▶ ☐

To revoke a prior tax information authorization(s) without submitting a new authorization, see the line 6 instructions.

---

7   Signature of taxpayer. If signed by a corporate officer, partner, guardian, partnership representative, executor, receiver, administrator, trustee, or party other than the taxpayer, I certify that I have the authority to execute this form with respect to the tax matters and tax periods shown on line 3 above.

▶**IF NOT COMPLETE, SIGNED, AND DATED, THIS TAX INFORMATION AUTHORIZATION WILL BE RETURNED.**

▶**DON'T SIGN THIS FORM IF IT IS BLANK OR INCOMPLETE.**

Signature	Date
Print Name	Title (if applicable)

For Privacy Act and Paperwork Reduction Act Notice, see instructions.   Cat. No. 11596P   Form **8821** (Rev. 1-2018)

FIGURE 6.21   The IRS Tax Information Authorization Form 8821.

Each item of evidence should be placed in a suitable container, and this container should be properly identified and sealed. The laboratory can only aid in the investigation if evidence has been preserved ... As a general rule, to guarantee the value of the evidence collected, evidence should be packaged to:

1. Prevent loss: Package all evidence in such a manner that small items will not be lost from the container or in the seams or folds of a container. Envelopes are poor containers for small items such as paint chips, since they can leak out at the corners or become lodged in the folds and be difficult to remove without loss or damage. Pill boxes or plastic vials should be used for this type of evidence.
2. Prevent contamination: Separate items so that there is no mixing of items from various locations. NEVER place items from the scene and from the suspect in the same container. Each article of clothing from a victim or suspect of a crime should also be individually packaged and identified so that no trace evidence is transferred from one item to the next.
3. Prevent alteration: Handle and package the evidence in such a manner that it reaches the laboratory in the same condition as collected. Use common sense.[52]

Of course, some types of evidence are more prone to natural breakdown or contamination—such as blood and other bodily fluids. Special care and special packaging is essential to preservation. Other forms of evidence lose "freshness" and become "outdated" very quickly.[53] The FBI, in its *Handbook for Forensic Services*,[54] has published guidelines on how evidence should be packaged, processed, and mailed for any analysis. See Box 6.14[55] for samples of packaging and safety standards.

BOX 6.14   GUIDELINES AND BEST PRACTICES FOR PACKAGING, PROCESSING, AND MAILING OUT EVIDENCE (SOURCE: FBI)

Questions concerning radioactive materials evidence should be directed to 703-898-7186. Call 703-898-7186 prior to submitting evidence.

Rope or Cordage Examinations

Cordage examinations can determine if portions of rope/cord exhibit the same color, construction, and composition. The manufacturer of ropes/cords may also be determined.

Questions concerning rope or cordage evidence should be directed to 703-632-8449.
Collection and packaging concerns:

- When possible, submit the entire rope/cord.
- If the rope/cord must be cut, label which ends were cut during evidence collection.

Rubber Stamp Examinations

A rubber stamp impression can be compared with a known source.

Questions concerning rubber stamp examinations should be directed to 703-632-8444.
Collection and packaging considerations:

- Submit the rubber stamp to the Laboratory uncleaned.
- Documentary evidence must be preserved in the condition in which it was found. It must not be unnecessarily folded, torn, marked, soiled, stamped, or written on or handled excessively. Protect the evidence from inadvertent indented writing.

Safe Insulation Examinations

Safe insulation can be compared to a known source. Examinations of safe insulation sometimes can determine the manufacturer.

Questions concerning safe insulation evidence should be directed to 703-632-8449.
Collection and packaging considerations:

- Collect safe insulation samples from damaged areas. Safe insulation can adhere to people, clothing, tools, bags, and stolen items and can transfer to vehicles. If possible, submit the evidence to the Laboratory for examiners to remove the debris. Package each item of evidence in a separate leakproof container. Do not process tools for latent prints.
- Ship known and questioned debris separately to avoid contamination. Submit known and questioned debris in leakproof containers such as film canisters or plastic pill bottles. Do not use paper or glass containers. Pack to keep lumps intact.

Serial Number (Altered) Examinations

Altered or restamped serial or identification numbers, including markings on metal, wood, plastic, and fiberglass, may contain toolmarks of value. If toolmarks are present and no suspect tool is submitted, it may be possible to produce a list of possible tools. When toolmarks of value are present, a comparison can be made with suspect dies.

The Laboratory can provide on-scene serial number restoration of obliterated or suspect areas on stolen vehicles and heavy equipment. Depending on the type of metal surface, a thermal or chemical method, along with specialized techniques, is used to assist in restoring and visualizing an obliterated stamping.

Questions concerning serial number evidence should be directed to 703-632-8442.
42 Handbook of Forensic Services 2013
   Collection and packaging considerations:

- For bulky items, if possible, remove the section containing the serial number and submit to Laboratory.
- If it is not possible to remove the section containing the serial number, take several photographs and make several casts of the suspect area to submit to the Laboratory.
  - Take several photographs and document the location of the area that is being cast.
  - Use an acrylic-surface replica cast kit. Call the Laboratory at 703-632-8442 regarding the appropriate cast kit.
  - Prior to cleaning the surface, cast the surface in its original state. Allow cast to set and label appropriately.
  - Clean the area. Remove paint or dirt with a solvent such as acetone, gasoline, or paint remover. Use Naval Jelly to remove rust. Use a soft brush. Do not use a wire brush.
  - Build a dam around the stamped characters to retain the acrylic liquid while it sets. Use a soft and pliable dam material such as modeling clay. Ensure there are no voids in the dam.
  - The acrylic liquid will take several minutes to set. If paint, foreign debris, and/ or rust are on the cast, make additional casts. These casts should be labeled sequentially and documented appropriately.
  - Pack the cast(s) to prevent any damage.

Shoe Print and Tire Tread Examinations

Shoe print or tire tread impressions are routinely left at crime scenes. These impressions are retained on surfaces in two- and three-dimensional forms. Almost all impressions, including partial impressions, have value for forensic comparisons. Examinations of shoe print and tire tread impressions could result in the positive identification of the shoes of the suspect(s) or tire(s) from the vehicle(s) of the suspect(s).

Whenever possible, submit the evidence bearing the original impression. If this evidence cannot be submitted to the Laboratory, see below for techniques on lifting two-dimensional and casting three-dimensional impressions.

A file of manufacturer's outsole designs and a file of tire tread patterns and other reference material can be searched to determine brand names and manufacturers. For shoe print and tire tread file searches, submit quality photographs of the impressions (see below for photography information). If photographs are not available, submit casts, lifts, or the original evidence.

Electronic images of shoe print or tire tread impressions may be submitted for file searches via email, along with a request letter on your agency's letterhead, to shoeprintsearch@ic.fbi. gov. The request letter should include suspect's name, victim's name, type of crime, date of crime, brief synopsis of crime, agency case number, and contact information. Email attachments are limited to 5 MB; therefore, it may be necessary to submit the request in multiple emails.

Questions concerning shoe print and tire tread evidence should be directed to 703-632-8444.
Collection and packaging considerations:

- For shoe print and tire tread comparisons, submit original evidence whenever possible (shoes, tires, photographic negatives, CDs with images, casts, lifts).
- Air-dry and package evidence separately in paper bags. Ensure the collector's initials, dates, and other relevant information is on the evidence container.
- Electrostatic lifts should be taped inside a clean, legal-size file folder or other laminated folder.
- Casts should be placed in paper bags and then covered with bubble wrap to minimize breakage when shipped to the Laboratory.

Capturing shoe print/tire tread images

- Questions concerning shoe print/tire tread photography should be directed to **703-632-8087**. Due to insufficient image detail, general crime scene photographs are not suitable for shoe print/tire tread impression examinations. Examination quality photographs require extreme close-up photographs.
- A SLR 12 MP (or higher) digital camera or 35 mm film camera body should be used. Use a tripod and a cable/electronic release to avoid vibration of the camera.
- RAW uncompressed, RAW lossless compression, and TIFF lossless compression are the only acceptable file formats. JPEG file format is not acceptable.
- Set the ISO to 400 ISO and select the proper White balance to capture the impression in its correct color. The White balance selection is controlled by the lighting condition (daylight or incandescent lighting).
- Select either Aperture Priority or Manual mode to control depth of field and select an f/stop setting of f/16 or f/22.
- If possible, use a fixed focal length lens that is double the normal focal length for your camera (e.g., use a 100 mm or 105 mm lens for 35 mm film or a 35 mm full frame sensor). If that lens is not available, use the normal lens for film or sensor size (e.g., use a 50 mm or 60 mm lens with 35 mm film or DSLR with a full frame sensor or a 35mm lens with DSLR with DX or APS-C sensor size). If neither option is available, use a zoom lens with the zoom set at double the normal focal length. Once the focal length and focus are selected, use a piece of tape to secure the lens barrel so the lens setting does not change due to the effects of gravity.

- Place a linear scale such as a ruler next to the full length of the impressions and on the same plane as the impression. If the impression is in a medium such as snow, sand, or soil, consider pressing the scale adjacent to the impression into the medium so that it is at the same plane as the bottom level of the impression. Also place a label in the photograph to correlate the impression with the crime scene notes and general crime scene photographs.
  - For tire treads, use a long tape measure as a scale and photograph the impression in overlapping segments to capture a full revolution (approximately 7 to 9 feet) of the tire.

- Fill the viewfinder with the impression and scale in landscape orientation. Position the camera directly over the impression with the film plane of the camera parallel to the surface of the impression.
- Adjust the focus of the macro lens in manual mode focusing on the bottom of the impression.
- Attach an electronic flash with long extension cord to the camera and position at a very low angle for oblique lighting, 10- to 15-degrees above the ground to enhance the detail of the impression. For consistent and even illumination, hold the flash at least 5 to 7 feet from the impression. Block out any bright ambient light with a sunscreen to maximize the lighting effect from the electronic flash unit for maximum detail.
- For shoe impressions, take a minimum of three images with oblique lighting at least 120-degree increments around the entire impression. For tire impressions, take four images, positioning the flash to illuminate the impression from all four sides.
- Copy the image files from the camera to a hard drive, CD, or DVD and verify images were successfully copied before deleting from camera. Best practice is to make at least two copies marked as "original/master," stored separately. If possible, create two additional copies marked "original/master working copy," for viewing, processing, and printing.

Capturing shoe print/tire tread images in snow

- First, attempt to photograph the impressions as if in soil.
- Impressions in snow are difficult to photograph because of lack of contrast. To increase contrast, lightly spray snow impressions with Snow Print Wax or with colored spray paint. Hold the spray can at least 2 to 3 feet from the impression so the force of the aerosol does not damage the impression.
- Direct a light application of the spray at a 30- to 45-degree angle so the colored paint strikes only the high points of the impression.
- Highlighted impressions will absorb heat from the sun and must be shielded until photographed and cast to prevent melting.
- After spraying, photograph impressions using above instructions.

Casting three-dimensional impressions

- Casting a three-dimensional impression in soil, sand, or snow is necessary to capture detail for examination. Dental stone, with a compressive strength of 8,000 psi or greater, must be used for casting all impressions. The compressive strength is listed on the container along with the proper ratio of powder to water used for mixing. Dental stone is available through local dental supply houses. Colored dental stone is preferred.
- Plaster of paris, modeling plasters, and dental plasters are not sufficiently hard, do not resist abrasion when cleaned, and must not be used.
- The average footwear impression requires about 2 lbs of dental stone and approximately 10 oz of water. The average tire impression (about 18 to 24 inches in length) requires about

7 lbs of dental stone and about 35 oz water. Tire impressions can be cast up to 36 inches in length.

- After the dental stone and water have been mixed, the material should have the consistency of pancake batter or heavy cream. It may be necessary to adjust the amounts of dental stone and water used to obtain the desired consistency.
- Store dental stone in resealable plastic bags. An 8- by 12-inch resealable plastic bag can store 2 lbs of dental stone powder. With premeasured bags, casting impressions at the crime scene involves only adding water. The bag containing the dental stone powder can be used to mix and pour the dental stone. To make a cast, add the appropriate amount of water to the bag and close the top. Mix the casting material by vigorously massaging it through the bag for 3 to 5 minutes. Ensure that the material in the corners of the bag is also mixed.
- If the impressions are numerous or large, it may be necessary to mix larger quantities of dental stone in a bucket or bowl. The dental stone should be added slowly to the water and stirred continuously for 3 to 5 minutes.
- Casting material has sufficient weight and volume to erode and destroy detail if it is poured directly on top of the impression. The casting material should be poured on the ground next to the impression, allowing it to flow into the impression. The impression should be filled with casting material until it has overflowed. Once dried, the resulting cast should be ½ to 1 inch in thickness to minimize breakage when being transported to the Laboratory.

The integrity of evidence can also be protected by the use of tags, tapes, and various forms of labels.[56] Calling for a hands-off approach, evidence tamper tapes warn prospective individuals to keep out unless authorized. Property evidence tags are usually tied to the bag, box, or other packaging; they account for the exact chain of possession—from whom, to where, and what date and time is recorded. See Figures 6.22[57] and 6.23.[58]

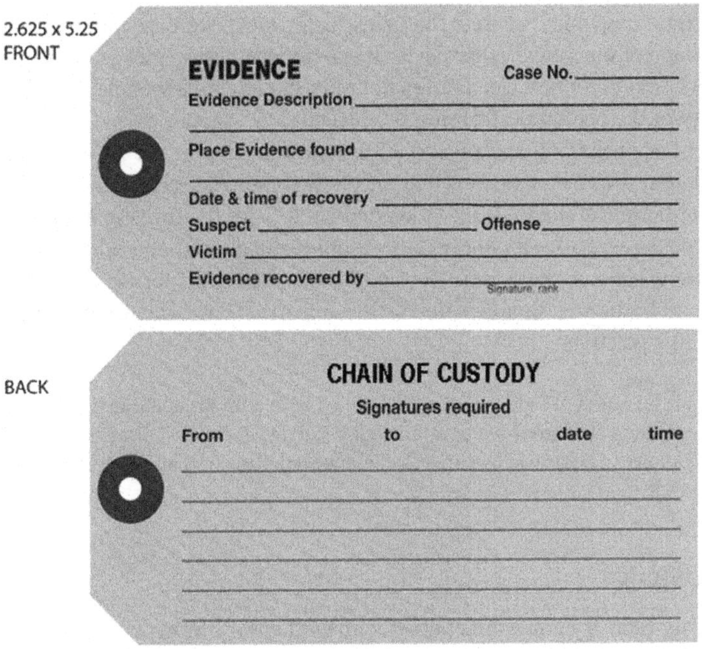

FIGURE 6.22 Property evidence tags. (Used with permission, St. Louis Tag.)

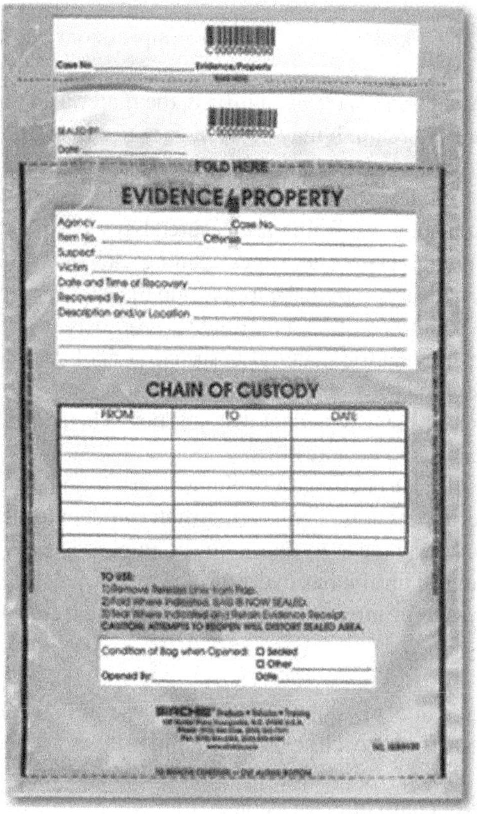

FIGURE 6.23 Integrity evidence bag. (Used with permission, Sirchie.)

In an age of communicable diseases, the investigator must exercise caution in handling materials and in the storage of fluids and other perishable evidence. Using gloves, syringe needles, plastic vials, eyedroppers, and other devices assures not only the unchallengeable quality of the evidence, but also the safety of the person performing the investigative function.

Web Exercise: For packaging and preservation requirements for the many of types of evidence, see the FBI's *Handbook of Forensic Services* at: www.fbi.gov/hq/lab/handbook/forensics.pdf.

Numerous commercial companies provide compact kits for the investigation of blood, collection of evidence in rape cases, ballistics analysis, gunshot residue tests, and other matter. Whatever the investigator chooses, if he or she is unsure of his or her skill or expertise in handling complicated evidence packages, he or she should defer to the expert.[59] The American Society for Industrial Security affirms this position.

> Collection and preservation of evidence are only a part of any professional investigation, but they frequently prove to be the most important part in solving a crime and prosecuting a suspect. An otherwise efficient investigation can be ruined by careless evidence handling or inadequate knowledge of this vital aspect of the work.[60]

6.9 CONCLUSION

The private security industry comes in contact with evidentiary forms each and every day as it processes various scenes. At the workplace, the industry investigates pilferage, breaking and entering, internal theft rings, workplace violence, and substance abuse. Violence in the workplace has now escalated to active shooter status and the evidentiary demands associated with those sorts of cases are legendary. The industry needs to know the fundamentals of evidence gathering, its preservation and maintenance, and the assurance that its chain of custody has not been breached. That is the thrust of this entire chapter—from crime scene visitation to an auto accident collision, private security operatives must know how to protect and preserve everything in a scene, From a forensic perspective, the investigator should acquire a rudimentary understanding of fingerprints, trace materials, biological fluids, rocks, soil, and other geological materials, fibers, hair, rope, string, thread, firearms, tools and tool mark evidence, questioned documents, and explosive materials, and how to collect and preserve those materials. In the forensic age, "evidence is technologically and mechanically sophisticated. It requires complex and sophisticated knowledge and instrumentation to understand or interpret it."[61]

Scene sketches, diagrams, photographs, and digital imagery are covered as well. As a final admonition, working closely with public law enforcement becomes quite apparent in these sorts of cases. Adhere to evidentiary and investigative protocol and work collegially with the public system to assure the private system can effectively investigate and collect evidence for subsequent adjudication or litigation.

NOTES

1. Charles P. Nemeth, *The Paralegal Resource Manual*, 3rd ed. (New York: McGraw-Hill, 2008): 338; Susan Geoghegan, "Lessons Learned in Evidence Management," *Law &Order* 62, no. 6 (2014): 26–28.
2. National Forensic Science Technology Center, *Crime Scene Investigation: A Guide for Law Enforcement* (2013), www.nfstc.org; George Schiro, "Collection and Preservation of Evidence," Crime Scene Investigator Network, accessed September 9, 2018, www.crime-scene-investigator.net/evidenc3.html; Wisconsin Dept of Justice, Crime Laboratory Bureau, *Physical Evidence Handbook* (2017), https://wilenet.org/html/crime-lab/physevbook/physical-evidence-handbook-2017.pdf; Salisbury University Police Department, "Chapter 83—Collection and Preservation of Evidence," www.salisbury.edu/police/Written_Directives/Chap83.pdf; Federal Bureau of Investigation, *Crime Scene Investigation: A Guide for Law Enforcement* (2000), https://archives.fbi.gov/archives/about-us/lab/forensic-science-communications/fsc/april2000/twgcsi.pdf; Indiana Law Enforcement Academy, *Criminal Investigation Manual*, www.in.gov/ilea/files/Criminal%20Investigation%20Manual%20Rev%202.pdf.
3. U.S. Department of Justice, National Institute of Justice, *Crime Scene Search and Physical Evidence Handbook* (U.S. Government Printing Office, 1973); National Forensic Science Technology Center (NFSTC), *Simplified Guide to Crime Scene Investigation* (2009), www.forensicsciencesimplified.org/csi/CrimeSceneInvestigation.pdf; FBI, "Crime Scene Investigation."
4. Ibid.: 15; see also NIJ, *Death Investigation: A Guide for the Scene Investigator* (2011), www.ncjrs.gov/pdffiles1/nij/234457.pdf; NFSTC, "Simplified Guide"; FBI, "Crime Scene Investigation."
5. Geoghegan, "Lessons Learned." See also Texas Department of Public Safety, *Crime Scene Response: Standard Operating Procedures* (2011), https://txdpslabs.qualtraxcloud.com/ShowDocument.aspx?ID=43042.
6. Ibid.; NFSTC, "Simplified Guide"; FBI, "Crime Scene Investigation."
7. United States Department of Justice, *Crime Scene Investigation: A Guide for Law Enforcement* (2000): 11.
8. Pennsylvania State Police, *Crime Laboratory* 2.1 (1985); Texas Department of Public Safety, Crime Laboratory Service, *Physical Evidence Handbook* (2007), www.crime-scene-investigator.net/evidence_manual_TX.pdf; Wisconsin DOJ, "Evidence Handbook."
9. For a fascinating look at the new world of electronic crime scenes, such as computer hard drives, and the need for first responders to exercise the same caution on approach to a crime scene, see National Institute of Justice, *Electronic Crime Scene Investigation: A Guide for First Responders*, 2nd ed. (2008).
10. See also National Institute of Justice, *Crime Scene Investigation: A Reference for Law Enforcement Training* (2004).
11. "Organization and Procedures for Search Operations," Crime Scene Investigator Network, accessed September 9, 2018, www.crime-scene-investigator.net/respon3.html. This information was adapted from the California Commission on Peace Officer Standards and Training's workbook for the "Forensic Technology for Law Enforcement" Telecourse presented on May 13, 1993.

12. NIJ, "Crime Scene Investigation": 14–16; U.S. Department of Justice, *A Guide for Explosion and Bombing Scene Investigation* (2000), accessed September 9, 2018, www.ncjrs.gov/pdffiles1/nij/181869.pdf.

13. Wisconsin DOJ, "Evidence Handbook": 261–263; US DOJ, "Explosion and Bombing"; G. Knowles, *Bomb Security Guide* (1976): 69.

14. See US DOJ, "Explosion and Bombing"; see also Michael Dellarocco, *Bombing Investigation: A Basic Primer*, April 1, 2001, accessed September 9, 2018, www.fireengineering.com/articles/print/volume-154/issue-4/features/bombing-investigation-a-basic-primer.html.

15. Ibid.: 115–116; Dellarocco, "Bombing Investigation."

16. Al Lohner, "Crime Scene Diagramming Software Steadily Gains Converts," *Law Enforcement Technology*, April 2002: 58, 60–62, 63; Wisconsin DOJ, "Evidence Handbook": 47–57.

17. US DOJ, "Evidence Handbook": 36; Wisconsin DOJ, "Evidence Handbook": 47–57.

18. Headquarters, Department of the Army, *Law Enforcement Investigations* (2005): 125, https://rdl.train.army.mil/soldierPortal/atia/adlsc/view/public/12038-1/FM/3-19.13/FM3_19X13.PDF; Wisconsin DOJ, "Evidence Handbook": 47–57.

19. Tacoma Police Department, *Forensic Services Policy and Procedure Manual* (2004): 4; Wisconsin DOJ, "Evidence Handbook": 47–57.

20. Army, "Investigations": 123; Wisconsin DOJ, "Evidence Handbook": 47–57.

21. Ibid.: 121; Wisconsin DOJ, "Evidence Handbook": 47–57.

22. Ibid.: 122; Wisconsin DOJ, "Evidence Handbook": 47–57.

23. Tim Dees, "Crime Scene Drawing Programs," *Law &Order*, August 2001: 12; Kent E. Boots, "Crime Scene Diagramming: Back to Basics," January 4, 2014, accessed September 9, 2018, www.forensicmag.com/article/2014/01/crime-scene-diagramming-back-basics.

24. The Forensic Sciences Foundation, *Death Investigation and Examination: Medicolegal Guidelines and Checklists* (1986): 13; Boots, "Back to Basics"; Wisconsin DOJ, "Evidence Handbook": 47–57.

25. See Dick Warrington, "Crime Scene Photography: Capturing the Scene," *Forensic Magazine*, August 1, 2009, www.forensicmag.com/article/2009/08/crime-scene-photography-capturing-scene.

26. C. Scott, 1 *Photographic Evidence* (1980) § 13 at 19; *A Simplified Guide to Crime Scene Photography* (2009), www.forensicsciencesimplified.org/photo/Photography.pdf; Dick Warrington, Crime Scene Photography: Capturing the Scene, *Forensic Magazine*, August 1, 2009, www.forensicmag.com/article/2009/08/crime-scene-photography-capturing-scene.

27. Ibid.: 344–345; National Forensic Science Technology Center, *A Simplified Guide to Crime Scene Photography* (2009), www.forensicsciencesimplified.org/photo/Photography.pdf; Warrington, "Capturing the Scene."

28. David A. Bright and Jane Goodman-Delahunty, "Gruesome Evidence and Emotion: Anger, Blame, and Jury Decision-Making," *Law &Human Behavior* 30 (2006): 183; Rebecca Hofstein Grady, Lauren Reiser, Robert J. Garcia, Christian Koeu, and Nicholas Scurich, "Impact of Gruesome Photographic Evidence on Legal Decisions: A Meta-Analysis," *Psychiatry, Psychology and Law* (2018), doi:10.1080/13218719.2018.1440468; "Gruesome Nature Renders Photographic Evidence Inadmissible in Criminal Trial," *Stanford Law Review* 4, no. 4 (July 1952): 589–591.

29. NFSTC, "Photography": 5.

30. PA State Police, "Crime Laboratory," 2.2; Wisconsin DOJ, "Evidence Handbook"; Indiana Law Enforcement Academy, *Criminal Investigation Manual*, accessed September 9, 2018, www.in.gov/ilea/files/Criminal%20Investigation%20Manual%20Rev%202.pdf.

31. Kathy Marks, "Sirchie Crime Scene Products &Equipment: The Total Crime Scene Solution," *Law &Order* 63, no. 6 (June 2015): 24–27.

32. US DOJ, "Evidence Handbook": 44–45; NFSTC, "Photography"; Warrington, "Capturing the Scene."

33. Forensic Sciences, "Death Investigation": 77; NFSTC, "Photography"; Warrington, "Capturing the Scene."

34. John J. Lentini, "What Fire Litigators Need to Know in 2017," *The SciTech Lawyer* (Summer 2017): 18.

35. US DOJ, "Evidence Handbook": 43; Lentini, "Fire Litigators."

36. For an interesting study of forensic key and lock analysis, especially as it relates to tool marks, see "Forensic Locksmithing: A Key to Solving Crime," *Forensic Examiner* 22, no. 2 (Summer 2013): 76–77.

37. US DOJ, "Evidence Handbook": 44; "Forensic Locksmithing"; Schiro, "Collection and Preservation."

38. American Society for Industrial Security, *Basic Guidelines for Security Investigations* (1981): 79; *POST Background Investigation Manual: Guidelines for the Investigator* (California Commission on Peace Officer Standards and Training, 2018), http://lib.post.ca.gov/Publications/bi.pdf; NIJ, "Death Investigation."

39. Read Hayes, "Strategies to Detect and Prevent Workplace Dishonesty," (ASIS International, 2008): 20, www.asisonline.org/globalassets/foundation/documents/crisp-reports/crisp-strategies-detect-prevent-workplace-dishonesty.pdf.

40. *Forensic Sciences*, "Death Investigation": 55.

41. "Alcohol Influence Report Form," New Jersey Division of Criminal Justice, accessed September 9, 2018, www.state.nj.us/lps/dcj/agguide/final_ai_form.pdf.

42. The International Association of Chiefs of Police (IACP), *Combating Workplace Violence* (2002): 1–2.

43. "Missing Person Report," State of California Department of Justice (2014), accessed September 9, 2018, http://lib.post.ca.gov/Publications/Missing_Persons_Forms/mp_report.pdf.

44. State of Illinois, *Instruction Booklet for Expunging and Sealing Court Forms* (2017): 12–15, www.illinoislegalaid.org/sites/default/files/legal_content/file_form_content/Worksheet%20for%20criminal%20records%20expungement%20and%20sealing.pdf.

45. "Summary of the HIPAA Privacy Rule," HHS.gov, accessed September 9, 2018, www.hhs.gov/hipaa/for-professionals/privacy/laws-regulations/index.html.

46. 45 C.F.R. §§ 160.102, 160.103.

47. "Medical Record Privacy," Electronic Privacy Information Center, accessed August 4, 2018, www.epic.org/privacy/medical/#consumer.

48. Halil Ibrahim Bulbul, H. Guclu Yavuzcan, and Mesut Ozel, "Digital Forensics: An Analytical Crime Scene Procedure Model (ACSPM)," *Forensic Science International* 233, nos. 1–3 (2013): 244, https://doi.org/10.1016/j.forsciint.2013.09.007.

49. The compelling nature of DNA evidence has surely heightened chain of custody concerns for both the public and private sector. See William P Kiley, "The Effects of DNA Advances on Police Property Rooms," *FBI Law Enforcement Bulletin*, March 2009: 20; O. Marius-Sorin and G. I. Madalin, "Biological Evidence, Clues and Answers for Criminal Activity," *Journal of Criminal Investigations* 10, no. 1 (2016): 66–69; Texas Department of Public Safety, Crime Laboratory Service, *Physical Evidence Handbook* (2007), www.crime-scene-investigator.net/evidence_manual_TX.pdf.

50. *Am. Jur. Trials* (1987): 555, 577.

51. PA State Police, "Crime Laboratory," 2.5; Texas Public Safety, "Crime Laboratory"; Wisconsin DOJ, "Evidence Handbook."

52. PA State Police, "Crime Laboratory," 2.5; Texas Public Safety, "Crime Laboratory"; Wisconsin DOJ, "Evidence Handbook."

53. See Marius-Sorin and Madalin, "Biological Evidence"; see also J. L. Sumpter, "Investigating Big Crimes in Small Towns," *Law &Order* 61, 6 (2013): 28–30.

54. Federal Bureau of Investigation, *Handbook for Forensic Services* (Washington, DC: U.S. Government Printing Office, 2013), www.fbi.gov/file-repository/handbook-of-forensic-services-pdf.pdf.

55. Ibid.: 42–45.

56. Ibid.

57. Evidence Tag #8, St. Louis Tag, 3201 Laclede Station Road, St. Louis, Missouri 63143.

58. Integrity Evidence Bag #IEB9120, Sirchie, 100 Hunter Place, Youngsville, NC 27596.

59. See Texas Department of Public Safety, *Best Practices: Collection, Packaging, Storage, Preservation, and Retrieval of Biological Evidence* (2012), accessed September 9, 2018, www.dps.texas.gov/CrimeLaboratory/documents/labBP01BestPractice.pdf.

60. ASIS, "Basic Guidelines": 28; Texas Public Safety, "Crime Laboratory"; NFSTC, "Law Enforcement."

61. Erin Murphy, "The Mismatch Between Twenty-First-Century Forensic Evidence and Our Antiquated Criminal Justice System," *Southern California Law Review* 87 (March 2014): 634.

7 Surveillance Techniques

7.1 PURPOSES AND FUNCTIONS

To surveil is to watch another, either by personal observation, technological means, or a combination of the two. Surveillance is an integral component for any security practice, but its object (the person surveilled), and the activities under scrutiny, are unknowing subjects. To have any effectiveness, surveillance needs to take place without notice or public awareness. The use of surveillance should be a blend of aggressive and cautious planning and tactics. Aggressive in the sense that it is one of the more remarkable tools in the security professional's toolbox which should be used with regularity and cautiously employed because of the privacy implications of its usage.

Surveillance complements traditional methods of investigative tracking and rests side by side with direct observation. Surveillance or covert observation serves a host of purposes, such as:

- To protect undercover officers or to corroborate their testimony
- To obtain evidence of a crime
- To obtain evidence of a civil wrong
- To locate persons
- To check on the reliability of informants, witnesses, and other parties
- To locate hidden property or contraband
- To obtain probable cause for search warrant processes
- To prevent the commission of an act or to apprehend a suspect in the commission of an act
- To obtain information for later use in interrogation
- To develop leads and information received from other sources
- To know at all times the whereabouts of an individual
- To obtain admissible legal evidence for use in court.

The International Foundation for Protection Officers defines surveillance practice as:

> … quite simply, observations conducted to gain information. This simple definition includes a plethora of techniques and methods that can be considered a form of surveillance. Many of these are recognizable through common knowledge produced by popular culture. The most well known methods include stationary surveillance, technical surveillance (typically covert video or audio recordings), electronic surveillance (digital observations, keystroke counting), and many more.[1]

The uses of surveillance by the security investigator are unlimited and only constrained by the investigator's area of practice and skill set.[2] And there is no denying its upward usage since the "use of CCTV by security companies is regarded as cost effective"[3] and a practice that always justifies the expenditure. Many private security firms stress its use in fraud analysis or thievery at the corporate or governmental level (See Figure 7.1[4]), others use it to discern crowd behavior and potential contagion.[5]

Surveillance can be classified according to its function. For example, surveillance could be strictly for the purposes of gathering intelligence about a specific person, crime, or activity. Surveillance may be a preliminary or preparatory step in an investigation, setting the stage for an eventual drug sweep or apprehension of retail thieves. Similarly, surveillance may serve as a backup for an undercover investigator's activities. This type of surveillance serves two primary purposes: first, the observation corroborates the undercover agent's activity and testimony; and second, if trouble erupts, the surveillance team assists the undercover operative. Finally, surveillance is an effective

○PRMG

About   Corporate Security   Investigations   Marijuana Security & Planning   Blog   Join our Team   Contact Us

How To Choose A Corporate Fraud Investigation Firm

Individuals searching for a corporate fraud investigator should seek a special investigations unit that excels in conducting undercover investigations, recording interviews and statements, and locating witnesses as well as investigating subrogation, larceny, theft, and embezzlement.

Corporate fraud investigation service providers work hand-in-hand with the proper authorities to obtain the true facts and build a case for termination and prosecution of the dishonest employee(s).

PRMG Corporate Fraud Investigation Services

PRMG agents have years of experience providing corporate fraud investigation services. We have experience conducting investigations for corporations in retail, insurance, shipping/receiving, and many others.

While each case is unique, our investigators have a set of investigative tools/services that we apply to situations as needed.

Some of the tools we regularly use in corporate fraud investigation are:

- Undercover Investigations

- Surveillance Investigators

- Employee Background Screening

- Forensic Interviewing

- GPS Tracking

- Many More

If you think that you may have a theft or fraud problem, don't wait!

FIGURE 7.1   Increasingly firms can be utilized in corporate fraud investigations. (Used with permission, Precision Risk Management Group.)

tool in post-purchase activity, especially in drug cases, receipt of stolen property or other fencing operations, internal corporate fraud, and business or industrial theft. Post-purchase surveillance has many applications in criminal settings including:

- To determine where the money or goods go after the sale or transaction
- To identify subsequent buyers or purchasers of stolen goods, drugs, or other materials
- To keep the suspect under observation in case the undercover officer was duped in a previous transaction

Surveillance goes far beyond human subjects as well, as data mining and shadowing are taking place in the virtual world at a pace never envisioned a decade ago. Intelligence agencies and law enforcement entities, security firms and their IT arms all engage in various sorts of intelligence surveillance.[6]

That the private security industry plays an important and critical role in the development, implementation, and utilization of surveillance can be best described as an understatement. For "technology develops at a pace that is virtually impossible for our law enforcement and security agencies to maintain."[7] This collegial mentality is further buttressed by the complexities of computer science, and "the combination of computing and communications, a new space for the mutual benefit of state and private enterprise was opened up."[8]

Web Exercise: Read the article on various types of surveillance at www.nowpi.com/surveillance/.

7.2   TACTICS AND STRATEGY IN SURVEILLANCE

Planning and preparation are key elements in surveillance practice. This portion of the chapter gauges the various procedural steps essential to intelligent surveillance policy and practice.

7.2.1   WHAT ARE THE STEPS OF SURVEILLANCE?

Successful surveillance requires—as do all aspects of criminal and civil investigation—four basic steps:

1. Planning
2. Organizing
3. Directing
4. Controlling[9]

Preparation is key to results-oriented investigative practice and surveillance is no exception to that rule. "The success of any surveillance operation relies heavily on preparation."[10]

To be effective, the investigative team plans and organizes its purpose and aim, and assesses the landscape and geography to determine the most suitable means of surveillance.[11] Intelligent planning assures a better use and a better result. Know the area you are responsible for—know its geography and all the subtleties of the location. Private investigator Joseph M. LaSorsa provides experience-based advice when he remarks:

> Familiarize yourself with the area. Check Google Earth imagery for all possible routes to and from the location. This will help you choose the best possible staging area—hopefully, a spot that will allow you to see your subject leaving, regardless of what route he takes. If your initial site recon reveals that there's no way to cover all the ways in and out, this lets you know that you'll need more than one vehicle to do the job.[12]

Before deploying, other questions should be asked and answered.

- Is there any alternative to surveillance?
- Do you know what information is needed from the surveillance?
- Have you decided what type of surveillance is needed?
- Do you know enough about the area of surveillance to determine equipment and manpower needs?
- Do you have the required equipment and manpower?
- Are proper forms available to record necessary information during the surveillance?
- Are all signals preestablished?[13]

Just as important, be certain the activity is lawful in the jurisdiction where the surveillance is conducted and be equally sure that its implementation will not trigger constitutional violations relating to the 4th Amendment or civil liability arising out of invasion of privacy torts.[14]

Web Exercise: For an interesting case that limits surveillance and tracking by GPS, read US v. Jones at: www.oyez.org/cases/2011/10-1259.

Be attuned to the legal and ethical dynamics of surveillance.[15]

Before launch be confident of its lawfulness. John Dale Hartman delineates the primary legal concerns and considerations:

- Were the agents in a place in which they had a right to be?
- Were the documentations limited to the view available to any other member of the general public?

- Did the agents do anything to enhance the secured view that exceeds the view available to the general public?
- Was the view secured from a position the employee could reasonably expect someone in the general public or another coworker to be in at any given time?
- Was the area in which the documentations were made one in which the employee could reasonably expect privacy from an outside view?
- Was the area one in which the agent was statutorily prohibited from making clandestine observations?
- Was the area one over which the employee maintains exclusive control or was access available to others?
- If the area involved a "private area," was the employee warned that activities were subject to observation and documentation?
- Were the efforts used by the agent limited to those objectively considered reasonable and unobtrusive or did the agent conduct an operation that can only be described as offensive, unreasonable, and blatant?
- Were the documentations limited to those related to the issue at hand?
- Were the documented activities ones that could be considered embarrassing to the subject?
- Was the reason for the surveillance related to legitimate business purposes and conducted for a legitimate cause or was an unlawful motive involved?
- Was the operation one that could violate an existing contract or intrude on an employee's right to collective bargaining?[16]

Privacy considerations may rest in civil remedies and damage claims—especially invasion of privacy. In this context, the investigator must act reasonably and within the bounds of customary legal standards. Surveillance which is overly intrusive confronts and undermines a person's basic expectation of privacy. The International Foundation for Protection Officers declares:

> Surveillance should never intrude on the subject's reasonable expectation of privacy. If the investigator is utilizing technology to observe into the subject's life where one normally could not observe, then perhaps there is an issue of privacy intrusion. Utilizing a digital zoom to see through sheer curtains of a living room and observe into a house, observing what is happening in the hallway or a back bedroom, may be considered a use of unique means that may be an invasion of privacy.[17]

Web Exercise: Watch the video on "Surveillance and Privacy Issues" at www.c-span.org/video/?312840-4/surveillance-privacy-issues.

At times, agents will work undercover, requiring additional emphasis on intelligent planning. Just as important, the assigned investigator needs not only the technical skills and equipment to succeed in the surveillance, but also the proper disposition and personality that can carry out this task. Industry professional Tom Shamshak delivers an excellent portrait for the competent professional who conducts surveillance.

> Surveillance is incredibly demanding and challenging. Private investigators who are successful at surveillance have to possess certain qualities. Someone with an outgoing personality, exceptional communication skills, the ability to take action, a good memory, an ability to blend into their surroundings and a strong attention to detail would be a good fit for surveillance. This person should also be honest, patient, observant, resourceful, flexible and focused.[18]

Before commencing an undercover activity, the investigator must be trained in these principles:

- Undercover investigators should never become emotionally or sexually involved with any of the subjects of the investigation. More than one case on record has been compromised this way.

- The undercover operator should not consume alcohol. Even though it may serve the purpose to have the subject do so, the undercover operator should not.
- The undercover investigator should never, under any circumstances, steal anything—even to become part of the group and even though the item may be returned to the client. The agent can help the subjects of the investigation take merchandise from a security room, and bring it to the edge of the receiving dock, but that's about it. The agent must never aid in actual removal of the item from the premises, or even load the merchandise in a vehicle. This has, and it will continue to have, a boomerang effect. The thief may suggest that the agent had been behind the whole thing, and management may believe it.
- The operative should not take security identification or other investigative identification on assignment.
- The undercover operator should leave nothing in the car that can reveal the identity of the operative. Do not leave notes in the glove compartment; one never knows when the subject or other person involved in the investigation will have access to the agent's car.

Because surveillance is a costly undertaking, the client, as well as the firm, must justify this form of expenditure. Does the client's problem lend itself to surveillance tactics? Is there an alternative mechanism for obtaining the same information? Will the surveillance activities place the client or agents of the firm in jeopardy?

7.2.2 THE PRECISE OBJECTIVE OF SURVEILLANCE

Effective surveillance sets goals and parameters. Solid surveillance practice keeps the endgame in view by laying out specific objectives for the action. While these objectives may change due to a change of circumstance or facts discovered, surveillance must not be a freewheeling discovery exercise. It must have an initial purpose in mind with full awareness that the purpose may be subject to change. At a minimum, the objective should correlate to the purpose of the surveillance. These ends and goals must be subject to revision where needed. Effective surveillance is flexible and adaptable and subject to continuous review.[19]

The ends of the surveillance will be as varied as the subject matter of that surveillance. More typical examples might be:

- Is the subject acting in accordance with a complete or partial disability claim?
- Is the subject faking or feigning injuries alleged in a workers' compensation or personal injury case?
- Is the subject operating a stolen property ring?
- Is the subject suspected of raiding cash registers?
- Is the subject suspected of shoplifting?
- Is the subject, in a retail establishment, suspected of passing goods and merchandise to friends through nonsecure exit points?
- Is the subject taking alcohol or narcotic substances into the workplace?
- Is the subject sexually harassing workers at his place of employment?

Surveillance should never be an unrestrained and unchecked activity or a prophetic hope that some sort of criminality or liability will emerge. Surveillance, rather than a mere fishing expedition, must target a particular goal or aim. "Careful planning is imperative. The plan must allow room for flexibility, but ensure direction is given to the effort from the start. It must make clear who and what the targets are and what elements of proof must be met."[20]

7.2.3 THE LOCATION OF SURVEILLANCE

Professional surveillance requires a full understanding of not only the subject but his or her surrounding environment. In a phrase, know your geography and territory before deployment. Become familiar with the geographic, cultural, and environmental qualities in which the target lives and works.[21] More specifically, be aware of entry and exit points at enclosed locations. Trace and track streets and byways. Precisely pinpoint the location of public law enforcement relative to the place of surveillance. Other relevant questions involving locale are.

- What is the character and quality of the neighborhood in which you are conducting surveillance?
- Can you easily be disguised, or are outsiders quickly labeled and identified? Which type of surveillance will work best depends on freedom of movement.
- Is auto surveillance possible or is stationary or foot surveillance more likely?
- What areas of cover might you adopt, such as rooming houses, hotels, or apartments?
- What public transportation is readily available?
- Given the density of the area, is it preferable to have multiple investigators at the location?
- Are maps, charts, or diagrams of the area readily available?
- Have you investigated possible ways to avoid observation or apprehension?

Be on the safe side before the issuance of any order of surveillance. Visit and inspect the locality and familiarize yourself with the neighborhood's style of dress, language, and other cultural nuances.

7.2.4 TIME OF SURVEILLANCE

The decision to commence surveillance activities is both organizational and tactical. The surveillance decision should also be based upon strategic considerations, such as:

- Is surveillance likely to be more effective at night or in the daytime?
- Which time of the day will result in less of an opportunity to be "burned" or found out?
- Will the time of day, such as rush hour, evening, or dusk, affect the amount of surveillance employed for the task?
- Are there difficulties with visibility, angle of observation, or clarity of direction at certain times of the day?
- Can auto surveillance be used more effectively at certain times rather than other types of surveillance?
- Will specialized equipment be needed to conduct surveillance?
- How does the location of surveillance affect the chosen time?

Also consider how long the surveillance is supposed to last. This can depend on a number of things, including:

- Budgetary considerations of the client
- The complexity or simplicity of the case in question
- The nature of the surveillance, whether it calls for more underground activities
- The sophistication of the subject being surveilled, causing greater sensitivity and patience in the surveillance process.

7.2.5 THE SUBJECT OR TARGET OF SURVEILLANCE

The surveillance subject can be either a person or a nonhuman entity, such as a plant, business, industry, or other installation. No matter who or what is under surveillance, that person or entity is labeled the "subject." "It can be a person, place, property, vehicle, group of persons, organization, or object."[22] Within this broad categorization fall the following:

- Persons suspected of criminal activity
- Persons suspected of fraud in a civil context
- Persons in need of evaluation in personal injury or workers' compensation cases
- Persons suspected of labor violations
- Persons involved in public riot or other disorder activities

On the other hand, the surveillance subject which is a place or a location could be any of these:

- The residence of a suspected felon
- Fencing locations for stolen goods
- Locations for terrorists in executive protection cases
- Houses of prostitution
- Houses of gambling
- Drug dens
- Illegal alien hideouts
- Illegal medical operations
- Auto body chop shops

The target of surveillance will impact the comprehensiveness of that surveillance. In other words, the drug dealer selling on a neighborhood street has less of an expectation of privacy than a citizen praying at the local church. The level of intrusion will depend on many factors although the extent of the intrusion will be guided by constitutional expectations of privacy.[23] A highly intrusive, technologically entranced surveillance of a home is a trickier proposition than the criminal on the street. The home or domicile affords the highest expectation of privacy. "Factors considered by the courts in addressing the permissibility of a view into the home include

- The time at which the view is secured
- The duration of the surveillance
- The distance to the target under surveillance
- The positioning of the investigator
- The use of the area under surveillance
- The distance between the activity and the residence
- The efforts taken by the subjects to ensure their privacy
- Whether the portal used to view the activity has curtains or blinds and whether they were drawn at the time
- Whether the activities in question were visible to the general public
- Whether the enhancement efforts were effected to confirm observations visible with unaided vision or whether the view would not be visible without an enhancement device
- The sophistication of the equipment used by the agents to secure the view
- Whether the view can be considered to violate the reasonable expectation of privacy maintained by the subject
- Whether the efforts made by the officers were to conceal themselves and not to enhance an otherwise unavailable view"[24]

Web Exercise: Read the article about five things private investigators cannot do at: www.trustify. info/blog/5-things-private-investigators-can-and-cant-do.

7.3 SURVEILLANCE: PREPARATORY STEPS

As already noted, effective surveillance requires advance planning and preparation. Although most competent investigators are capable of conducting reasonably good surveillance, the results and effectiveness will markedly grow when smaller details are attended to. Here are the more common issues in need of advance preparation.

Web Exercise: Being prepared and understanding the goal of a surveillance program go hand and hand. Read the article at www.buildings.com/article-details/articleid/21029/title/the-keys-to-implementing-an-effective-surveillance-system for elements to consider.

7.3.1 PERSONAL BEHAVIOR AND ATTIRE

The surveillance officer should have an ordinary appearance that blends into the territory. Any exceptional physical characteristics attract the subject's attention. The surveillance officer must be a natural player under all circumstances, acclimating into the environment subject to the surveillance. The agent must exhibit uncanny attentiveness and resourcefulness since unpredictability is a constant of the surveillance process. No matter how well it is planned and adopted, many events and conditions are unanticipated. The agent should have superior skills of observation and high memory retention. The agent needs absolute patience and mental endurance. Surveillance is not, at least in the majority of cases, a quick fix, as is depicted in television. Instead, the agent must be a painstaking, perseverant, and dogged observer of the subject.

In addition, investigators must always be mindful of their appearance and demeanor. A surveillant's clothing should not stand out from others in the environment, and it is highly recommended that the clothing selected be reversible. The agent must not be unnecessarily noticeable. The overall approach of the agent must be subdued, not attracting attention—not running, darting, or hiding, nor acting in a mysterious fashion.[25] In the same light, if auto surveillance is employed, the vehicle should be completely inconspicuous. Bright colors, loud exhaust systems, blatant antenna systems, and siren devices have no place in surveillance activities.

7.3.2 SURVEILLANCE EQUIPMENT

The agent must consider his or her technological needs before embarking on or commencing any surveillance activity. Having the right equipment is crucial to success. Equipment check is central to the planner. Review the checklist.

- Is there any need for radio or electronic monitoring equipment, cameras, or remote receivers?
- What types of specialized equipment could be of use to the surveillant?
- Are radio communications protected or subject to breaches in integrity?
- What type of photographic equipment is necessary?
- If electronic surveillance techniques are employed, what are the legal restrictions within your jurisdiction?

The complexity of the surveillance process has triggered a multimillion dollar industry that produces surveillance materials and equipment. This reliance on equipment is sometimes labeled "enhanced surveillance." See Figure 7.2.

For further research, consult *Surveillance &Society*, the international, interdisciplinary, open access, peer-reviewed journal of surveillance studies. *Surveillance &Society* exists to:

- Publish innovative and transdisciplinary work on surveillance
- Encourage understanding of approaches to surveillance in different academic disciplines

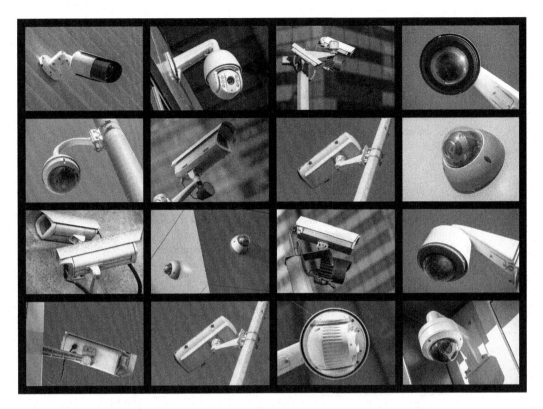

FIGURE 7.2   Surveillance systems globally have become a multibillion dollar industry. (Used with permission: Shutterstock.)

- Promote understanding of surveillance in wider society
- Encourage policy and political debate about surveillance[26]

Physical Security and Safety: A Field Guide for the Practitioner by Truett A. Ricks, Bobby E. Ricks, and Jeffrey Dingle provides a comprehensive examination of technology employed in security practice with excellent insight into the electronic aspect of surveillance.[27]

Some of the more dominant hardware and technology are summarized in the next section.

7.3.2.1   CCTV Equipment

A number of manufacturers produce high-resolution and high-sensitivity closed-circuit television systems for the purposes of ongoing surveillance. A needs analysis is an essential preparatory step for the investigator—discerning the landscape or subject to be surveilled with required equipment. Complete a CCTV needs survey represented at Table 7.1.[28]

With CCTV systems, each camera is wired directly into individual monitors. Figure 7.3[29] depicts the CCTV system.

CCTV technology as well as other innovations play a crucial role in both environmental and situational crime prevention. As citizens and criminals alike encounter CCTV, behavior changes or modifies. Some examples are:

- Effective deployment; CCTV directs security personnel to ambiguous situations, which may head off their development into real criminal acts
- Publicity; CCTV could symbolize efforts to take crime seriously, and the perception of those efforts may energize law-abiding citizens and/or deter others

TABLE 7.1

A CCTV System Design Survey

CCTV System Design Worksheet

Basic Questions for Addressing CCTV System Requirements

1) What areas require coverage by the CCTV system?
2) What are the highest value assets that need to be protected? For example:
   - High-value material property;
   - Critical infrastructure;
   - Intellectual property; and/or
   - Classified material or intelligence information.
3) Where are the sites of greatest vulnerability?
4) Does the information technology infrastructure adequately support the number of cameras?
5) Will the system integrate with an existing physical security system?
6) Will the system integrate with an existing electronic access control system?
7) Does the security budget cover regular maintenance, training, and upgrades to the system?

Source: DHS.

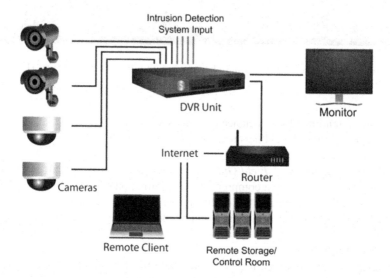

FIGURE 7.3   The design of a networked CCTV system. (Source: DHS.)

- Time for crime; CCTV may be perceived as reducing the time available to commit crime, preventing those crimes that require extended time and effort
- Memory jogging; the presence of CCTV may induce people to take elementary security precautions, such as locking their car, by jogging their memory about the possibility of being victimized
- Anticipated shaming; the presence of CCTV may induce people to take elementary security precautions, for fear that they will be shamed by being shown on CCTV as being careless
- Appeal to the cautious; cautious people may, for example, migrate to the areas containing CCTV to shop or leave their cars[30]

While CCTV is touted as an indispensable tool in security technology, overreliance may be unwise. Specific disadvantages can include:

1. The monitoring screen does not provide as faithful a reproduction of the scene as does direct vision. For this reason, small details are not discernible or are vague to the eye.
2. Dividing the guard's attention between several monitoring screens may not provide the continuity of coverage desired.
3. The resulting eye strain and the boredom of watching a monitor may cause a lack of attention on the part of the security guard.
4. The area viewed may contain so many obstructions that even several CCTV cameras could not give proper coverage; a roving guard or guard patrol would be a better choice in this case.
5. The camera is incapable of taking corrective actions in response to an event that is taking place. The time required to move a security guard or guards to the area may be too great.[31]

Many security companies have an impressive array of surveillance cameras, many of which are creatively disguised in such components as:

- Garbage cans
- Mailboxes
- Fence posts
- Car antennae
- Clocks
- Cigarette packs
- Exit signs
- Tie clips
- Cameras
- Pocketbooks

One effective strategy is to hide the camera's eye within an unassuming sprinkler system (see Figure 7.4).

Web Exercise: Surveillance practice is not without its problems. Read the article on the benefits and problems of CCTV systems in public places at www.popcenter.org/responses/video_surveillance.

7.3.2.2 Photographic/Video Equipment

Employing the photograph as a surveillance tool is wise; however, the agent will have the added pressure of operating photographic equipment correctly. "Good surveillance photographs require good police work plus good photographic techniques. Such techniques include the use of telephoto lenses, the use of infrared flashes or lamps, the processing of film for maximum film speed, and the use of motion picture and time lapse cameras."[32] Photographic surveillance can either be active or passive in nature. In the active category, the investigator is making a conscious decision to be on the scene with the correct equipment. The investigator must be attuned to the difficulties of normal light photography, taking into consideration distances, light, exposure, and climatic factors, and whether or not telephoto shutter speeds, depth of field, and other accessories are needed to take acceptable pictures. Telephoto lenses are also a necessity, although in the age of digital photography this is less so since modern digital cameras are amazingly accurate. It is becoming even more common for the private security industry to employ video recording devices as they become more economical for firms to own and operate.

Web Exercise: Watch the video on advice in choosing photographic equipment for the private investigator at https://youtu.be/BIjkGAkCMhk.

FIGURE 7.4 Cameras can be hidden in other devices including a sprinkler head. (Used with permission: Shutterstock.)

FIGURE 7.5 Motion sensors can trigger alarms or cameras to begin recording. (Used with permission: Shutterstock.)

Passive surveillance is mechanically commenced by the suspect himself with the use of motion detectors (Figure 7.5). Video technology has obviously impacted the industry's surveillance practices in a positive way. See Figure 7.5.

Many devices can sense the presence of an intruder and trigger the operation of a camera.

Photoelectric detector: Relies on a beam of light falling upon a photosensitive detector. If the beam is broken, the camera operates.

Audio detector: Relies on a microphone detector which triggers the camera when noises are made.

Vibration detector: Triggers camera operation with any sensitive detection of movement.

Capacitance detector: A capacitance field is established surrounding an area. A person who breaks the field triggers the camera.

Ultrasonic detector: Uses sound wave patterns to generate camera operation.[33]

The importance of photography in surveillance methods is unquestionable:

The surveillance investigator must obtain clear and identifiable photos or video images of the subject and the subject's actions. If the subject is not known, the investigator should obtain clear pictures and seek out someone, preferably the client, who can positively identify the subject. When surveillance involves several unknown subjects, in the case of a theft or burglary investigation, attempt to obtain clear close-ups and then create "mug shots" or electronic files for later identification.

All photographs must be considered clear enough to identify the subject. If the picture is not clear, the subject may successfully argue in court that the images and acts depicted are someone else. The investigator may lose the argument that he or she is credible because the subject cannot be positively identified. The subject will claim mistaken identity or coincidence.[34]

With all these preparatory steps in mind, and before starting any surveillance process, complete the surveillance checklist as outlined at Figure 7.6.

Surveillance evidence needs to be attentive to claims regarding its integrity and chain of custody. See Figure 7.7 for a surveillance photography log.

| Client: | _____ | Investigator: | _____ |
| Subject: | _____ | Location: | _____ |

Surveillance Checklist

To be checked by investigator: (1) When planning a Surveillance; (2) Immediately prior to departing en route to Surveillance; (3) When returning rental vehicle (to ensure all equipment has been removed); (4) When returning equipment to office (to ensure all equipment is accounted for).

——— 1. Dress Appropriately (Warmly, casually, dress clothes, etc. Also, should you have alternative change of clothes with you?)
——— 2. Binoculars
——— 3. Video Camera – extra cartridges and/or video cards; fully charged batteries; outlet adapter
——— 4. Digital camera – extra cards; fully charged and extra batteries
——— 5. Wrist watch
——— 6. Pen & Paper
——— 7. MP3 player
——— 8. Appropriate forms and signs (pretext interview book, traffic count forms, hand counter, magnetic signs for doors, traffic survey signs, etc.
——— 9. Food and drink
——— 10. Proper vehicle as indicated by area and cover with a full tank of gas
——— 11. Cellular phone fully charged with adapter
——— 12. Proper identification – company and personal ID; business cards, etc.
——— 13. Expense advances
——— 14. Reservations/lodging secured for out of town assignments
——— 15. Handcuffs (when appropriate)
——— 16. Handgun (When appropriate)
——— 17. Flashlight

Date(s) of Surveillance: _____

Commence: _____ Discontinue: _____

Remarks/Precautions: _____

_____

_____

FIGURE 7.6 A surveillance checklist is a good backup to ensure all items required for a surveillance operation are brought along.

Surveillance Photography Log

Investigator _____   Date of Report _____
Subject _____   Claim # _____
Alleged Impairment _____   Address _____

Camera Information
Owner _____   Make _____
Serial Number _____   Model _____

Memory Card Information
Make _____   Capacity _____
Type

Photo Record

File Name	Time	Description of Activities	No. Feet Exposed	Subject Distance

State exactly where photos were taken: Home ( ) Business ( ) Other Location ( )

Provide exact street address: _____

From what vantage point were pictures taken; i.e., across the street, adjacent building, etc.

_____
_____
_____
_____
_____
_____

FIGURE 7.7   An example of a surveillance photography log.

7.4 TYPES OF SURVEILLANCE

The methods and types of security surveillance, while often innovative and technologically advanced, have really stayed fairly standard over the last century. While it is true that the placement of surveillance devices continues to amaze the jaded security specialist, the tactics of person to person or automobile surveillance have remained pretty standard. Surveillance techniques and methods fall into two major categories:

Stationary: That in which the agent is either in a fixed location planted within or on a stake-out.
Moving: Moving either by foot or by vehicle in tight, close, loose, or rough proximity to the subject.

Moving surveillance can be either loose or close:

Loose Surveillance is when caution must be exercised—when the subject must not become aware or even suspicious [that] he is being followed.

Close Surveillance means simply to stay close to him because of contacts he may make, something he might pass to another person, or simply because of prevailing congested conditions.[35]

See Table 7.2.[36]

7.4.1 STATIONARY SURVEILLANCE

Although dramatized as the exciting police stakeout in the movies, stationary surveillance is usually a long and tedious process. The situation usually involves the security investigator who hopes to observe something "go down" such as a theft, robbery, drug deal, sexual assault, or other activities that are not easily detected or observed. Stationary surveillance requires substantial patience while waiting and watching, sometimes without any result over extended periods of time. One of the continuing frustrations of the security professional is in meeting the challenge that surveillance boredom causes. Protracted periods of stationary surveillance can result in extreme occupational burnout.

In stationary surveillance, a stakeout position is selected to observe the target. Typical stakeouts are:

- Adjacent or parallel rooms, apartments, or other locations in the field of vision
- Dummy vehicles
- Nondescript or inconspicuous vehicles

Even though the investigator is perpetually waiting and watching, watching and waiting, the rewards eventually come. In surveillance patience is a virtue! Do not prematurely disengage. The temptation to so do is often referred to as the "burned" complex, that is, a belief and assumption that the lack of activity means the subject is on to him or aware of his surveillance. The agent then believes that the hard work is a complete waste of time and becomes discouraged. When the agent acts in haste, the case is often lost. Be patient, take your time, and realize that a person who has adequately prepared the surveillance plan rarely gets caught.

Web Exercise: Read the short article on methods of surveillance at www.privateinvestigatormiami.us/pi-101-surveillance-techniques-used-private-investigation/.

7.4.2 MOVING SURVEILLANCE

7.4.2.1 Foot Surveillance

Foot surveillance is either individual or by team composition. Most experts believe that the team number should be no more than three. However, for economic and tactical reasons, a one-man

---

TABLE 7.2

A Visual Guide to Loose, Close, and Combined Surveillance

Surveillance Methods		
Loose	**Close**	**Combined**
Subject watched now and then; needed information can be gained by monitoring one facet of subject's activities.	Subject watched constantly; needed information must be gleaned by monitoring more than one facet of subject's activities.	Loose and close surveillance running concurrently on separate subjects or in sequence on one subject to gain more information.

Source: United States Army.

surveillance operation is sometimes the only acceptable method. Some companies recognize that one-man surveillance may be the cheaper option, but produce disappointing results, though acceptable given the expenditure.

7.4.2.1.1 Two-Person Technique

Two-person foot surveillance teams increase the chances for a positive finding. Two agents allow greater flexibility for a plan of operation; two agents also afford greater security against detection and reduce the risk of being spotted. If one comes under suspicion, he or she can duck out while the other takes over. See Figure 7.8[37] for a graphic portrayal of this method.

7.4.2.1.2 Three-Person Technique—the ABC Method

In some security circles, the three-person foot surveillance, referred to as the "ABC Method," is the most desirable strategy. By using three agents, the risk of losing the subject or being detected and identified is minimized. Personal and strategic flexibility in dealing with unanticipated events is the ABC Method's strongest asset. Two typical ABC scenarios are described below and illustrated in Figures 7.9 and 7.10.

FIGURE 7.8   An illustration of two-person surveillance operations. (Source: United States Army.)

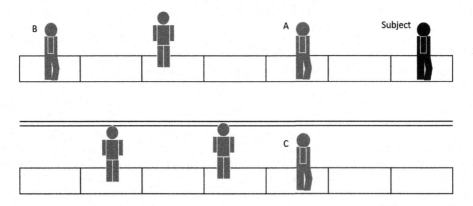

FIGURE 7.9   Basic ABC procedure—normal pedestrian traffic.

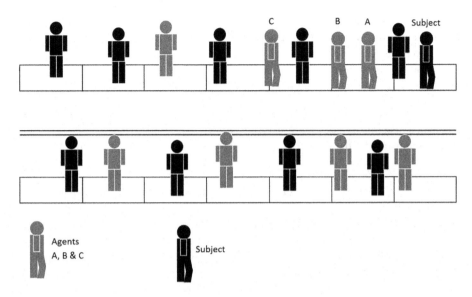

FIGURE 7.10   ABC procedure on very crowded street.

- Agent A is to the rear of the subject and with a reasonable distance between them. What is reasonable depends on the number of people on the street between Agent A and the subject. The fewer the people, the greater the distance should be. A common mistake of the new agent is to have too much distance between himself and the subject.
- Agent B follows Agent A. Agent B's responsibility is to keep Agent A in sight and to detect associates of the subject. The distance between Agents A and B is slightly more than the distance between Agent A and the subject.
- Agent C is on the opposite side of the street and slightly to the rear of the subject. Agent C's responsibility is to keep both the subject and Agent A in sight.
- All three agents are on the same side of the street as the subject
- Agent A should follow very close to the subject
- Agent B concentrates on keeping Agent A in view
- Agent C concentrates on keeping Agent B in view

The ABC Method works better than a one- or two-man surveillance because the subject is less likely to feel that he or she is being followed. Suspicions are aroused more easily with a one-man foot patrol. With the three-man method, if any of the agents is noticed, one of the three agents can easily drop out without causing the surveillance to end. See Figure 7.11[38] for another representation of a three-man surveillance method.

The ABC technique allows several choices when the subject turns the corner. Assume A and B are behind the subject and C is across the street when the subject turns the corner away from C. A could keep going straight and B would take the A position. C would move across to the B position. A would stay across the street, moving as C had done before.

Another approach would be for C to move into the A position. A would go across and take up the C position, while B keeps his own. What if the subject turns left and crosses the street toward C? C drops back and A continues in the original direction and becomes C. Then B moves into the A position, and C becomes B.[39]

Certain conduct might indicate the subject's suspicion of being followed. The suspect may:

- Reverse his direction
- Watch for your reflection

- Drop a piece of paper to see who picks it up
- Board a conveyance, then get off just before it leaves
- Walk around a corner and stop
- Use someone else to help him
- Use multi-exit buildings to escape you[40]

The suspect may also use a decoy, escape down an alley, take the last taxi, or even change his appearance, disguise himself, or lose himself in a crowd.

In some circumstances, the subject may confront the investigator. If this occurs:

- Act in a natural manner
- Act indignant and walk away from subject in the same direction the investigator/agent had been going before approached
- Determine if subject is following you by using a plate-glass window as a mirror
- Be sure the subject is not the investigator/agent's supervisor conducting a field investigation
- If subject is tailing the investigator/agent, the agent can lose the subject in an office building, subway, crowd, bus, taxi, etc.
- The investigator/agent must drop suspicious subject in a natural manner to create doubt in the subject's mind as to whether or not he was being followed

Web Exercise: Watch the short video about solo surveillance at https://youtu.be/qzzzYU7YwQk.

7.4.2.2 Auto Surveillance

Auto surveillance is a regular and reliable method of general intelligence gathering. Though it may be used to surveil premises and individuals on occasion, the primary function is in the surveillance of other vehicles. Naturally, the appearance of the vehicle should be subdued. It is strongly recommended that two agents be in the vehicle since driving restricts full and uninterrupted observational capacity. "The driver must have exceptional car handling ability; the second must be constantly alert and ready to assist the driver in maintaining surveillance."[41]

Except in rare and exceptional circumstances, the auto agents should not violate traffic laws and should fully cooperate if police intervene or seek identification. Public law enforcement officers are skilled in detecting vehicles on a contrived and steady tail of another vehicle.

FIGURE 7.11 A follows the subject and B follows A. C normally stays across the street and just to the rear of the subject. (Source: United States Army.)

Distance from the surveilled target is also a recurring concern in planning moving auto surveillance. Distance will largely depend on traffic conditions, topography, and the ability of the agent and the subject to move. Once behind the subject, the agent must use every means possible to avoid any prolonged viewing of his vehicle by the subject in his rearview mirror. By using other surveillance groups and vehicles (these vehicles being described as *cover vehicles*), the image projected in the rearview mirror can be confused (see Figure 7.12).

Auto surveillance technique and procedure is guided by the geographic or topographic area where surveillance is taking place. For example, compare and contrast the surveillance technique employed on an open highway versus city traffic. Predictably, dense city traffic can cause immense frustrations for the surveillant, such as when the subject vehicle makes abrupt traffic adjustments. The pattern of traffic lights, stop signs, and the amount of cars between the surveillant's vehicle and the subject have much to do with keeping position, not getting burned or identified, and witnessing events and activities in the subject's vehicle. On the open highway, such as an interstate or other four-lane road, multiple surveillance vehicles are generally wise practice since the subject of surveillance has a wider plane of view, thereby enabling him to identify or become accustomed to one particular automobile. In highway situations, it is more advantageous to have multiple surveillance vehicles. In the multiple-vehicle surveillance scheme, the *lead vehicle*—the actual pursuit car—is sometimes referred to as the "eyeball." Sound policy dictates that the other vehicles, depending on conditions, switch and give up their various positions to minimize the potential for detection. The laws of traffic etiquette and habit such as passing, moving to other lanes, acceleration or deceleration of the vehicle, or temporary pullover make a switch of position or control relatively easy.

7.4.2.2.1 Auto Surveillance Techniques

Obviously, a surveillance method that is easily detected is of little value to the private security investigator. Persons engaged in illegal, illicit, or questionable conduct tend to act defensively and with suspicious body language. In auto situations, the subject driver is generally on the lookout for persons who tail. The situations described below include tactical plans to minimize detection and carry out successful surveillance. However, these suggestions are general; events, conditions, circumstances, and territories may make these strategies inappropriate.

7.4.2.2.1.1 Open Highway/Interstate Highway   In individual situations, keep your distance, consider a change of hat, coat, or sunglasses, even changing license plates. A temporary pull-off onto the shoulder or at a rest stop may be appropriate. (See Figure 7.13).

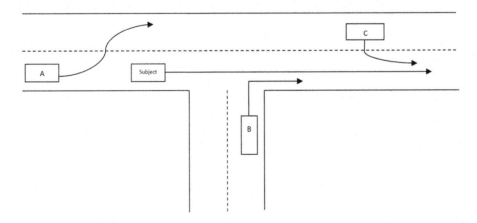

FIGURE 7.12 An illustration of vehicle surveillance.

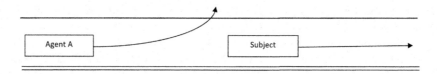

FIGURE 7.13 Pulling off may be appropriate to avoid detection.

7.4.2.2.1.2 Left Turn (Subject Left Lane; Agent Right Lane)   A switch of lanes may be obvious. Go through the intersection and make U-turn. If switch of lane is not likely to be detected, do so. (See Figure 7.14).

7.4.2.2.1.3 Left Turn (Subject in Lane without Traffic Signal)   If the agent mimics subject, detection is probable. Go through the intersection and make first feasible U-turn to get back into position behind the subject. (Figure 7.15).

In the left-turn situations described above, the agent has to proceed through the intersection, which heightens the risk of losing the subject. For this reason, one-man auto surveillance is often unsuccessful. By use of multiple surveillance vehicles, the lead car can pass through the intersection, and the second or third vehicle can follow the subject through the left turn.

7.4.2.2.1.4 Left Turn (Subject Passes through Green; Agent Stuck at Red)   In multiple-vehicle situations, lead vehicle, after proceeding through intersection and making contact with the other agents, must make an aggressive U-turn and attempt to reestablish surveillance (See Figure 7.16).

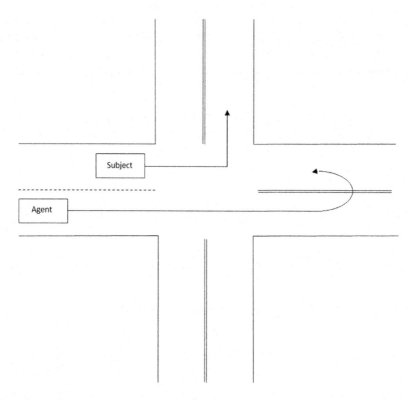

FIGURE 7.14 Subject is in the left lane making a left. The agent goes through an intersection then makes a U-turn.

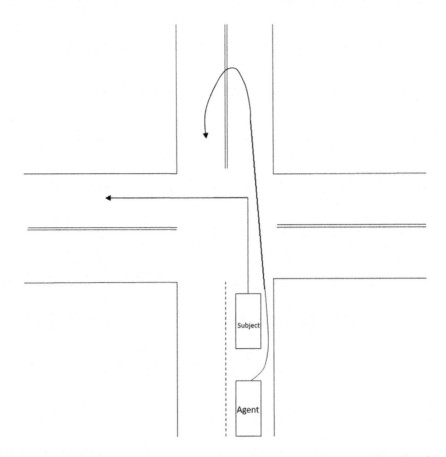

FIGURE 7.15 The subject takes a left across oncoming traffic. Again, the agent goes through an intersection then makes a U-turn.

7.4.2.2.1.5 Illegal or Improper Turn by Subject When the subject makes illegal turns, mimicry by the lead vehicle results in absolute and automatic detection. The lead vehicle should continue straight and make a U-turn (see Figure 7.15 above).

7.4.2.2.1.6 Multiple Surveillance (Changing Position of Vehicles) To avoid detection, alternate the positions of the lead and other surveillance vehicles. Do not change lead vehicle position until another agent is ready to, and capable of, assuming the lead position (Figure 7.17).

7.4.2.2.1.7 Traffic Light (Subject Runs through Red) Subjects often run traffic lights. Wait at the intersection and hope that the light will change quickly or that the subject vehicle will be caught at the next light. (See Figure 7.18).

7.4.2.2.1.8 U-Turn by Subject In cases of multiple auto surveillance, the lead team can notify the other surveillance vehicles, then continue straight, turn around and try to reestablish the tail (Figure 7.19).

7.4.2.2.1.9 Stopping beyond a Corner or on the Crest of a Hill by Subject To avoid detection, the lead vehicle must drive past the curb. In cases using multiple vehicle surveillance, the lead vehicle agent should relay the position and location of the subject to other surveillance agents (Figure 7.20).

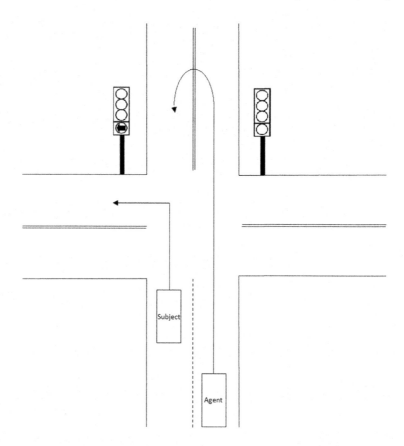

FIGURE 7.16   The subject takes a left across oncoming traffic. Again, the agent goes through an intersection then makes a U-turn.

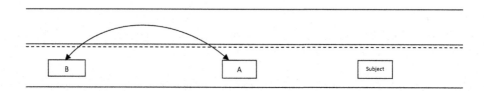

FIGURE 7.17   Alternate the positions of the lead and other surveillance vehicles.

7.4.2.2.1.10   Right or Left Turn into an Alley by Subject   Because an alley is not a normal inter-section, do not turn into the alley. Lead vehicle should stop before the alley. Meanwhile, the sec-ondary surveillant, the passenger in the lead vehicle can observe the subject and advise the other surveillance vehicle what the subject is doing (Figure 7.21).

7.4.2.2.1.11   Leading Surveillance   Leading surveillance requires several drivers and vehicles. This technique is a boxing-in strategy to keep the subject between a lead vehicle and other sur-veillance vehicles. Although it is not always an acceptable method, this technique works best in situations in which the subject's direction and eventual destination are known. By enclosing the subject vehicle in this manner, the surveillance vehicles following have more leeway in distance (Figure 7.22).

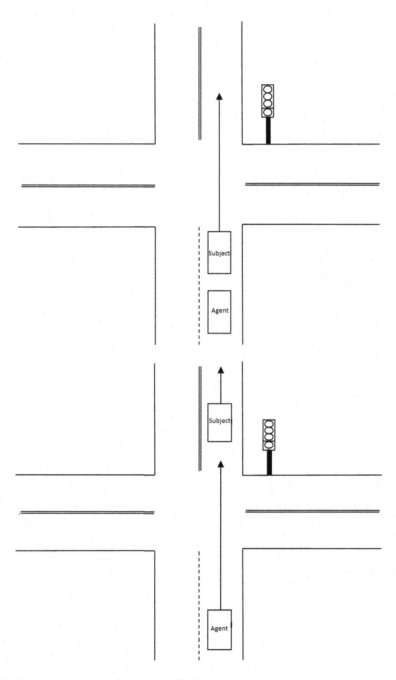

FIGURE 7.18 Following a subject through a traffic light.

7.4.2.2.1.12 Progressive Surveillance Progressive surveillance is not a continuous, ongoing, or predictable method of watching the subject's vehicle. When one is tracking or surveilling highly attuned, tail-conscious subjects, progressive surveillance is particularly effective. Progressive surveillance avoids the possibility of a subject identifying or witnessing routine practices by the surveillance vehicle. The method involves stationing surveillance vehicles at various points along a known or suspected route of travel, especially at intersections. The vehicles are hidden at these

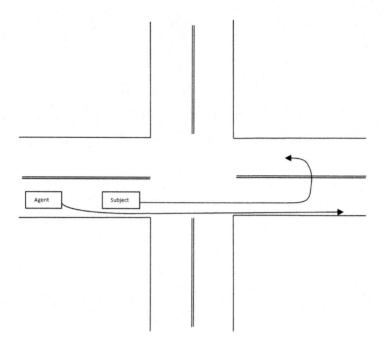

FIGURE 7.19 In the case of a U-turn by the subject, with multiple auto surveillance.

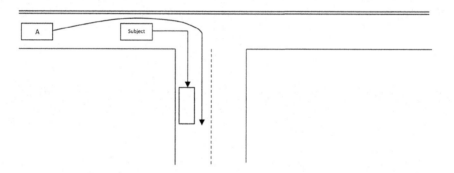

FIGURE 7.20 Stopping beyond a corner or on a crest of a hill.

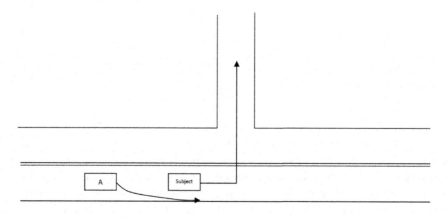

FIGURE 7.21 Diagram in the event subject turns into an alley.

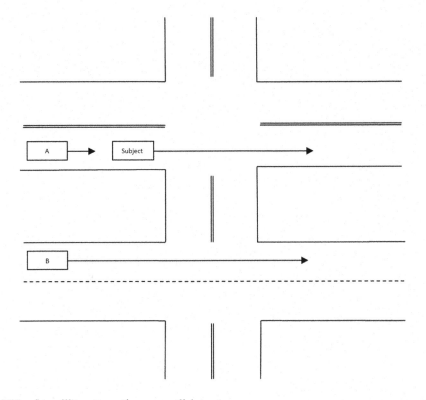

FIGURE 7.22 Leading surveillance requires several drivers and vehicles that results in a boxing-in technique.

intersections or agents are stationed on foot. If the subject fails to reach a particular intersection, progressive surveillance makes is possible to determine where he turned off. An example of progressive surveillance is:

First Day: One investigator follows subject to the bus stop and drops him.
Second Day: A different investigator is waiting for the subject at the bus stop and rides on the bus with him to his destination. He remains on the bus when subject alights.
Third Day: Another investigator is waiting when the subject gets off the bus and follows him either to his first stop or for a short distance and drops him, etc., etc.

Progressive surveillance is costly, but in cases where detection is likely or the subject catches on to surveillance quickly, it is strongly recommended.

7.4.2.2.1.13 Parallel Surveillance Figure 7.23 shows vehicles operating on parallel streets. The technique is remarkably useful in removing multiple surveillance vehicles from the subject';s view on a street with little or no traffic and gives greater flexibility to agents when turns occur. Multiple

FIGURE 7.23 Surveillance operating on parallel streets.

surveillance vehicles must adapt and adjust their positions as turns are made or acceleration or deceleration takes place. Constant contact is mandatory.

Web Exercise: Watch the video on vehicle surveillance at https://youtu.be/OAo9RVikLCE.

7.4.3 Hybrid and Other Special Surveillance Techniques

7.4.3.1 Foot and Auto Surveillance

Some combination between foot and auto surveillance is often advisable, particularly in congested urban areas. Figure 7.24 shows a subject vehicle being tailed by a surveillance vehicle on a suspected or known route. Note that, one block up, a foot surveillance agent awaits the subject vehicle's arrival.

As mentioned earlier, no surveillance vehicle should have only one agent, the driver. The demands of auto operation are a major distraction to an agent's observational skills. The second party in the vehicle, often referred to as the footman, has the following occupational responsibilities:

1. Watch the subject's car; keep the driver advised of its movement.
2. Place the subject under surveillance immediately if the subject should get out of his car. The driver will park the car and join him when he can. (See Figure 7.25.)
3. If the surveillance car is stopped by a light, the footman must keep the subject's car in sight. If the subject turns right or left at an intersection when the surveillance car is stopped, the footman should get out of the surveillance car and get to the corner in case the subject makes another turn. If necessary, the footman is to run to that corner. If the subject's car proceeds straight ahead and surveillance car is stopped at a light, the footman should alight so that he can watch the movements of the subject's vehicle, particularly if the subject turns right or left at the following intersection. (See Figure 7.26.)

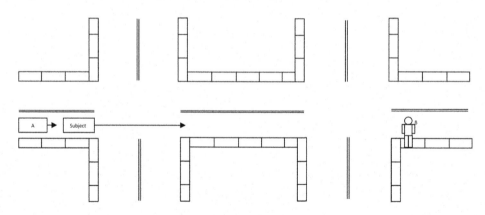

FIGURE 7.24 Combination foot and auto suveillance.

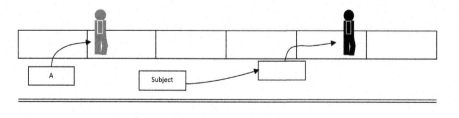

FIGURE 7.25 When the subject pulls over the car and gets out.

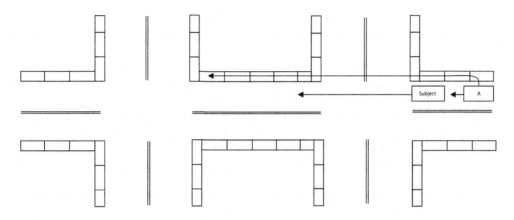

FIGURE 7.26 The footman gets out of the surveillance care to watch the movements of the subject's vehicle.

7.4.3.2 Surveillance at Bus Stops

Surveillance of a subject at a bus stop requires special attention. The following methods are suggested:

1. As the subject approaches the bus, get close rapidly so that you are as close to him as possible when the bus stops.
2. Enter the bus directly behind subject in order to be able to walk by him unseen when he takes his seat.
3. Always take a position to the rear of the bus and behind the subject.
4. Sit on the same side of the bus as the subject. We all look at those persons across from us.
5. If possible, remain seated when subject stands to leave the bus. Wait until he is alighting, then leave the bus with him. Subjects who are surveillance-conscious will walk to the door of the bus and then return to their seats, thereby catching the investigator off guard.

7.4.3.3 Use of Pretext

A pretext is an alleged, assumed, or feigned representation or introduction that conceals the real intention and purpose of the surveillance. A pretext is an acting job and is not to be confused with the technique of "roping," which refers to the investigator's capacity to draw out or obtain information without an individual realizing it. People are reluctant to give information to law enforcement officials (either public or private in nature); thus, pretexts are often necessary in performing the functions of investigation. A pretext is not a direct or affirmative misrepresentation, nor is it an affirmative allegation or impression of false authority or control. The investigator merely conceals his true purpose and affords the respondent an opportunity to talk and relay information. However, caution must be exercised because the operation of a pretext skims dangerously near the legal issues of privacy, obstruction of justice, and official misrepresentation.[42]

Pretexts should be adopted with these reservations:

- Only thoroughly experienced and trained investigators are assigned to surveillance and/or pretext work, especially in those instances where the subject has a suit pending for personal injuries alleged to have resulted from an accident of some nature.

- The pretext interview with the claimant should be limited to an identification of the subject and an observation of any apparent condition that would indicate that the claim is misrepresented.
- The pretext investigator is not to enter the claimant's residence if it can be avoided.
- The pretext investigator should never be on the surveillance team, for this would be likely to give away the surveillants. If manpower restraints make it necessary for the same person to be involved in pretext and surveillance, special care must be exercised to assure that the surveillance investigator and the designated investigator are not identified as the same person. The use of a hat, sunglasses, false mustache, change of clothes, etc. can all be used to disguise the investigator. The designated investigator must never allow his automobile to be seen by the subject.
- A surveillance will not be continued after the [pretext investigator] is assured the subject is aware of the surveillance.
- The investigators will not tell neighbors or other persons having no legitimate interest therein of the personal business or intimate activities of the subject under surveillance; or tell false stories about the subject.
- The investigators will not spy upon the subject in the privacy of the subject's home or take pictures of the subject under such circumstances.
- The investigators will strictly limit their picture-taking to activities that are inconsistent with the subject's claim.
- The investigators must not falsely represent themselves to be a federal, state, county, or city law enforcement officer, nor a newspaper reporter, nor an employee of or representative of a bona fide concern or organization.
- The investigators will not furnish a company's address or telephone number.
- The investigators will not furnish any information through which their identity might be established, nor permit anyone to obtain the license number of the automobile they are using.

Web Exercise: Read the article on pretexting laws and court cases at www.privateinvestigatoradvicehq.com/pretexting-laws/.

7.4.3.3.1   Examples of Pretext

7.4.3.3.1.1   Personal Injury Accident   The security investigator represents that he or she is an agent of the National Accident Prevention Association, which acquires and studies data on reported accidents.

7.4.3.3.1.2   Bank Account   Call the bank indicating that you are a merchant checking whether or not sufficient funds exist to honor a check.

7.4.3.3.1.3   Character and Community Reputation   Indicate to neighbors that you are considering relocation to the area but are concerned about the character, reputation, and of the manner of living of your next-door neighbor.

7.4.3.3.1.4   Claim Settlement–Verification   Act as if you are a representative of the National Claims Bureau, which is a nonprofit entity created by the insurance industry to calculate and report on the amount of settlements reached in insurance cases.

7.4.3.3.1.5   Disability Case   The following pretexts may provide the investigator with information:

- Tell subject that one of your relatives suffered a similar injury or illness and that you have heard that the subject's therapeutic regimen and treatment had been most effective.

Could subject advise of doctors' names and results and whether or not results were positive.

- Say that you are conducting a survey to determine the rate of unemployment in a particular trade occupation.
- Indicate that you are a contractor and had heard that person being surveyed was a skilled carpenter or tradesman. Ask whether or not the individual has any interest in doing work on the side.

7.4.3.3.1.6 Acquiring a Handwriting Sample   The following pretexts may allow the investigator to acquire a writing sample:

- Advise the subject that you are conducting a survey for a consumer group, Manufacturer's Trade Association, and that you need to obtain certain data. Ask for a signature after the survey has been completed.
- Ask person to sign a petition for a worthwhile (but fictitious) cause.

7.4.3.3.1.7 Location of Persons   The following pretexts may help locate a suspect:

- Indicate to a neighbor of the subject that you were once a roommate or close friend of subject and that you are trying to retrieve goods that were borrowed by the subject.
- Indicate that you were once a co-employee with the subject and that you had shared tools and other belongings and seek return of said items.

7.4.3.3.1.8 Video Surveillance Pictures   The following pretexts may allow the investigator to take pictures of the suspect:

- One investigator walks up to the suspect and says that his or her car has broken down (or needs directions, etc.) while the other agent in vehicle operates a camera in a discreet manner.
- Give the impression that you are a freelance writer, photographer, and filmmaker and that you are engaged in the collection of information for a national magazine or in the preparation of a film for educational purposes.

7.4.3.3.1.9 Occupation or Employment of Subject   The following pretexts may ascertain the subject's occupation:

- Call subject's residence acting as if you are employed by a private nongovernmental employment agency. Preferably talk with someone other than the subject asking if he or she has acquired a position and what that position is.
- Say that you are conducting a national survey for a business and industrial concern that seeks qualified employees in the area in which the company will be located.

7.4.3.3.1.10 Stockholder or Shareholder Suit   Indicate that you represent a firm (located in a distant city) that plans to contract with the subject's firm, but has heard rumors and innuendo regarding legal problems and difficulties.

7.4.3.3.1.11 Suicide/Murder of Business Owner   Make clear that you represent a principal who is interested in purchasing the business once owned by the deceased but are in need of information regarding total assets and liabilities. During the course of the discussion, indicate that the deceased should have done much more business and inquire if he knew if the deceased had any personal difficulties such as domestic squabbling, financial troubles, or ongoing illnesses.

The above pretexts are merely introductory suggestions regarding circumstances and events that arise in private investigation. Always be attentive to the ethical and legal boundaries these activities encompass. Investigators must be on their guard not to violate accepted standards of conduct.

Web Exercise: Watch the video on the number one pretext fundamental at https://youtu.be/SCQAABblaOs.

7.5 SURVEILLANCE FORMS AND REPORTS

As in all facets of private investigation, report writing, and note taking, accurate documentation is essential for any professional investigation. The daily grind of surveillance needs to be reported and recorded for later reference and compared with historically accumulated data and evidence. Most firms regularly keep a surveillance log which will serve as a cover sheet to a more substantial report. An example is at Figure 7.27.

Surveillance Log Cover Sheet

Subject _____   Conducted by (Investigators) _____
Address _____   _____
Telephone _____   Case No. _____
Social Security # _____   Case Name _____
Date of Birth _____
Description _____

Type of Injury _____

Vehicles _____
_____   Date _____

Persons Observed   Times Observed

Synopsis:
☐ Subject Observed   ☐ Contact Observed   ☐ Photos Attempted
☐ Subject not observed   ☐ Unusual activity   ☐ Assessment data obtained
_____ Hours   _____ Minutes = Total time on subject

Administrative Data:

Equipment:
Van: _____   Starting Mileage:_____ Finish Mileage:_____
Photos   Yes _____   No_____
Video   Yes _____   No_____

FIGURE 7.27 An example of a surveillance log cover sheet.

Field notes are of the utmost importance in the eventual construction and drafting of a surveillance report. "Complete notes are invaluable later for developing leads and for carrying out the substantive work of the investigation."[43] The surveillance officer must always remember that note taking serves as the foundational support for whatever eventual documentation is submitted to the client. The surveillance report probably makes the biggest impression on a client. Keep in mind these points regarding notes:

1. Surveillance reports are compiled from investigator's notes.
2. Notes must be accurate, exact, and thorough—investigator may have to testify from or about them.
3. Notes should show investigator's initials and dates.
4. Notes should reflect events listed opposite a time caption in chronological order, to the nearest minute.
5. Notes must be handed in with the investigator's report.
6. The supervisor must check investigator's notes with his report to determine:
   a.   If time captions are correct, and
   b.   If any pertinent information was left out of the report.[44]

The culmination of surveillance activities results in either a daily, weekly, or summary surveil-lance report. Review Figure 7.28, titled "Daily Surveillance Report," written in a memorandum

Daily Surveillance Report

To:

From:

RE: Surveillance of

On: [Date]

(Paragraph 1)

   Summary of debriefing to include date, time, information received from supervisor

(Paragraph 2)

   Proposed method of surveillance.

(Paragraph 3)

   Any deviation from plan and reason for such.

(Paragraph 4)

   Activity Log

Example:

6/22/18

8:00 a.m.   Smith exits residence and enters car. (Include color, make, model, year if known, and registration.

8:03 a.m.   Smith drives to CoGo's convenience store via Main Street and enters the store.

8:06 a.m.   Smith exits the store, carrying two medium - sized bags. (photograph taken)

FIGURE 7.28   Sample Daily Surveillance Report.

in chronological date, time, and activity format. Note the sequential and conceptual order of presentation. Paragraph 1 calls for a summary or debriefing of the activities undertaken. Paragraph 2 requests a discussion on the proposed method of surveillance. Paragraph 3 seeks an explanation for a deviation from said plan. At paragraph 4, the activity log commences.

Another proposed format of construction for a surveillance report is at Box 7.1. Some differences in style are apparent. First, this example uses a synopsis format as seen on the first page of the report. Second, this report places more emphasis on factual and comprehensive writing (e.g., see the 8:15 a.m. designation). This type of detailed authorship is most commendable. Other specific points include:

- The investigator is required to type all reports.
- The investigator must includeall descriptions of cars and people.
- The investigator must always describe the person being followed and what he is wearing the first time he is observed, and at the beginning of each day, and any changes of clothing thereafter.
- The surveillance report must note photographic or video evidence gathered on the assignment and file appropriate forms and documentation.[45]

BOX 7.1   AN ALTERNATIVE, NARRATIVE STYLE SURVEILLANCE REPORT

XYZ Insurance
Claimant: Jim Smith
Worker's Compensation Claim Investigation
Claim No. 1234A BCD
Wednesday, June, 17, 2018

Synopsis:

Jim Smith was observed on this date working under the hood of his pickup truck. It was a particularly hot day, with temperatures up to 96 degrees.

In the early afternoon he was observed walking briskly with a sure stride; then he was observed pulling weeds in his garden, bending over at the waist to do so, and hanging clothes onto a clothesline in his backyard.

Smith was also observed bending forward to raise the door of his garage with his right hand grasping a small piece of rope. After placing several objects into the back seat of an automobile, he reached upward over his head with his right hand to grasp the rope attached to the garage door handle. He yanked the cord downward, pulling the garage door shut in one easy motion. He returned to the driver's seat of the automobile and drove away.

At no time did Smith's face reflect signs of pain or discomfort, and he did not exhibit any signs of strain or difficulty.

Reading of this entire report is recommended.

COMPANY: XYZ Insurance	OFFICE: Wilmington
CLAIMANT: Jim Smith	CLAIM NO.: 1234A BCD

INVESTIGATION TYPE: Worker's Compensation Claim Investigation
CONFIDENTIAL

	City	Day of week	Date

COMMENCED: 5:30 am   DISCONTINUED: 7:00 pm

Received details and commenced surveillance of Jim Smith, known to reside at 67 Oak Street, Anytown, DE, 00000.

5:30 am	This investigator, after receiving details of this assignment, departed Wilmington en route to Anytown, DE.
8:02 am	Arrived in Anytown and proceeded to Anytown Post Office, 100 W. Main Street.
8:15 am	Contacted the Anytown Post Office, who provided directions to the Smith residence. These directions are as follows:
	Take Main Street going east through town 2.2 miles. At the intersection of E. Main Street and Oak Street turn right onto Oak Street. The Smith residence is the third house on the left. A mailbox with the house number, 67, is at the end of the driveway.
8:32 am	Proceeded to the vicinity of the subject's residence and found it to be a suburban, middle-class residential area, consisting of mostly wood-frame, one and two story structures. The estimated value of these homes is between $75,000 and $85,000.
9:00 am	Located the Smith house. The subject's residence is described as a red sided two story home with an enclosed front porch. There is a paved driveway to the right of the residence leading to a small-frame garage located to the right rear of the home. The garage stands apart from the home and is sided red.
	The residence appears to be well maintained. The lawn and shrubbery show signs of regular care; there is a small flower garden and vegetable garden, also showing signs of care. The vegetable garden is located at the rear of the property.
	The Smith residence, consisting of .75 acres, is estimated to be valued at $75,000.
	Parked in the driveway, heading toward the garage is a:
	1999 Chevrolet Silverado pickup truck, silver in color, current Delaware license number 000 XXXX.
9:01 am	While initially driving by the Smith residence, I observed that the hood of the above-described pickup truck was raised. Sitting on the edge of the truck's left front fender, bending slightly over the engine, was an individual described as:
	Male, white, age 44, 5′8″ tall, 178 lbs., muscular build with pot belly, deeply tanned, close-cropped light brown hair, wearing no shirt and faded blue jeans
	Believed to be Jim Smith, and hereafter referred to as Smith.
	It should be noted that the weather is clear and sunny, the temperature averaging 96 degrees Fahrenheit, and humidity high.
9:42 am	I have established surveillance of the Smith residence. Smith is not in sight at this time. The hood of the pickup truck is now down, Smith apparently having returned to his house. Noted at this time, parked in the driveway to the left of the silver pickup truck is a:
	Shiny, red 2005 Chevrolet Cobalt, current Delaware license number 111 ZZZZ.
10:11 am	I observed a female described as:
	White, age 25, 5′4″ tall, 155 lbs, chunky build, pale complexion, dark, shoulder-length wavy hair, wearing light colored, short sleeved top with dark colored slacks.
	This female left Smith's residence with several, small, active children. They entered the above-described Cobalt and she drove away.
11:17 am	Activity at the Smith residence observed since the departure of the Cobalt.
	A moderate, continuing flow of local traffic, pickup trucks and automobiles, passed the Smith residence.
12:00 pm	Still no activity observed at the Smith residence since the Cobalt's departure at 10:11 am.
12:35 pm	Smith, now wearing a white, sweat-stained T-shirt, walked briskly from the rear of the house across the yard to the flower garden on the right side of the house. Smith walked with a sure stride, his upper torso appeared to be slightly stiff as he walked, his arms swinging mechanically, close to his body.
12:36 pm	Smith was observed for 8 minutes pulling weeds from the flower garden. This physical movement involved his bending forward at the waist, knees slightly crooked, his arms extended forward toward the ground, using both hands to pull and discard weeds. Smith, in the bent-over position, moving very slowly forward along the edge of the garden, raised upright only twice during this 8 minute period, apparently to arch his back and stretch. During this period, Smith was observed weeding his garden, he slowly inched forward a total of 3 feet along the garden's edge.

12:43 pm	At this time, Smith raised upright and immediately proceeded to walk from the garden to the tool shed (approximately 17 feet), with no obvious hesitation or difficulty.
12:45 pm	Smith, after leaving the tool shed, was briefly observed hanging several pieces of clothing on the outside clothesline on the left, rear side of the house. When observed, he was using both arms to hang the clothes, his hands raised to head level in front of his body. This activity lasted approximately 2 minutes.
12:54 pm	I observed an automobile, described as:

Blue, 2008 Ford Mustang, current Delaware license number 123 ZYXW

drive into the paved driveway and park next to the silver pickup truck. A man described as:

White, age 72, 5′3″ tall, 148 lbs., bony build with hunchback, pale complexion, short white hair, wearing dark colored hat, white long-sleeved shirt and overalls, alighted from this automobile and walked slowly into the Smith house.

12:58 pm	Smith and the elderly man described above left the house, the older man returning to the blue automobile, and Smith walking toward the garage door. Again, Smith walked in a confident manner, a grin on his face, showing no apparent distress.
12:59 pm	Smith, at the closed garage door, bent forward to the ground and gripped a small piece of rope attached to the door handle in his right hand. Smith then, in one, smooth, unbroken motion, swiftly raised upright, raising the garage door completely open.
1:00 pm	Smith entered the garage (empty of cars) and picked up in his right hand a large plastic container the size of a clothes basket and an unidentified object in his left hand. With these objects in his hand, Smith walked swiftly, approximately 30 feet to the back of the blue car.
1:01 pm	Smith opened the trunk and bent forward over the rear of the car at a 90 degree angle and placed the objects in the car. He then raised upright and closed the trunk and walked back to the garage in the above-described manner.
1:02 pm	Smith then reached upward over his head with his right hand to grasp the cord attached to the garage door handle. He yanked the cord downward, pulling the garage door shut in one easy motion.
1:03 pm	Smith returned to the blue car, climbing into the driver's seat with no apparent hesitation. Smith had a constant smile on his face, showing no signs of discomfort or strain while walking, opening and closing the garage door, or getting into the blue automobile.
1:04 pm	Smith, driving the blue automobile, backed into the driveway, then drove forward onto the road. He then drove the blue automobile out of my sight.
2:15 pm	Smith had not returned to the house.
3:00 pm	As no further activity was observed, I departed the area en route to Wilmington, discontinuing surveillance for this day.
5:20 pm	Arrived at the Wilmington office and began report preparation.
7:00 pm	Concluded this report and discontinued work for the day.

SUPERVISOR'S NOTE: The license plate of the silver Chevrolet pickup truck (DE 000 XXXX) and the red Chevrolet Cobalt (DE 111 ZZZZ) were found to be registered to Jim Smith at 67 Oak Street, Anytown, DE, 00000.

Additional surveillance is recommended to further document the activity of Jim Smith.

Final until further advised.

7.6 CONCLUSION

This chapter's main focus was on the practices and procedures relating to surveillance. How surveillance serves the private security industry and the investigative team is quite obvious from its many uses in many types of cases. Special discussion of how surveillance practice assists in the resolution of crimes, disability claims and injury claims, illegal fencing and other property operations, retail theft and other economic crime were all highlighted. In addition, readers were given a broad and detailed assessment of how surveillance methods lead to effective surveillance results. Full coverage of the many types of surveillance was posed including stationery one-person stakeouts to multiparty observation. Other coverage stressed how the automobile can be used to ferret out every sort of bad person and the many harms they inflict. Graphic diagrams which illustrate these techniques were posed throughout the chapter and practical tools for surveillance practice fully made available.

NOTES

1. International Foundation for Protection Officers, "Surveillance: Concepts and Practices for Fraud, Security and Crime Investigation" (2005): 1, accessed September 9, 2018, www.hitsinstitute.com/pdf/surveillance.pdf.; see also Rod Gehl and Darryl Plecas, *Introduction to Criminal Investigation: Processes, Practices &Thinking* (University of Fraser Valley, BC, 2018); Charles P. Nemeth, *Private Security: Principles and Practice* (Boca Raton, FL: CRC Press, 2018).
2. Michael A Gips, "Image Is Everything in Stopping Crime," *Security Management*, February 2004: 12; "Public Cameras Yet to Be Real-Time Intelligence for Security," *Corporate Security*, January 31, 2007: 6.
3. David Aspland, "The Other Side of 'Big Brother': CCTV Surveillance and Intelligence Gathering by Private Police," *Journal of Cases on Information Technology* 13, no. 2 (April–June 2011): 34, http://dx.doi.org/10.4018/jcit.2011040103.
4. PRMG Security, 2899 E. Big Beaver Rd. Suite 135, Troy, MI 48083, accessed September 9, 2018, http://prmgsecurity.com/corporate-fraud-investigation.
5. Hidefumi Nishiyama, "Crowd Surveillance: The (In)Securitization of the Urban Body," *Security Dialogue* 49, no. 3 (2018): 200–216.
6. See Torin Monahan, "The Future of Security? Surveillance Operations at Homeland Security Fusion Centers," *Social Justice* 37, nos. 2–3 (2010): 84–98.
7. Robert Liscouski, "Surveillance Is Not a Dirty Word," *Security* 51, no. 8 (August 2014): 37.
8. Kirstie S. Ball, and David Murakami Wood, "Political Economies of Surveillance," *Surveillance &Society* 11, no. 1 (2013): 1–3; Bill Zalud, "12 Cost-Effective Video Strategies," *Security* 52, no. 11 (November 2015): 87–89.
9. Pinkerton's, Inc., *Surveillance Manual* 2 (1990); Ball and Wood, "Political Economies"; IFPO, "Surveillance."
10. Eddie Cruz, "Foot Surveillance: Keeping Your Cover," *Pursuit Magazine*, April 11, 2017, http://pursuit-mag.com/foot-surveillance-keeping-your-cover/.
11. K. C. Scott-Brown and P. D. J. Cronin, "Detect the Unexpected: A Science for Surveillance," *Policing* 31 (2008): 395; Tom Shamshak, "Private Investigator Basics Part 3: Surveillance," PInow.com, May 21, 2012, www.pinow.com/articles/1195/private-investigator-basics-surveillance; Cruz, "Foot Surveillance"; IFPO, "Surveillance"; Council of the Inspectors General on Integrity and Efficiency, *Guidelines on Undercover Operations* (2013), www.ignet.gov/sites/default/files/files/guidelines-under-cover-operations-june-2013.pdf.
12. Joseph M. LaSorsa, "25 Tips for Surveillance Operatives: On Tactics, Equipment, and Reports," *Pursuit Magazine*, April 5, 2016, http://pursuitmag.com/surveillance-tactics-equipment-reports/.
13. W. Bennett and K. Hess, *Criminal Investigation* (1981): 235; LaSorsa, "25 Tips"; IFPO, "Surveillance"; Inspectors General, "Undercover Operations."
14. For the brave new world of surveillance legal challenges—consider how drones will test our usual boundaries. See Deven R. Desai, "Constitutional Limits on Surveillance: Associational Freedom in the Age of Data Hoarding," *Notre Dame Law Review* 90 (December 2014): 579.
15. Ibid.; David Gray and Danielle Citron, "The Right to Quantitative Privacy," *Minnesota Law Review* 98 (November 2013): 62.
16. Ibid.; Gray and Citron, "Quantitative Privacy"; John Dale Hartman, *Legal Guidelines for Covert Surveillance Operations in the Private Sector* (1993): 168–169.
17. IFPO, "Surveillance"; see also "Setting limits on video surveillance in public places," Securityinfowatch.com, April 2015; Desai, "Constitutional Limits."
18. Shamshak, "Basics Part 3."
19. Inspectors General, "Undercover Operations."
20. Department of the Army, *US Army Field Manual 19-20 Investigative Process*: 21, http://library.enlist-ment.us/field-manuals/series-2/FM19_20/CH2.PDF.

21. National Institute of Justice, *Video Surveillance of Public Places*, February 2006; "Setting limits on video surveillance"; Brandon C. Welsh, David P. Farrington, and Sema A. Taheri, "Effectiveness and Social Costs of Public Area Surveillance for Crime Prevention," *Annual Review of Law and Social Science* 11 (2015): 111–130.

22. W. Bennett and K. Hess, *Criminal Investigation* (West Publishing, 1981): 225; LaSorsa, "25 Tips"; IFPO, "Surveillance"; Inspectors General, "Undercover Operations."

23. Colin Shaff, "Is the Court Allergic to Katz? Problems Posed by New Methods of Electronic Surveillance to the 'Reasonable-Expectation-of-Privacy' Test," *Southern California Interdisciplinary Law Journal* 23, no. 2 (2014): 409–450.

24. Hartman, "Legal Guidelines": 32–33; Gray and Citron, "Quantitative Privacy"; Shaff, "Allergic to Katz?"; Joel R. Reidenberg, "Privacy in Public," *University of Miami Law Review* 69 (Fall 2014): 141.

25. Pinkerton's, Inc., *Investigations Department Training Manual* (1990): 114; Department of the Army, *Army Military Police Reference and Training Manual MP2004*: 2–45; Department of the Army, *US Army Military Police Law and Order Operations FM19–10*; Army, "Investigative Process."

26. "Announcements," *Surveillance &Society*, accessed September 9, 2018, https://ojs.library.queensu.ca/index.php/surveillance-and-society/index.

27. Truett A. Ricks, Bobby E. Ricks, and Jeffrey Dingle, *Physical Security and Safety: A Field Guide for the Practitioner* (Boca Raton, FL: CRC Press, 2014), www.crcpress.com; for an interesting web location that features the intricacies of casino surveillance, visit Casino Surveillance News at www.casinosurveillancenews.com.

28. U.S. Department of Homeland Security, *CCTV Technology Handbook* (July 2013), Table 2.1, www.dhs.gov/sites/default/files/publications/CCTV-Tech-HBK_0713-508.pdf.

29. Ibid.: 9.

30. Brandon C. Welsh, David P. Farrington, and Sema A. Taheri, "Effectiveness and Social Costs of Public Area Surveillance for Crime Prevention," *Annual Review of Law and Social Science* 11 (2015): 111–130, www-annualreviews-org.ez.lib.jjay.cuny.edu/doi/full/10.1146/annurev-lawsocsci-120814-121649.

31. Carl A. Roper, *Physical Security and the Inspection Process* (1997): 165; Ricks, Ricks, and Dingle, "Security and Safety."

32. Eastman Kodak Co., *Photographic Surveillance Techniques for Law Enforcement Agencies* (1972); Raymond Siljander and Lance Juusola, *Clandestine Photography—Basic to Advanced Daytime and Nighttime Manual Surveillance Photography Techniques—For Military Special Operations Forces, Law Enforcement, Intelligence Agencies and Investigators*, (Charles C. Thomas Publisher Ltd., 2012); LaSorsa, "25 Tips"; Shamshak, "Basics Part 3."

33. Kodak, "Surveillance": 17; Siljander and Juusola, "Clandestine"; LaSorsa, "25 Tips"; Shamshak, "Basics Part 3."

34. IFPO, "Surveillance."

35. Army, "Investigative Process"; Inspectors General, "Undercover Operations."

36. Army, "Investigative Process."

37. Ibid.: 17.

38. Ibid.

39. Ibid.: 18.

40. Ibid.; Inspectors General, "Undercover Operations."

41. Ibid.; Inspectors General, "Undercover Operations."

42. Bill Pellerin, "Pretext as a Necessary Tool for Investigations," Texas Investigative Network, accessed September 9, 2018, www.texasinvestigators.com/pretext-necessary-tool-investigations/.

43. ASIS, "Basic Guidelines": 44; Army, "Investigative Process."

44. Pinkerton's, "Surveillance": 9; Army, "Investigative Process."

45. See "5 Tips for Surveillance Photography," Saber Security, February 6, 2015, https://sabersecuritytraining.com/5-tips-surveillance-photography.

8 Report Writing

8.1 INTRODUCTION

Despite its tendency to be laborious, report writing is a core and mandatory function for private investigators throughout the investigative process. Report writing—that is, the compilation, drafting, and authorship of various reports and documents relating to an investigative case—serves as the formal record of investigative steps and findings. Reports are crucial to historical accuracy and assure an objective appraisal of events and conditions surrounding the case as it unfolds. Reports also promote professional best practices for the security industry by forcing the compiler to weigh progress or lack thereof or to think alternatively about the facts thus far experienced. The quality of report writing remains a top priority: as Tim Dees puts it, one of the "ills that complicate the lives of police recruits and the people who train them, report writing has long been at the top of the list."[1] Security investigators need not overcomplicate facts and conditions under review but always try to stay clear, focused, and factual in all things reported. Good report writing must adhere to the premise "the simpler, the better."[2] This chapter evaluates best methods in report compilation and makes suggestions as to how the author and the firm and client represented will benefit by taking this task very seriously.

8.1.1 REPORT WRITING PROMOTES EFFICIENCY IN THE INVESTIGATIVE PROCESS

Reports and record keeping promote productivity and efficiency in the typical security agency's operation and the many duties and tasks it undertakes. "There is a direct relationship between the efficiency of a security operation and the quality of its records and record procedures ... In meeting these demands, the security operation must function according to plans that provide for detailed records regarding each phase of its operational responsibility."[3]

Reports generate two fundamental ends: first, that initial steps of the investigation are memorialized; second, that subsequent investigative actions are not a rehash of the first steps taken. As case investigation progresses, it is difficult to remember every fact and nuance discovered and these reports keep the investigator on an accurate and efficient path.

Reports, which are shared among all the interested parties, tend to foster a universal understanding and a climate for knowledgeable collaboration.[4] The reports keep the investigative team and management close to the plan of action chosen and the investigative processes already completed.

Bennett and Hess, long-time experts in the investigative realm, properly hold that "[Y]our reports, like your notes, are a permanent record that communicates important information to many others. They are used, not simply filed away."[5] Without reports, the case and its assigned personnel will likely lose their uniform understanding of events and conditions surrounding the case, and rather than operate with one vision, the lack of documentation will foster an individualism that will be hard to predict and advance. Security firms, like police departments, are increasingly reliant upon software programs to assure efficiency in the draft and final report, and such software programs go a long way towards assuring efficiency.[6]

Web Exercise: Review and evaluate a popular report writing software program at www.silver-tracsoftware.com/security-incident-reporting-software.

8.1.2 REPORTS AND MEMORY

Both short-term and long-term memory are subject to a variety of forces which impact clarity and recall and for this reason alone, the report solidifies memory as closely as possible. Note taking at the scene, and creation of the report as soon as possible after an event, reduces the risk of factual inaccuracy. Notes and field notations provide a factual foundation for an eventual report. "These contemporaneous notes are a vital part of report writing, because they serve as the launching pad from which officers create their reports."[7] Case documentation, fully accepting the fallibility of human memory, provides a permanent locale for later reference. "The need to retrieve information contained in a report may occur within hours or days after it is written or perhaps even years later. A quick and effective technique for evaluating a security system is to determine how many questions concerning past activity are answered by personal memory as opposed to answers supplied according to documented facts."[8] The passage of time, the fading capacity to remember, and the diversity of external influences, such as varied opinions, all undermine the quality of memory alone and the urgent need for a documentary record.[9]

8.1.3 INVESTIGATIVE REPORTS AND ORGANIZATIONAL METHOD

Reports and report writing foster a formal understanding of the case rather than an extemporaneous finding, and because of this, the investigator is always better organized. Reports, by their very construction, force the investigator to sequence and catalog events and circumstances surrounding a case. Experienced investigators learn to write "sequentially"—relaying facts and conditions in a chronological, step-by-step sequencing which traces the life of any investigation.[10] While oral communication tends to be spontaneous, communicating thoughts in written form requires a more formal organizational approach. Each report prompts the investigator to target the "who, what, when, where, and how" of a case and author language that reflects the fundamental queries of any skilled investigator.

From an administrative perspective, reports and documentation organize the functions, such as assignments, expenses, payroll, photographic or investigative findings common to and generated by the security firm. R. Gallati, in *Introduction to Private Security*, emphasizes the importance of records:

> Basically, the security budget and security public relations are dependent upon records. Communications are not going to be up to standard unless they are based upon adequate files. Without proper records, you simply are not going to be able to tell where you have been, where you are, or where you are going.[11]

Consider some of the records that maintain the structural operation of a private security firm.

- Incident reports
- Memorandum files
- Expenditure records
- Equipment files
- Personnel files
- Logs and other sequential documentation
- Intelligence files
- Investigative and evidentiary records
- Statistical files
- Arrest and other action reports

In essence, formal documentation mirrors the task and functions of the private investigator and gives a formal mechanism to track and trace a case's progress.

8.1.4 INVESTIGATIVE REPORTS AS PROOF OF SERVICES RENDERED

A very beneficial byproduct of records regards the proof of the firm's services rendered. Security companies are first and foremost a business enterprise and need to generate sufficient income and revenue to stay alive. In this way, the security operation is vastly different from its governmental counterpart that depends on government sources of revenue which pay less attention to the profit-loss ratio. The security industry has no such luxury and must author records that prove primarily a correlation between time expended and fees charged. On top of this, reports reassure clients of progress made and where in the cycle of investigation the case might be. A report corroborates the assertions of the security provider that it did X or Y. Sophisticated clients, especially those with business and industrial concerns, are investing a sizeable chunk of money for security services and have a rightful expectation of a documentary record of said activities. Permanent records reflect the firm's efforts.

Records and reports can foster a client's goodwill with the firm and educate the client on the nature of investigative results. Hence, the report is not only a tool of investigation, but also a critical communicative aid between client and investigator. Pinkerton's, Inc. stresses this fact to its agents when it states:

> We consider client reports to be the most important responsibility that an investigator and handling manager has. No matter how well or professionally an investigation is conducted, the report is what the client receives. They will use this report to hire, fire, suspend, discontinue compensation payments, settle a claim, go to court, continue an investigation, obtain peace of mind, prosecute, and to determine if they will pay our bill.[12]

Reports are "critical communicative tools" between the client and investigator and a means to "educate" the client.[13] Confirming this position regarding report writing, author Robert Gallati states: "Security, as we have previously stated, must continually be 'sold'; otherwise it may not receive the attention it warrants. In order to sell anything, one must communicate; in order to persuade, one must educate while communicating."[14]

Finally, reports can serve as a defense mechanism in the event the client alleges nonperformance. Since most note taking and report writing is rote or autonomic in completion, the evidentiary reliability of the document is quite favorable—so much so that its author need not advance the document in a legal setting. Reports often fall under the "business records" exception of the Hearsay Rule.

8.2 INVESTIGATIVE REPORT WRITING: STANDARDS FOR AUTHORSHIP

Report writing is as effective as its quality of content and adherence to the rules of proper grammatical construction. Solid report writing depends on many factors including proper grammar and usage, clarity of exposition and narrative, and the accuracy of the historical and present record. Reports should be fresh and reliable products, the result not solely of spontaneous thinking but instead after thoughtful reflection and review. Reports should always stress objective reality rather than subjective assumptions and hunches.[15] Every report should be guided by a logical process, a careful assessment as to its accuracy and a reconciliation of personal observation and memory. Finally every report needs continuous and passionate scrutiny as to grammar and expository construction. Every report should be reviewed and re-reviewed. Dr. Mary Dowd lays out this expectation:

> Well-written security reports are more effective than sloppily written reports, which diminish your credibility. When editing, shorten the text by deleting superfluous words. Fix run on sentences, delete redundant statements, correct typos and fix grammatical errors. Reword any statements that may be misinterpreted, which can happen with awkward sentence structure. Generally, the subject of a sentence should start off the sentence, which creates a more effective security report. Technical writing is different from creative writing.[16]

Security firms and organizations should always support and foster the critical importance of the report writing process, not in some minimalist sense but as a crucial, core part of the investigative regimen. Reward and give recognition to those officers and investigators who author high-quality reports.[17]

8.2.1 Investigative Field Notes: A Preliminary Step

Field notes play a critical role in the draft of any subsequent report and are often the first mental impressions converted to actual written text. From first visitation to the last meeting at an investigative scene, the professional investigator writes down observations, questions, ideas, and thoughts that might arise at scene. Field notes are less formal than any subsequently filed and finished report although this early stage of the documentary process does not minimize their importance. Field notes are preliminary observations that shall be relied upon at a later time when a report is to be finalized. Notes are not the formal record but a tool leading to that formal document. In fact, field notes are often a mishmash of ideas, some eventually accepted while others discarded, and part and parcel to a collection process that leads to a finalized investigative report. See Figure 8.1.

As the terminology implies, field notes or note taking tends to a cryptic, abbreviated relation of facts and conditions relative to the case with aligned notations or queries. The standard lines of inquiry—the *who, what, when, where,* and *how* of the matter weave their way through the composition of field notes. Commonly discovered in field notes are background details that may or may not have relevance in the latter stages of the investigation, like:

- Weather
- Lighting conditions
- Clothing of victims/suspects
- Description of roads
- Location of roads
- Emergency medical personnel on the scene
- Statements
- Activities of other investigative personnel: forensic technicians, photographers, survey sketchers, police
- Important addresses and phone numbers
- Other relevant information

Notes start but do not finish the process of fact assimilation and at best serve as undergirding for a subsequent formal report, or supplement other documents like scene sketches and photographic or digital evidence or confirm or corroborate the existence of documentary evidence. Effective field notes are arranged in chronological order corresponding to the investigator's steps or sequence during the course of the investigation. What field notes include largely depends on the nature of the incident being investigated. For criminal activity, the author would make notes of:

- Date and time call received
- Time of arrival
- Names of officers present
- Names and complete demographic information of witnesses present
- Anything touched, moved, or altered
- Any statements made by witnesses to officers present
- Exact geographic location of scene
- Overall scene conditions
- Photographs taken, including photographer's name, time photos taken, scene depicted by photos, setting, film speed, etc.
- Real and physical evidence including description, identification marks, date, time, and exact location where found, by whom found, and custodian of evidence[18]

CASE NAME	CASE NUMBER
DATE / /	TIME AM PM
1. EVIDENCE	
2. WITNESSES	
3. GENERAL OBSERVATIONS	
INVESTIGATING OFFICIAL	SIGNATURE

FIGURE 8.1 A field notes template.

Web Exercise: Watch the video on taking field notes at https://youtu.be/V1Xk4bdUU_E.

Another example of a field notes format can be viewed at Figure 8.2.

The mental montage of information will be heavily relied upon by the investigator as the report document is finalized.

8.2.2 The Essential Qualities of an Investigative Report: Accurate, Brief, and Complete

Accuracy is a perpetual concern to the security professional in two contexts: first, whether or not the information included in the report is factually and legally correct; and second, whether or not the information contained in the report is technically correct. Each report must contain certain components whatever the format might be. Each report must tell a story accurately and objectively and include these parts:

1. All narratives should be written in chronological order.
2. Use a person's name if known, if not, use Suspect #1, Suspect #2, etc.
3. List each item in the Property section. Group similar items; items of great value or readily identifiable list separately with specific descriptions. When referring to property in the Narrative, use general terms.
4. The total value of property should be mentioned in the Narrative.
5. If a juvenile is a subject include the parent/guardian and school information.
6. All subjects mentioned must be listed in the Subjects section, and vice versa.
7. All vehicles mentioned in the Narrative must be listed in the Vehicles section, and vice versa.
8. If a subject is not a local resident, obtain local address information, and note when the subject is leaving the area along with a permanent address.
9. Officers should obtain future contact information from victims and witnesses who may move before the trial.

10. All statements must have a synopsis in the narrative along with the person's name making the statement.
11. Detailed descriptions of suspects and missing persons should be included in the principals list of the report. General descriptions should be used in the narrative.[19]

Investigative reports filled with chronological or sequential gaps will provide little aid in recall and are dubious legally and factually. In fact, incomplete reports and notes can be utterly undermined during the testimonial phase of trial litigation. Thoroughness is imperative in all facets of report writing. Comprehensiveness in the authorship of an investigative report is equally critical since gaps or

Date:	Time:
Location:	
Description of Surroundings:	
Individuals involved:	
Other witnesses:	
Description of Incident:	

FIGURE 8.2   An alternate template for recording field notes.

holes in the report are bound to be challenged. As noted earlier, attention to style, rules of grammar and construction, and clarity of exposition need always be at the front burner of report writing. Cox and Brown use common sense and a bit of humor to drive home the stylistic aspect of report writing.

1. *Accuracy is important in word use as well as in information.* Poor word choice will get you into trouble. One officer wound up in court on three occasions trying to explain what he meant when he said that the suspect "crowded" him. Was he pushed, shoved up against the wall, verbally intimidated, or what? *Value judgments must be avoided, and brief details should be given instead.* For example, don't say, "The child seemed afraid of his father." Instead, give the facts that led you to this assumption: "When the father came into the room, the boy stopped talking and began to cry. The father smiled and offered the boy candy, but the son backed up to his mother and clung to her, crying harder."
2. *Brevity is important, as long as it is not used at the cost of accuracy or completeness.* This applies to words, too. Never use a complicated word when a simple one will do. The active form is shorter and generally more accurate than the passive form.
3. *Completeness is essential.* One of the stories used recently on this point is that of the young lawyer Abraham Lincoln, who won a case because he proved that the moon was not shining on a night that the presumed suspect was supposedly identified by the full light of the moon. Do not assume anything, even the obvious. A recent case in Australia made the front page of a newspaper for its rather humorous point: A man was alleged to be drunk, and the report stated that the officer observed the man's eyes to be bloodshot.

   "Both of them?" asked the defense attorney. Looking at the now clear-eyed defendant the officer said firmly, "Yes, both of them." Whereupon the defendant removed his clear, artificial eye and rolled it on the table. Case dismissed.[20]

Every investigative report writer needs to pay close attention to spelling errors, the misuse of words and terms, and the logical and orderly flow of the report's presentation. Grammatical rigor is central to professional report writing. Conciseness, brevity of thought and idea, and an objective presentation are critical attributes as well. The investigative report should also be free of opinions, conjecture, emotional qualities, and personal vendetta or object. The stress has to be utterly factual.[21]

Before submitting a report to a client or supervisor, the investigator should take the time to read and review its contents thoroughly. In making the final assessment, the investigator should make sure the report is:

- Factual
- Clear
- Accurate
- Grammatically correct
- Objective
- Written in standard English
- Complete
- Legible
- Concise

8.2.3 INVESTIGATIVE REPORT DESIGN

Effective report writing also requires familiarity with the basic styles and formats of report design. The *checklist* format, the most abbreviated and least narrative of all report systems, simply calls upon the author to check by mark, asterisk, or initial, the information requested. Numerous examples of the checklist format are included throughout this text. The *narrative* format requires the greatest level of composition. A typical example of an arrest report, at Figure 8.3,[22] provides a substantial space for a recitation of the facts leading up to and justifying the arrest.

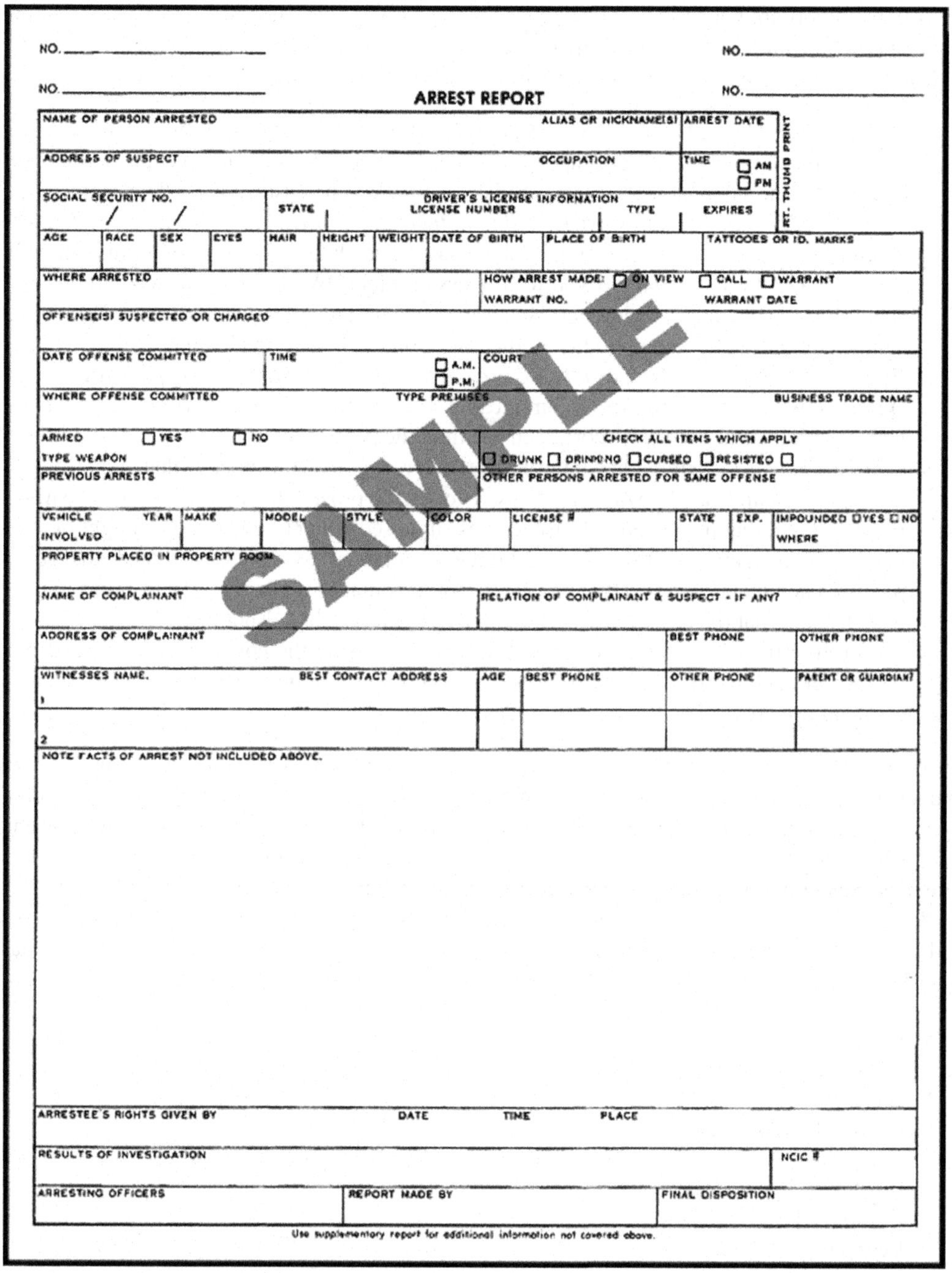

NO. ____ NO. ____

NO. ____ NO. ____

ARREST REPORT

NAME OF PERSON ARRESTED | ALIAS OR NICKNAME(S) | ARREST DATE | RT. THUMB PRINT

ADDRESS OF SUSPECT | OCCUPATION | TIME ☐ AM ☐ PM

SOCIAL SECURITY NO. / / | DRIVER'S LICENSE INFORMATION: STATE | LICENSE NUMBER | TYPE | EXPIRES

AGE | RACE | SEX | EYES | HAIR | HEIGHT | WEIGHT | DATE OF BIRTH | PLACE OF BIRTH | TATTOOES OR ID. MARKS

WHERE ARRESTED | HOW ARREST MADE: ☐ ON VIEW ☐ CALL ☐ WARRANT | WARRANT NO. | WARRANT DATE

OFFENSE(S) SUSPECTED OR CHARGED

DATE OFFENSE COMMITTED | TIME ☐ A.M. ☐ P.M. | COURT

WHERE OFFENSE COMMITTED | TYPE PREMISES | BUSINESS TRADE NAME

ARMED ☐ YES ☐ NO | TYPE WEAPON | CHECK ALL ITEMS WHICH APPLY ☐ DRUNK ☐ DRINKING ☐ CURSED ☐ RESISTED ☐

PREVIOUS ARRESTS | OTHER PERSONS ARRESTED FOR SAME OFFENSE

VEHICLE INVOLVED | YEAR | MAKE | MODEL | STYLE | COLOR | LICENSE # | STATE | EXP. | IMPOUNDED ☐ YES ☐ NO | WHERE

PROPERTY PLACED IN PROPERTY ROOM

NAME OF COMPLAINANT | RELATION OF COMPLAINANT & SUSPECT - IF ANY?

ADDRESS OF COMPLAINANT | BEST PHONE | OTHER PHONE

WITNESSES NAME. | BEST CONTACT ADDRESS | AGE | BEST PHONE | OTHER PHONE | PARENT OR GUARDIAN?

1

2

NOTE FACTS OF ARREST NOT INCLUDED ABOVE.

ARRESTEE'S RIGHTS GIVEN BY | DATE | TIME | PLACE

RESULTS OF INVESTIGATION | NCIC #

ARRESTING OFFICERS | REPORT MADE BY | FINAL DISPOSITION

Use supplementary report for additional information not covered above.

SAMPLE

FIGURE 8.3 Typical example of a basic arrest report. (Used with permission, G.F. Thompson.)

Some reports are intentionally designed to call upon the investigator to make a deduction, a finding, or a conclusion regarding certain matters. Sometimes a list of alternative explanations or descriptions might be requested. *Interpretative* questionnaires can call for deductive or inferential conclusions regarding a suspect description, motive, or *modus operandi* (method of operation or MO). See Figure 8.4.[23]

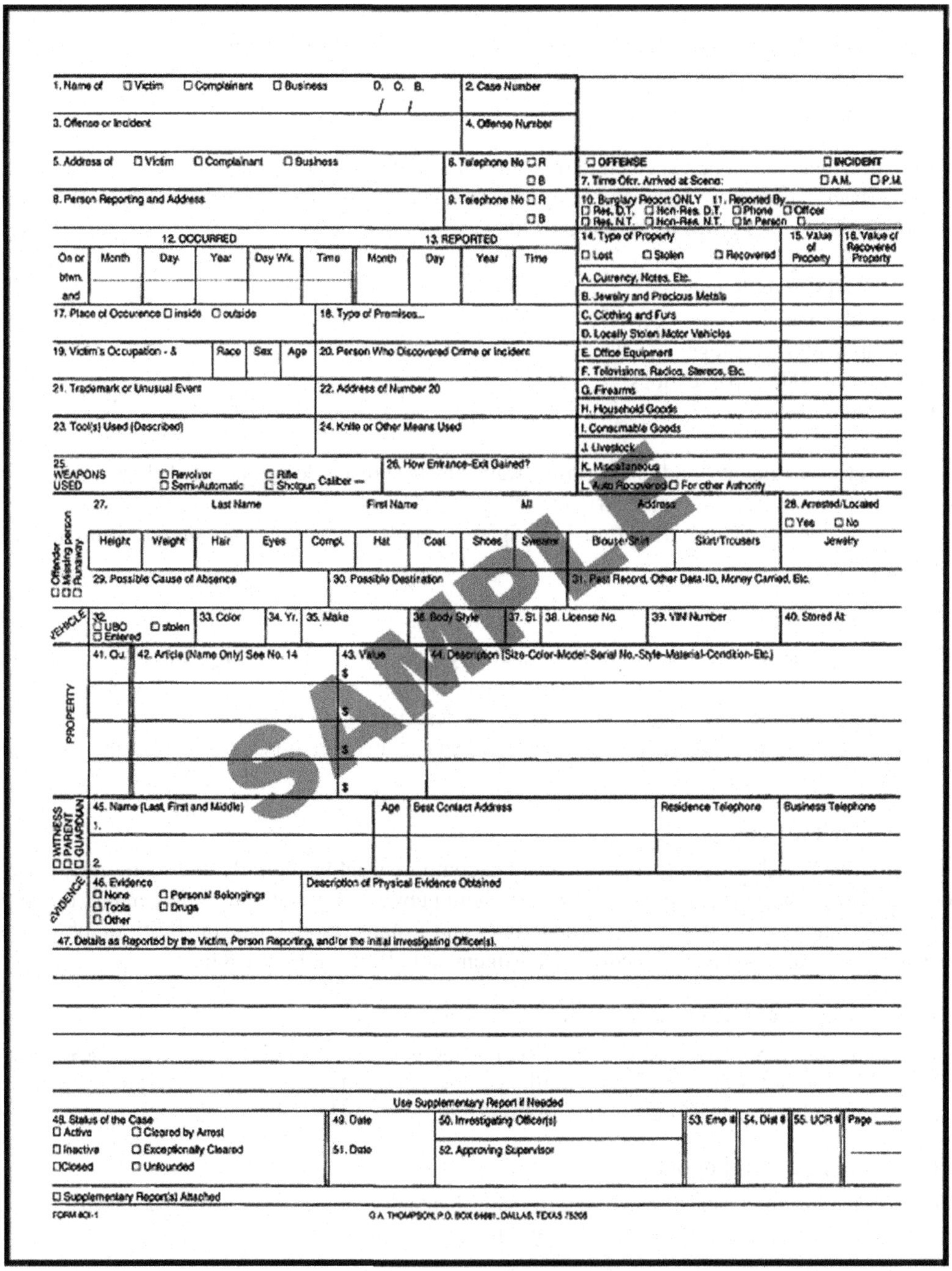
1. Name of ☐ Victim ☐ Complainant ☐ Business D. O. B. / /
2. Case Number
3. Offense or Incident
4. Offense Number
5. Address of ☐ Victim ☐ Complainant ☐ Business
6. Telephone No ☐ R ☐ B
☐ OFFENSE ☐ INCIDENT
7. Time Ofcr. Arrived at Scene: ☐ A.M. ☐ P.M.
8. Person Reporting and Address
9. Telephone No ☐ R ☐ B
10. Burglary Report ONLY ☐ Res. D.T. ☐ Non-Res. D.T. ☐ Res. N.T. ☐ Non-Res. N.T.
11. Reported By ☐ Phone ☐ Officer ☐ In Person ☐

12. OCCURRED						13. REPORTED			
On or btwn. and	Month	Day	Year	Day Wk.	Time	Month	Day	Year	Time

14. Type of Property ☐ Lost ☐ Stolen ☐ Recovered	15. Value of Property	16. Value of Recovered Property
A. Currency, Notes, Etc.		
B. Jewelry and Precious Metals		
C. Clothing and Furs		
D. Locally Stolen Motor Vehicles		
E. Office Equipment		
F. Televisions, Radios, Stereos, Etc.		
G. Firearms		
H. Household Goods		
I. Consumable Goods		
J. Livestock		
K. Miscellaneous		
L. Auto Recovered ☐ For other Authority		

17. Place of Occurence ☐ inside ☐ outside
18. Type of Premises...
19. Victim's Occupation - & | Race | Sex | Age
20. Person Who Discovered Crime or Incident
21. Trademark or Unusual Event
22. Address of Number 20
23. Tool(s) Used (Described)
24. Knife or Other Means Used
25. WEAPONS USED ☐ Revolver ☐ Semi-Automatic ☐ Rifle ☐ Shotgun Caliber —
26. How Entrance-Exit Gained?

☐ Offender ☐ Missing person ☐ Runaway
27. Last Name | First Name | MI | Address
28. Arrested/Located ☐ Yes ☐ No

Height	Weight	Hair	Eyes	Compl.	Hat	Coat	Shoes	Sweater	Blouse/Shirt	Skirt/Trousers	Jewelry

29. Possible Cause of Absence
30. Possible Destination
31. Past Record, Other Data-ID, Money Carried, Etc.

VEHICLE
32. ☐ UBO ☐ Entered ☐ stolen | 33. Color | 34. Yr. | 35. Make | 36. Body Style | 37. St. | 38. License No. | 39. VIN Number | 40. Stored At

PROPERTY

41. Qu.	42. Article (Name Only) See No. 14	43. Value	44. Description (Size-Color-Model-Serial No.-Style-Material-Condition-Etc.)
		$	
		$	
		$	
		$	

☐ WITNESS ☐ PARENT ☐ GUARDIAN

45. Name (Last, First and Middle)	Age	Best Contact Address	Residence Telephone	Business Telephone
1.				
2.				

EVIDENCE
46. Evidence ☐ None ☐ Tools ☐ Other ☐ Personal Belongings ☐ Drugs
Description of Physical Evidence Obtained

47. Details as Reported by the Victim, Person Reporting, and/or the initial investigating Officer(s).

Use Supplementary Report if Needed

48. Status of the Case ☐ Active ☐ Inactive ☐ Closed ☐ Cleared by Arrest ☐ Exceptionally Cleared ☐ Unfounded
49. Date
50. Investigating Officer(s)
51. Date
52. Approving Supervisor
53. Emp # | 54. Dist # | 55. UCR # | Page ____

☐ Supplementary Report(s) Attached

FORM 8OI-1 G.A. THOMPSON, P.O. BOX 64681, DALLAS, TEXAS 75206

FIGURE 8.4 An example of an interpretive questionnaire. (Used with permission, G.F. Thompson.)

8.3 STANDARD REPORTS FOR THE PRIVATE INVESTIGATOR

In the this section, the reader will encounter a series of the more commonly encountered forms and documents authored by and used by the security investigator and the private security industry. Many such forms are discoverable at other sections of this text, such as pertinent suggestions on initial interview, surveillance, office administration, and others that relate to day-to-day investigative process. Many of the suggested forms are standardized in the industry and used no matter what the subject matter of the case. Others are uniquely tailored to specific activities.

8.3.1 INVESTIGATIVE ACTIVITY REPORTS

Private investigators can be expected to track and chronologically post the substance of their activities over specific periods of time, and according to specific activities. In some circles, these reports are called activity logs or even timesheets. Other examples are:

- Shift logs or daily logs
- Vehicle logs
- Visitor/contractor logs
- Material control passes/logs
- Incident reports[24]

All of these documents tend to be administrative by design and less concerned about conclusions or deductions in the merits of any particular case.

Web Exercise: Read the article on investigative report writing at www.pimall.com/nais/nl/n. reportwlc.html.

8.3.1.1 Daily Reports

Some investigators are asked to fill out daily activity reports, which relay the times of scene arrival and departure, as well as investigative action taken throughout the course of the day. Some reports note the activity under investigation and request a description of the action taken. A daily report, filed by security departments, combines checklist and narrative methods of report composition. See Figure 8.5.

8.3.1.2 Review Reports

It is customary practice in the security industry to compose weekly, monthly, and even yearly review documents regarding investigative activities. In both public and private law enforcement, this type of documentation serves to measure productivity and foster personal accountability in job performance. An annual summary of security department activities is at Figure 8.6.

8.3.1.3 Patrol and Observation Reports

Many of the security investigator's functions rely upon the skills and techniques of observation whether on foot, in a vehicle, or by surveillance posts or stations. Figure 8.7 contains those lines necessary to compose a brief description of time, date, and conduct observed.

8.3.1.4 Surveillance Reports

For a full discussion on surveillance reports, see Chapter 7, but suffice to say, those entrusted with the surveillance task must regularly report on the results.

8.3.1.5 Missing Person Reports

Missing persons are a concern for both public and private law enforcement personnel. The missing person report, at Figure 8.8,[25] concentrates on information that could deliver leads to solve these cases.

Figure 8.9, Search for Current Whereabouts, should be of assistance to the private investigator on the hunt for a missing person or "skip witness." The report summarizes the extensive steps to be done during the search.

Web Exercise: What the video at https://youtu.be/ZslHIT48mJc for tips on locating skip witnesses.

SECURITY DEPARTMENT OFFICER'S DAILY REPORT								
REPORT OF		SHIELD NO		SHIFT FROM	AM PM	TO	AM PM	S M T W DATE T F S
RELIEVED OFFICER	AT AM PM		RELIEVED BY OFFICER	AT AM PM		RADIO NUMBER		TOTAL HRS.
ITEMS NO. 1 THROUGH 13 MUST BE CHECKED YES OR NO. ITEMS CHECKED YES MUST BE EXPLAINED UNDER DETAILS.				DETAILS REPORT BELOW THE DETAILS OF EACH ITEM CHECKED YES AND ALL OTHER UNUSUAL OCCURRENCES OR MATTERS OF INTEREST. LIST LICENSE NUMBER OF ALL PARKING VIOLATORS				
	WERE THERE ANY	YES	NO					
1	FIRE HAZARDS							
2	SMOKING VIOLATIONS							
3	DOORS OR WINDOWS OPEN OR BROKEN							
4	VAULTS OR SAFES OPEN							
5	TRESSPASSER(S)							
6	SUSPICIOUS ACTIVITIES							
7	THEFTS-ATTEMPTED							
8	THEFTS-COMMITTED							
9	PROPERTY DAMAGE							
10	SECURITY LIGHTS OFF							
11	PARKING VIOLATIONS							
12	EXITS BLOCKED							
13	SAFETY HAZARDS							
EXAMINED BY				OPERATION INSPECTED BY				
INITIALS SGT. LT. CAPT. SEC. OFF.				SIGNED				
DATE							OFFICER SIGNATURE	

FIGURE 8.5   An example of a daily report.

SECURITY DEPT. YEARLY ACTIVITIES REPORT		
DATE _____		
	20	20
A　THEFTS/MISSING		
1. COMPANY		
2. EMPLOYEE		
B　MALICIOUS DAMAGE TO PROPERTY		
1. COMPANY		
2. EMPLOYEE		
C　TAMPERING WITH EQUIPMENT		
D　FOREIGN CAPS/TABS/OBJECTS		
E　CONCEALED SHORTAGE		
F　PRODUCT PROBLEMS		
1. DIVERSION		
2. OTHER		
G　CRANK CALLS/LETTERS		
H　MOTOR VEHICLE ACCIDENTS		
I　EMPLOYEE PROBLEMS		
J　ASSAULT & BATTERY		
K　MEETINGS/CONFERENCES/COURT		
L　NARCOTICS		
M　CONFIDENTIAL		
N　LARCENY FROM AUTO		
O　WAREHOUSE/TRUCK CHECKS		
P　CO-OPS		
1. COMPANY		
2. OUTSIDE AGENCIES		
Q　CONTINUED INVESTIGATIONS		
R　OTHER		

FIGURE 8.6　An example of a yearly summary activities report for a security department.

Patrol & Observation Request

Date _____ Requesting Officer _____

Time _____ Termination Date _____

Location _____

Reason For Request _____

Officer's Observation

Officer _____ Observation _____

Time _____ Date _____

Officer _____ Observation _____

Time _____ Date _____

Officer _____ Observation _____

Time _____ Date _____

Officer _____ Observation _____

Time _____ Date _____

Officer _____ Observation _____

Time _____ Date _____

Officer _____ Observation _____

Time _____ Date _____

Officer _____ Observation _____

Time _____ Date _____

Officer _____ Observation _____

Time _____ Date _____

FIGURE 8.7 A sample patrol and observation request form.

MISSING PERSON REPORT

Date

Case No.

TYPE OF MISSING - PERSON	
D = DISABILITY	
I = INVOLUNTARY	
E = ENDANGERED	
J = JUVENILE	
V = DISASTER VICTIM	

Name:
Last / First / Middle / Suffix

Sex: M = Male   F = Female

Race:
☐ White   ☐ Alaskan
☐ Black   ☐ American Indian
☐ Unknown   ☐ Asian/Pacific Islander

DOB: Month Day Year ☐☐/☐☐/☐☐

State of Birth

Height: Ft. Inches

Weight: Pounds

Eyes:
☐ BLU = Blue   ☐ GRY = Gray   ☐ MAR = Maroon
☐ BRO = Brown   ☐ GRN = Green   ☐ PNK = Pink
☐ BLK = Black   ☐ HAZ = Hazel   ☐ XXX = Unknown

Hair:
☐ BLK = Black   ☐ WHI = White
☐ BRO = Brown   ☐ SDY = Sandy
☐ BLN = Blond   ☐ GRY = Gray
☐ RED = Red   ☐ XXX = Unknown

Scars, Mark, Tattoo

Social Security #

DRILICNO: State   Yr. Exp.

NCIC FPCLASS: RT   RI   RM   RR   RL   LT   LI   LM   LR   LL

Blood Type:
☐ A Pos   ☐ B Pos   ☐ AB Pos   ☐ O Pos
☐ A Neg   ☐ B Neg   ☐ AB Neg   ☐ O Neg

Circumcision ☐ Yes ☐ No

Footprints Available ☐ Yes ☐ No

Body X-rays Available ☐ Yes ☐ No

Build:
☐ Very thin   ☐ Muscular
☐ Thin   ☐ Heavy/Stocky
☐ Medium   ☐ Obese

Date of Last Contact
Month Day Year / /

Does the missing person have corrected vision ☐ Yes ☐ No
☐ Glasses?   ☐ Contact lenses?

Corrective Vision RX

Type of contact lenses and color:
☐ Hard   ☐ Longwear   ☐ Blue   ☐ Gray   ☐ Clear
☐ Soft   ☐ Semi   ☐ Brown   ☐ Green

Does the missing person have any broken or healed bones, artificial body parts, or missing body parts?   ☐ Yes   ☐ No   if so, describe

LICENSE PLATE AND VEHICLE INFORMATION

License Plate Number   State   Yr. Exp.   Type

Vehicle Identification #   Year

Make   Model   Style   Color   Other

OTHER INFORMATION

Reporting Agency   Reporting Officer

Complainant's Name   Complainant's Address   Complainant's Telephone Number

Relationship of Complainant to Missing Person   Missing Person's Address   Missing Person's Aliases

Missing Person's Occupation   Miscellaneous Number(s)

Below is a list of clothing and personal effects. Please indicate those items that have been found with the person or body. Include style, type, size, color, condition, etc.

Item	Style/Type	Size	Color	Markings	Item	Style/Type	Size	Color	Markings
Head Gear					Shoes/Boots/Sneakers				
Scarf/Tie/Gloves					Underwear				
Coat/Jacket/Vest					Bra/Girdle/Slip				
Sweater					Stockings/Pantyhose				
Shirt/Blouse					Wallet/Purse				
Pants/Skirt					Money				
Belt/Suspenders					Jewelry	See Back			
Socks					Other				

ALL DENTAL INFORMATION SHOULD BE RECORDED ON THE DENTAL RECORD REPORT.

FIGURE 8.8   A sample missing person report. (Used with permission, G.F. Thompson.)

SEARCH FOR CURRENT WHEREABOUTS

NAME OF ACTOR _____   PLACE OF EMPLOYMENT _____

ADDRESS _____

TELEPHONE NO _____   CELLULAR _____

DATES RESIDENCE CHECKED _____   OFFICER _____

PERSON CONTACTED _____

ON _____ BY _____ TIME _____   HOW CONTACTED _____

ON _____ BY _____ TIME _____   RESULT _____

ON _____ BY _____ TIME _____

ON _____ BY _____ TIME _____

A   RELATIVES

B   NEIGHBORS

C   TELEPHONE COMPANY

D   BUREAU OF MOTOR VEHICLES

E   POST OFFICE

F   PROBATION OFFICE

G   PENITENTIARY

H   CITY IDENTIFICATION BUREAU

I   BUREAU OF CRIMINAL IDENTIFICATION

J   COUNTY JAIL

K   OTHER (Specify)

1   _____

2   _____

3   _____

4   _____

DATE _____	DATE _____
OFFICER _____	OFFICER _____
PERSON CONTACTED _____	PERSON CONTACTED _____
HOW CONTACTED _____	HOW CONTACTED _____
RESULT _____	RESULT _____
DATE _____	DATE _____
OFFICER _____	OFFICER _____
PERSON CONTACTED _____	PERSON CONTACTED _____
HOW CONTACTED _____	HOW CONTACTED _____
RESULT _____	RESULT _____
DATE _____	DATE _____
OFFICER _____	OFFICER _____
PERSON CONTACTED _____	PERSON CONTACTED _____
HOW CONTACTED _____	HOW CONTACTED _____
RESULT _____	RESULT _____

(If more than six contacts, use separate sheet)

Sworn to and subscribed before me this _____ day of _____, 20____.

The above is a true and correct summary of the search I conducted on the abovenamed Actor.

SEAL MAGISTRATE OR NOTARY _____   POLICE OFFICER _____

FIGURE 8.9   An example of a Search for Current Whereabouts report.

8.3.1.6   Undercover Investigation Reports

The undercover investigative report calls for the most elaborate form of narrative. Review an excerpt from an undercover report at Box 8.1.

BOX 8.1   AN EXAMPLE OF AN UNDERCOVER INVESTIGATIVE REPORT WHICH ENTAILS A DETAILED NARRATIVE

#219

Saturday, June 27, 2018

PROGRESS REPORT: Verbal report of these finding was given to the client on Monday, June 29, 2018. Marvin openly admitted to having stolen several watches and said a female supplied him with these watches. Strong admitted to having stolen PlayStation 4 game disks, which he sold for half (1/2) price on the street to purchase himself some drugs. After lunch, Jones stated that last Saturday, right after work, he observed Keeney drive from the back side of the parking lot to the shipping dock doors, where unusual activity involving Keeney and Griswald occurred. According to Jones, he thinks that Griswald and Keeney worked together to commit a theft. Dalton, who was aided by Don Sheridan, removed two (2) half barrel bar-b-que pits from the pit area of the shipping dock and proceeded to carry them outside the facility by way of the shipping dock garage doors. Dalton indicated that he had been given two grills by Griswald to keep.

Reading of the entire report is recommended.

At the start of today's shift, Gram, Strong, Jones, Dalton, Sheridan, Christine and John were all present for Saturday work. Roger, Nelson and Walker reported to the workplace late. Griswald, the Plant Manager, was noted to be present at the warehouse today. A new employee was also observed briefly on the dock at the start of the shift. He is described as:

Male, black, age 22, 5'11" tall, 170 lbs., medium build, dark complexion, short curly black hair, thin mustache, wearing a white t-shirt, blue jeans and tennis shoes.

Although not all of the departments throughout receiving were working this date, all of the shipping dock employees observed worked diligently in their efforts to get processed merchandise loaded into trailers, as well as handling two (2) truckloads of Fort Worth merchandise that were unloaded, sorted and tagged for shipment.

At approximately 8:53 am, Merril and Jones discontinued their work efforts and proceeded to the cafeteria on the lower level of the facility where doughnuts were being served for employees who worked today. Employees from other work areas were also noted arriving in the cafeteria prior to the hour of 9:00 am. During this break, Marvin openly stated to a group of employees that he had committed a theft of several watches. Marvin contended that a female employee supplied him with...

8.3.1.7   Bomb Search Reports

Private security investigators involved in executive protection and prevention of terrorism are often assigned bomb responsibilities. Explosive devices are a constant concern for those entrusted with the safety of others. See Table 8.1.

8.3.1.8   Inspection Reports

Inspection reports are helpful tools to the client—keeping them posted or aware of potential harmful conditions that give rise to civil liability. For example, the safety and security of a parking authority or public building, or a given product design, can be gleaned from inspection documentation.

TABLE 8.1

An Example of a Bomb Search Report

Bomb Search Report	
REMEMBER: Keep well spaced apart.	
Do not search in adjacent areas.	
DO NOT TOUCH SUSPICIOUS OR OUT-OF-PLACE OJECTS.	
Area searched:	
Suspicious object found at	
Description of object	
Sketch of object	
Did the object have a visible or ticking clock timer?	Yes/No
Did you see or smell a burning fuse?	Yes/No
Did you see trip wires or booby traps?	Yes/No
At exactly what time did you find the object?	
Sketch of object's position	
Is the object easily accessible?	Yes/No
DRAW YOUR EXACT ROUTE TO AND FROM THE OBJECT	
Did you continue searching the area for other devices?	Yes/No
Did you see other suspicious objects?	Yes/No
Has area around the object (above/below) been evacuated?	Yes/No
Are there people near the object?	Yes/No
If yes, how many people are there?	
Are all evacuees accounted for?	Yes/No
Is the suspicious object near fuel/explosives, valuable equipment?	Yes/No
HAND THIS FORM TO THE BOMB SQUAD WHEN THEY ARRIVE.	
Name:	Rank:

A failure to inspect may lead to an inference of negligence in civil actions and an inspection proto-col defends against that averment or cause of action. Inspection reports can be as uncomplicated as the Safety Inspection Checklist at Figure 8.10, to a slightly more demanding version of a building inspection report, which calls upon the author to make remarks or to note corrective action taken. See Figure 8.11.

8.3.1.9 Security Incident Reports

When a wrongdoing is discovered, most security firms compose what is known as an Incident Report (see Figure 8.12). The security investigator's first contact with a case often involves a review of this document. A much more simplified, checklist version of an incident report is at Figure 8.13.

8.3.1.10 Investigative Reports

Investigative report forms portray many scenarios and, as has been discussed throughout this chap-ter, the contents largely depend upon the parties and subject matter of the investigation. While the format might be uniform it is very unlikely that one report will ever be identical to another report.[26] In cases of missing property, a report addressing the circumstances and events surrounding the loss would be completed. Some reports summarize the client's complaint. See Figure 8.14.

Drafted with a checklist design, the Motor Vehicle Accident Checklist at Box 8.2[27] assures that the initial as well as subsequent parties assigned have full and complete access to information. A more complete document, titled Investigation Report, quite similar to a public police offense report, is at Figure 8.15.

SAFETY INSPECTION CHECKLIST

Plant or department _____ Date _____

This list is intended as only a reminder. Look for other unsafe acts and conditions, and then report them so that corrective   action can be taken. Not particularly whether unsafe acts or conditions that have caused accidents have been corrected. Note also whether potential accident causes, marked "X" on previous inspection, have been corrected.

(✓) Indicates Satisfactory   (X) Indicates Unsatisfactory

1. **Fire Protection**   7. **Machinery**
   Extinguishing equipment   ☐   Point of operation guards   ☐
   Standpipes, hoses, sprinkler heads and valves ☐   Belts, pulleys, gears, shafts, etc.   ☐
   Exits, stairs and signs   ☐   Oiling, cleaning and adjusting   ☐
   Storage of flammable material   ☐   Maintenance and oil leakage   ☐

2. **Housekeeping**   8. **Pressure equipment**
   Aisles, stairs and floors   ☐   Steam Equipment   ☐
   Storage and piling of material   ☐   Air receivers and compressors   ☐
   Wash and locker rooms   ☐   Gas cylinders and hose   ☐
   Light and ventilation   ☐ 9. **Unsafe Practices**
   Disposal of waste   ☐   Excessive speed of vehicles   ☐
   Yards and parking lots   ☐   Improper Lifting   ☐

3. **Tools**   Smoking in danger areas   ☐
   Power tools, wiring   ☐   Horseplay   ☐
   Hand tools   ☐   Running in aisles or on stairs   ☐
   Use and storage of tools   ☐   Improper use of air hoses   ☐

4. **Personal Protective Equipment**   Removing machine or other guards   ☐
   Goggles or face shields   ☐   Work on unguarded moving machinery   ☐
   Safety shoes   ☐ 10. **First Aid**
   Gloves   ☐   First aid kits and rooms   ☐
   Respirators or gas masks   ☐   Stretchers and fire blankets   ☐
   Protective clothing   ☐   Emergency showers   ☐
                                                         All injuries reported   ☐
5. **Material Handling Equipment**
   Power trucks, hand trucks   ☐ 11. **Miscellaneous**
   Elevators   ☐   Acids and caustics   ☐
   Cranes and hoists   ☐   New processes, chemicals and solvents ☐
   Conveyors   ☐   Dusts, vapors or fumes   ☐
   Cables, ropes, chains, slings   ☐   Ladders and scaffolds   ☐

6. **Bulletin Boards**
   Neat and attractive   ☐
   Display changed regularly   ☐
   Well illuminated   ☐

Signed

Use reverse side for detailed comments or recommendations

FIGURE 8.10   A sample Safety Inspection Checklist.

BUILDING SECURITY INSPECTION REPORT

A Security Inspection was made at _____ on date and at the time shown below. Conditions, if any, having a bearing on the protection of Company property are also noted below.

Security Representative _____

District _____ Date _____ 20 ____

Complete address of property inspected _____ Time   From   -AM

Central Office ( )   District ( )   Garage ( )   Locker ( )   Work Center ( )   _____ -PM

Carrier Hut ( )   Vehicle ( )   Acctg. Bldg. ( )   Commercial Bldg. ( )   To   -AM
_____ -PM

Regular Means of Admittance: Guard ( )   Locked doors or gate ( )   Door Tele. ( )

Code key set ( )   Cable box lock ( )   Sesame lock ( )

No.	Item	Satisfactory	Unsatisfactory	Remarks-Briefly describe conditions that prompted "unsatisfactory" classification and corrective action taken
1.	Appropriate illumination			
2.	Condition of locks			
3.	Condition of fences			
4.	Condition of gates			
5.	Basement entrances			
6.	Outside doors			
7.	Windows			
8.	Guard services			
9.	Storage – Cable			
10.	Material storage, Cages			
11.	Tool storage			
12.	Talking set storage, Cages			
13.	Car or bin doors unlocked			
14.	Fire hazards			
15.	Identification & accountability of others found on premises / Employees / Non-employees			
16.	Responsible department advised: Date: Title: Name			
17.	Repeated Condition: Number ( ) above			

Use other side if necessary

FIGURE 8.11   A sample building security inspection report.

SECURITY DEPARTMENT INCIDENT REPORT

OFFENSE CATEGORY		DATE-TIME RECEIVED	DAY OF WK.	DATE MO. DAY YR	TIME AM PM	INVESTIGATION NO.
FORCED ENTRY		COMPLAINANT'S NAME				HOME PHONE
THEFT	PERS.PROP.					
	COMPANY PROP	ADDRESS				BUSINESS PHONE
	COIN MACHINE					
	AUTO	STATUS				
ROBBERY		☐ VISITOR	☐ EMPLOYEE		☐ OTHER (SPECIFY)	
ASSAULT		DATE-TIME OF OFFENSE		DAY OF WK	DATE MO. DAY YR	TIME AM PM
RAPE						
MANSLAUGHTER		PLACE			WEAPON USED	
DISTURBANCE						
TRAFFIC		TRADEMARK				
OTHER (SPECIFY)						

VICTIM'S NAME		ADDRESS	

SEX ☐ M ☐ F	AGE	RACE	STATUS	☐ VISITOR	☐ EMPLOYEE	☐ OTHER (SPECIFY)
MECIAL TREATMENT ☐ YES (EXPLAIN) ☐ NO				DESCRIPTION OF LOST PROPERTY		VALUE

DESCRIPTION OF OFFENDERS

NO. 1	SEX ☐ M ☐ F	RACE	HEIGHT	BUILD	EYES	HAIR	GLASSES ☐ YES ☐ NO	COMPLEXION
	MARKS				AGE	HAT	COAT	SHIRT

NO. 2	SEX ☐ M ☐ F	RACE	HEIGHT	BUILD	EYES	HAIR	GLASSES ☐ YES ☐ NO	COMPLEXION
	MARKS				AGE	HAT	COAT	SHIRT

WITNESS NAME 1.	ADDRESS	TELEPHONE
WITNESS NAME 2.	ADDRESS	TELEPHONE

LAW ENFORCEMENT AGENCY NOTIFIED	TIME	PERSON
1.	AM PM	
2.	AM PM	

NAME OF PERSON ARRESTED 1.	ADDRESS
NAME OF PERSON ARRESTED 2.	ADDRESS

CHARGES

1.	2.

WAS PHYICAL FORCE USED?	☐ YES	☐ NO

SIGNATURE OF REPORTING OFFICER DATE	FOR SECURITY OFFICE USE ONLY APPROVED _____ DATE NAME CARD COMPLETED _____

FIGURE 8.12   An example of a standard incident report.

NARRATIVE – BE SPECIFIC IN WRITING OF THIS REPORT. BE SURE TO USE THE GUIDELINES: WHO, WHAT, WHEN, WHY, WHERE AND HOW. DESCRIBE OFFENSE IN DETAIL. INCLUDE STATEMENTS UTTERED BY VICTIM, WITNESSES AND SUSPECTS. DESCRIBE SCENE OF OFFENSE AND CONTRIBUTORY COND ITIONS SUCH AS POOR LIGHTING, EXTREME ISOLATION, ETC. LIST EVIDENCE FOUND AT SCENE AND ALL OTHER RELEVANT INFORMATION SUCH AS SOBRIETY OF VICTIM, WITNESSES AND SUSPECTS, SAFEGUARD REPORT FOR REFERENCE.

FOR SECURITY DEPARTMENT USE ONLY

THIS OFFENSE IS DECLARED:
UNFOUNDED ☐
CLEARED BY ARREST ☐   SIGNED _____   DATE _____
EXCEPTIONALLY CLEARED ☐   SECURITY DIRECTOR
INACTIVE (NOT CLEARED) ☐

FIGURE 8.12 (CONTINUED)

SECURITY DEPARTMENT
INCIDENT REPORT

NATURE OF INCIDENT   REPORT NO.

☐   Theft Of Property   ☐   Liquor Violation

☐   Vandalism   ☐   Other _____

☐   Trespassing   Date And Time Of Report
                               _____
                                                         Date And Time Of Incident
☐   Time Card Violation   _____
                                                         Location Of Incident
☐   Unauthorized Entry/Exit

REPORT IN DETAIL:	WHO	WHAT	WHEN	WHERE	HOW	WHY
Complainant		Clock Or Social Security No		Department Or Address		
Offender		Clock Or Social Security No		Department Or Address		
Witness		Clock Or Social Security No		Department Or Address		

DESCRIPTION OF INCIDENT: _____

_____
_____
_____
_____
_____
_____
_____
_____
_____
_____
_____
_____
_____
_____
_____
_____
_____
_____
_____
_____
_____

Estimate of Theft or Damage $_____   Reported by:

Continued on Reverse side?   ☐ Yes   ☐ No   _____

                                               Security Officer   Badge No.

FIGURE 8.13   A more simplified, checklist version of an incident report.

CLEAR FORM

MISSING, DAMAGED OR STOLEN PROPERTY REPORT

NOTE: If property has been stolen or is lost, destroyed or damaged as a result of negligence, this form should be completed and sent to the Office of the Attorney General within 72 hours of the occurrance.

Name of agency / institution		Agency no.

Place of occurrence	City	County
Police agency notified	Police report number	Disposal code	Estimated value at date of loss

SERIAL NUMBER(S)	PURCHASE DATE	PURCHASE VALUE

STATE PROPERTY NUMBER	COMPONENT NUMBER	DESCRIPTION	LOCATION

Person(s) responsible for asset(s)	Property Manager name	Property Manager phone

Report in detail (including what security measures were in place at the time.)

Please check one box.

☐ Our investigation of the circumstances surrounding the state property listed herein indicates reasonable cause to believe that the loss, destruction, or damage to this property **was** through the negligence of the person(s) charged with the care and custody of this property.

☐ Our investigation of the circumstances surrounding the state property listed herein indicates reasonable cause to believe that the loss, destruction, or damage to this property **was not** through the negligence of the person(s) charged with the care and custody of this property.

This form should be signed and dated by the agency/institution head or designated representative. If a designated representative completes this form, the rank of that individual should be greater than that of the property manager.

sign here ▶   Date

Printed name and title

Retain this form for your files. If the property was missing, damaged, or stolen due to employee negligence, submit a copy of this form and a copy of the police report, if applicable, to the Office of the Attorney General.

FIGURE 8.14 A sample missing, damaged, or stolen property report.

INVESTIGATION REPORT

1 Referral/Connecting/Property Slip #	2 Code	3 UCR Code	4 Trans Disc No		5 Case Number	

6 Crime ☐ Accident ☐	7 Patrol District	8 NJS	9 Victim's Name			
			10 Race		11 Sex	12 Age

13 Date/Time Between At	14 hr.	15 Wk.	16 Mo.	17 Day	18 Year	19 Home address – City – State	Phone

20 Location		21 Employer-School	22 Business Phone

23 Time Unit Notified	24 Person Reporting Crime	25 Age	26 Date and Time

27 Type of Premises	28 Code	29 Weapons-Tools	30 Code	31 Address	32 Phone

33 Vehicle	34 Year	35 Make	36 Body Type	37 Color	38 Reg. Number & State	39 Serial Number

Value Stolen Prop	40 Currency	41 Jewelry	42 Furs	43 Clothing	44 Auto	45 Misc.

46 Total Value Stolen	47 Total Value Recovered	48 Teletype Yes ☐ No ☐	49 Alarm No.	50 Weather	51 Status Crime	52 Status Case

53 Cleared by Arrest				
	Adult ☐	Juvenile ☐	Adult and Juvenile ☐	Narcotics Involved ☐

LIST INVOLVED – LIST AND IDENTIFY ADDITIONAL VICTIMS – DESCRIBE PERPETRATORS OR SUSPECTS – ACTION TAKEN INCLUDES FINDINGS AND OBSERVATIONS OF INVESTIGATOR – PHYSICAL EVIDENCE FOUND – WHERE – BY WHOM – DISPOSITION AND TECHNICAL SERVICES PERFORMED – INTERVIEW OF VICTIMS – WITNESSES – PERSONS CONTACTED – SUSPECTS – LIST – DESCRIBE STOLEN PROPERTY – VALUE – COURT ACTION – ATTACH STATEMENTS

54 Person Involved	Address	Phone No.	Race	Sex	DOB	Arrest Suspect Witness
						☐
						☐
						☐
						☐
						☐

NARRATIVE:

61 Case No.

55 Type Name	56 Badge Number	57 Page____ of ____ Pages	58 Date of Report
Signature_____	59 Typist		60 Desk Supervisor

FIGURE 8.15   A detailed Investigation Report.

BOX 8.2   AN EXAMPLE MOTOR VEHICLE ACCIDENT CHECKLIST (SOURCE: U.S. NAVY.)

Motor Vehicle Accident Checklist

- Vehicle(s) identified, including vehicle identification number (VIN), license plate number, make, model, year, and color.
- Identify the driver(s) and owner(s), to include the name, age, addresses (home and work), and telephone numbers.

- For military members indicate their military status at the time of the accident (e.g., active duty, TAD, leave, liberty, etc.), their grade/rank, and the name, address, location and Unit Identification Code (UIC) of their unit.
- If an individual died or is incapacitated as a result of the accident, provide similar identifying information for the next-of-kin or legal representative.
- If a Government vehicle was involved, identify the unit to which the vehicle was assigned, and the individual at the unit who authorized use of the vehicle, and its authorized purpose.
- Private vehicle involved: name, address, policy numbers and telephone number of the insurer of the vehicle, including the amount and type of insurance carried.
- Time of the accident.
  - Light and weather conditions.
  - Effect on driving conditions.
- Location of accident (e.g., highway number, direction of travel, milepost number, street name, intersection).
  - Road and terrain factors, road characteristics.
  - Any obstructions to the driver's vision.
- Speed of the vehicles involved as evidenced by testimony of witnesses, skid marks, condition of road, and the damage to the vehicles.
- Actions of other vehicles involved in the accident, including any part played by them in creating the conditions that resulted in the accident.
- Traffic conditions at the scene and their effect on the accident.
- Traffic laws and regulations in force pertinent to the accident, including traffic safety devices, signs, and marking? (e.g., school zone, no passing zone, railroad crossing, reduced speed limit).
  - Any regulations to use safety devices installed in the vehicles (e.g., seat belts, child carriers).
  - Copies of statues, ordinances, or regulations should be made an enclosure.
- Mechanical condition of the vehicles involved.
- If a mechanical defect or condition (e.g., faulty or worn brakes/tires), is determined to have contributed to the accident, include the relevant maintenance history of the vehicle.
- Physical condition of the driver(s), including intoxication, fatigue, use of medications or drugs, or other medical conditions, number of hours of sleep prior to the accident, number of hours worked.
  - The amount of alcohol consumed, results of any blood alcohol or other test for intoxication.
  - Any medications or drugs taken prior to the accident.
  - Any unusual stress or abnormal condition that might have affected the driver's alertness.
  - The opinion section should address any reasonable inferences that may be drawn from these facts relevant to the cause of the accident.
- Driving experience of the driver(s) both generally and in the type of vehicles being driven, to include the state which licensed the driver.
- Any previous loss of driving privileges and driving-related convictions.
- Safety devices installed and whether they were being used at the time of the accident.
- Conduct of passenger(s). Opinions may include reasonable inferences on the effect of any passenger's conduct on the driver(s).
- Facts and opinions relevant to knowledge by any passenger of any impairment of the driver at the time the passenger entered or had a reasonable opportunity to leave the vehicle.
- Damage to vehicle fully described (including photos, if available) and repair costs.

- Damage to other property (including photos, if available) and repair costs.
- Nature and extent of personal injuries and medical cost, documented by relevant medical records, bills, and receipts.
- If death resulted, indicate cause of death to include a copy of the death certificate and any autopsy reports as enclosures.
- Name, age, address, and telephone number of any witnesses to the accident.
  - A description of their (witnesses) location in relation to the accident scene, their ability to observe from that location, and what they saw.

- Name, address, and telephone number of any law enforcement official who investigated the accident.
  - Copy of any law enforcement or police report made concerning the accident should be included as an enclosure and the custodian of the original report should be indicated.

- Any civilian or military criminal charges brought as a result of the accident and the ultimate resolution of those charges.
- An opinion regarding the probable cause of the accident. If the evidence is insufficient to establish probable cause, those factors which in the opinion of the investigating officer contributed to the accident should be listed.
- An opinion regarding the contributory or comparative negligence of any party, if any.
- If not included in the facts relevant to military or criminal charges filed, an opinion concerning any laws, articles of the UCMJ, or regulations violated.
- Whether or not the vehicles are economically repairable, and if not, their salvage value.
- Whether or not the driver (in case of Government vehicle) was acting within the scope of employment pursuant to state law, and whether injuries sustained by military members were incurred in the line of duty or as result of misconduct.
- Whether or not disciplinary action should be taken.
- If Government property has been damaged, a recommendation as to the disposition of the property.
- Should the Government initiate a claim?
- Pertinent recommendations on matters of safety procedures.

NOTE: Motor vehicle accidents involving Government vehicles almost always involve the potential for claims for or against the Government. In such cases, refer to the "Claims" Checklist in this handbook and include all the facts and opinions required.

8.3.1.11 Traffic Reports

Traffic control violations, for those firms entrusted and empowered in this area, should be accurately catalogued. See Figure 8.16.

8.3.1.12 Property Reports

In both retail and insurance settings, the private investigator is concerned about the internal and external effects of pilferage and other property offenses. The field investigator must catalog and accurately describe the stolen property in question. The Stolen Property Report requires not only an itemization, but also detailed characteristics such as model, size, serial number, age, and value. See Figure 8.17.

Evidence that is found, seized, and secured in the field needs to be itemized for the purposes of assuring the proper chain of custody and acceptable identification. Report forms that itemize property track the journey of the evidence once seized. A record or receipt system is most advisable in

TRAFFIC VIOLATION LOG		Period:		Date:	
Operation:		Designation:		Page: of:	
TIME/DATE	VEHICLE DESCRIPTION	LICENSE/PERMIT	TYPE	COUNT	LOCATION

FIGURE 8.16 A sample Traffic Violation Log.

order to assure that there is no break in the chain of custody and that the evidence taken by private security operatives has not substantially changed in condition or form. The entry and exit of the evidence from storage, lab, or other protected facilities should be tracked by log and chronological time frame.

8.3.1.13 Basic Security Survey

If called upon to determine a breach of security in a government installation, business, or industrial concern, investigators frequently compile a security survey. The security survey document, such as

STOLEN PROPERTY REPORT

1. Victim's Name (Last, First, Middle)		2. Complaint No.
3. Victim's Address	4. Phone	5. Cell Phone
6. Address of Crime	7. Date of Crime	8. Date of Report

DESCRIPTION OF LOST/STOLEN PROPERTY

Quantity	Complete Item Description (Make, Model, Shape, Identifying Marks)	Color	Men's or Women's	Size	Serial No.	Model No.	Age	Value

I understand that copies of this form may be distributed as necessary to requesting insurance agencies and further that all items listed have, to the best of my knowledge, been stolen.

_____   _____
         Signature   Date

10. Victim Remarks	OFFICE USE ONLY
	Date Received by
11. Instructions for completing form: a. Complete items 1-10 (except Complaint No.) neatly and accurately b. Complete include a detailed description, including photographs or drawings. c. Each item must include an approximate age and value. d. Please request additional forms for additional listings. e. Return this form as soon as possible to: _____	Unit Referred to: Reproduced by: Reviewer:

12. Reporting Office No.	13 NCIC Entry by	14. Department Entry by	Page of

FIGURE 8.17 An example Stolen Property Report.

that at Figure 8.15, forms a permanent impression of a company's current security status. It is relied upon by policymakers and business officers in strategic decision making. The survey of the facility, place, or location is a comprehensive analysis of the entire physical plant, the perimeter, and its current level of security or lack thereof. See Table 8.2.

Web Exercise: Watch the video on a physical security assessment at https://youtu.be/SLw6Rrn6tsc.

TABLE 8.2

A Typical Facility and Site Risk Assessment and Security Survey

Risk Assessment Facility Checklist

	Yes	No	N/A	Notes
Windows	Yes	No	N/A	Notes
Note: All windows should be secured no matter how small or remote they are.				Including Sky Lights
Are basement windows clear of shrubbery and other obstructions?				
Are basement and grade level windows protected by:				
Bars?				
Wire Mesh?				
Window Locks?				
Wire Mesh?				
Plexiglas?				
Lexan?				
Other? (Explain)				
Are all windows, including those above ground level:				
Properly fitted with a locking device?				
Checked each night to make sure each window is closed and securely locked?				
Lights	Yes	No	N/A	Notes
Are exterior lights installed to illuminate the exterior of buildings and their alley ways?				
Are interior lights left on at night?				
Are entrance lights left burning at night so intruders will be clearly visible when forcibly attempting to enter premises?				
Are lights left burning in strategic locations to allow people passing by and/or police to see easily into the premises from foot or vehicle?				
Are timing devices used to turn lights on and off at preset times to give the impression the premises are occupied?				
Locks/Doors	Yes	No	N/A	Notes
Are all exterior doors equipped with proper locks?				
Are exterior doors of solid core construction?				
Are hinges, which are exposed on a door's exterior, equipped with non-removal able hinge pins?				
Are doors to adjoining building locked at night?				
Are all exterior doors kept locked to prevent entry?				
Is there a routine check each night to make sure all doors are locked?				
Intrusion Devices	Yes	No	N/A	Notes
Do you have a security alarm?				
If you have a system, is it approved by Underwriters Laboratories, Inc.?				
Was it properly installed by licensed workers?				
Is your security alarm system checked regularly?				
Does your system cover your hazardous points fully?				
Is your Alarm System:				
Connected to a central alarm station?				
Connected to an automatic dialing attachment?				
Local Alarms?				
Closed Circuit TV System	Yes	No	N/A	Notes
Do you have a security camera system?				
Does the system record 7 days or more? Tape or Digital Recorder				

(Continued)

TABLE 8.2 (CONTINUED)
A Typical Facility and Site Risk Assessment and Security Survey

Does the CCTV have motion detection?

Does the motion detection tie into the alarm system?

Does the camera placement cover all entry/exit points and vital areas?

Does the system cover the parking lot? If yes, are low light cameras required?

Can your system print photos or make video of critical incidents?

	Yes	No	N/A	Notes
Fire Suppression				
Are all fire extinguishers in a accessible position?				
Are all fire extinguishers tested and up to date?				
Is there a sprinkler system?				
Has it been tested recently?				
Is Emergency lighting in place and tested every month?				
Are smoke detection devices in place and tested every month?				
Are all fire exits properly marked?				
Are all appliances of in break/kitchen areas?				
Children's Area/Day Care				
Does the Children's area have a restricted entry point?				
Are there windows in all children's classroom areas?				
Is the diaper changing area in a secure location?				
Are there restroom facilities in the children's area?				
Do the doors for the storage area lock to keep toddlers out?				
Is the children's outside area protected by a chain linked fence and gate?				
General Security Measures				

Do you maintain a written or photographic inventory of all valuables and records on the premises?

Are personnel assigned to check exits, entrances, and windows to make sure they are secure before leaving at night?

Are precious objects, vessels and other valuables kept in a safe, vault or locked cabinet when not being used?

When staff or volunteers with access to keys or safe combinations terminate their status, are locks and/or combinations changed?

Do you have a security guard?

If so, did you investigate this guard before hiring him/her?

Are ladders, boxes and other equipment put away after use so that they are not left for use by anyone intent on criminal behavior?

Are premises used in the evening for meetings and other activities? (Evening activities generally reduce the possibility of burglaries/theft)

Have you arranged for a regular police patrol or a security force check at night?

Are the premises available for use 24-hours a-day?

Entire building?

Partial Section of building (Explain)

If a section of the building is open for use 24 hours a day, is movement from this section to other sections of the building restricted?

Describe security measures taken if answer to above is yes.

Completed By _____ Date _____

8.3.2 Major Criminal Documentation

8.3.2.1 The Offense Report

The offense report, often referred to as the *general crime report*, is the first major document completed in the examination and investigation of a *criminal* case. An offense report such as that provided at Figure 8.18 calls for a fairly comprehensive examination of the *actus reus*—the illegal conduct under review. For example, Item 28, the narrative column, calls upon the report writer to

OFFENSE REPORT	17 Rep Area	1 Victim's Name (Last, First, Middle)		1A M.O. No.	2 Complaint No.
18 Attachments ☐ Supplemental ☐ Property ☐ Arrest ☐ Vehicle ☐ Other___	19 Time Disp	3 Victim's Address City			4 Res. Phone
	20 Time Clear	5 Victim's Place of Employment or School			6 Bus. Phone
21 Weather		7 Victim's Sex – Race- Age	8 Location of Crime (Address)		
22 Describe Location of Offense		9 Reporting Person Sex – Race- Age			10 Res. Phone
23 Requested ☐ Crim. Inv. ☐ Traffic ☐ Juvenile ☐ Request to patrol ☐ Other ___		11 Reporting Person's Address City			12 Bus. Phone
		13 Day, Date and Time Occurred		14 Date and Time reported	
		15 Crime or Incident		15A Crime Compensation ☐ YES ☐ NO	16 UCR

Witness Parent Guardia	24 Name	Age	Best Contact Address		Best Phone	Other Phone
	(1)					
	(2)					

Missing Persons Suspects	25 Name - Address	Sex	Race	DOB	Ht	Wt	Hair	Eyes	Other	Clothing
	(1)									
	(2)									
	(3)									

Vehicle Involved	26 Year – Make - Model	Color(s)	Reg No. – State - Year		Identifying Characteristics

27 Property ☐ Lost ☐ Stolen ☐ Damaged ☐ Other	Quan.	Description – Size – Color – Model – Style – Material - Condition	Serial No	Where Located	Age	Total Value

Item No	28 NARRATIVE (1) CONTINUATION OF ABOVE ITEMS (INDICATE ITEM NUMBER CONTINUED AT LEFT), INCLUDE ADDITIONAL VICTIMS, WITNESSES AND SUSPECTS AS OUTLINED ABOVE (2) DESCRIBE DETAILS OF INCIDENT (3) DESCRIBE EVIDENCE AND PROPERTY AND INDICATE DISPOSITION (4) M.O. – HOW DONE – FORCE USED – AT WHAT POINT – WITH WHAT TOOL OR WEAPON – OTHER ACTS

	OFFICE USE ONLY	
	34 Date	35 Reproduced by

29 Reporting Officer	No	30 Status ☐ UNFOUNDED ☐ CLEARED & CLOSED ☐ OPEN ☐ SUSPENDED		36 Unit Referred to	
31 2nd Officer	No	32 Supervisor Approving	33 Daily Bulletin ☐ YES ☐ NO	37 Reviewer	Page of

FIGURE 8.18 An example offense report or general crime report.

fill in details of the criminal conduct. In order to corroborate this position, suspects, contacts, and other personnel involved in the case are catalogued. If the report document does not have sufficient space, most security firms have a continuation sheet or a supplemental report form. The supplemental report can be used to update the status of an investigation.

8.3.2.2   Arrest Report

Private security investigators have the same powers of arrest as any citizen and in most jurisdictions are held to a reasonable suspicion standard.[28] Individuals are required to document all arrests for liability and recordkeeping purposes. Police simply take over after a suspect has been arrested. Despite this looser legal standard governing arrest, and search and seizure activities, for private police, the individual agents and the industry itself must be vigilant and regular about its activities. Documentation not only prompts regularity in due process but also cuts down on abuse. For security, the lawsuit is the deterrent to abusive policing. The NCPA reminds the investigator of its sharp teeth:

> Lawsuits are more potent against private enforcers than public enforcers. Victims of erroneous arrests and prosecutions can successfully sue private agents for damages. Although a wrongfully arrested person may have little status or money, lawyers are available on a contingency basis and the arrestor's employer usually would be a suable (insured) "deep pocket." The employer is responsible for the on-the-job damages of his or her employees under the doctrine of respondent superior. Nor will abusive firms receive many contracts for enforcement services. Competition and the common law promote quality protective services at prices customers are willing to pay.[29]

An example of an arrest document that a private security investigator would complete is at Figure 8.19.

8.3.2.3   Defendant's Statement

As a precautionary measure, even though not legally required of all, private security companies, before eliciting information or interrogating witnesses, should warn or advise interviewees of their legal rights. There has been some challenge to the non-applicability of constitutional (Miranda) protections in the private sector.[30] Courts are increasingly hearing cases which allege a blurring of private and public police, especially when private and public officers work closely on a particular case. Arguments involving entanglement, public function, and using private officers to skirt or avoid constitutional strictures are now very common.[31] These relationships, whereby private security, not bound by constitutional principles, provide public officers with evidence they could have not secured otherwise, is referenced as the "platinum platter doctrine."[32] Mutual cooperation or assistance on a case may inadvertently provide a constitutional basis for a defendant at a later date.

To assure testimonial admissibility, some private security investigators relay the Miranda warning (see Box 8.3). These rights may be waived, but the waiver must be made voluntarily, knowingly, and intelligently (see Box 8.4).

ARREST REPORT	14 Rep Area	1 Suspect's Name (Last, First, Middle)		1A M.O. No.	2 Complaint No.

15 Location of Arrest	3 Suspect's Address	City	4 Arrest No/Grade

16 Describe Type of Premises	5 Sex Race DOB Ht Wt Hair Eyes	6 ID No.

17 Day, Date/Time Arrested	7 NCIC Check Time	8 Social Security No.

18 Breathalyzer/Operator/Time/ Reading	19 Parent/Guardian/Time Notified ☐YES ☐NO	9 Place of Birth	10 Weapon (Describe) Serial No.

20 Resist? ☐YES ☐NO	21 Narcotic? ☐YES ☐NO	22 Armed? ☐YES ☐NO	11 Occupation	12 Res. Phone	13 Bus. Phone

23 Where suspect Employed or School	24 Day, Date/Time Occurred	25 Date/Time Reported

26 Suspect Operators License No. State	27 Formal Charges	28 UCR

29 Hold Placed on Vehicle ☐YES ☐NO Towed to	30 Charges Changed to	Date/Time

31 Vehicle Involved Year/Make/Model Color(s)	Reg. No./State/Year	31A Vehicle Registered Owner Address

CODE: C-COMPLAINANT   V-VICTIM   W-WITNESS   P-PARENT/GUARDIAN   CO-SUSPECT

32 Name	Code	Residence	City	Res. Phone	Bus. Phone
(1)					
(2)					
(3)					
(4)					
(5)					

33 Arrest Procedure
(A) Arrested ____Hrs. (B) Rights ____ Hrs. (C) Transported ____ Hrs. (D) Arrived ____ Hrs.
(E) Processed & Rights ____ Hrs. (F) Interviewed ____ Hrs. (G) Arraigned ____ Hrs. (H) Released/Committed ____Hrs.
(I) Implied Consent Law ____ Hrs.

Item. No.	34 Narrative (1) Continuation of above items (indicate "Item Number" at left) (2) Describe Details of incident not listed above (3) Identify additional witnesses, victims, etc. from Block No. 32.

35 Transporting Officer	No	36 Arresting Officer	No	37 Booking Officer	No
38 Transporting Officer	No	39 Arresting Officer	No	40 Searched by	No

41 Suspect's Money	42 Supervisor Approving	43 Daily Bulletin ☐YES ☐NO	Page of

FIGURE 8.19 An example of an arrest report that includes extensive detail regarding the criminal conduct.

44 OFFICER'S OBSERVATIONS

ODOR OF ALCOHOL: STRONG☐ MODERATE☐ FAINT☐ OTHER _____

COMPLEXION: FLUSHED☐ MOTTLED☐ PALE☐ NORMAL☐ OTHER _____

EYES: BLOODSHOT☐ WATERY☐ GLASSY☐ CONTRACTED☐ DILATED☐ OTHER_____
    WEARING GLASSES☐ CONTACT LENSES☐

SPEECH: INCOHERENT☐ CONFUSED☐ JERKY☐ PROFANE☐ STUTTERING☐ GOOD☐ OTHER _____

BALANCE: STAGGERING☐ SWAYING☐ UNABLE TO STAND☐ NEEDED ASSISTANCE TO WALK☐ OTHER_____

MENTAL ATTITUDE: POLITE☐ EXCITED☐ TALKATIVE☐ HILARIOUS☐ COMBATIVE☐ STUPEFIED☐ OTHER_____

CLOTHING CONDITION: DISORDERLY☐ ORDERLY☐ SOILD BY VOMIT☐ SOILED BY URINE☐ PARTLY DRESSED☐ OTHER_____

CLOTHING (*Describe Clothing And Color Of Garments*)_____
_____

DEFENDANT INJURED? Yes☐ No☐   Retained in Hospital? Yes☐ No☐   Doctor_____

NATURE OF INJURIES_____
_____

45 REASON FOR STOP

DRIVING TOO FAST/SLOW☐   ACCIDENT☐   DRIVING IN ANAPPROPRIATE AREA☐   WEAVING/DRIFTING☐

NEARLY STRIKING CAR OR OBJECT☐   WIDE RADIUS TURN☐   STOPS WITHOUT CAUSE☐   LOOKS INTOXICATED☐

NOT IN MARKED LANE☐   EQUIPMENT VIOLATION☐   RAN STOP SIGN/LIGHT☐   FOLLOWING TOO CLOSELY☐

BRIGHT/NO LIGHTS☐

OTHER_____

46 FIELD TEST

1	**2**	**3**	MARK LEVEL
WALK AND TURN	**ONE LEG STAND**	**ALCOTEST**	OF DISCOLORATION
☐CAN'T KEEP BALANCE WHILE LISTENING TO INSTRUCTIONS	☐SWAYING WHILE BALANCING		
☐STARTS BEFORE INSTRUCTIONS FINISHED	☐USES ARMS TO BALANCE		
☐STOPS WHILE WALKING TO STEADY	☐QUITE UNSTEADY		
☐DOES NOT TOUCH HEEL TO TOE	☐PUTS FOOT DOWN		
☐LOSES BALANCE WHILE WALKING	☐CANNOT/REFUSES TEST		
☐INCORRECT NUMBER OF STEPS			
☐CANNOT/REFUSES TO DO TEST			

INSTRUCTIONS READ PER MTL FORM _____☐

47 CHEMICAL TESTING

TIME OF TEST _____

CHEMICAL BREATH TEST: ADMINISTERED BY _____ SERIAL#_____

DEVICE _____ SERIAL #_____

RESULTS_____

URINE TEST SAMPLE: OBTAINED BY_____

SAMPLE STORED IN_____

BLOOD SAMPLE: TAKEN BY_____ AT_____HOSPITAL

SAMPLE STORED IN _____ AT _____ FOR TRANSPORTATION

TO_____ LAB _____

FIGURE 8.19 (CONTINUED)

BOX 8.3   THE MIRANDA WARNING

Warning

Before you are asked any question, you must understand your rights.

You have the right to remain silent.
Anything you say will be used against you in court.

You have the right to talk to a lawyer for advice before we ask you any questions and to have him or her with you during questioning.

If you cannot afford a lawyer, one will be appointed free of charge, at any time.

If you decide to answer questions now, without a lawyer present, you will still have the right to stop answering at any time. You also have the right to stop answering at any time until you talk to a lawyer.

This statement of my rights has been read to me by the undersigned officer and I understand what my rights are.

Signed_____ Date_____ Time_____

Witness: _____

Witness: _____

BOX 8.4   A SAMPLE WAIVER FORM DENOTING AN INDIVIDUAL HAS ELECTED TO WAIVE THEIR RIGHTS

Waiver

This statement of my rights has been read to me by the undersigned officer, and I understand what my rights are. I am willing to make a statement and answer questions. I do not want a lawyer. I understand and know what I am doing. No promises or threats have been made to me, and no pressure or coercion of any kind has been used against me.

Signed_____ Date_____ Time_____

Witness: _____

Witness: _____

If a suspect's vehicle, personal effects, or other property are going to be searched, it is advisable, before commencing a search, to document and record the consent of the suspected party. The same constitutional challenge, as noted above, has been made, though unsuccessfully, in 4th Amendment cases.[33] See Box 8.5.

BOX 8.5   AN EXAMPLE OF A CONSENT TO SEARCH FORM

Consent To Search

[DATE]

STATE OF

COUNTY OF

I, _____, having been informed of my constitutional right not to have a search made of my automobile hereinafter mentioned without a search warrant and of my right to refuse to consent to such a search, hereby authorize _____ _____ and _____, officers of the _____ Police Department, in _____ _____, _____, to conduct a complete search of my automobile, a _____ _____, registration number _____. These officers are authorized by me to take from my automobile any letters, papers, materials or other property which may have been involved in an unlawful act. I realize that anything found by said officers that I cannot account for may be used as evidence against me in the event of a court trial.

    This written permission is being given by me to the above-named police officers voluntarily and without threats or promises of any kind.

    Signed_____ Date_____ Time_____

    Witness: _____

    Witness: _____

Once these constitutional issues have been addressed, acquire a statement from the suspect or witness. Witness statement documents come in many formats. Box 8.6 provides one example.

BOX 8.6   AN EXAMPLE OF A WITNESS STATEMENT FORM

Witness Statement

I, _____, Age_____,

Sex_____, Occupation _____ Address _____

_____, do hereby make the following statement of my own free will and accord concerning _____

_____, which occurred

on the _____ day of _____,

20_____.

Time:_____

_____

_____

_____

_____

_____

_____

_____

_____

_____

_____

_____

_____

_____

_____

_____

_____

_____

_____

_____

_____

Web Exercise: Watch the informative video on witness statements at https://youtu.be/hSpp69qB83E.

8.4 CONCLUSION

This chapter introduces the many facets and requirements of report writing and document preparation for the private investigator. Reports, in their many formats, from field notes to security surveys, are examined. All reports are evaluated in light of general recommendations on construction for clarity and eventual admissibility. The chapter also highlights a series of forms that are commonly utilized by the private security industry and relays recommendations on how to properly prepare. Finally, the sequential and organizational benefits to the security investigator and firm regarding the authorship of reports are fully stressed.

NOTES

1. Tim Dees, "Report Writing Aids," *Law &Order*, December 2003: 18; see Rory J. McMahon, *Practical Handbook for Private Investigators* (Boca Raton, FL: CRC Press, 2001): 135.
2. Jean Reynolds, "The Myths of Report Writing," *Law &Order* 62, no. 2 (February 2014): 54.
3. Russell Colling, *Hospital Security*, 2nd ed. (Butterworth-Heinemann, 1982): 235; see how the rise of technology has influenced report writing in: Bryan Roberts, "The Keyboard Is Mightier than the Sword," *Journal of California Law Enforcement* 41 (2007): 14; Robert Garigue and Marc Stefaniu, "Best Practices for Security Report Writing," adapted from Robert Garigue and Marc Stefaniu, "Information Security Governance Reporting," *Information Systems Security* 12, no. 4 (September/October 2003): 36–40.
4. For an interesting analysis on the distinction or difference between solely individual reports versus collaborative reports amongst a team, see Annelies Vredeveldt, Linda Kesteloo, and Peter J. van Koppen, "Writing Alone or Together: Police Officers' Collaborative Reports of an Incident," *Criminal Justice &Behavior* 45, no. 7 (2018): 1071–1092, https://doi-org.ez.lib.jjay.cuny.edu/10.1177/0093854818771721.
5. Bennett and Hess, "Investigation": 79; William Evan Gillespie, "Report Writing as an Essential Tool to Investigations" (IFPO, January 2011), www.ifpo.org/wp-content/uploads/2013/08/Gillespie_Report_Writing.pdf; Applied Police Training and Certification, *Report Writing Guidelines for Incident Report Writing* (2009), accessed September 9, 2018, http://ddq74coujkv1i.cloudfront.net/pdfs/reportwriting-manual.pdf.
6. "Information Technology: More Police Departments Use Software Programs to Help Officers File Reports," *Law Enforcement Employment Bulletin* (May 2007): 1.
7. B. J. Bourg, "Seven Steps to Effective Report Writing," *Law &Order* 58, no. 11 (2010): 66–69.
8. Colling, "Hospital": 234; Corrections, Public Safety and Policing Ministry of Justice and Attorney General, *Corrections, Public Safety and Policing, Private Investigator and Security Guard Training Manual* (2008): Chapter 7, http://jjspaofazssecurity.yolasite.com/resources/pisg-manual-07.pdf; McMahon, "Practical Handbook": 135.
9. See Julie Schroeder, Bonnie Grohe, and Rene Pogue, "The Impact of Criterion Writing Evaluation Technology on Criminal Justice Student Writing Skills," *Journal of Criminal Justice Education* 19, no. 3 (2008): 432–445.
10. Frank Kerns, "7 Tips to Improve Security Officers' Incident Report Writing Skills," *Security Magazine*, February 28, 2017, www.securitymagazine.com/articles/87863-tips-to-improve-security-officers-incident-report-writing-skills.
11. R. Gallati, *Introduction to Private Security* (1983): 262; "Conquer the seven sins of security report writing," *Healthcare Security and Emergency Management*, November 1, 2004, www.hcpro.com/HOM-43520-742/Conquer-the-seven-sins-of-security-report-writing.html; Garigue and Stefaniu, "Best Practices."
12. Pinkerton's, Inc., *Investigator's Guide: Report Writing* (1990): 5.
13. Charles P. Nemeth, *Private Security: An Introduction to Principles and Practice* (Boca Raton, FL: CRC Press, 2018): 405.

14. Gallati, "Introduction": 256; Liz Martinez, "How to Train Your Security Staff for Successful Report Writing," SecurityInfoWatch, April 19, 2005, www.securityinfowatch.com/article/10608649/how-to-train-your-security-staff-for-successful-report-writing; Robert D. Sollars, "Security Report Writing: Tips for Creating Pro Security Reports," November 30, 2015, www.silvertracsoftware.com/extra/-security-officer-report-writing-and-creating-professional-reports.

15. See Martinez, "Successful Report Writing."

16. Mary Dowd, "How to Effectively Write Reports as a Security Officer," Chron.com, June 29, 2018, https://work.chron.com/effectively-write-reports-security-officer-20169.html.

17. See Chris Anderson, "How to Improve Report Writing," Security Officer's Guide, August 19, 2015, www.silvertracsoftware.com/extra/049-super-easy-ways-to-improve-your-security-officer-report-writing.

18. Gallati stresses the importance of taking good notes: The investigator must acquire the habit of making complete, comprehensive notes. They must not trust their memory. They are to place their initials and the date on each page as well as number them. They should be in chronological order (Gallati, "Introduction": 2).

19. APTAC, "Report Writing Guidelines."

20. C. Cox and J. Brown, *Report Writing For Criminal Justice Professionals* (Anderson Publishing, 1992): 14–15.

21. Dowd, "Effectively Write Reports."

22. "Form LE-7," G.A. Thompson Co., P.O. Box 720254, Dallas, TX 75372.

23. "Form OI-1," G.A. Thompson Co., P.O. Box 720254, Dallas, TX 75372.

24. Ralph F. Brislin, *The Effective Security Officer's Training Manual* (Butterworth-Heinemann, 1995): 101–102; McMahon, "Practical Handbook": 135; Gillespie, "Report Writing."

25. "Form MPR-1," G.A. Thompson Co., P.O. Box 720254, Dallas, TX 75372.

26. See Gillespie, "Report Writing."

27. Naval Justice School, *JAGMAN Investigations Handbook* (2016): XI-5–XI-7, www.dtic.mil/dtic/tr/fulltext/u2/1014458.pdf.

28. Charles P. Nemeth, *Private Security and the Law*, 5th ed. (Boca Raton, FL: CRC Press, 2018): 96 et seq.

29. National Center for Policy Analysis, "Potential Abuses under Private Law Enforcement," www.public-policy.org/~ncpa/studies/s181/s181j.html; see also Charles P. Nemeth and K. C. Poulin, *Private Security and Public Safety: A Community Based Approach* (2005): 294.

30. Nemeth, "Private Security Law": 112.

31. Nemeth, "Private Security Law": 189.

32. Nemeth, "Private Security Law": 115.

33. Ibid.

9 Investigative Method and Technique: Theft/Property Offenses

9.1 INTRODUCTION

Property offenses have a monumental impact on both personal and business environments. The impact of economic crime and its related costs are difficult to fully define and appreciate because the criminal conduct relating to property has many definitions and codifications.[1] "Shoplifting is a persistent problem for many retailers. It is a major source of 'shrinkage', the umbrella term used to denote preventable losses attributed to theft, fraud, error, damage or wastage."[2] The consensus as to what constitutes shrinkage is not fully uniform with varying conclusions about value, book or actual value, inventory cost—all impacting eventual computations.[3] According to estimates from the Global Retail Theft Barometer,[4] the cost of retail crime globally exceeded $214 billion in 2014–15.[5]

The methodologies employed to carry out this form of theft are a mix of the creative and the aggressive. Shoplifting is no longer a minor, incidental offense but one with highly charged, negative impacts. Shoplifting generally falls in these forms and formats:

Palming: Stealing small items and concealing them in the palm of the hand.

Switching prices: Putting price tags from low cost goods onto more expensive goods.

Steaming: A large gang enters a shop, intimidates, threatens, or distracts staff in order to steal large quantities of goods before running off. It can be dangerous to tackle these people, as they are likely to resort to violence.

Staff collusion: Staff working in conjunction with the thieves by turning a blind eye to theft or colluding in the crime.[6]

At both the national and international level, the problem of retail theft and shrinkage is staggering. See Figure 9.1.[7]

Beyond obvious financial losses to retailers, the effects of retail crime can be far reaching.[8] In extreme cases, chronic crime levels can force businesses to close, thereby limiting employment opportunities and the availability of goods and services.[9] Moreover, the costs of high crime levels ultimately fall on the consumer through elevated prices, comprising what Bamfield and Hollinger[10] call a "crime tax."[11] And retail businesses are increasingly experiencing theft at levels of violence and organization never previously witnessed. Like roving bands and gangs, the act of collective and violent retail theft has become a major security challenge for the retail and commercial entity.[12] Organized retail theft is a fast growing and very distressing reality that store owners must contend with, for the "loot" of these raids is put up for fast sale and fast profits. For example, "ORC gangs heist merchandise that can be turned for a quick profit … such as emergency contraception, pregnancy tests, Nexium, sleep aids, wrinkle creams, razors and baby formula"[13] to name a few. See Figure 9.2.[14]

Theft, retail shoplifting, organized retail crime, corporate fraud, cybercrime, and other forms of white-collar crime not only harm profit potential in the commercial marketplace, but also undermine institutional and employer trust and, unfortunately, cause an indirect escalation of prices inevitably passed on to consumers.[15] Economic crime impacts society in many indirect ways, in

The highest loss
by country

1 US
$36.79 billion

2 China
$26.06 billion

3 Japan
$14.90 billion

■ GLOBAL SHRINKAGE – BY COUNTRY

Among the top 10 countries with least shrinkage rates, eight are located in Europe; these include countries such as Norway, Switzerland, France, Poland, and the UK. Countries with the highest shrinkage rates include Mexico, the Netherlands, Finland, Japan, and China.

Retailers lost $36.79 billion due to shrinkage in the US —the highest among all countries— followed by China ($26.06 billion), and Japan ($14.90 billion).

Out of all the countries where a like-for-like analysis⁷ was possible, 7 witnessed an decrease in shrinkage during 2014–2015, as compared with 2013–2014, while 10 witnessed an increase. 6 out of these 7 countries that witnessed an decrease are located in Europe, except Australia.

In 2014–2015 US witnessed the highest erosion (0.69 pps).

FIGURE 9.1   Global shrinkage loss by country (Used with permission, Checkpoint Systems.)

For the first time, 100% of surveyed retailers believe their company has been the victim of organized retail crime.

95%	96%	94%	88%	97%	100%
2011	2012	2013	2014	2015	2016

▼ **More than 8 in 10 report that ORC activity has increased in the past 12 months.**

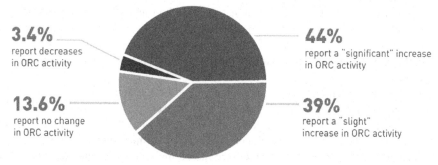

3.4%
report decreases
in ORC activity

44%
report a "significant" increase
in ORC activity

13.6%
report no change
in ORC activity

39%
report a "slight"
increase in ORC activity

FIGURE 9.2   Organized Retail Crime survey (Used with permission, National Retail Federation.)

business, government, and the common and public good. A listing of the negative effects illustrates the corrosive impact of property and other economic crime.

Business effects[16]
- Increased costs of insurance and security protection
- Costs of internal audit activities to detect crime
- Cost of investigation and prosecution of suspects measured in terms of lost time of security and management personnel
- Reduced profits

- Increased selling prices and weakened competitive standing
- Loss of productivity
- Loss of business reputation
- Deterioration in quality of service
- Threats to the survival of small business

Local government effects[17]
- Costs of investigation and prosecution of suspects
- Increased costs of prosecuting sophisticated (e.g., embezzlement) and technology-related (e.g., computer) crime
- Costs of correctional programs to deal with economic crime offenders
- Cost of crime prevention programs
- cost of crime reporting and mandated security programs
- Loss of tax revenue (e.g., loss of sales tax, untaxed income of perpetrator, and tax deductions allowed to business for crime-related losses)

Public effects[18]
- Increased costs of consumer goods and services to offset crime losses
- Loss of investor equity
- Increased taxes
- Reduced employment due to business failures

While there may be considerable disagreement as to the exact amounts of economic losses due to theft and other property offenses, it is a certainty that "[C]rimes victimize all businesses, small or large, retail, wholesale, manufacturing, or service."[19]

Loss of inventory from stores—due to causes including shoplifting and employee theft—cost the U.S. retail industry nearly $48.9 billion in 2016.

The National Retail Security Survey, conducted annually by the National Retail Federation trade group, found that the average inventory shrink rate increased to 1.44% in 2016. That figure—which measures missing inventory—includes items that go missing because of shoplifting, theft by employees, administrative errors, vendor fraud and other unknown loss.

Most missing inventory (36.5%) was attributed to shoplifting by outside customers, followed by employee theft (30%). Administrative errors accounted for 21.3% of inventory shrink, while vendor fraud accounted for 5.4%.

The survey—which included 83 retailers, some of which have multiple brands—found that the average cost per shoplifting incident doubled to $798.48. The average cost per employee theft incident was $1,922.80. The survey attributed that, in part, to a decrease in punitive action against shoplifters and employees.[20]

Case clearance rates—the rate at which cases are closed through a resolution and identification of the perpetrator—are low in property crime categorizations when compared to other, especially felonious criminality. Police resources and energies are more likely to be allotted for major personal crimes such as murder, rape, and robbery. With violent crime capturing the bulk of our interest, property offenses seem minor by design. As the push for lighter penalties increases, such as in shoplifting, the sting or severity of property crime dissipates.[21] In some jurisdictions, the effective deterrence approaches have caused drops in crime rates.[22]

Politicians and legislators have had a hand in this too. Instead of referring to it as a traditional larceny, that is, the unlawful taking of another's property, legislators have constructed and designed a new statute for shoplifting that is less felonious than an actual larceny, or in the alternative have raised the felony or misdemeanor guidelines to make formal prosecution less likely.[23] Others argue that a "business" is really not a crime "victim" in the same sense as a person and because of this distinction, the energies of the justice systems are misplaced and misguided when trying to formally charge and prosecute the shoplifter.[24] Prosecution clearance rates, a measure of successful convictions, are even less impressive.[25]

Private security companies that provide residential security systems have a heavy burden in identifying and apprehending residential burglars. Aside from apprehension and identification, the security officer is also obliged to assist the client in the recovery of lost property. In an overwhelming number of cases, property lost in burglary cases (particularly those that involve little use of force) is rarely recovered. What is not arguable is that the costs of these forms of crime negatively impact a wide array of constituencies.[26] "The impact of the many crimes against business cannot be ignored, since losses or shrinkages of the magnitude described cannot be tolerated. Crime against business has reached such proportions that it has been recognized as a major contributing factor in some business closings and corporate bankruptcies. The business community must begin to emphasize aggressive policies and procedures that anticipate and fight criminal opportunities that are particularly common to the business world."[27]

The main focus of this chapter regards the real and unceasing challenge of property crime and how the private security industry has taken a lead in its prevention and deterrence. Part of the industry's historic purpose and rationale centers on asset protection, and property offenses are a direct confrontation with that mission. Throughout these pages, the stress will be on retail theft and shoplifting, other forms of larceny, auto theft, fraud, and the new dimension of cyber crime.

9.2 SHOPLIFTING AND RETAIL THEFT

A plague of shoplifting occurs each and every day in the American economy. What cultural factors prompt this negative activity and is there any way of thwarting the onslaught? How do the thieves and actors rationalize their criminality? How can the private security industry minimize the damage or mitigate the harm? See Figure 9.3.[28]

9.2.1 RATIONALIZATIONS AND JUSTIFICATIONS FOR SHOPLIFTING AND RETAIL THEFT

Business planners and other entrepreneurs take for granted a certain level of internal and external pilferage and shoplifting. Shoplifting has reached epidemic proportions due to a host of factors—cultural tolerance, sheer volume, a lack of remedy and corresponding consequence, and a legal system incapable of handling the rush of cases. In addition to these explanations, the perpetrators have rationalized away the criminality of shoplifting—urging a tolerant view that does not reach the

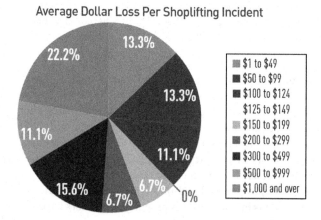

FIGURE 9.3   2017 National Retail Security survey (Used with permission, National Retail Federation.)

traditional threshold of crime and punishment.[29] The act of shoplifting or retail theft has become so common that in many circles there is a cry for decriminalization.

Web Exercise: The National Association of Shoplifting Prevention gives keen insight into the motivation of shoplifters at: www.shopliftingprevention.org/.

Its perpetrators are often skilled at posing rationalizations that seek to excuse this illegal conduct. The rationalizations and justifications can be categorized as follows:

1. That shoplifting is not stealing but simply borrowing
2. That shoplifting is a sign of the times
3. That shoplifting is a correct, moral act
4. That shoplifting is an indirect benefit or reward of the job
5. That shoplifting is not a crime but instead a political act in a class struggle

Shoplifters have diverse motivations for the act and just as many excuses that explain it away—as something more in the province of nuisance rather than crime. Robert O'Block, in his book *Security and Crime Prevention*, distinguishes between amateur and professional shoplifters.

Shoplifting occurs for a variety of reasons, including desperation, impulse, peer pressure, revenge, or (rarely) kleptomania. Persons who shoplift for these reasons are generally amateurs and represent a majority over professional shoplifters, amateurs comprising about 85 percent of all shoplifters.[30]

Whatever rationalization is conveyed, the act of shoplifting or retail theft has become so common that in many circles it is synonymous with decriminalized conduct.

Aside from motivations, shoplifters can be classified according to type. They can be categorized as follows:

1. The amateur adult shoplifter
2. The juvenile shoplifter
3. The professional shoplifter
4. The kleptomaniac
5. The shoplifter-addict
6. The vagrant and the alcoholic shoplifter[31]

In *Corporate Fraud: The Basics of Prevention and Detection*, thieves and shoplifters are categorized according to motivation rather than personality. The standard rationalizations are referred to as "personal inducements," with the following synopsis indicating the motivations:

1. Economic—to fulfill actual or perceived economic needs
2. Ideological—to take revenge against those with ideological differences
3. Egocentric—to prove that they are clever and knowledgeable or because they have an extravagant sense of self-importance
4. Psychotic—out of a distorted sense of reality, e.g., delusions[32]

Whatever the type or the motivation, it is a tough challenge for any American enterprise.

9.2.2 SHOPLIFTING METHODS

Every investigator should become familiar with the techniques and methods of shoplifting and its related deceptions. As a rule, shoplifters must rely upon their hands to commit acts of thievery. In the cyberworld, theft is committed virtually even though the net result occurs. Shoplifters are keenly attuned to and aware of their environment and, in scanning territory, they have a tendency to look quickly from side to side before committing the theft act. Because the shoplifter is performing an illegal act and is under the strain of trying to do so without getting caught, the physical movements and motions of the shoplifter tend to be less fluid and are instead quick, jerky, and sporadic. Body language speaks loudly. Shoplifters also use diversion, decoys, and disturbances that distract the eyes of salesclerks and other responsible personnel. Shoplifters regularly engage in these deceptive tactics:

1. Palming is the simplest and most common method for theft. Palming is often aided by the use of a package, handkerchief, or glove. An accomplice may stand to screen the shoplifter.
2. Purses and pockets are common concealing places for shoplifted items. Look closely at shopping bags and boxes from other stores, umbrellas, school books, knitting bags, strollers, baby carriages, sample cases, briefcases, overnight bags, and lunch boxes.
3. A loose coat can conceal items.
4. A full skirt can conceal items. A proficient professional can "crotch carry" as much as a 25-lb. ham or eight cartons of cigarettes.
5. Rubber bands can be snapped around bundles of ties, stockings, or socks.
6. Hats, gloves, scarves, coats, sweaters, and purses can be worn out of the store.
7. Coats or sweaters may be thrown down over merchandise desired, and then picked up with the merchandise concealed inside.
8. Jewelry and other accessories can be dropped into clothing or inserted into the hair.
9. In fitting rooms, tight or closely fitting garments can be put on under street clothes. Packages and purses can be rearranged to conceal the addition of a dress or blouse.
10. Intentional confusion with merchandise: handling so much clothing or products that sales personnel lose track; using accomplices or another party to distract sales personnel.
11. Price switching: taking a price from one product with a higher price and relabeling with a lower price label.
12. Stepping around the end of the counter, using the excuse of wanting to see something, in order to steal expensive articles from the unlocked side of a showcase.
13. Distracting sales personnel by persistent bell ringing while accomplice steals merchandise.
14. Removing small items from a display case and hiding them in another portion of the store for later retrieval by an accomplice.[33]

The deception employed varies by the merchant's environment and the product targeted by the thief. Security personnel must become adept at discerning the common clues that thieves and property offenders so often display. Watch out for:

1. Customer who enters the market with an empty paper bag in her purse, fills the bag with merchandise, and walks through an unused checkout line. If questioned, suspect assures the clerk that he or she has already been checked out.
2. Boxed items that are easily opened and reclosed may have more valuable items placed inside.
3. Produce bags are an easy mark for the shoplifter who brings his or her own crayon or stapler. This is called "price marking" and could occur on almost any product, but is very popular on meat items. (Today, many stores use computerized pricing.)
4. Supermarket shoplifters have been known to open an expensive package of tea and pour the contents into a pocketbook where it settles at the bottom.
5. A customer places an item in her purse and at the checkout counter asks for credit, explaining that another member of the family bought the item by mistake. If the clerk refuses the refund because of no receipt, the shoplifter wins. The shoplifter, of course, also wins if the store grants a refund.

6. Another variation of price switching is "cap switching." With prices frequently stamped on the caps, a shopper with a desire to steal will simply exchange the cap on a large size container for that on a small container.[34]

Security investigators will note differences in shoplifting not only by establishment and product but also by department. The attractiveness and expense of goods directly correlates to the level and intensity of shoplifting.

9.2.3 SHOPLIFTING IDENTIFICATION

To identify and catch shoplifters, keen senses and developed skills of human observation are necessary.[35] By both direct and inferential conduct, the investigator can make reasonable, probable cause judgments relative as to suspected parties if he or she watches closely. Examples that tip off the observer are:

- Persons entering stores with heavy overcoats, out of season.
- Persons wearing baggy pants, full or pleated skirts (when current styles do not dictate the wearing of such apparel).
- Persons demonstrating darting eye movement and who conspicuously stretch their neck in all directions. Many professional shoplifters often do not give any clues other than eye movement.
- Persons who exit the store with undue hurriedness.
- Customers who do not seem interested in merchandise about which they have asked.
- Customers who do not seem to know what they want and change their mind frequently about merchandise.
- Individuals who leave the store with an unusual gait or who tie their shoes or pull up their socks frequently, or make any other unusual body movements that might assist them in concealing articles.
- Customers who walk behind or reach into display counters.
- A disinterested customer who waits for a friend or spouse to shop.
- Customers who constantly keep one hand in an outer coat pocket.
- Customers who make a scene to distract clerks, so that an accomplice can remove property without paying for it.[36]

In addition to the initial observations, security personnel should watch for other conditions, circumstances, and behavioral characteristics of suspects:

- Customers who ask to be shown more articles than a clerk can keep track of.
- Repeatedly sending a clerk away for more merchandise.
- Two or more customers shuffling articles at the same time and at the same counter.
- Two or three persons grouped together around a counter, thereby restricting the view of the sales clerk.
- Examining articles in corners and odd locations.
- Continuously dropping articles on the floor.
- Holding identical pieces of merchandise for comparison.
- Holding or crumbling merchandise.
- Hesitation or sudden decisions at elevators.
- Making exits via back stairways.
- Movement throughout the store but constantly reappearing at one counter.
- Large groups of teenagers entering and splitting into smaller groups.

- Removing tags from merchandise.
- Nervous actions such as moistening dry lips or perspiring excessively.
- Startled looks.[37]

The security firm or consultant should aggressively advise the merchant about ways to deter shoplifting. In fact, sophisticated security practices provide a "predictive" capacity—to know how the acts typically go on. Security professionals can "predict future buying behavior, physical, cyber and intelligence security operations centers (SOCs) work to predict and thwart events that would negatively impact business continuity, infrastructure and stakeholders."[38] The private security firm should educate merchants on how to mitigate theft and how to prevent theft by situational and environmental design.[39] Physical space can be fashioned to prevent ready and easy theft. Added technology at points of ingress and egress assist too. Merchants have many lines of defense:

- Train employees in the methods of shoplifting.
- Offer employees a reward for deterring shoplifting.
- All customers should be greeted immediately upon entering the store.
- Maximize visibility by raising cash register area, use convex mirrors, one-way mirrors and closed-circuit television cameras.
- Use an electronic article surveillance system (EAS).
- Post signs in plain view stating that all shoplifters will be prosecuted.
- Keep cash registers locked and monitored at all times.
- Use cable tie-downs.
- Watch for price switching.
- Monitor all delivery men.
- Cashiers should check every item sold that might hide other merchandise.
- Have the cashier staple the customer's bag closed with the sales receipt attached.[40]

9.2.4 SHOPLIFTING INVESTIGATION

Shoplifting protocols mix all of these approaches with a wise and patient security investigator—one who waits until the evidence can be proven in accordance with the crime's basic elements. Apprehend with caution; show restraint in taking any party into custody until and only when the investigator is sure of the facts and the needed evidence to prove the allegation. J. Cleary, in *Prosecuting the Shoplifter: A Loss Prevention Strategy*, outlines elements for successfully investigating and prosecuting a shoplifting case:

1. *Logically and systematically gather evidence.* When cases are lost in court, it is usually because of insufficient evidence. This means that the store manager or security person overlooked some facts in the store, facts now needed as evidence at trial. The ability to produce facts logically and systematically in the store that can be relied on at trial as evidence to prove the elements of the offense is a necessary skill.
2. *Make decisions based on evidence produced in the store.* The essence of selective prosecution as authorized by the merchant's privilege is the ability to make decisions based on evidence found in the store. A retail employee must learn to see when the evidence supports the decision to prosecute a case. Sometimes the evidence will not be enough to support a decision to prosecute and supports the decision to release the suspect.
3. *Produce the two types of evidence needed to obtain convictions.* Merchants must learn how to produce the two types of store prosecution evidence needed to obtain a conviction for shoplifting in any state. Eyewitness evidence is produced by watching the suspect on a sales floor conceal merchandise or switch a price tag or assist a companion who is

concealing merchandise. The physical evidence is always produced after the suspect has first been detained on probable cause.

4. *Understand the legal meaning of the suspect's explanation.* Even veteran security people sometimes forget that the suspect's explanation is also evidence: defense evidence. Merchants must become good listeners. They will see that store managers and security people produce evidence with their ears, as well as with their eyes. As all those with even slight experience in dealing with shoplifting suspects know, very rarely will the person admit guilt. Most of the time people deny that they are shoplifting.

5. *Speak in terms of evidence.* In court, judges, prosecutors, and defense lawyers speak in terms of evidence. Thus, store managers and retail security persons must learn the language of evidence in their stores while they are handling the case and deciding whether to file a formal charge. Merchants will be shown how to discuss a shoplifting case in their stores in terms of what the evidence will prove in court. If the store manager or security person is speaking in terms of "suspicion" or "opinion," the chances of filing a clear case and losing it are much greater.[41]

The investigator must ensure and preserve the quality, content, and integrity of the evidence (see Chapter 6), by protecting the chain of custody. J. Kirk Bearfoot, in *Employee Theft Investigation*, offers sage advice on assuring an unassailable chain of custody:

> The main point is to be able to show who had sole custody of the goods during any given time span, and to prove that no one else was in a position to tamper with or alter the evidence in any way. It is also suggested that the written report of the agent involved in the handling of the contraband should indicate the marking of such evidence for identification. If possible, the nature of the identifying marks and their location on the contraband should be included. In this way, the written report stands to corroborate the actual identification mark on the evidence and thus greatly bolsters the entire case.[42]

From these suggestions, the investigator takes the work of retail thief in stages: first, identifying the offenses; second, being confident the elements of those offenses have been proven by the facts; third, exhibiting patience in both the allegation and the apprehension, and lastly learning from the defendant's own behavior patterns to be sure the customer is not merely a customer but a suspect.

9.3 INTERNAL THEFT BY EMPLOYEES

Internal theft, waste, and fraud by employees account for the largest part of shrinkage in many companies. Within the retail setting, internal theft rates are astronomical.[43] See Figure 9.4.

Of course, retailers everywhere deal with shrinkage, but there is one big difference between the United States and the rest of the world: Globally, dishonest employees are behind about 28% of inventory losses, while shoplifters account for a markedly higher 39%. Not so stateside, the study says, where employee theft accounts for 43% of lost revenue. That's about $18 billion, or $2.3 billion more than the cost of five-finger discounts taken by customers.

Some stores get ripped off more than others. Discounters, for example, experience higher rates of employee theft than home improvement stores or supermarkets do. Moreover, rather than simply walk off with merchandise or pocket cash, most workers who steal do so in subtler ways.

"Usually it happens during checkout, when an associate manipulates a transaction to benefit themselves or someone else," says Deyle. Employees might, for instance, enter refunds, discounts, or voided transactions into a cash register. They can also "cancel transactions, modify prices, or say someone used a coupon when they didn't."[44] Retail shrinkage can take a variety of forms, starting at the cash register, extending to the vendor and readily occurring in the front, administrative offices. See Figure 9.5.[45]

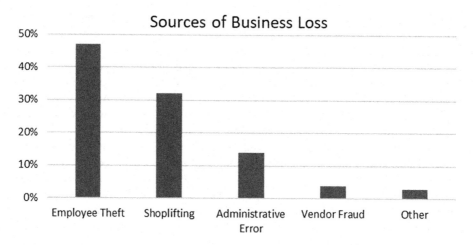

FIGURE 9.4   Sample Daily Surveillance Report (Used with permission, National Retail Federation).

Global Retail Shrinkage – by Source, 2013–2014 and 2014–2015 (all respondents)

Source	% Share (2014–2015)	% Share[12] (2013–2014)	Shrinkage by Value ($ billion, 2014–2015)
Dishonest Employee Theft	39%	28%	48.12
Shoplifting	38%	39%	46.89
Vendor/Supplier Fraud	7%	13%	8.64
Administrative and Non-crime Loss	16%	21%	19.74

FIGURE 9.5   Global retail shrinkage by source, Global Retail Theft Barometer (Used with permission, Checkpoint Systems).

Security firms must anticipate and plan for internal theft and recommend various protocols to minimize its impact for the client.[46]

9.3.1   REASONS AND RATIONALES FOR INTERNAL THEFT

Considerable differences of opinion exist as to why internal pilferage and other forms of employee thievery have risen so markedly. Some theorists hold that employees and, for that matter, employers, have lost all sense of loyalty to one another and to the company. As Barefoot remarks:

Unlike Japanese firms, which generally enjoy a high degree of loyalty on the part of their employees, the typical American employer has seen employee loyalty dwindle to a point where it can no longer be considered a viable factor in any well-balanced security program.[47]

How do employees rationalize their illegal conduct? To discern motive constitutes a critical step in policy making for any security team—discovering why people shoplift or engage in other commercial property crime is crucial for any investigator. Some industry analysts see a lack of awareness as to the "why" and a shortfall in the behavioral context of these offenses.[48]

Some experts have fashioned some standard rationales like:

- Real or perceived financial need
- Revenge
- Temptation and opportunity
- Workplace norms[49]

Many public and private law enforcement officials note that the employee's rationale is often "Everybody does it. Why shouldn't I?" Private security investigators have to understand and contend with this type of reasoning since it permeates the thief's moral decision making. Then again, a security firm that turns the other way in every retail theft case, trying to be tolerant and out of the mainstream justice processing, may be inadvertently setting up a tolerance threshold that promotes the activity. In short, actions without consequences lead to other actions without consequences.

9.3.2 THEFT STRATEGIES

How theft is consummated depends largely on positions, opportunities, and levels of access. The variety of tactics varies according to place, product, and capacity. Employees, committing internal theft, have many paths to criminality and commit thievery and fraudulent acts depending on individual circumstances and conditions. And there is little doubt that internal employee theft evolves as commerce and technology do. For example, who would ever have envisioned the "gift card" swindle schemes or accessing information at mobile checkout points.[50] Other crimes might involve:

- Merchandise swindles
- Embezzlement
- Organized crime schemes
- Commercial bribery and kickbacks
- Credit card fraud
- Receiving stolen goods
- Expense account fraud
- Price switching
- Medical and health care frauds
- Shoplifting
- Charitable and religious frauds
- Mortgage milking
- Insurance fraud
- Forgery and other document tampering
- False security fraud[51]

Employee theft strategies and tactics are multidimensional, including:

- Passing merchandise across the counter to an accomplice
- Putting merchandise in concealed places

- Under-ringing cash registers
- Overcharging a customer and pocketing the difference
- Theft of merchandise through unsupervised exits
- Failure to register sales
- Writing false refunds
- Collusion with delivery men and drivers
- Stealing from the warehouse or stockroom
- Stealing from returned goods and layaway
- Voiding a sales check and then pocketing the money
- Cashing fraudulent checks for accomplices
- Giving fraudulent refunds to accomplices
- Failing to record returned purchases and stealing an equal amount of cash
- Falsifying sales records to take cash
- Concealing thefts by falsifying store records
- Taking money from cash registers
- Giving employee discounts to unauthorized parties
- Concealing stolen goods in trash or other containers
- Shipping clerks mailing goods to their own address
- Wearing store clothing and accessories home at the end of a shift
- Intentionally damaging goods in order to buy them at discount
- Buying damaged merchandise at discount prices and later substituting damaged goods for first quality merchandise
- Stealing checks made payable to cash
- Picking up receipts discarded by customers and using them for refunds
- Stealing during early or late store hours
- Stealing from the dock or other exit areas
- Forging checks
- Keeping collections on uncollectible accounts
- Receiving kickbacks from suppliers[52]

9.3.3 Investigating Theft

Many methods are highly effective when investigating theft by employees or the public at large. That starts on the assumption that literally every person may be capable of committing theft. The American Society for Industrial Security warns investigators that even a company's most trusted employees must not be overlooked in the process of investigating an action.

[T]he investigator must consider all possible suspects, not eliminating anyone because they seem honest. In a pre-employment interview, all the signs may indicate that an employee can be trusted. However, people change, and negative attitudes toward the company can develop for many reasons. An updated background investigation may reveal that the employee has become a victim of alcohol or drug abuse, is in a financial bind, or is being strongly influenced by unsavory associates.[53]

When conducting an investigation of internal theft among retail store clerks, one should consider the following questions:

1. Are all sales being rung up and the monies deposited in the cash register?
2. Is the cash register kept closed at all times other than when a transaction takes place?
3. Are the clerks giving the employee discount privileges to non-store employees?
4. Are the employee purchase procedures being followed?
5. Is there an unusually close relationship between clerks in different departments, and do they handle each other's employee purchases?

6. Are the clerks following the store procedures on refunds and exchanges?
7. Are the clerks familiar with pricing within their department, thereby limiting the possibility of "price switching" by customers?
8. Are the proper taxes being charged?
9. Are the clerks wearing store merchandise, such as jewelry, and "forgetting" to return it?
10. Are clerks placing store merchandise under the counter to be purchased by them at some later date?[54]

Web Exercise: Watch the video on types of employee theft at https://youtu.be/uN4V-zNyFiI.

The investigator should also observe the conduct of the suspected employee. Look for behavior that sends up a red flag:

- Cash drawers are "under".
- Cash drawers are "over" or always correct.
- Constant and consistent errors.
- No-sale transactions.
- Trends. Is your cash loss intermittent?[55]

Certain evidence may directly implicate a suspect.

1. Big-ticket purchases or significant change in employee spending habits or lifestyle
2. Change in work habits
3. Purposefully trying to work independently or unsupervised
4. Problems with payroll, travel, and expense records
5. Missing items
6. Excessive absences
7. Suspicious cars, especially cars parked near back doors or dumpsters
8. Change in employee behavior
9. Pattern of friends or family showing up, or family and friends who insist they only go through employee's checkout line.
10. Change in voids, over rings, cash drawer overs/shorts
11. An increase in damaged merchandise or misplaced product[56]

Seasoned investigators get used to these and many other clues and this is why highly skilled investigators are so cherished by business and industry. Management also has a significant role in the prevention and deterrence of internal thievery especially during the hiring and screening process. Management obligation rests on integrity screening—being sure, or as sure as one feasibly can be, that new hires are less likely to pilfer. A host of techniques are available, as listed in Table 9.1.[57]

9.3.4 Obtaining Confessions or Statements

Once the evidentiary basis appears solid, and depending on the jurisdiction, the merchant and his investigator/officers have the right to temporarily detain and question the suspect. On top of this, the merchant may contact appropriate authorities for official processing. However, many companies prefer to informally handle these cases due to cost and other factors. Experienced investigators know they need to get their facts straight and documentation perfectly organized. Wise suggestions include:

- Prepare all the paperwork in advance, including their dismissal paperwork and, if possible, their final check.
- Keep a witness in the room. Typically, another store manager or HR person.

TABLE 9.1

2017   Survey of Employee Integrity Screening Options Used by Retailers

	2017	% Point Difference from 2016
Multiple interviews	91.0%	2.0 ▲
Criminal conviction checks	85.1%	−4.1 ▼
Verify past employment history	73.1%	11.6 ▲
Personal reference checks	58.2%	−0.3 ▼
Education verification	43.3%	7.9 ▲
Drug screening (laboratory)	40.3%	−15.1 ▼
Driving history	28.4%	−13.1 ▼
Credit checks	26.9%	−6.9 ▼
Computerassisted interview	20.9%	4.0 ▲
Preemployment honesty testing	14.9%	−0.5 ▼
Mutual protection association	9.0%	−3.3 ▼
Handwriting analysis	3.0%	3.0 ▲
Workers' compensation claims	1.5%	−3.1 ▼

Used with permission, National Retail Federation.

- Begin the interview by telling the employee you just wish to review some LP procedures.
- Though you should already know as much as you can ahead of time, don't tip your cards. Using various tactics, you may be able to get the employee to confess to crimes you didn't know they had committed.
- If you are going to prosecute the employee legally, call the cops after the employee has confessed, but continue the interview until the police arrive. And do note: Your employee is legally allowed to get up and leave the meeting with you at any time, and you must do nothing to prevent them from doing so.[58]

Before moving too fast and too far, it may make sense to question the suspect and root out something incriminating in the form of a statement. Since private security personnel are not subject to Miranda-style constitutional oversight, that questioning need not have warnings—unless the security investigator is working closely with the police.[59]

There is much to be concerned about when questioning suspects—both legally and personally. Of course, while the constitution may not apply, civil remedies in the form of unlawful restraint, false imprisonment, defamation and slander, or malicious prosecution surely do.[60.] Case law and jury awards are replete with cases involving excessive force, sexual harassment, and the infliction of mental distress. Use common sense. Joseph Di Domenico, a long-time practitioner, notes the following regarding the investigator's conduct as he or she seeks the statement from a suspected thief.

1. The interview should be conducted in private.
2. Female store detectives should handle the interviews of shoplifting suspects who are children or female.
3. The store detective should ask the questions in a polite manner, without threats, force, or extending any promises to the suspect.
4. Store detectives should never make promises that they know they cannot or will not keep.
5. If the suspect requests to call a spouse, or even the police, either allow the suspect to make the call, or else put the call through for the person.
6. Do not treat the suspect like a "prisoner."

7. If a shoplifting suspect indicates to the store detective that certain medication is required because the suspect is under a doctor's care, the store detective should summon the store nurse, if there is a nurse on the staff. If the store has no nurse in attendance, the detective must exercise good judgment.

8. Do not lock the office door or post a guard in front of the door, which would give the impression that the subject is not free to leave at any time.

9. The completion of the case history form should be approached with some discretion.

10. When endeavoring to get the individual to sign the preprinted statement of admission form, explain to the subject that the form contains in print the oral admission made by the person.

11. The store detective should keep in mind that, in about 99 percent of the cases that will not be prosecuted by the store for some reason or other, one thing the shoplifter values more than any other factor is confidentiality.[61]

See Table 9.2 for a checklist when preparing for a workplace theft investigation.

9.4 BURGLARY AND THE PRIVATE INVESTIGATOR

Of major interest to the security industry is the crime of burglary, a crime whose felonious intent may be oriented toward property, but which always requires illegal entry into a domicile or other structure. Below is the traditional, common law definition of burglary—such crimes are now defined statutorily.

1. The premises must be the dwelling house of another.
2. There must be a breaking of some part of the house itself. The breaking can be constructive, as well as actual.
3. There must be an entry. The slightest entry of a hand or even an instrument suffices.
4. The breaking and entering must both be at night, but need not be on the same night.
5. There must be an intent to commit a felony in the house and such intent must accompany both the breaking and entry. The intended felony need not be committed.[62]

Statutory modifications of these elements have been quite common. A definition of "dwelling house" has been liberally construed and includes the following: chicken coop, cow stable, hog house, barn, smoke house, mill house, and any other area of any other building or occupied structure, including most commercial structures.[63] The term "breaking" does not require an actual destruction of property, merely the breaking of a plane or point of entrance in the occupied structure. Additionally, most jurisdictions have reassessed the nighttime determination and made the requirement nonmandatory. Many jurisdictions, however, make the time of the intrusion applicable to the gradation of the offense or the severity of possible punishment.[64]

Burglary is not necessarily a property offense—in the sense of stealing some asset—although it may be. Felons break and enter for a host of reasons including property theft, but the burglary definition includes the commission of "any felony therein." So the motivation could be physical assault or sexual assault. Appellate decisions have served to remind us of the requirement that the entry be spurred on by an intent to commit any felony within the dwelling.[65]

The investigation of burglary requires the same general investigative approach as all other offenses. Proof of the felony's elements are tied to the objective facts collected. Be concerned with these steps:

1. Carefully check the scene of the burglary for latent fingerprints.
2. If fingerprints are obtained, fingerprint all employees for the purpose of elimination.
3. Check polished floor surfaces or any papers on the floor, for any trace of footprints.

TABLE 9.2

Investigation Checklist for Workplace Complaints

Preventing, Investigating and Remedying Workplace Complaints
Investigation Checklist

I. Preventing Workplace Complaints
- ☐ Critical policies
  - ☐ Sexual and Other Harassment
  - ☐ Workplace Violence
  - ☐ Code of Conduct and Ethics Standards
  - ☐ Electronic and Other Communications
- ☐ Examples of situations that may merit an investigation
  - ☐ Suspected substance abuse
  - ☐ Attitude problems
  - ☐ Discrimination/harassment complaints
  - ☐ Threats
  - ☐ Vandalism and other sabotage
  - ☐ Violation of policies
  - ☐ Workplace theft
  - ☐ Safety problems
  - ☐ Anti-competitive activities
- ☐ Effective complaint procedure
  - ☐ Designate knowledgeable and sensitive individuals to receive complaints.
  - ☐ Inform and remind employees of complaint process.
  - ☐ Allow oral complaints.
- ☐ Training
  - ☐ Employees
  - ☐ Managers

II. Preparing For An Investigation
- ☐ Design and implement an investigation plan.
  - ☐ Maintain a short list of potential investigators.
  - ☐ Investigator should be knowledgeable about state and federal employment laws.
  - ☐ Investigator must conduct a thorough investigation.
  - ☐ Must be objective.
  - ☐ Determine if outside counsel should investigate (i.e., possibly for complaints concerning senior management, etc.).
- ☐ Design and implement a process for collecting/securing evidence.
- ☐ Information flow/status reports.
  - ☐ Determine who receives information.

III. Investigating Workplace Complaints
- ☐ Investigation ground rules
  - ☐ Begin investigation as soon as practicable after employee complains or once the company has reason to believe that inappropriate conduct, violation of policy, etc. has occurred.
  - ☐ Involve Human Resources/senior management.
  - ☐ Consult with outside counsel at outset and throughout investigation to protect investigation by attorney-client privilege to the extent possible.
  - ☐ Determine if employees are represented by a union. If so, collective bargaining agreements grievance procedures and <u>Weingarten</u> rights apply. (<u>See</u> XI below.)
- ☐ Follow your investigation plan.
  - ☐ Select an investigator - Investigator should keep an open mind and speak to everyone involved before making a determination.
  - ☐ Collect and secure evidence.
    - ☐ Review personnel file(s) of both Complainant and alleged Offender to determine if there are previous complaints or recent disciplinary action.
    - ☐ Journals.
    - ☐ Recordings.
    - ☐ Photographs.
    - ☐ Voice mails.
    - ☐ E-mails.

(Continued)

TABLE 9.2 (CONTINUED)

Investigation Checklist for Workplace Complaints

      ☐ Telephone records.

      ☐ Receipts.

      ☐ Other relevant documents.

      ☐ Other relevant evidence.

   ☐ Identify potential witnesses - Determine appropriate order of interviews on a case-by-case basis.

  ☐ Maintain investigative file with detailed notes of each interview and each step of the investigation process.

  ☐ Conduct witness interviews.

  ☐ Have a witness (preferably the same witness) present at all interviews.

IV. Interviewing the Complainant

  ☐ Explain the investigation process. You want to obtain facts and clarify any issues in order to reach a fair solution.

  ☐ Discuss confidentiality, expressing that you will maintain confidentiality to the extent possible and information will be disseminated only on a "need to know" basis. Do not promise absolute confidentiality, as it will impede your obligation to conduct a thorough investigation. Explain legal duty to investigate allegations even if Complainant does not want you to.

  ☐ Review relevant policies with Complainant.

      ☐ Review the Company's no retaliation policy. Explain what constitutes retaliation, if necessary.

  ☐ Questions

      ☐ First, let Complainant give his/her story. Take notes. Record all details, such as date, time and place of conduct, witnesses or others involved, and any documents mentioned.

      ☐ In questioning Complainant, begin with general questions and move on to specific questions.

         ☐ General, non-leading questions.

            ☐ How long have you worked with alleged Offender?

            ☐ How would you describe your relationship with him/her (i.e., manager/subordinate)?

         ☐ More specific questions.

            ☐ When did the incident occur? (date, time and place)

         ☐ Highly specific questions.

            ☐ Describe the incident (details, including exact words, if applicable).

            ☐ Who was involved in the incident? What was each person's involvement?

            ☐ To whom have you spoken regarding the incident?

            ☐ Has anything like this happened before?

            ☐ How did the incident affect you?

            ☐ How would you like to see the matter resolved?

         ☐ Go through all relevant events chronologically, again, to be sure that you have a record of all details of complained of conduct, including exact words, if possible: who said what to whom; what was his/her response; and so on.

         ☐ Determine identity of all persons involved in conduct (consider asking for contact information if necessary and appropriate).

         ☐ Determine identity of any witnesses to conduct (consider asking for contact information if necessary and appropriate).

         ☐ Complainant's response to the conduct.

            ☐ Response to alleged offender.

            ☐ Comments to others.

         ☐ Explore whether Complainant knows if any other employees have been subjected to the same or similar conduct.

         ☐ Explore how Complainant would like the situation resolved. (*Do not promise requested resolution - any resolution will be based on all facts and circumstances.*)

      ☐ Obtain any documents or evidence.

      ☐ Invite the Complainant to contact you with any additional information.

V. Interim Remedies

  ☐ Determine whether the Complainant and the alleged Offender should be separated, pending the investigation.

  ☐ Separate the parties.

      ☐ Leave of absence.

      ☐ Suspension (with or without pay).

      ☐ Eliminate supervisory authority.

      ☐ Instruct alleged Offender to cease conduct.

(Continued)

TABLE 9.2 (CONTINUED)

Investigation Checklist for Workplace Complaints

VI. Interviewing the Alleged Offender
- ☐ Inform the alleged Offender of the allegations against him/her.
  - ☐ You may not have to identify the Complainant if the allegations are of general unacceptable behavior.
- ☐ Explain the investigation process — obtain facts, clarify any issues in order to reach a fair resolution.
- ☐ Review the Company's relevant policies; including the possibility of disciplinary action if the Company concludes that inappropriate conduct or a violation of Company policy occurred.
  - ☐ Review the Company's no retaliation policy. Explain what constitutes retaliation, if necessary.
- ☐ Discuss confidentiality - will maintain confidentiality to the extent possible and information will be disseminated only on a "need to know" basis. Do not promise absolute confidentiality - will impede your obligation to conduct a thorough investigation.
- ☐ Questions
- ☐ Begin with general, non-leading questions, move on to specific questions, make sure you obtain all the facts related to the complaint and the alleged Offender's response thereto.
  - ☐ General, non-leading questions.
    - ☐ How long have you worked with Complainant?
    - ☐ How would you describe your relationship with him/her (i.e., manager/subordinate)?
  - ☐ More specific questions.
    - ☐ When did the incident occur? (date, time and place)
  - ☐ Highly specific questions.
    - ☐ Describe the incident (details, including exact words, if applicable).
    - ☐ Who was involved in the incident? What was each person's involvement?
    - ☐ To whom have you spoken regarding the incident?
    - ☐ Has anything like this happened before?
    - ☐ How did the incident affect you?
    - ☐ How would you like to see the matter resolved?
  - ☐ Obtain any documents or evidence.
  - ☐ Invite the alleged Offender to contact you with any additional information.

VII. Reassess Interim Remedies
- ☐ Further assess whether interim remedies are necessary, pending the investigation. You may want to consult with outside counsel.
  - ☐ Separate the parties.
  - ☐ Leave of absence.
  - ☐ Suspension (with or without pay).
  - ☐ Eliminate supervisory authority.
  - ☐ Instinct alleged offender (and/or Complainant) to cease conduct.

VIII. Interviewing Witnesses
- ☐ Explain that the Company has received a complaint of inappropriate conduct, violation of policy, etc.
- ☐ Explain the investigation process - obtain facts, clarify any issues in order to reach a fair solution.
- ☐ Discuss confidentiality, expressing that you will maintain confidentiality to the extent possible and information will be disseminated only on a "need to know" basis. Do not promise absolute confidentiality, as it will impede your obligation to conduct a thorough investigation.
- ☐ Review the Company's no retaliation policy. Explain what constitutes retaliation, if necessary.
- ☐ Questions.
  - ☐ In questioning witness, begin with general, non-leading questions. Move on to specific questions. Make sure you obtain all the facts relating to the Complaint.
    - ☐ General, non-leading questions.
      - ☐ How long have you worked with Complainant?
      - ☐ How would you describe your relationship with him/her (i.e., manager/subordinate)?
    - ☐ More specific questions.
      - ☐ When did the incident occur? (date, time and place)
    - ☐ Highly specific questions.
      - ☐ Describe the incident (details, including exact words, if applicable).
      - ☐ Who was involved in the incident? What was each person's involvement?
      - ☐ To whom have you spoken regarding the incident?

(Continued)

TABLE 9.2 (CONTINUED)

Investigation Checklist for Workplace Complaints

    ☐ Has anything like this happened before?

    ☐ How did the incident affect you?

    ☐ How would you like to see the matter resolved?

☐ Obtain any documents or evidence.

☐ Invite the witness to contact you with any additional information.

IX. Prepare a Final Written Report

☐ Review all notes, statements and evidence.

☐ Determine whether any further interviews are required.

☐ Analyze each person's story and assess credibility.

☐ Determine whether a violation of Company policy or inappropriate conduct has occurred.

☐ Prepare draft report, detail steps taken and reasons for conclusions. Do not make legal conclusions, i.e., sexual harassment occurred.

    ☐ All drafts should be addressed and forwarded to outside counsel.

    ☐ Discuss with outside counsel what to do with investigation notes.

X. Remedying Workplace Complaints

☐ Inform Complainant and alleged Offender of conclusions.

☐ Impose appropriate disciplinary action, if necessary. (Determine who may be subject to disciplinary action, e.g., Complainant, alleged Offender, third parties.)

    ☐ Potential disciplinary action:

        ☐ Verbal warning.

        ☐ Written warning.

        ☐ Second written warning.

        ☐ Suspension (with or without pay).

        ☐ Termination.

☐ Follow-up with Complainant to ascertain whether he/she has experienced retaliation or further inappropriate behavior.

☐ Follow-up with alleged Offender to ensure that disciplinary action, if any, is effective.

XI. Information Regarding Union Employees

☐ Weingarten Rights - Union employees may have a representative present during an interview that might reasonably lead to disciplinary action. Nonunion employees do not have this right.

☐ Collective Bargaining Agreements (CBAs) supersede handbook policies, to the extent that CBAs and policies are inconsistent.

☐ Be mindful of any grievance procedure for Union employees.

---

4. Check the area surrounding the burglarized building for tire marks or footprints that may be connected with the burglary.

5. Obtain an accurate, detailed description of all missing property or monies.

6. Check the loss-payable clauses of any insurance carried.

7. Interview all persons having access to the premises. This step should include the night watchman, the patrolman, or the trooper working the area, the last person to leave the premises prior to the burglary, and the person who discovered and reported the burglary.

8. Attempt to trace the source of any tools recovered.

9. If explosives are recovered, do not attempt to transport them. Contact the appropriate unit.

10. Take scale photographs of the attacked safe (if applicable).

11. If possible, obtain the make, serial number, size, and weight of the safe (if applicable).

12. If a suspect is arrested and charged with burglary at or near the scene of the crime, immediately obtain access to all the clothing he is wearing … Clothing may contain safe insulation, paint fragments, or metal particles.

13. If the suspect is in an automobile when apprehended, mark any recovered tools for identification and forward them with all other evidence.[66]

In surveying the area subject to the burglary, be on the lookout for tools, instruments, and mechanical means and aids used to accomplish the breaking and entry.[67] A list of common burglary tools includes the following:

- Wrecking bar or pry bar
- Diamond core bits
- Tapered punches
- Tire irons
- Core drills and bits
- Abrasive saws, chisels, wood bits
- Hammers and sledgehammers
- Pliers or wire cutters
- Pipe wrench
- Can opener or plate gripper
- Vise grip
- Bolt cutters
- Keyhole saw
- Oxy acetylene outfits
- Hacksaw and blade
- Crowbars
- Electric drills
- Screwdrivers

Private security plays a critical role in the reduction of business theft and burglary.[68] Business, industry, and individuals can unwittingly contribute to opportunities for burglary and other property offenses. Burglars look for many advantages, some of which include:

- Dark areas
- Shrubs in front of windows
- Doors that are not secured
- Lack of security cameras[69]

The best approach is to establish a theft/burglary deterrence program.[70] In facility or perimeter protection, the security specialist takes on a wide array of responsibilities. Surveillance systems play a key role since perpetrators are inhibited by the eye of surveillance.[71] Other, salient, common-sense suggestions include:

- Make sure all outside entrances and inside security doors have deadbolt locks. If you use padlocks, they should be made of steel and kept locked at all times. Remember to remove serial numbers from your locks, to prevent unauthorized keys from being made.
- All outside or security doors should be metal-lined and secured with metal security crossbars. Pin all exposed hinges to prevent removal.
- Windows should have secure locks and burglar-resistant glass. Consider installing metal grates on all your windows except display windows.
- Remove all expensive items from window displays at night and make sure you can see easily into your business after closing.
- Light the inside and outside of your business, especially around doors, windows, skylights, or other entry points. Consider installing covers over exterior lights and power sources to deter tampering.
- Check the parking lot for good lighting and unobstructed views.
- Keep your cash register in plain view from the outside of your business, so it can be monitored by police during the day or at night. Leave it open and empty after closing.

- Be sure your safe is fireproof and securely anchored. It should be kept in plain view. Leave it open when it's empty, use it to lock up valuables when you close. Remember to change the combination when an employee who has had access to it leaves your business.
- Before you invest in an alarm system, check with several companies and decide what level of security fits your needs. Contact your local law enforcement agency to recommend established companies. Learn how to use your system properly. Check the system daily, and run a test when closing.[72]

The checklist at Table 9.3 will be of great utility to the security investigator.

TABLE 9.3

Burglary Investigation Checklist

Name:_____ Address: _____

BURGLARY PREVENTION CHECKLIST

PREVENTION TIPS	OK	NEEDED	RECOMMEND REPLACEMENT
Doors:			
Strong Pin tumbler locks:			
-Front Door			
-Back Door			
-Side Door			
-Basement Door			
Chain Latch:			
-Front Door			
-Back Door			
-Side Door			
-Basement Door			
Heavy-Duty Hinges:			
-Front Door			
-Back Door			
-Side Door			
-Basement Door			
Peephole:			
-Front Door			
-Back Door			
Doors with Windows:			
Need key to open inside and out			
Mailbox/Mail Slot in Door			
Garage Door Pin tumbler Lock			
Windows:			
All windows with Pin tumblers			
Bar or Strip of Wood (Patio Door)			
Bars or Grillworks:			
"Out-of-the-Way" windows			
Garage Windows			
Basement Windows			
Keys:			
Change tumblers when you move in or out if keys are lost			
Don't give out duplicate keys			
Keep home and automobile keys separate			
Don't put name and address on keys			
Keep house key hidden outside			

9.5   DEFENSIVE TECHNIQUES TO MINIMIZE PROPERTY LOSSES FROM THEFT AND BURGLARY

9.5.1   TACTICS AND STRATEGIES

A highly skilled theft and property investigator possesses two fundamental traits: first, the investigator knows the territory to which he or she is assigned, and second, the investigator is capable of analyzing patterns of loss. Of course this requires that the investigator know the people and personalities involved, the geographic location, its layout and overall operation. In the case of residential establishments, the home security industry's growth reflects a bona fide niche in communities all across America. To be sure, strong residential security systems go a long way towards burglary prevention.[73] A skilled private security investigator can advise the retail establishment how goods are being pilfered and at the same time make recommendations on how to remedy this economic pilferage. To accomplish this dual goal, some security protocols should be undertaken.

9.5.1.1   Site Security Surveys and Their Application

Security surveys provide the client with an assessment of security vulnerabilities by gauging and reviewing the current state of the facility, highlighting security strengths and weaknesses, making recommendations on corrective action for better safety and security, and laying out the current state of the environmental design of that location. The security survey has many purposes though none is more compelling that deterrence of criminal activity. Upon completion of a field survey, a permanent record can be kept on file. See the business or commercial survey at Table 9.4.[74]

9.5.1.2   Determining Organizational Characteristics

Investigators, especially those working in institutional settings, should have a feel for the organizational and administrative makeup of their clients. Companies that are loosely organized and have administrative problems will be more likely to have serious problems with internal theft and pilferage. The National Institute of Justice urges:

> [T]he control of employee taking of property seems to be a problem that the business organization must keep visible on its list of priorities and objectives. It cannot be ignored or relegated to a topic of temporary or minimal importance, nor should it be assigned as a task for a specialized portion of the organization's management team. This research suggests that only by exhibiting a conspicuous and consistent climate of concern about the control of internal theft at all occupational levels can an organization hope to have a significant effect on the behavior of its employees.[75]

The entire corporate or institutional environment influences an investigator's judgment. To perform the job properly, the investigator must know how management operates, how it intends to pursue parties that are apprehended, and how it oversees the scheme of things. Companies that treat their employees poorly, that provide little or no feedback on performance, and that do not restrict or restrain conduct or behavior, risk far greater losses due to employee misconduct. In essence, a lack of control results in an almost chaotic environment. As a rule of thumb, if employees feel the scrutiny of management, that there are repercussions to illegal and immoral conduct, and that the company has invested significant time and energy in assuring the protection of its assets, it is less likely that criminal conduct will occur. The company that invests resources in the detection and prevention of criminality will most likely be rewarded with lower internal theft rates. The measures in Table 9.5 should provide obstacles to internal theft.

9.5.1.3   Theft Tests

Testing for internal and external shoplifting and pilferage falls into two major categories: honesty and service tests. When conducting an honesty test, the investigator determines whether employees are stealing cash during customer purchase transactions. In service testing, the investigator reports

TABLE 9.4
Commercial or Business Security Survey

Exterior Grounds

Yes	No	
☐	☐	Is there a fence around the property or a clear definition of Territoriality?
☐	☐	If there is a fence, is it tall enough and maintained in good repair?
☐	☐	Is there a reliable system for locking fence gates at night or when the facility is not occupied by personnel.
☐	☐	Are fence gates maintained in a good state of repair, including hinges and locks?
☐	☐	Are fences obstructed by weeds or other ground cover?
☐	☐	Are there any unused or unneeded fence gates?
☐	☐	Are there any trees, poles or other features that help a burglar climb over a fence?
☐	☐	If appropriate, are there "No Trespassing" signs on the fence and/or gate?
☐	☐	Are shrubs and bushes and other plant growth within four (4) feet of any sidewalks, driveways or building entrances maintained at a height of not more than two (2) feet?
☐	☐	Are shrubs and bushes and other plant growth between four (4) and eight (8) feet from any sidewalks, driveways or building entrances maintained at a height of not more than four (4) feet?
☐	☐	Are trees trimmed so that lower branches are at least six (6) feet off the ground?
☐	☐	In parking areas, are trees trimmed so that they do not block out or obscure the light from light fixtures?
☐	☐	Are trees trimmed so they cannot be used to gain access to an upper level of the building?
☐	☐	Are spiny (thorny) plants used as ground cover along fences and under first floor windows of the building?

Exterior Lighting

Yes	No	
☐	☐	Are building parking lots sufficiently illuminated?
☐	☐	Are walkways and building entrances well lighted?
☐	☐	Are all sides of the building adequately illuminated?
☐	☐	Are lighting standards well marked or identified to facilitate the reporting of inoperative lighting?
☐	☐	Is there a clear definition of who is responsible for reporting inoperative lighting?
☐	☐	Are electrical switch boxes secured?
☐	☐	Is lighting directed or positioned in such a manner as to blind patrol officer?
☐	☐	Are light fixture protective lenses vandal resistant?

Building Exterior

Yes	No	
☐	☐	Are fire escapes and exits designed so they are difficult to access from the exterior of the building?
☐	☐	Can access be gained to the roof or upper level windows by climbing up downspouts or other building attachments?
☐	☐	Are telephone and power lines to the building located high enough so they are not easily accessible?
☐	☐	Are there unprotected skylights that could provide access into the building?
☐	☐	Are rubbish or trash container areas fenced and locked?
☐	☐	Are random spot checks of outgoing trash made?
☐	☐	Are fan openings and ventilator shafts adequately secured?
☐	☐	Can access into the building be gained from an adjacent building?

(Continued)

TABLE 9.4 (CONTINUED)
Commercial or Business Security Survey

Parking Areas

Yes	No	
☐	☐	Is it possible for employees to remove property from the building and place it in their motor vehicle without being detected?
☐	☐	Are parking lots conducive to patrol observation?
☐	☐	Are parking lots monitored by closed-circuit television?
☐	☐	Are those who park in employee parking lots required to register their vehicles and display a parking permit?

Exterior Doors

Yes	No	
☐	☐	Are all exterior doors sturdy and resistant to forced entry?
☐	☐	If exterior doors swing outward and have exposed hinge pins, have removable pins been replaced with non-removable hinge pins?
☐	☐	Are door frames well constructed and in good condition?
☐	☐	Do all exterior doors fit tightly within their door frames?
☐	☐	Do exterior doors have wide angle (180°) door viewers?
☐	☐	For doors with glass within 40″ of the lock equipped with double-cylinder dead bolts?
☐	☐	For double exterior doors, is there an astragal (strong metallic cover slip) covering the space between the two doors?
☐	☐	Are exterior door strike plates reinforced or heavy duty and secured with screws at least 3″ long?
☐	☐	Are exterior doors equipped with door re- enforcers - a metal channel that wraps around the door at the lock area?

Yes	No	
☐	☐	Are deadbolt locks with at least a 1″ throw installed on all exterior doors?
☐	☐	Are unused exterior doors properly secured?

Exterior Windows

Yes	No	
☐	☐	Do all exterior windows have adequate locks?
☐	☐	Are unused windows permanently sealed or protected by bars or grillwork?
☐	☐	Are all windows within 14 feet of the ground protected with bars, grills or other protective coverings?
☐	☐	Are all vents or similar openings having a glass area of one square foot or more secured with protective coverings?

(Continued)

TABLE 9.4 (CONTINUED)
Commercial or Business Security Survey

☐	☐	Are all windows with 14 feet of the ground that are not protected with bars, grills or other protective coverings protected by an electronic alarm system?
☐	☐	Have any double hung windows within the building been pinned?
☐	☐	Have crank handles been removed form casement windows?
☐	☐	Do windows leading to a basement or subsurface level have security bars, grills or auxiliary locks?

Interior Lighting

Yes	No	
☐	☐	Is interior lighting, particularly in high risk areas, adequate?
☐	☐	Is there an auxiliary power source for interior lighting, particularly in hallways, restroom and other common areas?
☐	☐	Is interior security lighting controlled by a timer rather than a wall switch?

Interior Doors

Yes	No	
☐	☐	Are interior doors sturdy and resistant to forced entry?
☐	☐	Do all interior doors fit tightly within their door frames?
☐	☐	If interior doors swing outward and have exposed hinge pins, have removable pins been replaced with non-removable pins?
☐	☐	Does each interior door have a workable locking device?

Access Management

Yes	No	
☐	☐	Is there a written and consistently enforced key management policy?
☐	☐	Is there a record of all keys issued, particularly master keys?
☐	☐	Is there an enforced policy against unauthorized duplication of keys?
☐	☐	Are loss or theft of keys promptly reported?
☐	☐	Are periodic key audits conducted?
☐	☐	Is there an effective key recovery policy when employees retire, resign, are discharged or suspended?
☐	☐	Are duplicate keys stored in a secure location?
☐	☐	Is there clear responsibility for key issuance and responsibility?

Ceiling Construction

Yes	No	
☐	☐	Are there suspended ceilings with removable panels within the facility?
☐	☐	Do walls of hallways, offices, storage areas, etc., rise completely to the subfloor of the second floor or roof so entry cannot be achieved by climbing over the wall?
☐	☐	Has wire mesh been placed over the removable panels of suspended ceilings?
☐	☐	Have panels of suspended ceilings been glued in place?

Mechanical Equipment Rooms

Yes	No	
☐	☐	Is access to building mechanical rooms adequately controlled?
☐	☐	Are all gas, water, sprinkler and other valves securely locked?
☐	☐	Are large electrical switches padlocked?

Safes

Yes	No	
☐	☐	Is there a safe used for money or valuable property storage?
☐	☐	If "yes," is the safe burglar resistant (able to withstand an attack with burglary tools or a torch for 30 minutes)? Is the safe secured to the floor or imbedded in concrete?

(Continued)

TABLE 9.4 (CONTINUED)

Commercial or Business Security Survey

☐	☐	Is the safe protected by an electronic alarm system?
☐	☐	If the safe has wheels or casters, have they been removed?
☐	☐	Is the safe lighted at night?
☐	☐	Is the safe located where it can be observed by patrolling police or security officers?
☐	☐	Is the safe combination changed whenever an employee with knowledge of the combination is involuntarily terminated?

Security Alarm System

Yes	No	
☐	☐	Does the facility have an electronic alarm system?
☐	☐	Was the alarm system installed by an experienced, reputable and reliable alarm installation company?
☐	☐	Is the security alarm system monitored by a professional alarm monitoring company?
☐	☐	If the alarm system is more than five (5) years old, has the equipment been evaluated for upgrading or updating?
☐	☐	Have appropriate employees of the business been trained how to properly arm and disarm the alarm system?
☐	☐	Does the alarm system have a back-up power source (battery/generator)?

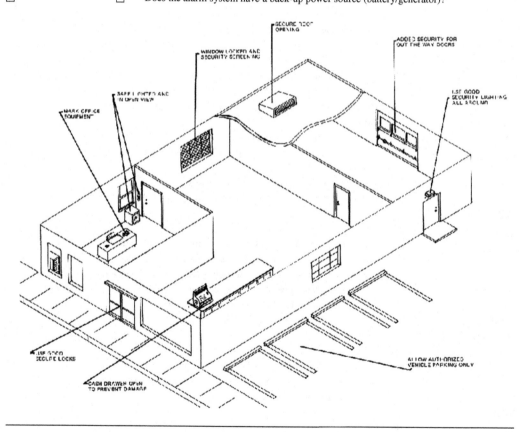

TABLE 9.5

Measures that Can Reduce the Risk and Prevent Internal Theft

A. Prevention measures
 1. Internal accounting controls
  a. Separation of duties
  b. Rotation of duties
  c. Periodic internal audits and surprise inspections
  d. Development and documentation of policies, procedures, systems, programs, and program modifications
  e. Establishment of dual signature authorities, dollar authorization limits per signatory, expiration date, and check amount limits
  f. Off-line entry controls and limits
  g. Batch totals, hash totals
 2. Computer access controls
  a. Identification defenses
   (1) Key or card inserts
   (2) Passwords and code numbers
   (3) Exclusion—repeated error lockout
   (4) Time activator/deactivator
   (5) Periodic code and password changes
  b. Authentication defenses
   (1) Random personal data
   (2) Voice, fingerprint, or palm geometry recognition
   (3) Callbacks
  c. Establishment of authorizations by levels of authority or levels of security (compartmentalization and "need to know")
B. Detection measures
 1. Exceptions in logging systems
  a. Out of sequence, out of priority, and aborted runs and entries
  b. Out-of-pattern transactions: too high, too low, too many, too often, too few, unusual file access (odd times and places)
  c. Attempted access beyond authorization level
  d. Repeated attempts to gain access improperly—wrong password, entry code, etc.
  e. Parity and redundancy checks
 2. Management information system
  a. Monitoring operational performance levels for
   (1) the variations from plans and standards
   (2) deviations from accepted or mandated policies, procedures, and practices
   (3) deviations from past quantitative relationships, i.e., ratios, proportions, percentages, trends, past performance levels, indices, etc.
 3. Intelligence gathering
  a. Monitoring employee attitudes, values, and job satisfaction level
  b. Soliciting random feedback from or surveying customers, vendors, and suppliers for evidence of dissatisfaction, inefficiency, inconsistency with policies, corruption, or dishonesty by employees

to management how he or she was treated during a specific transaction while observations were made.

Web Exercise: Visit Jack Hayes International—a firm that specializes in assisting business with inventory shrinkage and retail theft controls at: http://hayesinternational.com/2013/08/increasing-profitability-by-lowering-shrinklosses/.

9.5.1.3.1 Honesty Testing

To detect theft, deception, fraud, pilferage, or other illegal conduct on the part of employees, investigators conduct honesty testing. In this type of test, the investigator simultaneously buys two of the same item. Prices can be the same or different. The investigator notes the register reading for the previous sale. The investigator then selects two of the same item and pays the employee the exact amount for the entire purchase. The investigator should then observe whether or not the cash register drawer was opened or closed before, after, or at the time of the purchase. In addition, the investigator should check whether or not the employee issued a receipt. The investigator should formally document these facts, the subsequent items purchased, and their related costs. Other notations worthy of mention:

- Whether the purchase was wrapped or payment was received from the investigator.
- Did the clerk call back the amount of the purchase or the amount of money tendered?
- Did you receive correct change?
- Was the amount of the sale correctly recorded on the register?

Troubling or suspicious conduct should be reflected in the report. An example of a document recording honesty testing is shown in Figure 9.6.

Web Exercise: Watch the following video on shoplifting and retail shrinkage at https://youtu.be/ixLhRnf6fkM.

SHOPPING INVESTIGATION REPORT

Firm _____ Store No. _____ Case No. _____
Address _____ City _____ State _____
Date _____ Time _____ Opr. _____ Report No. _____

NAME
NUMBER
LETTER_____
Sex_____ Age_____
Height _____ Weight _____
Build_____
Eyes_____ Nose_____
Teeth_____
Complexion_____
Hair Color_____
Style_____
Glasses_____
Jewelry_____
Other_____

SALESPERSON'S APPEARANCE
_____ Well Groomed
_____ Passable
_____ Average
_____ Unimpressive
_____ Unkempt
_____ Other

SALESPERSON'S ATTITUDE
_____ Enthusiastic
_____ Pleasant
_____ Routine
_____ Indifferent
_____ Antagonistic
_____ Served Promptly
_____ Suggested other items
_____ Offered a "thank you"
_____ Other

Reg loc.no: _____
Reg read: _____
Other cust/oprs/salespeople: _____

PAYMENT MADE

	$20	$10	$5	$1	50¢	25¢	10¢	5¢	1¢	
1. Pur										Trans #_____
2. Pur										Trans #_____

DESCRIPTION OF TRANSACTION
_____
_____
_____
_____
_____
_____
_____
_____
_____
_____
_____
_____
_____

PURCHASES MADE
_____
_____
_____
_____
_____
_____
Total

FIGURE 9.6 A shopping investigation report for investigators assessing a retail employee's performance.

9.5.1.3.1.1   The Combination Buy   In a combination buy, the investigator buys two or more different items at the same time and pays the employee the exact amount for the entire purchase. Observe and record whether or not the employee rings up all, part, or none of the transaction. The investigator records whether a receipt was received for the purchase. In a follow-up report, the investigator inserts findings regarding the exact time of the purchase and the reading on the register before the clerk rang up the transaction. (This is helpful if the employee fails to give you a receipt.) By knowing the amount on the register prior to your purchase, it will be easy to check the sale for which no receipt was received.

9.5.1.3.1.2   The Double Buy   In effecting a double buy, the investigator buys one or more items. The transaction should result in paying an uneven amount of money, larger than the price of the goods in total, resulting in change. Because an overage of funds exists, the cash register tabulates the difference, and a receipt is remitted to the investigator. In this scenario, the investigator receives a receipt to identify either the cash register used or reference to its employee operator. This serves the first purpose of the double-buy process, namely, identification.

The second phase of the double-buy investigation tests the honesty of the employee. After the employee has returned change, the investigator purchases an additional item. In buying the second item, the exact purchase price should be paid. The investigator should request that the employee put the second purchase in the same bag used for the first purchase. (The employee may even suggest this.) The investigator should be alert at this point to record whether a second receipt was received.

Pinkerton's, Inc. relates other sensible information regarding the double-buy process:

> Use common sense when making a double buy. It would not be normal, for example, to spend 39 cents on the first buy and ten dollars on your second buy … Plan your approach and articles to be purchased prior to making your first buy. In this way you can control the type of goods in the first part so the bag will be large enough to hold the goods bought on the second part … In picking items for your second buy in a double buy, try to locate goods as far away as possible from the register … It is also possible to wear out or take out an unwrapped item which you have purchased on the second part of a double-buy test. This could be the case when buying at a jewelry department.[76]

As one final caution, in a double-buy test, the second purchase must occur immediately after the first purchase so that the factual chain and monetary sequence are not interrupted by other purchasers. The investigator should not act in a contrived or awkward manner; they should appear completely disinterested and aloof. Upon the second buy, the investigator should immediately leave the retail area without waiting for a receipt (but if the employee harkens you to accept it, do so).

9.5.1.3.1.3   The Exchange Buy   When customers have difficulty in choosing between multiple products, dishonest employees succumb to temptation. In the exchange buy, the investigator has two or more items to consider. In the investigator's original decision, the choice is to purchase the less costly item. The investigator then pays the employee with an uneven amount of money. Upon receipt of change, package, and sales receipt, the investigator, acting as a bewildered customer, changes heart and decides to take the higher-priced item. The purchaser (investigator) then must pay the difference between the lower-priced item and the higher-priced item. At this juncture, the investigator should watch carefully to see whether or not the employee records, registers, or makes notation of the difference between the two prices or simply pockets the difference.

9.5.1.3.1.4   The Refund Buy   Investigators who perform the refund test return an item to the selling department. After receipt of the cash or credit refund, the money is then used to make an even money purchase. The objective of the refund buy is to test the store's system by attempting to get a refund without a receipt. If the employee will not grant the refund without the receipt, the investigator can then "discover" the receipt and complete the transaction.

Author Read Hayes, in the ASIS Foundation's CRISP Report *Strategies to Detect and Prevent Workplace Dishonesty* provides salient advice on preventing employees committing retail fraud at Box 9.1.[77]

BOX 9.1   STRATEGIES TO DETER AND PREVENT EMPLOYEE RETAIL FRAUD. (REPRINTED WITH PERMISSION OF ASIS INTERNATIONAL © 2018.)

1. Never allow employees to bring their purses or packages onto the selling floor. Only clear plastic purses with essential personal items should be allowed in work areas.
2. Store high-priced and very high-loss overstock items in separate, locked, and monitored security cages for better protection. Maintain a log that documents access to the area.
3. Consider using closed-circuit television (CCTV) and/or roaming security agents in both store and distribution facilities to assist in detection and deterrence of employee theft. Because employees are often intimately aware of "hiding spots" in the store, any type of surveillance—natural or mechanical—should be thorough, covering as much of the floor as possible.
4. Offer store discounts to employees and their relatives. This can facilitate legitimate purchasing.
5. Control allocation of price guns and check prices on employee purchases to discourage unauthorized markdowns by employees and customers.
6. Authorize and verify all shipments by an employee who is not responsible for controlling inventories.
7. Require all employees to enter and leave the workplace through a designated employee entrance monitored by a security guard or management personnel.
8. Provide a room for overcoats and unusually large packages. Post a sign at this entrance warning employees that pilferage is a crime, and those caught will be prosecuted.
9. Lock roll-up receiving doors at the bottom, not at their pull chains, since employees can easily use dollies to hoist the doors open and then slide merchandise through the gap.
10. Secure all doors not used for regular customer traffic per local fire regulations and install panic alarms. Test panic doors monthly.
11. Hook doors up to a central alarm system to record openings and closings for patterns.
12. Ensure a manager observes and documents all freight deliveries made at either the distribution facility or the store.
13. Restrict access to supply areas and ensure these areas are monitored by a security guard.
14. Ensure that employees who enter the supply area are accompanied by a warehouse employee, and that they complete a sign-in sheet recording name, time of entrance and departure, and merchandise removed.
15. Keep customer returns and damaged items in a secure, monitored area.
16. Keep stockroom merchandise in neat stacks, not disorderly piles, so it is easy to spot missing items. Bad housekeeping is a quick tip-off to possible employee theft.
17. Restrict personal or unnecessary employee use of office equipment, company gas pumps, telephones, internet, email, postage meters, and other facilities designed for company use.
18. Monitor utility, internet use, and phone bills for patterns.
19. Escort guests and employees from other companies to their appointments.
20. Rotate employees of one department to a different department to take inventory. Ensure that inventory is supervised by a member of management.

21. Keep merchandise in neat, orderly displays. Never stack high-loss items near doors or operable windows.
22. Clearly and permanently mark company equipment with the company's name.
23. Ensure that tools and equipment are inventoried and locked up by a supervisor at the end of each workday.
24. Be suspicious of company equipment or merchandise that appears out of place. Encourage employees to report out-of-place items to management.
25. Inventory high-priced merchandise on processing lines in distribution facilities. Keep it in secured areas.

9.5.1.3.2 Service Testing

In service testing, the scrutinized employee is assessed on diverse issues:

- Approach
- Suggested purchase
- Appearance
- Service effect
- Courtesy
- Product knowledge
- Salesmanship
- Closing of the sale

Service testing should take the following questions into account:

- How much of a product was purchased?
- What is the description of the merchandise?
- What is the price of the merchandise?
- What is the tax or other special assessment on the merchandise?
- What was the total amount paid?
- What money denominations were used as payment?
- Was the money handled at the register in compliance with the store's system?
- Was a receipt issued and what were its contents?
- Did the clerk charge the correct price and give the correct change?
- Was the clerk busy? Orderly? Clean?
- How did the employee act? Careless? Complaining? Professional?

Testing an employee's service level is a circumstantial tool for management, targeting employees who are weak in customer service, or who are disgruntled, difficult, and likely to cause problems for the business enterprise.[78]

9.6 MISSING OR STOLEN PROPERTY

In cases of retail theft and business pilferage, the personal property document at Figure 9.7 is of considerable assistance. If a case of missing personal property leads to the allegation of theft or shoplifting, most security departments will have a "Report of Theft" document. Figure 9.8 contains space for comments not only about the theft, but also solicits recommendations for response.

Tracking the location of property that was seized by private security operatives assures a proper chain of custody. Use Figure 9.9 is a sample of a property control receipt used to trace the movement of property.

PERSONAL PROPERTY MISSING

REPORTED BY	BADGE	DEPT.		DATE REPORTED		TIME

ADDRESS (IF NON-EMPLOYEE)	REPORTED TO
	ESTIMATED VALUE OF ARTICLE

LOCATION OF OCCURRENCE

DESCRIBE ARTICLE IN DETAIL

BY WHOM WAS LOSS DISCOVERED?	DATE	TIME

BY WHOM WAS ARTICLE LAST SEEN?	DATE	TIME

WAS ARTICLE IN LOCKED CONTAINER?	IN LOCKED ROOM?	WERE LOCKS FORCED?

HOW DID LOSS OCCUR?

REMARKS

DISPOSITION

☐   RETURNED TO OWNER

                                                        ☐   OTHER, DESCRIBE _____

☐   RETURNED TO FINDER

RETURNED TO (SIGNATURE)	DATE	INVESTIGATED BY
		SECURITY OFFICE

FIGURE 9.7   Report of missing personal property.

Security Department
REPORT OF THEFT OR
LOSS OF PROPERTY

File #

1. Complainant's Name	2 Location and Tele. Ext.	3 Date Reported
4. Description of Item		Company Property ☐ Personal Property ☐

5. Model #	6. Serial #	7. Company Inventory No.	8. Value

9. Estimated Time of Theft

10. Last Known Location (Bdlg., Floor, Office)	11. Property Assigned to or Owned by

12. Describe Precautions Taken to Protect Property

13. Furnish Additional Details

14. Details Concerning Police Report

	15. Report Prepared by	16. Date

17. Recommended Action

FIGURE 9.8   A standard report of theft or loss of property.

PROPERTY CONTROL RECEIPT		
NAME	TITLE	SIGNATURE
LOCATION		TELEPHONE EXTENSION

PROPERTY SURRENDER AUTHORITY		
NAME	TITLE	SIGNATURE

REMOVAL TYPE:
☐ PERMANENT ☐ TEMPORARY ☐ OTHER

ITEM	COUNT	DESCRIPTION	ISSUE DATE	RECOVER DATE

FIGURE 9.9 Sample property control receipt.

TABLE 9.6

A Report of Losses Example, in the Event That Multiple Losses or Thefts Must be Tracked

SECURITY DEPARTMENT			REPORT OF LOSSES		MONTH OF _____ 20____		
DATE OF REPORT	DATE OF LOSS	NAME	STATUS	NATURE OF LOSS	VALUE	LOSS OR THEFT	RECOVERED

Security firms operating within larger corporations, educational institutions, hotels and motels, and transport companies generally have more than one incident to report in a typical workday. Use of a special form to report losses is an outstanding way to track complicated and voluminous information. Table 9.6 shows one style of this type of report.

9.7 CONCLUSION

Private security plays in integral role in the prevention, deterrence, and detection of theft and property offenses. The permissiveness of the legal system's reaction to property offenses, the rationalizations and justifications espoused by retail thieves and shoplifters and their diverse methods and techniques, and the increase in internal theft in the business environment, in an employer/employee context and in other corporate settings, are all indicative of the importance of having well-trained security officers and investigators. The specific recommendations, tactics, and strategies regarding the investigation of theft and property offenses covered here should help security professionals dealing with these prolific, serious crimes.

NOTES

1. Robert D. McCrie, "Shoplifting: Managing the Problem," *Security Letter*, July 2006: 4; Read Hayes and King Rogers, "Catch Them If You Can," *Security Management*, October 2003: 80; see: PwC, *Global Economic Crime and Fraud Survey* (2018), www.pwc.com/gx/en/forensics/

global-economic-crime-and-fraud-survey-2018.pdf; Katie Reilly, "Shoplifting and Other Fraud Cost Retailers Nearly $50 Billion Last Year," Time.com, June 22, 2017, http://time.com/money/4829684/shoplifting-fraud-retail-survey.

2. Adrian Beck, "Shrinkage and radio frequency identification (RFID): prospects, problems and practicalities," in *The Handbook of Security*, ed. M. Gill (Basingstoke, UK: Palgrave MacMillan, 2006).

3. See Adrian Beck, "Moving Beyond Shrinkage: Developing a Definition and Typology of Total Retail Loss," *Security Journal* 31, no. 1 (February 2018): 93–110.

4. Global Retail Theft Barometer (2015), www.odesus.gr/images/nea/eidhseis/2015/3.Global-Retail-Theft-Barometer-2015/GRTB%202015_web.pdf.

5. See also Jack L. Hayes International, Inc., *30th Annual Retail Theft Survey*, http://hayesinternational.com/news/annual-retail-theft-survey.

6. Garda, *Retail Security Guide* 20, www.garda.ie/en/Crime-Prevention/Retail-Security-Guide.pdf.

7. "Theft Barometer (2015)": 20.

8. See Nicole Leinbach-Reyhle, "New Report Identifies US Retailers Lose $60 Billion a Year, Employee Theft Top Concern," Forbes, October 7, 2015, www.forbes.com/sites/nicoleleinbachreyhle.

9. M. Hopkins and M. Gill, "Business, crime and crime prevention: emerging debates and future challenges," in *Handbook of Crime Prevention and Community Safety* 2nd ed., eds. N. Tilley and A. Sidebottom (Abingdon, UK: Routledge, 2017): 373–393.

10. J. Bamfield and R. C. Hollinger, "Managing Losses in the Retail Store: A Comparison of Loss Prevention Activity in the United States and Great Britain," *Security Journal* 7 (1996): 61–70.

11. Aiden Sidebottom, Amy Thornton, Lisa Tompson, Jyoti Belur, Nick Tilley, and Kate Bowers, "A Systematic Review of Tagging as a Method to Reduce Theft in Retail Environments," *Crime Science: An Interdisciplinary Journal* 6, no. 7 (2017): 1, https://doi.org/10.1186/s40163-017-0068-y.

12. See E. Finkel, "Organized Retail Crime on the Rise—and Perennial Challenges Remain," *Security* 54, no. 3 (2017): 58–60, 62.

13. L. Martìnez, "Taking the Bite out of Organized Retail Crime," *Security Technology Executive* 24 (September 2014): 20.

14. National Retail Federation, *Organized Retail Crime Survey* (2016): 7, accessed September 9, 2018, https://nrf.com/system/tdf/Documents/retail%20library/2016-NRF-Organized-Retail-Crime-Survey_Report.pdf?file=1&title=2016%20Organized%20Retail%20Crime%20Survey.

15. C. Meyer, "Monitoring the Floor," *Security* 51, no. 4 (2014): 56, 58.

16. William C. Cunningham and Todd H. Taylor, *The Hallcrest Report: Private Security and Police in America* (Chancellor, 1985): 19; Linda A. Bressler and Martin S. Bressler, "Accounting for Profit: How Crime Activity Can Cost You Your Business," *Global Journal of Business Disciplines* 1, no. 2 (2017): 21.

17. Ibid.; Nicole V. Lasky, Bonnie S. Fisher, and Jacques Scott, "'Thinking Thief' in the Crime Prevention Arms Race: Lessons Learned from Shoplifters," *Security Journal* 30, no. 3 (July 2017): 772–792, http://dx.doi.org.ez.lib.jjay.cuny.edu/10.1057/sj.2015.21.

18. Ibid.; Paul R. Zimmerman, "The Deterrence of Crime through Private Security Efforts: Theory and Evidence," *International Review of Law and Economics* 37 (March 2014): 66–75, https://doi.org/10.1016/j.irle.2013.06.003.

19. Robert O'Block, *Security and Crime Prevention* (Mosby, 1981): 156; M. McCourt, "The Predictive Revolution," *Security* 51, no. 11 (2014): 20; Matt Hopkins, "Business, Victimisation and Victimology: Reflections on Contemporary Patterns of Commercial Victimisation and the Concept of Businesses as 'Ideal Victims'," *International Review of Victimology* 22, no. 2 (May 2016): 161–178, http://journals.sagepub.com.ez.lib.jjay.cuny.edu/doi/pdf/10.1177/0269758016628948.

20. Katie Reilly, "Shoplifting and Other Fraud Cost Retailers Nearly $50 Billion Last Year," Time.com, June 22, 2017, http://time.com/money/4829684/shoplifting-fraud-retail-survey.

21. Bill Turner, "Shoplifting Penalties Rarely Benefit Retailers These Days," *LPM Insider*, July 2, 2018, https://losspreventionmedia.com/insider/shoplifting-organized-retail-crime/changes-in-shoplifting-penalties-make-it-tougher-for-retailers/. There has been a trend to decriminalization. See Charles P. Nemeth, *Criminal Law*, 2nd ed. (2011).

22. For example, see R. Brown, *Explaining the Property Crime Drop: The Offender Perspective* (Canberra: Australian Institute of Criminology, 2015).

23. See Turner, "Shoplifting Penalties."

24. See Hopkins, "Business, victimisation and victimology."

25. Turner, "Shoplifting Penalties"; Ben Stevens, "Shoplifting nearly doubled last year due to "effective decriminalisation," *Retail Gazette*, March 22, 2018, www.retailgazette.co.uk/blog/2018/03/shoplifting-nearly-doubled-last-year-due-effective-decriminalisation.

26. See Bressler and Bressler, "Accounting for Profit."
27. O'Block, "Crime Prevention": 157; Beck, "Moving beyond shrinkage"; PwC, "Global Economic Crime"; Reilly, "Cost Retailers."
28. National Retail Federation, *2017 National Retail Security Survey*, 6 (2017), https://nrf.com/system/tdf/Documents/NRSS-Industry-Research-Survey-2017.pdf?file=1&title=National%20Retail%20Security%20Survey%202017.
29. Robert McCrie, "Retail Mgmt.: Center Helps LP Directors &Aids Shoplifters to Break Habits," *Security Letter*, November 3, 2008; "Loss Prevention: Portrait of Effective Anti-Shoplifting Programs," *Security Letter*, October 15, 2008: 2; Turner, "Shoplifting Penalties"; Stevens, "Shoplifting nearly doubled."
30. O'Block, "Crime Prevention": 158.
31. Kansas Bureau of Investigations, "Shoplifting: Another Word for Stealing," accessed September 9, 2018, www.kansas.gov/kbi/PDF/brochures/Shoplifting.pdf.
32. J. Bologna, *Corporate Fraud: The Basics of Prevention and Detection* (1984): 82; "Shoplifting, employee theft top reasons for $44B retail loss in 2014," RetailCustomerExperience.com, June 29, 2015.
33. Kansas Bureau, "Shoplifting"; Maryland Security Professionals, "Common Grocery Store Shoplifting Techniques and How to Combat Them," January 10, 2018, https://marylandsecurity.net/security/common-grocery-store-shoplifting-techniques-and-how-to-combat-them/; Florissant, MO Police Department, "Shoplifting," www.florissantmo.com/egov/documents/f3bfaf93_2770_c331_55de_bc08b51d9569.pdf.
34. Ronald V. Clarke and Gohar Petrossian, *Shoplifting: Problem Specific Guides Series*, 2nd ed. (2013), www.popcenter.org/problems/pdfs/Shoplifting.pdf; Kansas Bureau, "Shoplifting"; Maryland, "Shoplifting Techniques"; Florissant, MO, "Shoplifting."
35. See Joseph Petrocelli, "Shoplifting," *Police*, December 2008: 16; C. Meyer, "Monitoring the floor," *Security* 51, no. 4 (2014): 56–56, 58; Clarke and Petrossian, "Shoplifting."
36. Clarke and Petrossian, "Shoplifting"; Kansas Bureau, "Shoplifting"; Maryland, "Shoplifting Techniques"; Florissant, MO, "Shoplifting."
37. Clarke and Petrossian, "Shoplifting"; Kansas Bureau, "Shoplifting"; Maryland, "Shoplifting Techniques"; Florissant, MO, "Shoplifting."
38. McCourt, "Predictive Revolution."
39. See Clarke and Petrossian, "Shoplifting"; see also C. Carmel-Gilfilen, "Bridging Security and Good Design: Understanding Perceptions of Expert and Novice Shoplifters," *Security Journal* 26, no. 1 (2013): 80–105, doi:http://dx.doi.org.ez.lib.jjay.cuny.edu/10.1057/sj.2011.34.
40. Mark Gleckman, "Crime Prevention/Community Relations," in *The Security Supervisor Training Manual*, eds. Sandi J. Davies and Ronald R. Minion (1995); Clarke and Petrossian, "Shoplifting"; Maryland, "Shoplifting Techniques"; Florissant, MO, "Shoplifting."
41. J. Cleary, *Prosecuting the Shoplifter: A Loss Prevention Strategy* (1986): 19–21.
42. J. Kirk Barefoot, *Employee Theft Investigation* (1979): 81.
43. Leinbach-Reyhle, "New Report."
44. Anne Fisher, "U.S. retail workers are No. 1...in employee theft," Fortune, January 26, 2015, http://fortune.com/2015/01/26/us-retail-worker-theft.
45. "Theft Barometer (2015)": 25.
46. See "Retailer Security Chief Pushes Proactive Approach," *Corporate Security*, January 31, 2008: 8; Francesca Nicasio, "How to Prevent and Handle Internal Theft in Retail Stores," *Vend*, April 30, 2018, https://blog.vendhq.com/post/64901830752/prevent-and-handle-internal-theft-retail; see also C. W. Von Bergen et al., "The Truth about Honesty Testing," http://homepages.se.edu/cvonbergen/files/2012/11/The-Truth-About-Honesty-Testing.pdf.
47. Barefoot, "Undercover": 8.
48. See D. Ritchey, "'Tis the Season," *Security* 52, no. 12 (2015): 10–12.
49. "Why employees steal, and how to handle it," *HR Specialist*, April 13, 2016, www.thehrspecialist.com/23224/why-employees-steal-and-how-to-handle-it; Brandon Gaille, "Types of Employee Theft and Office Theft Statistics," May 26, 2017, https://brandongaille.com/types-employee-theft-and-office-theft-statistics/.
50. See Garett Seivold, "5 Ways Employees Are Stealing from Your Stores Right Now," *LPM Insider*, January 4, 2018, https://losspreventionmedia.com/insider/employee-theft/5-ways-employees-are-stealing-from-your-stores-right-now.
51. Nicasio, "Internal Theft"; Seivold, "5 Ways"; "Employee Theft: Statistics, Interviewing Techniques and Tips to Optimize Your Employee Theft Policy," *LPM Reports*, accessed September 9, 2018, https://losspreventionmedia.com/free-reports/employee-theft-statistics-interviewing-techniques-and-tips-to-optimize-your-employee-theft-policy.

52. O'Block, "Crime Prevention": 184–185; Nicasio, "Internal Theft"; Seivold, "5 Ways"; *LPM Reports*, "Employee Theft."

53. American Society for Industrial Security, *Basic Guidelines for Security Investigations* (1981): 91. See John H. Christman and Charles A. Sennewald, *Shoplifting: Managing The Problem* (2006); *LPM Reports*, "Employee Theft."

54. Pinkerton's Inc., *Investigations Department Training Manual* (1990): 155–156; Nicasio, "Internal Theft."

55. "Identifying the warning signs of internal theft," *Tellermate*, August 11, 2016, www.tellermate.com/us/news-and-resources/identifying-warning-signs-internal-theft/.

56. Michele Eby, "11 Warning Signs that Your Employees May Be Ripping You Off," *Media Partners*, www.media-partners.com/articles/eleven_warning_signs_that_your_employees_may_be_ripping_you_off.htm.

57. National Retail Federation, *2017 National Retail Security Survey* (2017): 11, https://nrf.com/system/tdf/Documents/NRSS-Industry-Research-Survey-2017.pdf?file=1&title=National%20Retail%20Security%20Survey%202017 at page; see also: Read Hayes, "Strategies to Detect and Prevent Workplace Dishonesty," (2008), www.asisonline.org/globalassets/foundation/documents/crisp-reports/crisp-strategies-detect-prevent-workplace-dishonesty.pdf.

58. Nicasio, "Internal Theft."

59. Charles P. Nemeth, *Private Security and the Law*, 5th ed. (Boca Raton, FL: CRC Press, 2018).

60. Ibid.

61. J. Di Domenico, *Investigative Technique for the Retail Security Investigator* (Lebhar-Friedman Books, 1979): 135.

62. W. L. Clark and W. L. Marshall, *A Treatise on the Law of Crimes* (Callaghan, 1967): 984.

63. Ibid.: 986–987.

64. See N.Y. Crim. Law § 221.2 (McKinney, 1962).

65. See William Coates, "Criminal Intention of Burglary," *N.C.L. Rev.* 2, (1924): 110; see also Champlin v. State, 84 Wis. 2d 621, 267 N.W. 2d 295 (1978); State v. Oritz, 92 N.M. 166, 584 P. 2d 1306 (1978).

66. Pennsylvania State Police, Bureau of Training and Education, *Investigation of Safe Burglaries* (1972): 1–2; Amaury Murgado, "How to Investigate a Burglary," *Police Magazine*, February 9, 2017, www.policemag.com/channel/careers-training/articles/2017/02/how-to-investigate.aspx.

67. For some thoughtful suggestions on burglary investigations, see Murgado, "Investigate a Burglary."

68. See Charles P. Nemeth and K. C. Poulin, *Private Security and Public Safety: A Community Based Approach* (2005): 71–72.

69. "How Burglars Choose Their Targets," *Protect America*, November 15, 2017, www.protectamerica.com/home-security-blog/spotlight/how-burglars-choose-their-targets_15029.

70. See A. Tseloni, R. Thompson, L. Grove, N. Tilley, and G. Farrell, "The Effectiveness of Burglary Security Devices," *Security Journal* 30, no. 2 (2017): 646–664, doi:http://dx.doi.org.ez.lib.jjay.cuny.edu/10.1057/sj.2014.30; see also "Most effective burglary deterrents, according to the burglar." *Security Distributing &Marketing*, March 2014: 18.

71. C. Meyer, "Monitoring the Floor," *Security* 51, no. 4 (2014): 56–58.

72. Merchants Insurance Group, "Business Owner Burglary and Robbery Prevention Tips," June 20, 2017, www.merchantsgroup.com/business-owner-burglary-robbery-prevention-tips/; Tseloni, Thompson, Grove, Tilley, and Farrell, "Security Devices."

73. See Jeffrey Roth, "The Role of Perceived Effectiveness in Home Security Choices," *Security Journal* 31, no. 3 (July 2018): 708–725.

74. Barrow County Sheriff's Office, "Business Security Checklist," www.barrowsheriff.com/forms/BusinessSecurityChecklistv2.pdf.

75. U.S. Department of Justice, National Institute of Justice, *Theft by Employees in Work Organizations* (1983): 2.

76. Pinkerton's, Inc., "Training Manual": 165.

77. Hayes, "Strategies," Appendix C: 34–35.

78. See also Sidebottom, Thornton, Tompson, Belur, Tilley, and Bowers, "A systematic review": 1.

10 Investigative Method and Technique: Insurance Cases

10.1 INTRODUCTION

The insurance industry has an ongoing need for the services of private security professionals, particularly private investigators. Part of this reality is driven by the sheer volume of fraudulent conduct within the various facets of insurance practice. The Association of Certified Fraud Examiners (ACFE) delineates the most common versions of fraud:

- Agent and broker schemes
- Underwriting irregularities
- Vehicle insurance schemes
- Property schemes
- Life insurance schemes
- Liability schemes
- Health insurance schemes
- Workers' compensation schemes[1]

Insurance fraud can occur at various levels of the insurance contract and policy applications. The ACFE summarizes four stages where the fraud ripens:

- Individuals applying for insurance
- Policyholders
- Third-party claimants
- Professionals who provide services to claimants[2]

While the larger carriers have investigators on staff, many insurers have come to depend on an independent contractor relationship in commercial, casualty, auto, and workers' compensation settings. In times of catastrophe such as hurricanes and other large natural disasters, the insurance industry has to rely on external investigative services simply because of the volume of cases.[3] Private security's contribution and involvement in insurance practice and procedure has been and is formidable, the range of services including but not limited to:

- Interviewing claimants and witnesses
- Claim assessment and analysis
- Damage assessments
- Record searches
- Securing statements
- Credit bureaus
- Securing medical and autopsy reports
- Court records
- Subpoena service
- Motor vehicle records
- Locating witnesses
- Activity checks

- Establishing criminal histories
- Background investigations

Investigative practice in the insurance industry generally involves four basic types of insurance: life, fire, marine, and casualty. In general terms, investigators analyze harm, damage, and even tragedy (in insurance parlance, "casualty"). An insured and insurer are contractual parties to an explicit, well-defined agreement, the *insurance policy*. As a result, when a claim occurs, the insurance company needs verification of the status, credibility, and authenticity of the claim in order to determine whether or not there is legal liability. Private security firms are frequently asked to perform these authoritative reviews.

Insurance claims usually comprise these four areas of casualty coverage:

- Death
- Property damage
- Personal/bodily injury
- Illness and disability

Whatever the type of insurance claim, the underlying investigation determines the truth by obtaining the facts and recording the information.[4]

Insurance companies are primarily concerned with clear and accurate factual representations, which in turn permit their legal counsel to make judgments, develop tactical strategies, or formulate settlement positions. Traditional lines of inquiry in the insurance sector include:

- Did the event (e.g., the accident causing the claim) actually occur?
- Is the insured liable?
- What is the extent of the injury or damage?
- Who was at fault?
- What is the claimant's medical history or prior injuries?
- Is the claimant truly disabled?
- What are the character, reputation, and credibility of witnesses for the claimant?
- Can surveillance produce results regarding the claimant's physical condition?
- In an uninsured motorist case, are there assets that can be attached?[5]

It is the responsibility of the investigator to target and formulate early answers to these types of queries, so that the insurer and the insured obtain the legal and factual picture to be resolved.

10.2   INVESTIGATIVE APPLICATION AND METHOD IN SPECIFIC CASES

Each insurance investigation involves the basic issues outlined in the previous section. Even so, the investigator must tailor the investigation based not only on the parties and entities involved, but also on the particular subject matter. So a wind or hail case will obviously be different than an arson scenario, as would a death by suicide from an auto accident fatality case. Aside from the entry point information common to all insurance cases, the investigator needs to fashion his or her documentation to the unique subject matter, developing a series of forms, checklists, and other documentary tools that can assist in the performance of investigative work. In addition, the modern investigator employs cutting-edge technology during the investigative process including drones, GPS equipment, mapping, and remote surveillance—all of which should only be conducted in full legal compliance.[6]

10.2.1   INSURANCE PROPERTY CLAIMS IN FIRE AND ARSON

In fire casualty and property policies, a frequent inquiry involves whether or not damage to property, goods, or other collateral is a compensable claim. If arson has been ruled out, the policy provisions on fire liability are usually pretty straightforward, and matters of valuation and deductibles the only issues in need of resolution. Proof of arson is not something easily concluded for as experienced investigators often remark, fire investigation is a "mixture of art and science ... since the identification and interpretation of burn patterns was the 'art' of the profession. Today, there is a greater emphasis on fire science and engineering than ever before."[7]

Arson investigation is a much more complicated problem for the investigator and the qualifications and skill set of the fire investigator varies widely. John Lentini paints a picture of an investigative class that needs uniformity and standardized qualifications.

> The reality is that the fire investigation profession has within its ranks a large number of individuals who don't know what they're doing, and are blissfully unaware of the work of fire scientists who have been trying for years to get across the crucial point that fire patterns must be interpreted differently when the fire has fully engulfed a room. The only word for such individuals is "hacks." Hacks work cheap and they work quickly, but when they make an arson determination, it will often fail to withstand even mild scrutiny.[8]

Web Exercise: Visit the NIJ Guide for Investigating Fire and Arson:

www.nij.gov/topics/law-enforcement/investigations/crime-scene/guides/fire-arson/Pages/welcome.aspx.

The crime of arson is often committed by the insured. Arson is a multimillion dollar drain on businesses, governmental entities, and individuals. When investigators review fire-damaged structures, owners' names appear on the initial suspect list. Burning to defraud the insurer is particularly likely in economically depressed areas or when an owner is under extraordinary financial pressure. The investigator should consider these possible motives:

- Fraud
- Juvenile theft
- Effort to hide other crimes
- Riot
- Jealousy
- Vandalism
- Revenge
- Thrill (pyromania)
- Terrorism[9]

Establishing motive is a priority for the investigator.[10] Motives or mitigating factors that point to a fire set by the insured may include:

1. Is there a need for cash?
2. Is there a reason to terminate the lease?
3. Is there cause to relocate a business?
4. Is there an unprofitable contract?
5. What is the profit picture?
6. What are people saying?
7. What type of neighborhood is the building located in?
8. Is the fire advantageous to anyone?
9. What other crimes might have been perpetrated?
10. Is there other trouble or difficulty in the neighborhood?
11. Is arson a common crime in the neighborhood?
12. Was insurance recently increased?

Much of what can be gleaned from a fire investigation relies upon a mix of scientific analysis and human intelligence. Witnesses are crucial to proof of deliberate fire because so many locales where fire occurs are inhabited or a working business enterprise. The investigator must ask the right questions of the right people on or near the scene of a fire. A suggested format and series of fire witnesses includes these lines of inquiry:

- Name?
- What apartment unit were you in?
- Were you home at the time of the fire?
- Were there any other people in the apartment with you?
- Were you awake at the time of the fire?
- How were you alerted to the fire?
- What action did you perform after being alerted to the fire?
- What path did you take to egress the building?
- Did you smell smoke prior to/during your egress?
- Did you see smoke prior to/during your egress?
- Did you see smoke in the hallway?
- Did you see flames prior to/during your egress?
- Did you hear any smoke alarms activating?
- Location of activating smoke alarms?
- Were you injured?[11]

A comprehensive document regarding motivation and other issues relative to the proof of an arson insurance investigation case is at Table 10.1.

TABLE 10.1

A List of Where to Get Information, through Interviews, for a Fire and Arson Investigation

Sources of Interview Information

The following is a list of some of the possible witnesses to acts committed in connection with an arson-for-profit scheme and the types of questions they should be asked:

I. Interview of Witnesses at Scene of Fire

A. Possible Witnesses:
- Tenants of building
- Tenants of surrounding buildings
- Businessmen in building
- Businessmen in surrounding buildings
- Customers in businesses in building
- Customers in businesses in surrounding buildings
- Passersby including: bus route drivers, taxi drivers, deliverymen, garbage collectors, police patrol, people waiting for buses and taxis.

B. Questions to be Asked:
- Did you observe the fire?
- At what time did you first observe the fire?
- In what part of building did you observe the fire?
- What called your attention to the building?
- Did you see anyone entering or leaving the building prior to the fire?
- Did you recognize them?
- Can you describe them?
- Did you observe any vehicles in the area of the fire?

(Continued)

TABLE 10.1 (CONTINUED)

A List of Where to Get Information, through Interviews, for a Fire and Arson Investigation

- Can you describe them?
- Can you describe the smoke and the color of the flame?
- How quickly did the fire spread?
- Was the building burning in more than one place?
- Did you detect any unusual odors?
- Did you observe anything else?
- What else did you observe?

II. Interview of Fire Officers and/or Firefighters at Scene

A. Questions to be Asked:

- What time was alarm received?
- What time did you arrive at scene of fire?
- Was your route to the scene blocked?
- What was the extent of burning when you arrived?
- Were doors and windows locked?
- Was the entrance and/or passageways blocked?
- What kind of fire was it?
- What was the spread speed of the fire?
- In what area(s) did the fire start?
- What was the proximity of the fire to the roof?
- Was there evidence of the use of an accelerant?
- Was there any evidence of arson recovered?
- Did the building have a fire alarm system?
- Was it operating?
- Was there any evidence of tampering with the alarm system?
- Did the building have a sprinkler system?
- Did it operate?
- Was there any evidence of tampering with the sprinkler system?
- Was there anyone present in the building when you arrived?
- Who was that person in the building?
- Did he or she say anything to you?
- Were there any people present at the scene when you arrived?
- Who were they?
- Did you observe any vehicles at the scene or leaving when you arrived?
- Can you describe them?
- Were there contents in the building?
- Was there evidence of contents removed?
- Was the owner present?
- Did the owner make a statement?
- What did the owner say?
- What is the prior fire history of the building?
- What is the prior fire history of the area?

III. Interview of Insurance Personnel

The profit in many arson-for-profit cases is the payment from an insurance policy or policies. There are three classes of people who may be interviewed in order to determine if the profit centers around an insurance claim. They are the insurance agent/broker, the insurance adjuster, and the insurance investigator.

A. Questions to Ask the Agent or Broker:

- Who is the insured?
- Is there more than one insured?
- Is the insured the beneficiary?
- What type of policy was issued?

(Continued)

TABLE 10.1 (CONTINUED)

A List of Where to Get Information, through Interviews, for a Fire and Arson Investigation

- What is the amount of the policy?
- When was it issued?
- When does it expire?
- What is the premium cost?
- Are payments up-to-date?
- Have there been any increases in the amount of coverage?
- What amount?
- When did increase take effect?
- What was the reason for the increase?
- Are there any special provisions in the policy (e.g., interruption of business or rental income)?
- What are they, and when did they take effect?
- Has the insured ever received a cancellation notice on this property? If so, when? Why?
- Does the insured have any other policies?
- Were there previous losses at the location of the fire?
- Were there losses at other locations owned by the insured?

B. Questions to Ask the Insurance Claims Adjustor:
- Did you take a sworn statement from the insured?
- Did the insured submit documents regarding proof of loss, value of contents, bills of lading, value of building, etc.?
- Did you inspect the fire scene?
- Did you inspect the fire scene with a public insurance adjustor?
- Did you and the public adjuster agree on the cost figure in the loss?
- Have you dealt with this public adjuster before?
- Has the adjuster represented this owner before?
- Has the insured had any other losses with this company? If so, provide details.

C. Questions to Ask the Insurance Adjuster:
- Were you able to determine the cause of the fire?
- Did you collect any evidence?
- Who analyzed the evidence?
- What were the results of the analysis?
- Was the cause of the fire inconsistent with state of building as known through underwriting examination?
- Have you investigated past fires involving the location?
- Have you investigated past fires involving the insured?
- What were the results of the investigations?
- Have you had prior investigations involving the public adjuster?
- Have you had prior investigations involving buildings handled by the same insurance agent/broker?
- What were the results of these investigations?
- Does this fire fit into a pattern of fires of recent origin in the area?
- What are the similarities?
- What are the differences?
- Have you taken any statements in connection with this burning?
- Whose statements did you take?
- What do they reveal?

There may be restrictions on the amount of information insurance personnel can turn over without a subpoena, but the investigator should be able to determine enough to indicate whether the issuance of a subpoena or search warrant would prove fruitful.

IV. Other Witnesses Concerning Finances of Insured
- How long have you known the owner/insured?

There are a number of other people who may have information relating to the finances of the owner which may indicate how they stood to profit from the burning. These witnesses would include business associates, creditors, and competitors. Following are the types of questions these witnesses may be able to answer:

(Continued)

TABLE 10.1 (CONTINUED)

A List of Where to Get Information, through Interviews, for a Fire and Arson Investigation

- What is the nature of your relationship with the owner?
- Do you have any information on the financial position of the business?
- Is the owner competitive with similar businesses?
- Have there been recent technological advances which would threaten the business's position?
- Has there been a recent increase in competition which would affect the business's position?
- Have changes in the economy affected the business's position?
- Has the owner experienced recent difficulty in paying creditors?
- Has the owner's amount of debt increased recently?
- Has the business lost any key employees recently?
- Has the location of the business changed for the worse recently?
- Has the owner increased the mortgage or taken out a second or third mortgage?
- Has the owner had difficulty making mortgage payments?
- Do you have any other information about the owner's financial position?

Proof of arson is difficult without credible, forensic physical evidence and for the most part, this type of investigation calls for a specialization beyond the skill set of the traditional investigator.[12] First, the International Association of Arson Investigators® (IAAI®) is an international professional association of more than 9,000 fire investigation professionals, united by a strong commitment to suppress the crime of arson through professional fire investigation. See Figure 10.1.[13]

FIGURE 10.1 The International Association of Arson Investigators® (IAAI®) is a leading organization for fire investigation resources. (Used with permission, International Association of Arson Investigators, Inc.)

Next, the National Association of Fire Investigators is a nonprofit association of fire investigation professionals dedicated to the education of fire investigators worldwide. NAFI has led the charge to bring fire investigation science into the 21st century, and offers a wide variety of training programs based on the National Fire Protection Association's (NFPA) 921 investigation guide. See Figure 10.2.[14]

The purpose of the International Association of Fire Investigators (IAFI) is to provide a platform for association, training, education, and assisting and improving the professional performance of fire investigation professionals who operate in international venues. Additionally, the IAFI provides a means of recognizing the expertise, experience, and position of those members who lead their fellows. See Figure 10.3.[15]

FIGURE 10.2   The landing page of the National Association of Fire Investigators, another great resource for professionals in the field. (Used with permission, National Association of Fire Investigators.)

FIGURE 10.3   The International Association of Fire Investigators is another global organization that provides professional membership and resources. (Used with permission, International Association of Fire Investigators.)

Investigators should use a checklist similar to that shown at Table 10.2[16] when reviewing actual sites and locations. The investigator should be looking for anything at the scene that does not belong or the absence of anything that does belong.

Private investigators compile fire inspection reports on houses, boats, autos, and other insurable property. For a comprehensive fire report on a residence, see Box 10.1.[17]

TABLE 10.2
A Detailed Checklist to Use at Fire Sites and Locations

Contact first responders and establish presence.
- Identify and contact the current incident commander and present identification.
- Conduct a briefing with the incident commander to determine who has jurisdiction and authorization (legal right of entry) and to identify other personnel at the scene (e.g., law enforcement, firefighting, emergency medical services, hazardous materials personnel and utility services personnel).
- Determine the level of assistance required and whether additional personnel are needed.
- Determine initial scene safety prior to entry through observations and discussions with first responders. Consider environmental as well as personnel safety concerns. Assess changes in safety conditions resulting from suppression efforts.

Define the scene's boundaries.
- Make a preliminary scene assessment (an overall tour of the fire scene to determine the extent of the damage, proceeding from areas of least damage to areas of greater damage) to identify areas that warrant further examination, being careful not to disturb evidence.
- Inspect and protect adjacent areas that may include nonfire evidence (e.g., bodies, bloodstains, latent prints or tool marks) or additional fire-related evidence (e.g., unsuccessful ignition sources, fuel containers and ignitable liquids).
- Mark or reevaluate the perimeter and establish the procedures for controlling access to the scene.

Identify and interview witness(es) at the scene.
- Contact the incident commander, identify first responders and first-in firefighters, and arrange to document their observations either in writing or through recorded interviews.
- Determine who reported the fire. Secure a tape or transcript of the report if available.
- Identify the owner of the building/scene, any occupants, and the person responsible for property management.
- Identify who was last to leave the building/scene and what occurred immediately before they left.
- Identify and interview other witnesses (e.g., neighbors and bystanders) and record their statements.

Assess scene security at the time of the fire.
- Ask first responders where an entry was made, what steps were taken to gain entry to the building or vehicle, and whether any systems had been activated when they arrived at the scene.
- Observe and document the condition of doors, windows, other openings, and fire separations (e.g., fire doors). Attempt to determine whether they were open, closed or compromised at the time of the fire.
- Observe and document the position of timers, switches, valves, and control units for utilities, detection systems, and suppression systems, as well as any alterations to those positions by first responders.
- Contact security and suppression system monitoring agencies to obtain information and available documentation about the design and function of the systems.

Identify the resources required to process the scene.
- Identify a distinct origin (location where the fire started) and an obvious fire cause (ignition source, first fuel ignited, and circumstances of the event that brought the two together).
- If neither the origin nor the cause is immediately obvious, or if there is clear evidence of an incendiary cause, the investigator should
  - Conduct a scene examination in accordance with NFPA 921 and other guidelines.
  - Seek someone with the expertise required.
- Know when to request the assistance of specialized personnel and to obtain specialized equipment as required to assist with the investigation. Standard equipment should include the following:
  - Barrier tape.
  - Clean, unused evidence containers (e.g., cans, glass jars, nylon or polyester bags).

(Continued)

TABLE 10.2 (CONTINUED)
A Detailed Checklist to Use at Fire Sites and Locations

- Compass.
- Decontamination equipment (e.g., buckets, pans and detergent).
- Evidence tags, labels and tape.
- Gloves (disposable gloves and work gloves).
- Handtools (e.g., hammers, screwdrivers, knives and crowbars).
- Lights (e.g., flashlights, spotlights).
- Marker cones or flags.
- Personal protective equipment.
- Photographic equipment.
- Rakes, brooms, spades, etc.
- Tape measures.
- Writing equipment (e.g., notebooks, pens, pencils and permanent markers).

BOX 10.1   AN EXAMPLE OF A COMPREHENSIVE
FIRE REPORT ON A RESIDENCE

CASE NUMBER: #123456

DATE: 9/18/19

Summary of Incident

On September 18, 2019, Investigators Smith and Brown responded to 123 East 1st Street, incident #12, at the request of Chief Jones. The dispatch time was 1200 hours, arrival at the scene was 1230 hours. Investigators observed a wood-frame construction, single-story, one-family residence. The investigation revealed that the fire had originated in the bathroom adjacent to the bathtub. The indicators observed and the evidence taken and analyzed revealed the fire was started by the distribution of a flammable accelerant (gasoline) and ignited by an open flame (lighter). A suspect was identified by two witnesses (W-1 and W-2). The suspect was seen breaking into the house, distributing a liquid, and setting the fire with a lighter. Both witnesses (W-1 and W-2) identified the suspect (S-1) by name and identified him in a photo lineup. The motive for the fire was spite/revenge. The suspect (S-1) had been evicted on September 17, 2019.

Laboratory Analysis

Taken into evidence was a gasoline can, lighter, and crowbar. Fingerprints were taken from all three exhibits and identified the suspect (S-1) as the person handling each item. Furthermore, a gas station manager (W-3) identified the suspect (S-1) filling a container similar to the one taken into evidence. Laboratory analysis revealed that the flammable liquid was gasoline and had the same octane rating as described by the gas station manager (W-3).

Witnesses

W-1 John A. Smith, 345 E. 2nd St. Fun City, MA 00000, 300/111-2222. DOB 1-1-11, Occupation - Lawyer.

W-2 John A. Doe, 444 E. 3rd St. Sun City, MA 00000, 300/222-3333. DOB 2-2-22, Occupation - Doctor

W-3 James A. Smith, 555 W. 4th St. Moon City, MA 00000, 300/444-5555, DOB 3-3-33, Occupation - Gas station manager

Statements Made by Witnesses

Witnesses 1 and 2 both identified suspect entering house, distributing liquid, and setting the fire.

Witness 3 can identify the suspect purchasing and filling container with regular gasoline, octane rating of 87.

Statement Made by Suspect

No statement made, suspect taken into custody and Miranda warning given immediately on September 19, 2019 at 1200 hours.

Statutes Violated

MA Penal Code 111222: Deliberately setting fire to a dwelling of another. Bail/Fine $5,000.

MA Penal Code 1234: Unlawful entry - burglary. Bail/Fine $5,000

MA Penal Code 45678: Distribution of a flammable liquid in setting an incendiary fire. Bail/Fine $10,000.

Total Bail/Fine $18,500

The Unknown Fire Department doesn't recommend the suspect be released. (O.R. Release)

Web Exercise: Visit Interfire for an amazing resource center for fire investigators at: www.interfire.org/resourcecenter.asp.

10.2.2   WORKERS' COMPENSATION

Workers' compensation is a legislative remedy whereby injuries that occur in the workplace, within an employer/employee relationship, are not formally litigated and instead resolved according to a predetermined compensation formula. The question of fault is less an issue than the proof of injury at a workplace. It is a legislative response that replaces the common law principles of negligence and intentional torts with a strict liability, no-fault, statutory remedy. Employees who are injured on the job must be able to demonstrate that their injuries were work-related and within the scope of their employment. The problems with fraudulent claims are now legendary in investigative circles. "Fraudulent workers' compensation cases are on the rise and that likely will add to the several billion dollar annual price tag that already has insurers and employers reeling."[18]

So significant are these costs that insurers are now employing drones—unmanned aerial vehicles to track the activities of the fraudulent. Small, unmanned aerial vehicles may soon help ground some of those numbers.

As in disability cases, it is easy enough to feign injury and the resulting costs from escalating fraudulent claims have led to higher employer premiums.[19] In this setting, the investigator's chief aim and purpose is assuring the integrity of the claim and also mitigating existing injuries with proper treatment and remedial protocols.[20]

A work sheet collecting information regarding the compensability of a claim is at Box 10.2.[21]

BOX 10.2   A SAMPLE CLIENT DATA SHEET FROM A WORKER'S COMPENSATION CASE

CLIENT DATA SHEET – WORKER'S COMPENSATION CASE

IN RE: _____ Date Of Injury: _____

INS. CO: _____ Hearing Commissioner: _____

Hearing Date: _____

I.C. Docket No. _____

1. Full Name _____ S.S. No. _____ Age_____

2. Address_____ Telephone No_____

3. Name of Spouse or Nearest Kin and Address:_____

 Number of children:_____

4. Employer and Address:_____

 Job Held:_____

5. Hired In:_____ Length of Employment:_____

6. Work Week:_____ Hours per day:_____ Days per Week:_____

7. Wage Rate:_____ Per hour/day/week_____ For overtime:_____

8. Average Weekly Wage:_____ Extras Furnished:_____

9. Date of Accident:_____ Hour:_____

10. Paid for Date of Injury?_____ Started Losing Time:_____

11. Now receiving comp._____ Weeks paid at_____ per week

12. Place of accident_____ County_____

13. Description of Accident and Injury:_____

 _____

 Accident Details:_____

 _____

14. Any Part of Body Amputated?_____ Member and Point of Amputation:_____

15. Notice of Accident: Who:_____ Title:_____

 When:_____

16. Witnesses:_____

17. Doctors:_____

 Sent by:_____

18. Hospital:_____ From:_____ To:_____

19. Travel:_____

20. Returned to Work?_____ Date:_____ Rate of Pay:_____

21. Any statements or Recorded interviews given?_____ To Whom:_____

22. Other Attorneys Consulted?_____ Who:_____

23. Third Party Liability:_____

24. All Other Injuries and Claims:_____

25. Prior Health:_____

26. Date of Contract:_____ Referred by:_____

27. Additional Information:_____

 _____

 _____

Prior to the enactment of workers' compensation legislation, American law was more concerned with assessing or analyzing the negligent or intentional conduct of the employer, such as an employer who provided unsafe tools or equipment, fostered a dangerous work environment, or failed to warn of dangers in the work environment. These lines of advocacy have been legislatively swept away, and injuries are now adjudged on a strict liability basis, that is, an injury in the workplace will be compensable regardless of who is at fault. The Michigan State Code lays out some liability scenarios which edify how these principles apply:

(1) An employee, who receives a personal injury arising out of and in the course of employment by an employer who is subject to this act at the time of the injury, shall be paid compensation as provided in this act. A personal injury under this act is compensable if work causes, contributes to, or aggravates pathology in a manner so as to create a pathology that is medically distinguishable from any pathology that existed prior to the injury. In the case of death resulting from the personal injury to the employee, compensation shall be paid to the employee's dependents as provided in this act. Time of injury or date of injury as used in this act in the case of a disease or in the case of an injury not attributable to a single event is the last day of work in the employment in which the employee was last subjected to the conditions that resulted in the employee's disability or death.

(2) Mental disabilities and conditions of the aging process, including but not limited to heart and cardiovascular conditions and degenerative arthritis, are compensable if contributed to or aggravated or accelerated by the employment in a significant manner. Mental disabilities are compensable if arising out of actual events of employment, not unfounded perceptions thereof, and if the employee's perception of the actual events is reasonably grounded in fact or reality.

(3) An employee going to or from his or her work, while on the premises where the employee's work is to be performed, and within a reasonable time before and after his or her working hours, is presumed to be in the course of his or her employment. Notwithstanding this presumption, an injury incurred in the pursuit of an activity the major purpose of which is social or recreational is not covered under this act.[22]

As a result of this statutory construction, injuries on the job, from broken bones to lung disease, are subject to the provisions of the Worker's Disability Compensation Act. In most jurisdictions a schedule of benefits is published (see Box 10.3[23]).

BOX 10.3   AN EXCERPT OF THE SCHEDULE OF BENEFITS FROM THE WORKER'S DISABILITY COMPENSATION ACT FROM 1969

Worker's Disability Compensation Act Of 1969 (Excerpt)
Act 317 of 1969
418.361 Effect of imprisonment or commission of crime; scheduled disabilities; meaning of total and permanent disability; limitations; payment for loss of second member.
Sec. 361.

(1) An employer is not liable for compensation under section 301(7) or (8), 351, 371(1), or 401(5) or (6) for periods of time that the employee is unable to obtain or perform work because of imprisonment or commission of a crime.

(2) In cases included in the following schedule, the disability in each case shall be considered to continue for the period specified, and the compensation paid for the personal injury shall be 80% of the after-tax average weekly wage subject to the maximum and minimum rates of compensation under this act. The effect of any internal joint replacement surgery,

internal implant, or other similar medical procedure shall be considered in determining whether a specific loss has occurred. The specific loss period for the loss shall be considered as follows:

(a) Thumb, 65 weeks.
(b) First finger, 38 weeks.
(c) Second finger, 33 weeks.
(d) Third finger, 22 weeks.
(e) Fourth finger, 16 weeks.

The loss of the first phalange of the thumb, or of any finger, shall be considered to be equal to the loss of 1/2 of that thumb or finger, and compensation shall be 1/2 of the amount above specified.

The loss of more than 1 phalange shall be considered as the loss of the entire finger or thumb. The amount received for more than 1 finger shall not exceed the amount provided in this schedule for the loss of a hand.

(f) Great toe, 33 weeks.
(g) A toe other than the great toe, 11 weeks.

The loss of the first phalange of any toe shall be considered to be equal to the loss of 1/2 of that toe, and compensation shall be 1/2 of the amount above specified.

The loss of more than 1 phalange shall be considered as the loss of the entire toe.

(h) Hand, 215 weeks.
(i) Arm, 269 weeks.

An amputation between the elbow and wrist that is 6 or more inches below the elbow shall be considered a hand, and an amputation above that point shall be considered an arm.

(j) Foot, 162 weeks.
(k) Leg, 215 weeks.

An amputation between the knee and foot 7 or more inches below the tibial table (plateau) shall be considered a foot, and an amputation above that point shall be considered a leg.

(l) Eye, 162 weeks.

Eighty percent loss of vision of 1 eye shall constitute the total loss of that eye.

(3) Total and permanent disability, compensation for which is provided in section 351 means:

(a) Total and permanent loss of sight of both eyes.
(b) Loss of both legs or both feet at or above the ankle.
(c) Loss of both arms or both hands at or above the wrist.
(d) Loss of any 2 of the members or faculties in subdivision (a), (b), or (c).
(e) Permanent and complete paralysis of both legs or both arms or of 1 leg and 1 arm.
(f) Incurable insanity or imbecility.
(g) Permanent and total loss of industrial use of both legs or both hands or both arms or 1 leg and 1 arm; for the purpose of this subdivision such permanency shall be determined not less than 30 days before the expiration of 500 weeks from the date of injury.

(4) The amounts specified in this clause are all subject to the same limitations as to maximum and minimum as above stated. In case of the loss of 1 member while compensation is being paid for the loss of another member, compensation shall be paid for the loss of the second member for the period provided in this section. Payments for the loss of a second member shall begin at the conclusion of the payments for the first member.

History: 1969, Act 317, Eff. Dec. 31, 1969;—Am. 1980, Act 357, Eff. Jan. 1, 1982;—Am. 1985, Act 103, Imd. Eff. July 30, 1985;— Am. 2011, Act 266, Imd. Eff. Dec. 19, 2011.

Constitutionality: The statutory limitation in subsection (2)(g) of this section is not unconstitutional. Johnson v Harnischfeger Corp, 414 Mich 102; 323 NW2d 912 (1982).

Enacting section 2 of Act 266 of 2011 provides:

"Enacting section 2. This amendatory act applies to injuries incurred on or after its effective date."

Popular name: Act 317

Popular name: Heart and Lung Act

Upon initial interview and case assessment, the investigator's most pressing concern must be whether or not an injury exists and whether or not the injury is related to or arose from the work environment. To confirm the legitimacy of the claim, the investigator should consider using the techniques and tactics of surveillance—the most often used strategy to assure the credibility of a claim. Workers' compensation, disability, and proof of contested injuries should rely heavily on the use of photographic or video surveillance. The end result of this type of surveillance should, by visual means, verify or refute the authenticity of the claimant's condition. The best approach is to consider the injury from the claimant's point of view to determine exactly how the injury affects the ability to function. The more extreme the claimant's movements are and the more they conflict with those of a truly disabled person, the more important it is to record the claimant's action visually. The investigator should also document whether the claimant is able to perform activities that bear on the alleged injury. Types of actions to look for include:

1. Back injury
   - Subject is carrying bundles (such as groceries) in a normal fashion.
   - Subject is carrying anything of moderate weight in an awkward position (such as a large container of water in front of him with both hands).
   - Subject is leaning in an awkward position (such as out of a window to clean an upper pane of glass).
   - Subject is using his body to hold a heavy object in place or to apply pressure (such as applying pressure to an electric drill to bore a hole at the level of one's head or above).
2. Head injury
   - Subject is extremely active, physically, in extreme heat (such as working on a roof laying shingles).
   - Subject continuously moves his head in a quick, jerky fashion (such as one does in some strenuous dances).
   - Subject is involved in strenuous running.
3. Leg injury
   - Subject is walking in a quick, carefree manner (such as skipping or quickly crossing the street).
   - Subject is running.
   - Subject is freely and quickly climbing stairs without the assistance of a railing or cane.
   - Subject is found carrying a heavy object upstairs.
   - Subject gets up from an extended crouching position (such as one is in when washing a car or weeding a garden).
   - Subject remains in a crouching position for some time.
4. Arm injury
   - Subject is carrying something heavy at arm's length (such as a car tire).
   - Subject is seen grasping or pulling something (such as a large rock or root from the ground).
   - Subject is propping something of weight up (such as an extension ladder).
   - Subject is twisting something (such as wringing out a wet towel).
   - Subject is lifting something above the belt (such as loading luggage, groceries, or boxes into a vehicle).

5. Whiplash
  • Basically the same activities shown under headings for back injury and head injury with the addition of unusual movement of the neck.[24]

Box 10.4 includes detailed data on types of information to gather, pertinent medical information to find, and surveillance to report, as well as a summary of the investigator's findings.

BOX 10.4   A TEMPLATE FOR WORKER'S COMPENSATION INVESTIGATION FINAL REPORT

Worker's Compensation Investigation
FINAL REPORT

Client: [Name]   File No:
       [Title]   Date:
       [Company name]   Report by:
       [Address]

Report of investigation
Re: [Subject's name or other pertinent information]

Synopsis:
As requested by [client and address], a [type of investigation] was conducted on [subject's name] to determine …. The [investigation] and/or [activity] included [photographs or videos]. These efforts revealed ….

Details
A. Personal information:
   Name of subject and any aliases
   Address of subject
   Telephone number
   Date of birth
   Social Security number
   Height/weight
   Hair/eye color

B. Intelligence information
   A check of the [state] Department of Motor Vehicle Records revealed that the subject has a [current/expired/suspended] [state] driver's license, OLN [number], expiration [date]. Subject owns and/or uses the following vehicles:
   [year/make/model/color of car]
   [registration]

C. Interview results (if any)
   On [date] [name of interviewee] was interviewed. [name] is the [relationship] of the subject. The interview took place at [location]. The agent learned that [results of interview].
   or
   Interviews were not conducted [reason].

D. Medical information
   According to [source: include name, title, and address], the subject's medical condition is [explain].
E. Surveillance results

July 8, 2019
7:00 am – 10:00 am
7:35 am   On Wednesday, July 8, 2019, at 7:35 am agents arrived at 456 East Main Street, West Hills, PA and initiated a surveillance on subject. Agents observed a 2018 black Honda (PA registration ABC-1234) parked in front of the residence. Agents observed the residence to be a side-by-side duplex, orange brick, subject residing in the left side facing the house. The right side is unoccupied.
9:35 am   Agents unsuccessfully attempted to contact the subject by telephone. Agents listened to a recorded message indicating that subject was not at home. Agents terminated surveillance at approximately 10:00 am.

July 9, 2019
6:00 am – 12:00 pm
6:00 am   On Thursday, July 9, 2019 at 6:00 am agents arrived at 456 East Main Street, West Hills, PA and initiated a surveillance on subject. Subject's vehicle (2018 black Honda, PA registration ABC-1234) was parked on the street in front of the residence.
           At approximately 9:00 am, a pretext telephone call was placed to subject to verify her presence at the residence with positive results. Agents maintained surveillance until 12:00 pm and observed no movement. Surveillance was terminated at approximately 12:00 pm.

July 10, 2019
2:30 pm – 6:00 pm
2:30 pm   On Friday, July 10, 2019 at 2:30 pm agents arrived at 456 East Main Street, West Hills, PA and initiated a surveillance on subject. Agents observed subject enter vehicle (2018 black Honda, PA registration ABC-1234) and proceed to the West Hills Shopping Center where the subject entered the deli.
2:45 pm   At 2:45 pm the subject exited the deli with an unidentified white female, entered her vehicle and proceeded to the Richmond Shopping Center located at 123 East Main Street, Mars, PA. Subject parked in front of a MAC Banking Machine and made what appeared to be several transactions.
3:10 pm   At 3:10 pm the subject and companion returned to the West Hills Shopping Center and entered the Food King Supermarket.
3:55 pm   At 3:55 pm the subject exited the supermarket with one bag of groceries and proceeded to her vehicle and placed the groceries in the trunk of the car (Photograph #1). Subject then proceeded into the ice cream store.
4:05 pm   At 4:05 pm the subject exited the ice cream store, eating an ice cream cone, entered her vehicle and finished eating the cone (Photograph #2).
4:10 pm   At approximately 4:10 pm subject proceeded to a MAC Banking Machine located at 456 East Main Street. Subject made a transaction on the machine and proceeded home. Surveillance was terminated at approximately 5:45 pm.
F. Summary
Agents observed no apparent physical disability that would impair movement.
                                            or
Agents observed ....
                                   End of Report

10.2.3   DISABILITY CLAIMS

Insurance companies which issue disability policies have a recurring need for verification of disability claims. At the governmental level, particularly in the Social Security Administration,[25] outside review and analysis by investigators is standard operating procedure. The following elements are crucial to determine whether the claimant is really disabled:

1. Was claimant hospitalized?
   Where, when, and for how long?
   Name of attending physician.
2. Is claimant confined to his house?
   For what period of time is claimant bedridden?
3. Is claimant wearing any braces, aided by orthopedic equipment or other medical accoutrements as a result of the injury? Give description and names of medical aids, if possible.
4. What injuries can be documented?
5. Is the claimant restricted in his activities?
   Is the claimant working? Confirm status.
6. Has there been any time lost from work due to the accident?
   Give confirmation and facts.
7. Are there any previous accidents?
   Does the claimant have a significant past medical history?
8. Does the claimant drive?
9. In what activities is the claimant presently engaged?[26]

Web Exercise: Watch the video that answers the question "Will Social Security Send a Private Investigator to Challenge your Disabilty Claim?" at https://youtu.be/VpLoAfjCL10.

In addition to standard surveillance techniques discussed throughout this text, a disability claim investigation relies heavily upon an on-site claimant interview. The investigator need not fear personal confrontation or discussion with the claimant unless the insurance company has a strong certainty of subterfuge and fraud. A pretext of some kind is advisable, and a neighborhood investigation is likely to be the most informative.

With very few exceptions, the neighborhood investigation is performed under a pretext. A pretext means we do not identify ourselves as a representative of the client or of our own company, and we do not state the actual purpose of our inquiries.[27]

When questioning people, the investigator should be thoroughly prepared, orderly in presentation, and not appear intense or driven to a given end. The information elicited should come forth naturally from these third parties. Use of a checklist, such as that shown at Box 10.5, will ensure that the investigator focuses on appropriate lines of questioning.

BOX 10.5   A NEIGHBORHOOD INVESTIGATION CHECKLIST HELPS AN INVESTIGATOR TAKE AN APPROPRIATE LINE OF QUESTIONING

Neighborhood Investigation Checklist

1. How long have they known the subject?
2. Does a family relationship exist between the subject and the interviewee?
3. Present address (how long there); previous address.
4. How frequently is subject seen?
5. Age, race, and marital status (spouse's name).
6. Dependency status (include relationship, names, and approximate ages of dependents)

7. Is the subject employed? If so, where? If place of employment is not known, what time does he leave for work and what is his mode of travel? (Also, if employment status is unknown, does the subject leave his residence at about the same time every day?)

8. If unemployed, when and where did he last work; what were his duties, and why did he leave this employment? Does he appear able to work? What is his source of income? His normal occupation?

9. Are neighbors aware of any injuries or hospitalization? (Details, where, when, how long ago, etc.)

10. Health, prior to and subsequent to the injury in question.

11. Did the injury in question affect his normal activities (yard work, house repairs, car repairs, etc.)?

12. Present activities (golf, bowling, dancing, etc.)

13. Is spouse or are children employed? If so, where, how long, etc.

14. Property owned (residence, automobile, boat, truck, machinery, etc.)

15. Desirability as a neighbor and reputation (does subject drink alcohol, fight, gamble, use drugs, file suits, etc.?)

16. Names and addresses of personal references, friends, and relatives.

10.2.4 AUTO LIABILITY CLAIMS

Due to escalating costs of auto litigation and insurance claim analysis, the services of the private security industry are in high demand. Some insurance companies have adopted hardball strategies in contesting the claims and losses filed by lawyers; others make a reasonable effort to resolve.

The typical automobile insurance case finds its legal foundation in an auto insurance contract, that is, the agreement entered into between an insurer (the insurance company) and an insured (the claimant). A sample of a page of an auto insurance contract is at Box 10.6.

BOX 10.6   A SAMPLE OF A PAGE FROM AN AUTO INSURANCE CONTRACT

FIRST PARTY BENEFITS COVERAGE - <STATE>

The Definitions and General Provisions of this policy apply unless modified by this endorsement.

SCHEDULE	
BASIC FIRST PARTY BENEFITS	
Benefits	**Limit of Liability**
Medical Expense Benefit	Up to $10,000
Work Loss Benefit	Up to $4,000 subject to
Funeral Expense Benefit	a maximum of
	$1,000 per month
	Up to $15,000

The following options apply instead of Basic First Party Benefits as indicated below or in the Declarations:

☐ ADDED FIRST PARTY BENEFITS	**Limit of Liability**
Benefits	Up to $_____
Medical Expense Benefit	Up to $_____subject to
Work Loss Benefit	a maximum of
Funeral Expense Benefit	$_____per month
Accidental Death Benefit	Up to $_____
	Up to $_____

☐ COMBINATION FIRST PARTY BENEFITS	**Limit of Liability**
Benefits	Up to $_____
Maximum total Single Limit	No specific dollar amount
Subject to the following individual limits:	No specific dollar amount
Medical Expense Benefit	Up to $2,500
Work Loss Benefit	$25,000
Funeral Expense Benefit	
Accidental Death Benefit	

NOTE: IF ADDED FIRST PARTY BENEFITS or COMBINATION FIRST PARTY BENEFITS are not
shown as applicable in the Schedule or Declarations only BASIC FIRST PARTY BENEFITS apply.

The following exclusion applies as indicated below or in the Declarations:
☐ EXCLUSION OF WORK LOSS BENEFIT
The Work Loss Benefit does not apply

I. DEFINITIONS
With respect to First Party Benefits Coverage:
    "the Act" means the Pennsylvania Motor Vehicle Financial
    Responsibility Law of 1984, as amended.
In addition, the following words and phrases are defined for
    first party benefits coverage. They are bold-faced when used

"**Bodily injury**" means accidental
bodily harm to a person and that
person's resulting illness, disease or
death.
"**Insured**" means:
    1. You or your **family member**.
    2. Any other person:

10.2.4.1 Policy Declaration

The economic basis of the contractual obligation between the insured and the insurer is listed on a
policy declaration page. Most policy declaration pages are uniform in content and comprise these
categories:

- Bodily injury liability
- Collision protection
- Property damage liability
- Towing and labor costs
- Medical payments and benefits
- Funeral expenses
- Comprehensive coverage regarding personal effects
- Fire and theft
- Uninsured and underinsured motorist

Although dollar amounts influence the parameters of a potential lawsuit, the policy itself includes
contractual provisions which guide the obligations of the insured and the insurer. Three initial components are described in the insurance contract:

1. Specific agreements and coverages. (See the example shown at Box 10.6.)
2. Exclusions to coverage. (See Box 10.7.)
3. Covenants and other contingencies. (See Box 10.8.)

BOX 10.7   AN EXAMPLE OF A LIST OF VARIOUS EXCLUSIONS TO COVERAGE

Exclusions To Coverage
    We do not provide benefits for bodily injury:

1. Sustained by any person while intentionally causing or attempting to cause bodily injury to:
   a. himself;
   b. herself; or
   c. any other person;
   nor will we pay an Accidental Death Benefit on behalf of that person.
2. Sustained by any person while committing a felony.
3. Sustained by any person while seeking to elude lawful apprehension or arrest by a law enforcement official.
4. Sustained by any person while maintaining or using a motor vehicle knowingly converted by that person. However, this exclusion (4) does not apply to:
   a. you; or
   b. any family member.
5. Sustained by any person who, at the time of the accident:
   a. is the owner of one or more registered motor vehicles and none of the motor vehicles have in effect the financial responsibility required by the Act; or
   b. is occupying a motor vehicle owned by that person for which the financial responsibility required by the Act is not in effect.
6. Sustained by any person maintaining or using a motor vehicle while located for use as a residence or premises.
7. Sustained by any person injured as a result of conduct within the course of the business of repairing, servicing or otherwise maintaining motor vehicles. This exclusion (7) does not apply if the conduct is off the business premises.

BOX 10.8 AN EXAMPLE OF A LIMIT OF LIABILITY CLAUSE

Limit Of Liability

The limit of liability shown in the Schedule or in the Declarations for the first party benefits that apply is the most we will pay to or for each insured as the result of any one accident. This is the most we will pay regardless of the number of:

1. Claims made;
2. Vehicles or premiums shown in the Schedule or in the Declarations;
3. Vehicles involved in the accident; or
4. Insurers providing first party benefits.

If Combination First Party Benefits are afforded, we will apply the total limit of liability to provide any separate limits required by the Act for Basic First Party Benefits. This provision will not change our total limit of liability.

Any amount payable under First Party Benefits Coverage shall be excess over any amounts paid, payable or required to be provided to an Insured under any workers' compensation law or similar law.

The investigator may have many functions within auto liability claims investigation, but the primary function is to determine the facts. Decisions regarding liability, claims damages, and litigation are matters beyond the scope of investigative practice, but those entrusted with resolution of same weigh heavily upon the work of the investigator.[28]

Investigators assist the insurance company in the compilation of facts that lead to strategic decision making relative to litigation. In an automobile accident case, multiple remedies and causes of action may exist. The negligence action is not mutually exclusive but is predictably the cause of action first plead. Traditional negligence law asserts that certain careless acts, a breach of due care, result in actual injury and damage. The person who runs a stop sign or a red light, falls asleep at the wheel, or has his or her eyes distracted from the roadway, thereby causing injury, will be deemed to have breached the standard of care and conduct owed others in the operation of an automobile. Beyond negligence, other remedies must not be overlooked, such as:

1. *First party benefits*—Under contemporary no-fault provisions, an insured in a contractual capacity with his insurance company may collect benefits for injuries arising out of the ownership, operation, or utilization of a motor vehicle.
2. *Intentional torts*—Individuals who are not simply careless but intentional in their conduct, who inflict bodily injury, or who destroy property, can be sued on intentional tort theories such as assault, battery, trespass, or intentional infliction of mental distress.
3. *Underinsured or uninsured benefits*—If the tortfeasor's policy limits do not adequately compensate for injury, or the tortfeasor has no insurance (this is labeled "uninsured"), the insured's own policy may make up the inadequacy through its underinsurance or uninsured coverages. Frequently, competing carriers will insist on a right to consent to any settlement before payment of any underinsurance.

Web Exercise: Visit one of the many firms that operate in the auto claims portion of the insurance industry at: www.theeyewitness.com/auto-liability-investigations.html.

10.2.4.2   Processing the Auto Liability Case

Governing investigative action in auto accident and liability cases is the essential need to discover the sequence, the chain of events, and the flow of conditions that led to the collision or other injury. The chain of events leading to the accident generally consists of:

1. Principal event, the time, the place, and type of accident—for example, running off the road; collision on the road with a pedestrian
2. Perception of a hazard—the seeing, sensing, or hearing the unusual or unexpected movement or condition that could be taken as a sign of an accident about to happen
3. The point of perception—the time and place at which the unusual or unexpected movement or condition could have been perceived by a normal person
4. The point of no escape—the time and place beyond which the accident can no longer be prevented by the person who is watching
5. Maximum engagement—the time and position in which the objects in a collision are pushed together as far as they will be, and
6. The final position—the time and place when objects involved finally come to rest; this is the position before anything is moved[29]

Auto accident investigators must do all they can to maintain the final position of the persons or objects involved in the accident. Except for lifesaving issues and the minimization of property destruction, objects should remain in their final position to provide the most untainted picture of the accident scene. Insurance companies realize profits based on their capacity to analyze and reconstruct accident cases. Investigators, working on behalf of either the insured or the insurer, must possess the same level of dedication and proficiency. Where contributory negligence operates as a pure defense, reconstruction of the accident scene becomes an even more critical step in the investigative process.

Investigators need to document and complete memoranda outlining accident fact patterns because police reports and diagrams, as discussed in earlier sections of this text, serve as foundational pieces of evidence in the investigation of accident cases. Two types of forms regularly used to gather data are medical information sheets and accident data sheets. Samples of these types of forms are shown in Boxes 10.9 and 10.10.

BOX 10.9   AN EXAMPLE OF A MEDICAL DATA FORM

MEDICAL DATA

Please summarize the following items:

Description of Injuries:

History of Accident:

Progress:

Past Medical History:

Present Complaints:

Date	Nature	Permanency

BOX 10.10   AN EXAMPLE OF AN ACCIDENT DATA FORM

Accident Data Form

Your name

Accident date   Time   am/pm

Address   City   State   Zip

Police Dept.   Case #   Tickets Issued? ☐ Yes ☐ No

If yes, to whom?   Charges

Other Vehicle:

Year   Make   Model

Color   License Plate #   State

Driver of Other Vehicle:

Name   Apparent injuries? ☐ Yes ☐ No

Home Address   City   State   Zip

Home Phone   Business Phone

Drivers License #   State   Insurance Carrier

Age   Sex   Ht   Wt

Injury type

Registered Owner of Other Vehicle:

Name				Apparent injuries? ☐ Yes ☐ No
Home Address		City	State	Zip
Drivers License #	State	Insurance Carrier		

Passengers in Other Vehicle:

Name				Apparent injuries? ☐ Yes ☐ No
Home Address	City	State		Zip
Home phone		Business phone		
Drivers License #	State	Insurance Carrier		
Age	Sex		Ht	Wt
Injury type				
Position in vehicle at time of accident				

Name				Apparent injuries? ☐ Yes ☐ No
Home Address		City	State	Zip
Home phone		Business phone		
Drivers License #	State	Insurance Carrier		
Age	Sex		Ht	Wt
Injury type				
Position in vehicle at time of accident				

Witnesses:

Name				Apparent injuries? ☐ Yes ☐ No
Home Address		City	State	Zip
Home phone		Business phone		
Name				Apparent injuries? ☐ Yes ☐ No
Home Address		City	State	Zip
Home phone		Business phone		

10.2.4.2.1   Scene Sketch

Ask the client to diagram the accident as he or she remembers it. This type of active, graphic participation will help the client get the facts straight, and the investigator can verify and authenticate a client's story.

10.2.4.2.2   Photographing the Accident Scene

Although reports and documentation are necessary parts of investigative technique, photographs of the accident scene are vital pieces of evidence. Investigators should become proficient photographers or develop strong relationships with police photographers, or private photographers who work as independent contractors with police departments. Photographic coverage of an accident scene should provide a panorama and proper perspective which includes:

1. *Approach to the scene.* From the viewpoint of the driver or drivers involved. It may be necessary to make several photographs of the scene at different distances. Make these from the driver's eye level as he or she would be seated in the vehicle. Remember that the high cab of a tractor-trailer rig may place the driver as much as eight feet from the ground. Climb on a tow truck or station wagon tailgate to get the needed height.
2. *Eyewitness's viewpoint.* To corroborate eyewitness statements, make pictures of the scene from the eyewitness's position and eye level.

3. *Position of the vehicles.* Try to get shots of the final position of vehicles before they are moved. If they must be moved before they can be photographed, mark their positions with chalk or tape.
4. *Position of victims.* Where victims are thrown clear of the vehicles, get photographs of the position of a body or mark the position of an injured victim who is being removed for treatment.
5. *Point of impact.* If it is possible, determine and photograph the point of impact of the vehicle or vehicles involved in the accident. This may correspond to the final position of the vehicles, or it may be some distance from that point. Relate the two in a photograph if possible.
6. *Overall view of scene.* One or several pictures that relate the overall scene elements can be useful to the accident investigator. One viewpoint for such photographs is a high position overlooking the scene; a rooftop, an embankment, a bridge, or even a truck can provide a commanding position. Other overall shots can be made with the camera at eye level in the direction of vehicle travel and then by looking back through the scene from the opposite direction to show the area of approach.
7. *Close-ups of accident details.* Details of vehicle damage, skid marks, tire marks, worn or damaged tires, registration plates, oil-water-gasoline spills, and broken parts provide key information to aid the accident investigator. Photograph questionable items within the car such as wine, beer, and liquor bottles; narcotics; or firearms.[30]

The Center for Public Safety at Northwestern University, a preeminent research center on traffic investigation, suggests this accident scene photography protocol:
What to photograph

1. Vehicle identification
   a. Vehicle license plate
   b. Vehicle identification plate
   c. Vehicle's make and model

2. Contact damage area
   a. Overlap
   b. Collapse
   c. Direction of thrust

3. Induced damage area
4. Undamaged area
5. Interior—when needed
6. Vehicle lamps (if there is a question regarding #6 and #7, take picture)
7. Vehicle tires
8. Close-up photographs[31]

The Center also recommends that each picture be charted as to shutter speed, focal point, distance, and depth of field.

10.2.4.2.3 Auto Accident Reconstruction

Investigators involved in traffic accident investigation will be confronted with a myriad of problems from the simple to the complex. "Like many other specialized activities, traffic accident investigation may be done at various levels or degrees of technology depending on the needs and the resources available."[32] Northwestern University's Traffic Institute,[33] now known as the Center for

Public Safety, a private, nonprofit organization founded in 1936, has provided accident reconstruction services to law enforcement, criminal justice, private security, and highway transportation agencies. Private investigators wishing to enhance professional standing in accident reconstruction may wish to participate in one of the Traffic Institute's many educational programs. The webpage regarding its Crash Investigation Course is at Figure 10.4.[34]

The Center distinguishes five levels of traffic accident investigation:

1. Reporting
2. Supplementary data collection
3. Technical preparation
4. Professional reconstruction
5. Cause analysis

At the first level, the investigator *identifies* and *classifies* the accident conditions, persons, and property involved. Reports and other documents discussed throughout this text are filled out indicating time of day, location, environment, damage to vehicles and drivers, pedestrians, passengers, witnesses, and officials on the scene.

Companies such as SmartDraw and Virtual CRASH deliver virtual reconstructions such as Figures 10.5[35] and 10.6.[36]

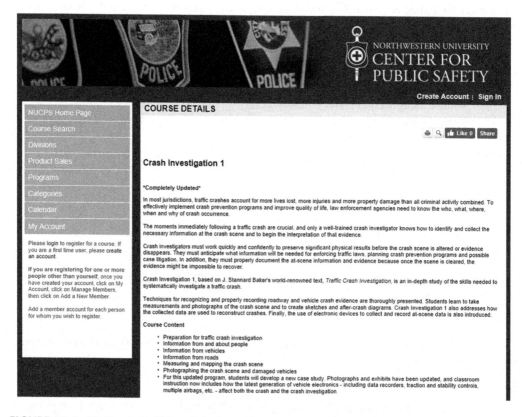

FIGURE 10.4 Northwestern University's Center for Public Safety is one university providing courses on accident reconstruction and crash investigation. (Used with permission, Northwestern University, Center for Public Safety.)

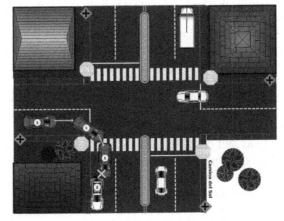

smartdraw   Home Diagrams Solutions Templates Features Buy Blog   Try it Now

Accident Reconstruction

1. WHAT IS AN ACCIDENT RECONSTRUCTION DRAWING? >

2. HOW TO DRAW AN ACCIDENT RECONSTRUCTION SKETCH >

3. ACCIDENT RECONSTRUCTION TUTORIAL VIDEO >

4. WHY CAR ACCIDENT DRAWINGS WIN CLAIMS >

5. ACCIDENT DIAGRAM EXAMPLES >

With SmartDraw, You Can Create More than 70 Different Types of Diagrams, Charts, and Visuals.

What is an Accident Reconstruction Drawing?

Accident reconstruction drawings are visual recreations or sketches of an accident. They normally depict the accident and the surrounding area, as well as the vehicles and people involved. They're created using eyewitness reports, photos, security footage, and physical evidence.

FIGURE 10.5 Companies like SmartDraw offer useful software to generate sketches recreating accident scenes. (Used with permission, SmartDraw, LLC.)

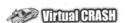

Virtual CRASH   HOME   PRODUCTS   INDUSTRIES   SALES   FREE TRIAL
SCHEDULE A DEMO   USER SUPPORT   MORE

How it works

Create the environment

Build surfaces from point clouds, total station measurements, or from scratch with our 3D modeling tools, and use our CAD tools to embellish and add important details.

Drop in objects

Drag and drop your vehicles, pedestrians, and other objects into your environment, use the incredibly intuitive controls to input simulation parameters or path animation data.

Execute and analyze

Run the simulation, or use the path animation tool, and watch Virtual CRASH execute your scenario. Easily refine your work using the real-time feedback from the ultra-fast physics engine. Use the graphing tool and data reports to help with your analysis.

Render

Once you've perfected your simulation or animation scenario, export still images or render a fully animated output with incredibly life-like detail.

FIGURE 10.6 Virtual CRASH is a provider of accident reconstruction software. (Used with permission, vCRASH, Americas, Inc.)

At the second level, the *supplementary data* phase, the initial accident report is supplemented by the following:

- Measurements to locate final positions of vehicles and bodies of persons killed or injured
- Measurements to locate tire marks, gouges, debris left on the road
- Photos of final positions of vehicles
- Photos of tire marks, gouges, and debris left on the road
- Descriptions of damage to vehicles and measurements of collision
- Photos of damage to vehicles
- Blood samples for alcohol tests
- Informal statements of people involved and other witnesses
- Preliminary matching of contact damage between vehicles and between vehicles and road surface or fixed objects
- Descriptions and photos of damage to such equipment as lamps, tires, batteries, safety belts, and obtaining these for test if possible
- Samples of paint and glass for examination
- Chemical tests for intoxication
- Autopsies to determine cause of death
- Medical descriptions of injuries[37]

Proceeding to the third level, *technical preparation*, the investigator begins to map out or graphically portray the incident. It may involve activities such as:

- Elementary ground photogrammetry
- Mapping from perspective template photos
- Matching vehicle damage areas and preparing maximum engagement, first contact, and disengagement diagrams
- Preparation of after-accident situation map
- Simple speed estimates from skid marks, yaw marks, and falls
- Determination of design speed and critical speed of curves and turns[38]

Yaw marks and other reference points can be photographically examined.

As discussed earlier, the investigator's comprehension of the accident site will be fostered by a scene sketch or other descriptive means. To construct an accident map, the investigator should follow the step-by-step instructions below.

1. Decide detail needed based on how map will be used:
    a. For *working* (reconstruction) *purposes*, minimum detail
    b. For *display* (court) *purposes*, additional detail for realism

2. Determine layout of roadways by inspection.
    a. Single roadway:
        (1) Straight or curved
        (2) Number of lanes
    b. Junction of two or more roadways:
        (1) Number of legs
        (2) Number of lanes in each leg
        (3) Which roadway edges align without offset or angle
        (4) What angles between roadways are not right angles
3. Draw on field sketch basic layout of roadways. Use light lines. Show approximate widths, angles, and curves (freehand).

4. Connect all edges which align by dashed line on field sketch.

5. If any leg is not square with the others, project one edge of it until it intercepts the edge of another leg to form an intercept.

6. Select reference point or points (RPs). Mark it on field sketch. Write description of RP on field sketch.

7. Mark accident RPs on field sketch if they are known.

8. Draw in edge returns (curves between edges of roadways), shoulders, sidewalks, etc., which may be needed.

9. Draw roadside objects which may be needed (fixed objects, etc.).

10. Draw in other things (buildings, fences, etc.) needed for display.

11. Indicate measurements to be made by dimension lines from coordinates or RPs to items 3, 5, 7, 8, 9, and 10 above. Show measurements in series as much as possible (a series of measures from one point along a line).

12. Show additional measurements for curves and angles.

13. Add check measurements between important points.

14. Mark road surface (RP, etc.) if needed. Use yellow crayon.

15. Make measurements indicated. Record on field sketch.

16. Note grades, elevations, and character of surface. Record if needed.

17. Show north by arrow. (Add accident identifiers.)

18. Identify location by road name and, if needed, distance and direction to recognizable landmark. Give city or county and state.

19. Sign and date field sketch.[39]

At the fourth level of accident scene investigation, professional reconstruction, the investigator—after gathering all information and graphically reproducing it—attempts to define the accident in order to pose an explanation. While not arriving at a specific cause or amassing enough evidence to deduce legal causation, the fourth level of accident analysis seeks "opinions, deductions, and inferences ... usually in the form of estimates of speed, position on the road, and visibility; descriptions of driving tactics (evasive action), strategy, communications, and how injuries were received; or proof of law violations and who was driving."[40]

In the final stage of accident reconstruction, "cause analysis," a conclusion as to the actual cause is determined. Conceptually, the accident reconstruction now defines circumstances and events, relays why the accident occurred, and gives direct or conditional explanations. The investigator's position can include, but is not restricted to, the following findings:

- Probable contribution of road or vehicle design deficiencies to accident, injury, and damage occurrence
- Probable contribution of bystanders to accident and injury occurrence
- Probable contribution of temporary road or vehicle conditions to accident and injury, and damage occurrence
- Probable contribution of temporary driver conditions (such as intoxication) to accident and injury occurrence
- Complete combination of probable and possible factors contributing to tactical (evasive action) failures in the highway transport system
- Complete combination of probable and possible factors contributing to strategy (precautionary measures) that prevented successful tactics or otherwise influenced the outcome of events
- Recommendations for prevention of future accidents with some of the same factors as the one under study[41]

Even a lifetime of field experience will not enable the investigator to claim perfection in auto accident analysis and reconstruction. As insurance companies seek ways of defending the onslaught of accident litigation, private security and its investigative cadre serve as the objective third party that provides information without bias or prejudice.

10.3   SPECIAL PROBLEMS: AUTO THEFT, FRAUD, AND PARTS PILFERAGE

Crime statistics point to an escalating rate of auto theft, a definitive rise in illegal trafficking in auto parts, the establishment of chop shops and underground operations that steal cars, strip them, and sell individual parts. The National Crime Insurance Bureau (NCIB) was formed in 1992 from a merger between the National Automobile Theft Bureau (NATB) and the Insurance Crime Prevention Institute (ICPI). The NATB—which managed vehicle theft investigations and developed vehicle theft databases for use by the insurance industry—dates to the early 20th century, while the ICPI investigated insurance fraud for approximately 20 years before joining with the NATB. The primary purpose of the NCIB is to lead a united effort of insurers, law enforcement agencies, and representatives of the public to prevent and combat insurance fraud and crime though data analytics, investigations, training, legislative advocacy, and public awareness.

Web Exercise: Visit the National Insurance Crime Bureau's website at www.nicb.org/.

To combat this plague of fraud, collusion, and thievery, the insurance industry, auto dealers, manufacturers, and legislative agencies have called upon the services of private investigators to pinpoint the location and identification of suspect motor vehicle practices. Investigators should cautiously evaluate an affidavit of vehicle theft, filed at either the local police department or insurance company for the purpose of claim reimbursement. Figure 10.7 shows one such form.

Investigators need to cautiously evaluate claims and allegations, especially when certain insured profiles and personalities appear. Be skeptical of an insured, a claimant, who:

- Gives address and phone number of a bar, hotel, or motel as a place where he can be contacted
- Is unavailable or difficult to contact
- Has family members or household who know nothing about the loss
- Avoids the use of the U.S. Mail
- Has income incompatible with the amount of the car payment
- Is a single male under 28 years of age
- Is unemployed
- Is in arrears with lienholder
- Has no prior business with the insurer
- Is in an extreme hurry to settle the claim
- Has made recent inquiry into policy coverages
- Wishes to retain title on a total loss

The type of vehicle is also instructive regarding potential fraud, theft, or collusion. Fraudulent activity favors selected types of vehicles due to demand and costs of parts in the underground marketplace. Some pertinent questions in this regard are:

- Is it a late model, expensive auto?
- Is the vehicle expensively customized?
- Are there expensive extras and accessories?
- Has the vehicle been rebuilt from a prior major collision claim?
- Is the vehicle inefficient on fuel?
- Is the Vehicle Identification Numbering (VIN) suspect?
- Does the recovered vehicle have no collision damage?
- Has the vehicle been stolen, subsequently recovered, and then shortly thereafter been burned?

Received	
Dispatched	
Arrived	

Police Department
Property Crimes Bureau
Auto Theft Detail
Stolen Vehicle Agreement & Affidavit

Case/Report number:_____

Name of registered owner of stolen vehicle (printed): _____
Name of reporting person (printed): _____
ID type: _____ID #:_____DOB: _____

Description of stolen vehicle:

MAKE_____MODEL_____YEAR_____
STYLE_____COLOR_____VIN _____
LICENSE_____STATE_____LIEN HOLDER _____
INSURANCE COMPANY_____POLICY#_____
FURTHER VEHICLE DESCRIPTION:_____

I _____ certify that the above-described vehicle was taken without my
knowledge or permission from_____ between the time span of
_____.

Due to the number of stolen vehicle reports the Police Department receives, it is necessary that:

- I immediately notify the P.D. if I become aware of the location of the stolen vehicle. ____(INITIAL)

- I agree to assist in the prosecution of the theft of my vehicle._____(INITIAL)

It is unlawful for a person to knowingly make to a law enforcement agency of either this state or a political subdivision of this state a false, fraudulent or unfounded report or statement or to knowingly misrepresent a fact for the purpose of interfering with the orderly operation of a law enforcement agency or misleading a peace officer. False Reporting to a law enforcement agency is a **class 1 misdemeanor** punishable up to six months in jail, $2,500 fine and three years probation. Furthermore, it is unlawful for a person to knowingly destroy, remove, conceal, encumber, convert, sell, transfer, control, or otherwise deal with property subject to a security interest with the intent to hinder or prevent the enforcement of that interest. Defrauding Secured Creditors is a **class 6 felony** punishable up to 1.5 years in jail, and up to a $150,000 fine.

IF THE AFFIDAVIT IS NOT TAKEN IN PERSON BY A LAW ENFORCEMENT OFFICER OR AGENCY, THE PERSON WHO ALLEGES THAT A THEFT OF MEANS OF TRANSPORTATION HAS OCCURRED SHALL MAIL OR DELIVER THE SIGNED AND NOTARIZED AFFIDAVIT TO THE APPROPRIATE LOCAL LAW ENFORCEMENT AGENCY WITHIN SEVEN (7) DAYS AFTER REPORTING THE THEFT. IF THE APPROPRIATE LAW ENFORCEMENT AGENCY DOES NOT RECEIVE THE SIGNED AND NOTARIZED AFFIDAVIT WITHIN THIRTY (30) DAYS AFTER THE INITIAL REPORT, THE VEHICLE INFORMATION SHALL BE REMOVED FROM THE DATABASES OF THE NATIONAL CRIME INFORMATION CENTER AND THE ARIZONA CRIMINAL JUSTICE INFORMATION SYSTEM.

_____
Signature of Reporting Person   Date/Time

_____
Complete Address

_____
Home Phone   Cell Phone   Work Phone

_____
Officer Signature   Serial #   Date/Time

Subscribed and sworn to me on this_____day of _____, 20____.
Notary Public_____

My Commission Expires:_____

FIGURE 10.7 A stolen vehicle theft agreement and affidavit.

In this way, the investigator is always searching patterns, trends, special characteristics, and unique factors that make it more likely than not a fraud might be occurring. Other factors to consider when making these judgments are:

- Type of car
- Time of the theft
- Day of the week
- Location of vehicle when stolen
- Suspects or vehicles seen
- Location of vehicle when recovered
- Condition of vehicle when recovered

Use the auto theft fraud indicator checklist at Box 10.11 as a guide to this type of investigation.

BOX 10.11   A COMPREHENSIVE LIST OF AUTO THEFT FRAUD INDICATORS FOR INVESTIGATORS

Auto Theft Fraud Indicators

1. Policy in effect ninety (90) days or less, or recent vehicle purchase.
2. Auto stolen while not in possession of insured.
3. In arrears with lienholder.
4. The vehicle was a previously recovered theft or the subject of a prior major collision claim.
5. Insured furnished address and phone number of a bar, hotel, or motel as a place to be contacted by the claims adjuster.
6. The insured has failed to report the theft to the police.
7. The insured is unable to identify himself (i.e., does not know his own social security or driver's license number)
8. Late notice of theft to insurance company or police.
9. Any discrepancy in VIN or license plate numbers.
10. Cash purchase from an individual rather than a dealer.
11. The vehicle was alleged to have been stolen prior to titling and registration.
12. The previous owner cannot be located or is unknown to the insured.
13. Mail address differs from garaging address on policy.
14. Date of coverage and date of claim are closely related.
15. Title or proof of ownership is a duplicate issue or from a distant state.
16. The insured has just recently titled the vehicle in his name.
17. The insured presents an assigned title, still in the name of the previous owner, as proof of his ownership.
18. The insured is unable to produce title or proof of ownership.
19. Time and location of loss are suspicious—usually away from insured's premises and in the evening.
20. The vehicle is reported to be expensively customized or a show model.
21. The vehicle has become unpopular for any reason (i.e., inefficient to operate, difficult to find repair parts, has received unfavorable press coverage concerning safety, etc.).
22. Members of the insured's family or household know nothing about the loss.
23. Insured has little or no liability coverage.
24. Insured quickly pressures for claim settlement including threats of complaints to Insurance Commissioner.
25. Demands car settlement in lieu of replacement.

Aside from auto theft, auto fraud—which involves intentional deceit and trickery, the investigator will also encounter intentional misstatements to cover up other illegal activity. Fraudulent reporting of a stolen vehicle may serve an ulterior and underhanded purpose such as:

1. To cover up a hit-and-run accident
2. To cover up a one-car accident to beat the deductible
3. To cover an accident in which operators are under the influence of alcohol or drugs
4. To cover the need for extensive repairs such as new transmission, new motor, new paint job
5. Has large vehicle with large gasoline consumption
6. To purchase a good vehicle, export it by selling to foreign country, then report as stolen
7. Import fraud—to allege purchase of a vehicle from outside the United States, obtain the vehicle, then report as stolen.
8. Strip fraud—to purchase a vehicle, strip unit of most of its parts, return it, and claim it was recovered in stripped condition

At a minimum, the investigator should always be dubious of auto theft claims when these factual scenarios exist:

- Ownership of the vehicle is very recent.
- Vehicle was purchased from a private individual.
- Vehicle was purchased out of state.
- The insured presents an assigned title with the previous owner's name still on it.
- Previous owner cannot be located.
- Payment for vehicle is made in cash.
- Duplicate title or no title is available.
- The loss occurred shortly after obtaining an insurance policy.
- Fire loss occurred at night in an out-of-the-way location.
- Notice of loss was not timely.
- Recovered vehicle had heavy collision damage.
- Reported to police rather than through insurance agency.
- Not reported to police at all.
- Loss occurred prior to final title and registration.

10.3.1 AUTO IDENTIFICATION SYSTEMS

Investigators have to become proficient in the workings of the various auto identification systems—from the emblazoned, impressed numbers on block and engine to the universal VIN designation and to new computer coding on vehicles which are a sort of auto DNA. Each of these systems has the capacity to connect the perpetrator to a particular vehicle.

10.3.1.1 VIN Systems

Automobiles are identified by several methods, including insurance identification number, title, registration, and other motor vehicle documentation. Identification of a vehicle at its point of manufacturing origin is accomplished through the Vehicle Identification Numbering (VIN) system. The VIN method of vehicle marking and identification is an impressive defense mechanism because foreign and domestic automakers make a concerted effort to inscribe, without chance of alteration or obliteration, identification numbers at selected points on a vehicle. These identification numbers are stamped and registered at the factory. The engine and vehicle identification numbers are used on legal documents and recorded upon transfer.

Web Exercise: Visit the NICB to learn about their VINCheck program at www.nicb.org/how-we-help/vincheck.

Under rules established by the National Highway Traffic Safety Administration, specifically Federal Motor Vehicle Safety Standard 115, commencing in 1981, all motor vehicles must adopt a vehicle identification numbering system. The VIN is a series of 17 alpha-numeric characters. For vehicles with a gross vehicle weight of 10,000 pounds or less, the VIN must be located inside the passenger compartment adjacent to the left windshield pillar and readable from the outside of the vehicle. For vehicles with a gross vehicle weight rating of more than 10,000 pounds, location and visibility requirements are not specified. All VINs shall appear clearly and indelibly upon either a part of the vehicle, other than the glazing, that is not designed to be removed except for repair or upon a separate label or plate which is permanently affixed to such a part. Figure 10.8 illustrates the basis of the VIN system.

Auto manufacturers designate specific areas on each model for identification number placement. See Figure 10.9.

10.3.1.2 Parts

Identification numbers are also placed on certain parts of a vehicle. Because of the high cost of parts replacement, the crude practices of chop shops and the ease with which engines, transmissions, and other selected parts can be sold, manufacturers have inscribed identification numbers on engines and transmissions. As a rule, the number is derivatively based upon the VIN.

As the price of replacement parts has risen, automobile manufacturers have embarked on parts identification programs. Probably the most advanced contribution is from General Motors Corporation, which, in 1980, established a special parts marking program by which parts such as luggage lids, fenders, doors, and other body panels are labeled. The labels consist of a special brand of security film, approximately 2.25 inches wide and 6.25 inches high. The label is designed so that once it is affixed to the surface, any attempt to remove it will result in the border pulling away from the window, which will destroy the integrity of the label. Under ordinary light, the label will appear

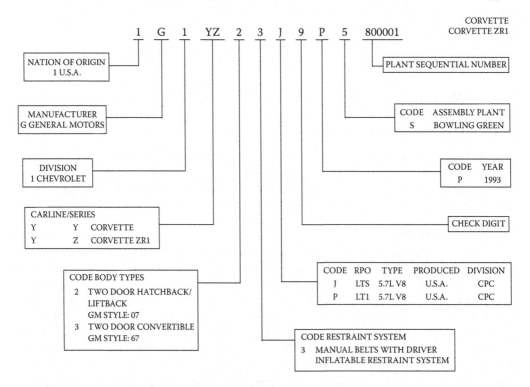

FIGURE 10.8   The Vehicle Identification Numbering (VIN) system.

MOST COMMON LOCATION

Driver Side Interior Dash

1969 and newer cars will have the VIN on the drivers side dash viewable through the windshield.

● Additional Possibilities
Trunk (under spare)
Driver Door Jam (open door)
Bach Wheel Well

Where is your VIN?

Here are some common suggestions. but not the only places that the VIN may appear. Consult your dealership or the vehicle manufacturere if you have problems locating your VIN.

Sample Vehicle Shown

Front of Engine Block
Raise hood and look at front of engine.

Stamped on Front End of Frame
You can see it by looking down between your front carb and your windshield washer unit. Most likely older cars.

FIGURE 10.9   Locations of VIN placement.

light blue in color. It can be authenticated by examination under retro-reflective light. This is accomplished by using an inexpensive retro-reflective viewer, available from several commercial sources, or by holding a flashlight parallel to and at the same level as the viewer's eye. Under retro-reflective light, an authentic label will display a pattern of GM logos across the entire face of the label. The lack of such a pattern or discontinuity in the pattern will indicate counterfeit products.

To stay on the cutting edge of this complex field, private investigators should strongly consider membership in the International Association of Auto Theft Investigators.

Web Exercise: Visit the Web location of the IAAYI at: www.iaati.org.

10.4   CONCLUSION

This chapter covered the most frequently encountered insurance investigations witnessed in the private security industry. Commencing with auto policy and its parameters of liability and ending with security measures to protect auto parts, the reader was exposed to many investigative regimens. In addition, the chapter fully covered workers' compensation, disability and accident analysis, and accident reconstruction. The chapter emphasizes the practical steps that need to be taken in these various settings and delivers a wide series of documents and practice forms.

NOTES

1. Association of Certified Fraud Examiners, Insurance Fraud Handbook (2018), accessed September 9, 2018, www.acfe.com/uploadedfiles/acfe_website/content/documents/insurance-fraud-handbook.pdf.
2. Ibid.: 1.
3. For information on the scope of the problem in the insurance industry, see FBI News, "Investigating Insurance Fraud: A $30-Billion-a-Year Racket," January 31, 2012, www.fbi.gov/news/stories/investigating-insurance-fraud.
4. See a protocol for investigative practice in four basic steps at Joseph L. Giacalone, "Four Basic Steps in Fraud Investigation," http://blogs.lexisnexis.com/public-safety/2015/06/fraud-investigation-basic-steps.

5. Pinkerton's Inc., *Investigation-Insurance Claims* (1990): 3; James E. Whitaker, *Insurance Fraud Handbook* (Association of Certified Fraud Examiners, 2018), www.acfe.com/uploadedfiles/acfe_website/content/documents/insurance-fraud-handbook.pdf; Giacalone, "Four Basic Steps."

6. See Denise Johnson, "Tips and Tools for Insurance Fraud Investigations," *Claims Journal*, June 5, 2014, www.claimsjournal.com/news/national/2014/06/05/249845.htm.

7. Steven W. Carman, "The State of Forensic Science: Science Trumps Art in Fire Investigation," *Texas Bar Journal* 74 (July 2011): 587.

8. J. J. Lentini, "The Evolution of Fire: Investigation and Its Impact on Arson Cases," *Criminal Justice* 27, no. 1 (2012): 12; see also Gregory E. Gorbett, Brian J. Meacham, Christopher B. Wood, and Nicholas A. Dembsey, "Use of Damage in Fire Investigation: A Review of Fire Patterns Analysis, Research and Future Direction," *Fire Science Reviews* 4, no. 4 (2015).

9. National Institute of Justice, *Sourcebook of Justice Statistics* (1988); Shelly King and Michael L. McCabe, "Whose Fire Scene Is This Anyway?" *Forensic Examiner* 20, no. 2 (Summer 2011): 74–77.

10. Richard N. Kocsis, "Arson: Exploring Motives and Possible Solutions," *Trends &Issues in Crime and Criminal Justice*, August 2002: 1; Johnson, "Tips and Tools"; Joseph L. Giacalone, "Four Basic Step in a Fraud Investigation," http://blogs.lexisnexis.com/public-safety/2015/06/fraud-investigation-basic-steps.

11. Justin A. Geiman and James M. Lord, "Systematic Analysis of Witness Statements for Fire Investigation," *Fire Technology* 48 (2012): 227, doi:10.1007/s10694-010-0208-3.

12. Mary R. Williams and Michael Sigman, "Performance Testing of Commercial Containers for Collection and Storage of Fire Debris Evidence," *Journal of Forensic Science* 52 (2007): 579; Steven W. Carman, "The State of Forensic Science: Science Trumps Art in Fire Investigation," *Texas Bar Journal* 74 (July 2011): 587; Lentini, "The evolution of fire."

13. International Association of Arson Investigators, Inc., accessed July 22, 2018, www.firearson.com.

14. National Association of Fire Investigators, accessed July 22, 2018, www.nafi.org.

15. International Association of Fire Investigators, accessed July 22, 2018, www.internationalassociationof-fireinvestigators.com.

16. "Arriving at the Fire and/or Arson Scene: Evaluating the Scene," Office of Justice Programs, National Institute of Justice, accessed July 22, 2018, www.nij.gov/topics/law-enforcement/investigations/crime-scene/guides/fire-arson/Pages/evaluate.aspx.

17. "Management for Arson Prevention and Control," (US Fire Administration and National Fire Academy.

18. Lori Chordas, "Eye in the sky: drones will soon fly to new heights to investigate fraudulent workers' compensation claims." *Best's Review*, March 2016: 96.

19. Rebecca A. Shafer, "'Loss' From Employer's Fraud on Insurers Is Unpaid Workers' Compensation Premiums," *Criminal Law Reporter* 83 (2008): 752; "Workers Comp Cost Containment Starts with Post-Injury Investigation," Lexis Nexis Legal News Room, October 24, 2013, www.lexisnexis.com/legalnewsroom/workers-compensation/b/recent-cases-news-trends-developments/archive/2013/10/24/workers-comp-cost-containment-starts-with-post-injury-investigation.aspx?Redirected=true;   Stacey Golden, "3 keys to a successful workers' compensation fraud investigation," July 23, 2015, *Property Casualty 360*, www.propertycasualty360.com/2015/07/23/3-keys-to-a-successful-workers-compensation-fraud/?slreturn=20180622132116; AMIS/Alliance Marketing &Insurance Services, AOE/COE Investigative Report &Investigation Procedure, www.amisinsurance.com/content/AOE-COE_investigative_report_and_investigation_procedures.php.

20. See: Shafer, "Cost Containment."

21. North Carolina Bar Foundation, *VI Practical Skills Course, Workers' Compensation* (1988) 36; Golden, "3 keys."; Steven Babitsky, "Investigating Workers' Compensation Claims," https://www.seak.com/blog/workers-compensation/investigating-workers-compensation-claims/

22. See MCL 418.301

23. MCL 418.361

24. Pinkerton's, Investigation, "Using Your Camera on an Insurance Investigation;" Steven Babitsky, "Investigating Workers' Compensation Claims," https://www.seak.com/blog/workers-compensation/investigating-workers-compensation-claims/; Golden, "3 keys."

25. Social Security Administration, Office of the Inspector General, "Cooperative Disability Investigations," https://oig.ssa.gov/cooperative-disability-investigations-cdi.

26. Ibid. at 4.

27. Ibid.

28. James E. Whitaker, *Insurance Fraud Handbook* (Association of Certified Fraud Examiners, 2018) http://www.acfe.com/uploadedfiles/acfe_website/content/documents/insurance-fraud-handbook.pdf; For an excellent series of resources for the Accident Investigator, visit: "Accident Reconstruction &Investigator Liability Insurance Coverage," Alliance Marketing &Insurance Services, http://www.amisinsurance.com/lines/accident_reconstruction_insurance.php

29. W. Strobl, The Investigator's Handbook (Butterworth Heinemann, 1984) 90; Whitaker, "Handbook."

30. Eastman Kodak Co., Photography in Traffic Accident Investigation (1979) 4; "Tips for Car Accident Scene Photography," Findlaw.com, accessed July 22, 2018, https://injury.findlaw.com/car-accidents/tips-for-car-accident-scene-photography.html; Falcon Transport, "Employee Handbook," accessed July 22, 2018, http://www.falcontransport.com/PDF%20Files/Handbook/Photos.pdf.

31. The Traffic Institute, *Vehicle Damage Photography* (SN 7717) 2–3; State of Texas, *Vehicle Damage Guide for Traffic Crash Investigators* (2015), ftp://ftp.dot.state.tx.us/pub/txdot-info/trf/crash_notifications/2015/crash-report-80.pdf.

32. The Traffic Institute, *Level of Traffic Accident Investigation* (SN 8000) 1; Texas, "Damage Guide."; Elvin Aycock, *Traffic Accident Reconstruction* (2010), accessed July 22, 2018,https://atu587.org/sites/default/files/Traffic%20Accident%20Reconstruction.pdf.

33. Northwestern University, The Center for Public Safety, 555 Clark St., Evanston, IL 60204.

34. "Crash Investigation I," Northwestern University, The Center for Public Safety, accessed September 12, 2018, https://registration.nucps.northwestern.edu/courseDisplay.cfm?schID=1301.

35. SmartDraw, https://www.smartdraw.com/accident-reconstruction.

36. Virtual Crash, http://www.vcrashusa.com/home.

37. Institute, "Investigation," 4; Texas, "Damage Guide."; Aycock, "Traffic Accident."

38. Institute, "Investigation," 5; Texas, "Damage Guide."; Aycock, "Traffic Accident."

39. The Traffic Institute, *Measuring for Maps* (SN 1097) 2; Texas, "Damage Guide."; Aycock, "Traffic Accident."

40. Institute, "Photography," 6; Texas, "Damage Guide."; Aycock, "Traffic Accident."

41. Institute, "Photography," 7; Texas, "Damage Guide."; Aycock, "Traffic Accident."

11 Investigative Method and Technique: Background Investigations

11.1 INTRODUCTION

The role of background investigations in the world of private security and its investigative arm ranks in the higher echelon of duties and responsibilities. A failure to conduct properly opens up the liability floodgates, triggers potential economic losses, and even poses threats to our national security. In 2013, a subcontractor for the United States government named Edward Snowden leaked classified information from the National Security Agency. Quickly following this security breach, the United States Congress launched two federal inquiries into what background investigation practices were being used that would let a person such as Snowden "slip through." What they found was that contractors like Snowden were not scrutinized to the same degree as regular government employees. Therefore, ironically, Snowden's intent to expose the government's surveillance systems actually provided the impetus for increased government scrutiny of new and ongoing background investigations[1] and in many ways increased the profile and importance of background investigations worldwide.

While the government may be concerned with the threat of espionage and terrorist activities, individuals, institutions, and businesses are all increasingly concerned about the identities, temperaments, and backgrounds of the people they hire and work with. Alcohol and drug addiction, the ease of document forgery, transcript alteration, and assumption of false names and backgrounds are all of concern, and consequently, background investigations make up an increasingly large portion of private security assignments.

Personal background checks are also important because of their capacity to measure what is at risk. Such investigations are necessary when giving an individual access to one's home or property, usually so that they can perform a service, e.g., a contractor or a full-time household employee such as a nanny or a housekeeper. Applications for these positions, and many others too large to enumerate, may contain false or other misleading information. By conducting thorough background checks, the homeowner increases the ability to protect possessions and keep loved ones safe. However, because personal background investigations are similar to but often—due to lack of resources—less extensive than business-related background investigations, this chapter focuses primarily on background checks conducted by businesses, institutions, and governments.

Within corporate settings, personnel departments greatly rely upon background reviews. Given the investment companies make in hire and placement, the need for a serious background investigation cannot be overemphasized. In response to 9/11, companies have increasingly relied on background checks for prospective employees. Generally conducted by a third party, basic checks include checks for a criminal record; date, source, and subject of educational credits; and dates and places of prior employment. But more and more often, companies are also gathering information on credit history, civil litigation, motor-vehicle record, even "mode of living" and character. According to William Cunningham and Todd Taylor, authors of the first *Hallcrest Report*:

> It is essential that a person hired for a specific position possesses the background, training, and skills stated in his or her résumé and employment application. Certain positions have special requirements for trust, deportment, confidentiality, and other character traits. For these positions, the organization must

be able to verify that there have been no previous adverse reflections on the candidate's character and that there are no tendencies toward inappropriate conduct.[2]

Business's natural hesitancy in believing an applicant's stated background displays intelligent discretion, especially when one considers the civil actions that can be brought against an employer who negligently retains and fails to terminate an employee.[3] In today's climate, the risks are both enormous and multiple, from checkered backgrounds of criminality to histories of abusive behavior, from a series of former employer terminations to disciplinary histories on the job, and allegations of harassment of any sort to a reputation for sexual impropriety, to name a few.

> Within the security community itself, there continues to be a lot of discussion on just how thoroughly this is accomplished. From the HR side, there can be questions regarding which background elements are relevant to the roles being hired, as well as cost and time affiliated with the processes.

> It's generally accepted that if a candidate falsifies major elements of their employment (i.e. education, employment history, etc.) on their application they will be rejected. The areas in which this is less clear are those related to ethics, reputation, professional and operational skills. These less obvious attributes are really the key identifiers in most job descriptions, but validating them becomes very nebulous.[4]

As J. Kirk Barefoot remarked:

> It is absolutely essential in building a healthy company to begin with the selection of persons who are inherently honest, or at least basically honest if the proper controls and procedures are in effect. Hiring persons who have a history of consistent employee theft only insures that security problems will continue to develop and that there will be always be plenty of work to occupy the investigation section of the security department.[5]

What's more, some businesses are too small to have security departments capable of conducting sophisticated background reviews, so initial background checks are truly their first and primary line of defense when it comes to protecting their business from internal theft. Yet many small businesses forgo this crucial hiring step as a cost-saving measure. In some cases, these efforts to save the few hundred dollars results in later, far more costly harm or even financial ruin or bankruptcy. Thus, background checks are central to business vitality and businesses that neglect such crucial hiring steps do so at their peril.

Finally, while businesses that are hiring may present the most obvious cases of needing to hire individuals or firms to help them conduct background checks, there are other circumstances when these investigations are warranted. In an age of terrorism and terrorists, the need to know exactly and precisely who the applicant or potential employee might be has never been more important. "Security professionals cannot assume the U.S. government has performed a background check on workers with a visa that relieves them of their due diligence obligation to conduct their own screening. Government efforts are not foolproof."[6]

Background checks have the capacity to protect investors in complex economic transactions and to prevent fraud and corruption in dealings with others, contract negotiations and compliance with national and international commerce standards.[7]

Background consulting firms are now common fixtures in business and industry.

At the federal and state level, individual private contractors, in some agencies, now conduct background investigations. For example, the Bureau of Alcohol, Tobacco, and Firearms uses private investigators to conduct background investigations. While the background investigation primarily pertains during the initial hiring phase for potential employment, these practices are now being employed post-employment. This type of perpetual screening has been termed "infinity" since "continuous screening, reoccurring screening and post-hire screening are synonymous and are used interchangeably. Infinity screening is taking hold because employers are beginning to learn and understand that pre-hire detection of problem behavior is not enough to forestall or foretell future bad behavior that creates risk for an organization."[8]

If an employee becomes a disciplinary problem while on the job an updated background check may make sense. In one case, an employee at a small business was caught stealing cash from the register. This employee planned to throw herself on the mercy of the court as a first-time offender, but by employing an investigator to look into this woman's background, the business owner learned that the employee already had a restitution agreement under a prior first-time offender engagement with another court. Furthermore, the investigator learned that she was also stealing money from a second, previous employer. In this scenario and others, the business owner corrals the necessary background information, both the good and the bad, to make subsequent decisions that are fully defensible.

11.2 BACKGROUND INVESTIGATION BASICS

While there are other circumstances when background investigations can be useful, their primary purpose and function is employee screening. Because employees actually and vicariously represent the business, especially when interacting with customers or clients, it is vital to the success and well-being of any business to make certain that its employees are honest, responsible, and reliable. Background investigations need to be sequential and corroborative. Jerry Brennan and Lynn Mattice suggest a step-by-step process in the background review.

1. Clearly state within the position description what your organization's expectation is regarding ethics and reputational issues that are relevant to the position.
2. Develop and ask relevant competency and behavioral questions during the interview process.
3. Obtain facts that can be substantiated.
4. Do not violate your organization's policy guidelines or the laws and regulations within the jurisdictions affected.
5. Encourage your organization to have a risk-based referencing process in place that goes beyond the basic transactional verifications.
6. Obtain the appropriate consents from the candidate.
7. Have a plan in place for how your organization will react should serious derogatory information be obtained, and put in practice an assessment methodology.
8. Make sure that your actions are ethically and legally defensible.[9]

Background investigations need be fair to all parties and those conducting these sorts of investigations should avoid special rules based on race, sex or gender, age or disability, creed, national origin and the like. "In all cases, make sure that you're treating everyone equally."[10]

That review commences with the resume—that early representation of self made to the employer. Resumes, for the most part, are honest portrayals of past and present positions although some resumes suffer from serious and inaccurate embellishment and even flat-out fraudulent representations. For example, claiming one has an academic degree from a selective institution needs to be verified, or representing some high-level certification or specialty cannot be taken at face value. Resume information needs to be corroborated and checked for accuracy. Furthermore, as corporate scandals have demonstrated, no company fully escapes the impact of employee misconduct. The damage from employee malfeasance can be devastating, ranging from financial losses to violation of law and regulatory jeopardy—all of which can ruin careers, reputations, and even the trust of existing and potential clients. Therefore, background checks are crucial for all businesses, large or small, to protect themselves from future calamity at the hands of their employees.

Web Exercise: Read the article about the different types of background checks and what they reveal at www.trustify.info/for-business/insight/different-types-of-background-checks.

Background assessment can take many forms, and the "screening procedures used should be based on the nature of the business, its resources for carrying out the procedures, and the security needs of the business."[11]

Oftentimes the level and depth of these screenings are categorized as standard background investigations or comprehensive due diligence investigations, with the former mostly comprised of verifying identification data and cross-checking with various databases, and the latter being more rigorous and thorough, sometimes involving human assets in gathering information about every aspect of an individual's adult life.[12] Complete descriptions of these two types of investigations can be found in Appendix A.

No matter what type of background investigation is conducted, consent must be gained from the party to be investigated in order for the investigation to proceed. Box 11.1 is an authorization to undertake a background investigation. As is evident on the form, various legal cases and legislation have mandated that it include clear statements about what the firm will do and why.

BOX 11.1   AN AUTHORIZATION AND RELEASE FORM TO ALLOW A BACKGROUND INVESTIGATION

Background Investigation Firm

BACKGROUND INVESTIGATION AUTHORIZATION AND RELEASE FORM

I hereby authorize BACKGROUND INVESTIATION FIRM (BIF) and its designated agents and representatives to conduct a background investigation, causing a consumer report and/or an investigative consumer report to be generated, for employment purposes.

I understand that the scope of the consumer report/investigative consumer report may include, but is not limited to, the following areas:

Verification of social security number; current and previous residences; employment history including all personnel files; education including transcripts; character references; credit history and reports; criminal history records from any criminal justice agency in any or all federal, state, county jurisdictions; birth records; motor vehicle records to include traffic citations and registration; and any other public records or to conduct interviews with third parties relative to my character, general reputation, personal characteristics, or mode of living.

I further authorize any individual, company, firm, corporation, or public agency (including the Social Security Administration and law enforcement agencies) to divulge any and all information, verbal or written, pertaining to me to (BIF) or its agents. I hereby release (BIF) its corporate affiliates, its employees, its authorized agents and representatives and all others involved in this background investigation from any liability in connection with any information they give or gather and any decisions made concerning my employment based on such information. Copies of this authorization are as valid as the original release signed by me. I believe to the best of my knowledge that all information I have provided is accurate and correct.

This release shall be in effect for the length of my employment. I understand that I have the right to request a written disclosure of the nature and scope of the investigation and I have the right to obtain a free copy of the consumer report if any adverse action/decision is made based on the information in the consumer report.

Print Name: _____

First   Middle   Last

Former Name(s):
Year most recently used   Name/Year   Name/Year*

Former Name(s):
Year most recently used   Name/Year   Name/Year*

Current Address Since: _____
Mo/Yr Street City State Zip

Previous Address From: _____
Mo/Yr Street City State Zip

Home Telephone Number: _____   Driver's License # / State: _____

Social Security Number: _____   Prof. License State / Type: _____

Date of Birth**: _____   Gender**: _____ Male _____ Female

Position Applying For: _____

**Information regarding age, sex, or race will not be used as part of any employment decision, and is being provided solely to assist in completing the background investigation.

Signature:_____   Date: _____

To be completed by client.

CLIENT NAME: _____   PHONE NUMBER: _____

EMAIL ADDRESS: _____   SIGNATURE: _____

Background Investigation Release Form (08/10/2015)

This type of background investigation waiver is a precondition of joining many companies. Overall, what the company is trying to discern is whether a potential employee is who he (or she) says he is, and whether he has a track record of criminal activity, data theft, violence, fraud, or negligence. By unearthing these elements in advance of hiring, the business reduces its chance of becoming a victim of any of these crimes.

The ability to determine the background of an individual in employment settings, surveillance operations, skip/trace analysis, or other matters depends upon access to the following types of records:

- Educational and school materials
- Employment information
- Neighborhood information
- Criminal background and court records
- Civil litigation and court records
- Credit and financial resources
- Personal references

Many security firms solely focus on this aspect of practice. See Figure 11.1.[13]

These sources of information have been discussed comprehensively in Chapter 5. This chapter's focus is a generic discussion of the investigative sequence used in establishing background history with specialized suggestions, forms, documents, and checklists of practical use to the private investigator. Figure 11.2 reviews the areas of a background investigation and can help the investigator refine the search process. An investigator's checklist, guiding the security professional through the facets of background checks, is shown in Figure 11.3. The investigator is reminded to adhere

Due Diligence Investigations

CIS aids clients in managing the risks of new investments and mergers and acquisitions by thoroughly screening potential business partners and target companies for signs of impropriety, misrepresentation, and other possible "deal-breakers". Our team of corporate investigative analysts can assist in determining the credibility of target companies and key executives through detailed investigation and assessment of criminal, civil, and financial histories. Our investigators can also assist in resolving key issues of concern through management and employee interviews, auditing of records and systems, forensic accounting, and digital forensic analysis.

Throughout the due diligence process, CIS investigators and analysts are especially attentive to confidentiality and the sensitivity of relations. Our experienced specialists know that one wrong move by an investigator can jeopardize a deal. By utilizing CIS investigative analysts, clients can be sure that critical investment and M&A decisions are based on accurate information while maintaining good relations and encouraging high enthusiasm for the deal.

Vendor Integrity

In most businesses today, reliable and ethical service by vendors is critical to maintaining sustained operations and profits. Mistakes in vendor selection and contracting can easily result in costly consequences such as lost productivity, fraud, civil liability, and damaged company image. CIS investigative analysts can aid companies in making informed vendor selection decisions by screening potential vendors for financial integrity, criminal history, work performance and capabilities, and legal history.

Background Investigations

In addition to due diligence and vendor integrity screening, CIS investigators can assist companies in screening the backgrounds of employees and contractors for indicators of criminality and potential violence. While many background investigation services only provide historical record data, our experienced investigators actively assist companies in analyzing background information to identify subtle patterns or indicators of potential problems that are often overlooked by human resources personnel.

FIGURE 11.1 Security firms can be invaluable in assessing the background of individuals on behalf of clients. (Used with permission, Critical Intervention Services, Inc.)

to federal, state, and local legislation bearing on background investigation practices and access to background information.

11.3 BACKGROUND ISSUES

From the outset, the investigator must understand the precise meaning of "background." Background encompasses a history of identity, personhood, and name verification coupled with residential

PRINT CHARACTERS LIKE THIS

ABCDE 98765

CORRECT INCORRECT

Applicant's First Name or Initial   Last Name

I understand that _____ ('COMPANY') will use _____ ('CONTRACTOR') to obtain a consumer report and/or investigative consumer report ("Report") as part of the hiring process. I also understand that if hired, to the extent permitted by law, COMPANY may obtain further Reports from CONTRACTOR so as to update, renew or extend my employment.

I understand _____ CONTRACTOR investigation may include obtaining information regarding my credit background, bankruptcies, lawsuits, judgments, paid tax liens, unlawful detainer actions, failure to pay spousal or child support, accounts placed for collection, character, general reputation, personal characteristics and standard of living, driving record and criminal record, subject to any limitations imposed by applicable federal and state law. I understand such information may be obtained through direct or indirect contact with former employers, schools, financial institutions, landlords and public agencies or other persons who may have such knowledge. If an investigative consumer report is being requested, I understand such information may be obtained through any means, including but not limited to personal interviews with my acquaintances and/or associates or with others whom I am acquainted.

The nature and scope of the investigation sought is indicated by the selected services below: **(Employer Use Only)**

☐ Criminal Background Check   ☐ Education Verification   ☐ Sex Offender Search

☐ SSN Trace   ☐ Employment Verification   ☐ OFAC/Terrorist Watch List

☐ Motor Vehicle Report   ☐ Personal Reference   ☐ Fraud & Abuse Control Info System (FACIS®)

☐ Consumer Credit Report   ☐ Professional License/Certification   ☐ Office of Inspector General Sanctions (OIG)

☐ Other Please List:

I acknowledge receipt of the attached summary of my rights under the Fair Credit Reporting Act and, as required by law, any related state summary of rights (collectively "Summaries of Rights").

This consent will not affect my ability to question or dispute the accuracy of any information contained in a Report. I understand if COMPANY makes a conditional decision to disqualify me based all or in part on my Report, I will be provided with a copy of the Report and another copy of the Summaries of Rights, and if I disagree with the accuracy of the purported disqualifying information in the Report, I must notify COMPANY within five business days of my receipt of the Report that I am challenging the accuracy of such information with

I hereby consent to this investigation and authorize COMPANY to procure a Report on my background.

In order to verify my identity for the purposes of Report preparation, I am voluntarily releasing my date of birth, social security number and the other information and fully understand that all employment decisions are based on legitimate non-discriminatory reasons.

The name, address and telephone number of the nearest unit of the consumer reporting agency designated to handle inquiries regarding the investigative consumer report is:

☐ **California, Maine, Massachusetts, Minnesota, New Jersey & Oklahoma Applicants Only:** I have the right to request a copy of any Report obtained by COMPANY from STERLING by checking the box. (Check only if you wish to receive a copy)

☐ **California, Connecticut, Maryland, Oregon and Washington State Applicants Only (AS APPLICABLE):** I further understand that COMPANY will not obtain information about my credit history, credit worthiness, credit standing, or credit capacity unless: (i) the information is required by law; (ii) I am seeking employment with a financial institution (California and Connecticut only – in California the financial institution must be subject to Sections 6801-6809 of the U.S. Code); (iii) I am seeking employment with a financial institution that accepts deposits that are insured by a federal agency, or an affiliate or subsidiary of the financial institution or a credit union share guaranty corporation that is approved by the Maryland Commissioner of Financial Regulation or an entity or an affiliate of the entity that is registered as an investment advisor with the United States Securities and Exchange Commission (Maryland only); (iv) **the information is substantially job related, and the bona fide reasons for using the information are disclosed to me in writing, (complete the question below)** (Connecticut, Maryland, Oregon and Washington only);(v) I am seeking employment as a covered police, officer , peace officer or other law enforcement position (California and Oregon only - in Oregon the police or peace officer position must be sought with a federally insured bank or credit union) , (vi) the COMPANY reasonably believes I have engaged in specific activity that constitutes a violation of law related to my employment (Connecticut only), (vii) I am seeking a position with the state Department of Justice (California only), (viii) I am seeking a position as an exempt managerial employee (California only), or (viii)) I am seeking employment in a position that involves regular access to personal

FIGURE 11.2 A form for prospective employees to sign and fill out that allows employers to perform a background check.

history, employment history, military background, legal and criminal background, as well as economic history relative to asset purchases, particularly homes and automobiles.[14]

Background is a composite of the subject under review, the sum of his or her parts so to speak and a method to match the historical person with the present picture being presented by the person under review. These assessments must not only account for a subject's national experience but also the international, more global history is definitely part of this review.[15]

A review of these various elements follows.

PRINT CHARACTERS LIKE THIS	CORRECT	INCORRECT
ABCDE 98765	●	⌀ ⊠ ◉

information of others (i.e., bank or credit card account information, social security numbers, dates of birth), other than regular solicitation of credit card applications at a retail establishment, I am seeking employment in a position that requires me to be a named signatory on the employer's bank or credit card or otherwise authorized to enter into financial contracts on behalf of the employer, I am seeking employment in a position that involves access to confidential or proprietary information of the Company or regular access to $10,000 or more in cash (California only).

Bona fide reasons why COMPANY considers credit information substantially job related (complete if this is the sole basis for obtaining credit information) or in California the COMPANY'S basis for the credit check.

_____

NY Applicants Only: I also acknowledge that I have received the attached copy of Article 23A of New York's Correction Law. I further understand that I may request a copy of any investigative consumer report by contacting   I further understand that I will be advised if any further checks are requested and provided the name and address of the consumer reporting agency.

California Applicants and Residents: If I am applying for employment in California or reside in California, I understand I have the right to visually inspect the files concerning me maintained by an investigative consumer reporting agency during normal business hours and upon reasonable notice. The inspection can be done in person, and, if I appear in person and furnish proper identification; I am entitled to a copy of the file for a fee not to exceed the actual costs of duplication. I am entitled to be accompanied by one person of my choosing, who shall furnish reasonable identification. The inspection can also be done via certified mail if I make a written request, with proper identification, for copies to be sent to a specified addressee. I can also request a summary of the information to be provided by telephone if I make a written request, with proper identification for telephone disclosure, and the toll charge, if any, for the telephone call is prepaid by or directly charged to me. I further understand that the investigative consumer reporting agency shall provide trained personnel to explain to me any of the information furnished to me; I shall receive from the investigative consumer reporting agency a written explanation of any coded information contained in files maintained on me. "Proper identification" as used in this paragraph means information generally deemed sufficient to identify a person, including documents such as a valid driver's license, social security account number, military identification card and credit cards. I understand that I can access the following website -   - to view   privacy practices, including information with respect to preparation and processing of investigative consumer reports and guidance as to whether my personal information will be sent outside the United States or its territories.

_____   _____

Signature: **Today's Date:**

FIGURE 11.2 (CONTINUED)

11.3.1 ESTABLISHING IDENTITY

The task of checking individual backgrounds and verifying identity, as in all facets of investigation, requires an orderly process. Box 11.2 lists the appropriate investigation sequence for identity analysis.

BACKGROUND VERIFICATION INFORMATION

Legal Name

First Name	Middle Initial	Last Name

Education Information (Highest Degree Attained)

Level of Education	
Name of School	
Year Graduated	Degree Awarded
School Phone/Location	
Have you used any other name while attending this institution? If yes, please indicate here:	

Employment Information (Please include previous 7 years of employment. Begin with most recent employer.)

Most Recent/Present Employer - Company Name		
Employed From		
Are You Presently Employed	☐ YES	☐ NO
Last Date Worked		
Position Title		
Company Address		

City	State	Zip Code

Supervisor	
Phone	
Reason for Leaving	

Company Name		
Employed From		
Last Date Worked		
Position Title		
Company Address		

City	State	Zip Code

Supervisor	
Phone	
Reason for Leaving	

I agree that the above information is correct and accurate and that no relevant information has been omitted.

_____   _____
Signature   Date

FIGURE 11.2 (CONTINUED)

Company Name		
Employed From		
Last Date Worked		
Position Title		
Company Address		
City	State	Zip Code
Supervisor		
Phone		
Reason for Leaving		

Company Name		
Employed From		
Last Date Worked		
Position Title		
Company Address		
City	State	Zip Code
Supervisor		
Phone		
Reason for Leaving		

Company Name		
Employed From		
Last Date Worked		
Position Title		
Company Address		
City	State	Zip Code
Supervisor		
Phone		
Reason for Leaving		

I agree that the above information is correct and accurate and that no relevant information has been omitted.

_____   _____

Signature   Date

FIGURE 11.2 (CONTINUED)

BACKGROUND INVESTIGATION CHECKLIST
PEACE OFFICER REQUIREMENTS

NAME				POSITION			

1. Documents Verified

TYPE OF DOCUMENT	DATE	BY	TYPE OF DOCUMENT	DATE	BY
Birth Date			Marriage Dissolution(s):		
Citizenship Requirement					
Educational Requirement					
Selective Svc Registration/Military Discharge					
Driver's License					

2. Reference Checks Completed

TYPE OF CONTACT	DATE PERSONAL CONTACT	LETTER MAILED	REPLY RECEIVED	BY	TYPE OF CONTACT	DATE PERSONAL CONTACT	LETTER MAILED	REPLY RECEIVED	BY
Relatives and References					**Employers, Supervisors, and Co-workers**				
Neighbors and Landlords					**Secondary References**				

FIGURE 11.3 A checklist to performing a background investigation.

BACKGROUND INVESTIGATION CHECKLIST continued
PEACE OFFICER REQUIREMENTS

NAME				POSITION			

3. Record Checks Completed

TYPE OF INQUIRY	DATE — LETTER MAILED	DATE — REPLY RECEIVED	BY	TYPE OF INQUIRY	DATE — LETTER MAILED	DATE — REPLY RECEIVED	BY
Educational Documents				**Legal Records**			
				FBI Record			
				CA Department of Justice			
				Firearms Clearance Letter			
Credit Records				Local LE Agency Checks:			
Military Records							
DMV Records							

4. Examinations Completed

TYPE OF SCREENING	DATE	BY	OTHER	DATE	BY
Medical Screening Completed					
Psychological Screening Completed					

5. Additional Actions Completed

TYPE OF ACTION	DATE	BY	COMMENTS
Applicant Orientation and Questionnaire Review (Optional)			
Applicant Discrepancy Interview, if any (Optional)			
Narrative Investigation Report Completed			

FIGURE 11.3 (CONTINUED)

BOX 11.2   THE INVESTIGATION SEQUENCE FOR AN IDENTITY ANALYSIS

1. Name Verification
   a. Telephone directory (either print or online)
   b. Credit records
   c. Pretext

2. Address Verification
   a. Telephone directory (either print or online)
   b. Credit records, etc.
   c. Pretext
   d. Utility bills
3. Voter Registration
   Check principals to identify full name, confirm address, place and date of birth, social security number (if available), spouse, and other residents of household.
4. Assumed/Fictitious Business Names
   In some states, this may be referred to as Fictitious Name, DBA (doing business as), or Fictitious Business Name.
5. Secretary of State
   Check Secretary of State records to confirm ownership of corporations and limited partnerships.
6. Property Tax Records
   Identify all properties, real and personal, owned by the individuals or companies at the time of the last tax roll, and obtain copies, if necessary.
7. County Clerk Records
   a. Pull all documents identified in the Appraisal/Assessor's Office.
   b. Obtain copies of all warranty deeds and deeds of trust for those properties identified.
   c. Check the indexes for any property transactions since the last tax roll up to the present date.
   d. Check indexes for properties sold in the last two years and obtain copies of the documents.
   e. Check indexes for liens and abstracts of judgments, to include releases, for the past five years, and obtain copies. Make notes of any other information identifiable with principals.
   f. Check for oil and gas information.
8. Filings
   Check Uniform Commercial Code filings (financing statements) at county and state levels, to identify assets other than real property.
9. Divorce Records
   Check divorce records at county level to obtain lists of property (assets) awarded in proceedings.
10. Bankruptcy
    Check bankruptcy records at servicing federal courts to obtain lists of assets and creditors, and statements of filings.
11. Federal Civil Cases
    Check federal civil records for judgments, pending cases, etc.

Access to records and information will vary by the locality but access, in every circumstance, is essential to success in the background investigation process. States and counties are somewhat more liberal than federal agencies in granting access to records. According to Bottom and Kostanoski:

Many public records are available to personnel directors and to security and loss control personnel. Each state has its own repository for workers' compensation claims. Each state has a central driver's license records center. Criminal records are available at the county level (over 3,000 in the United States) and at all state levels (with the exception of Nevada). Rules of access to these records vary from state to state. The vast majority of counties and/or state agencies will provide some information by telephone or letter. Computerized access to these records is expanding every year. All states and the District of Columbia will make driving records available to the public.[16]

Policies of access will depend on the type of institution as well. For example, educational institutions are guided by a host of privacy and data rules that make easy access an impossibility. While colleges and universities will allow confirmation of attendance or a degree granted, access to a transcript without the party's consent is nothing more than a pipedream. Federal agencies are more aggressively guided by "sunshine" or "right to know" policies than their state counterparts. As a result, federal records, such as criminal convictions, civil litigation records, federal tax liens, and bankruptcy filings are not difficult to acquire. Statutory designs and even internal agency and entity policies will have much to do with how much information can be garnered with or without the permission of the target.

11.3.2 EMPLOYMENT HISTORY

From the first day of application to the date of resignation, retirement, or termination, employment history manifests a great deal about the investigative subject. In employment settings, the application form serves as a significant tool in screening applicants and verifying the identities and conduct of present employees. The form should be a detailed document that is sensitive to legal issues. To accomplish its divergent purposes, an application should address a variety of topical concerns, including the applicant's name and address, citizenship, schooling, work experience, and other details. A comprehensive list of items that may be included on an employment application is:

- Request an applicant to write his/her name and address on an application.
- Ask an applicant if a complaint has been placed against him/her or if he/she has been indicted or convicted of a crime and under what name.
- Ask an applicant's age (only if the information is an occupational qualification).
- Explain to an applicant the hours and days he/she will be required to work.
- Ask if applicant is a U.S. citizen, or if he/she has the intent to become one.
- Ask about schooling, both academic and vocational.
- Inquire about relevant work experience.
- Inquire into his/her character and background.
- Ask for name, address, and relationship of person to be notified in case of an accident or emergency.
- Inquire into applicant's military experience in the U.S. armed forces. After hiring, ask to see discharge papers.
- Ask an applicant about memberships in organizations that may indicate race, religion, or national origin.
- Ask an applicant if he/she belongs to an organization advocating the overthrow of the U.S. government.
- Ask the sex of the applicant only where it constitutes a qualification for the job.[17]

Web Exercise: Read CNBC's article on why people fake their resumes at www.cnbc.com/2014/02/07/desperate-measures-why-some-people-fake-their-resumes.html.

Employers who design their own application forms need to be conscious of issues that raise red flags—particularly legal ones. Under some state and federal legislation, certain types of questions from prospective employers are inappropriate, such as an applicant's race, color, or religion. Federal consumer legislation in particular has restrictive guidelines regarding information an employer may or may not ask a prospective hire to reveal. This list includes:

- Asking an applicant whose name has been changed to disclose the original name
- Inquiring as to the birthplace of an applicant or applicant's family if outside the United States
- Requiring an applicant to produce discharge papers from the U.S. armed forces (before employment)

- Inquiring into foreign military experience
- Asking an applicant's age when it is not an occupational qualification or is not needed for state or federal minimum age laws
- Asking about an applicant's race or color
- Requiring an applicant to provide a photograph with the application
- Asking an applicant to disclose membership in organizations that may indicate race, religion, or national origin
- Asking a male applicant to provide the maiden name of his spouse or his mother
- Asking the place of residence of an applicant's spouse, parents, or relatives
- Inquiring whether an applicant's spouse or parents are naturalized or native citizens
- Asking an applicant his religion[18]

Federal consumer legislation promulgates guidelines regarding what may not be asked on a job application. These items include:

- Records of arrests, indictments, or conviction of crimes where the disposition of the case, release, or parole has been more than seven years prior to the date of application
- Any bankruptcies that have been more than fourteen years before the application
- Any paid tax liens, legal suits, or judgments, or other such information that has a harmful effect[19]

The use of court records to get an accurate portrayal of a subject is wise investigative strategy. Pay close attention to the many rules which guide access to those types of records. Use Box 11.3[20] as a guide.

BOX 11.3   TIP SHEET FOR SEARCH OF COURT RECORDS (USED WITH PERMISSION, BRB PUBLICATIONS, LLC.)

Tip Sheet for Searching Court Records

Below are a series of tips that should be kept in mind as you perform your record searching at the courts.

1. Learn the Index & Record Systems

    Most civil courts index records by both plaintiffs and defendants, but some only index by the defendant name. A plaintiff search is useful, for example, to determine if someone is especially litigious.

2. Understand the Search Requirements

    There is a strong tendency for courts to overstate their search requirements. For civil cases, the usual reasonable requirement is a defendant (or plaintiff) name – full name if it is a common name – and the time frame to search – e.g., 1993-2002. For criminal cases, the court may require more identification, such as date of birth (DOB), to ascertain the correct individual.

3. Be Aware of Restricted Records

    Courts have types of case records, such as juvenile and adoptions, which are not released without a court order. Records may also be sealed from view or expunged. The presiding judge often makes a determination of whether a particular record type is available to the public. Some criminal court records include the arresting officer's report. In some locations this information is regarded as public record, while in other locations the police report may be sealed.

4. Watch for Multiple Courts at Same Location

When the general jurisdiction and limited jurisdiction courts are in the same building and use the same support staff, chances are the record databases are combined as well. But that does not necessarily mean you will receive a search of both databases and pay for one search unless you ask for it. Do not assume.

5. Watch for Overlapping Jurisdictions

In some states, the general jurisdiction court and the limited jurisdiction court have overlapping dollar amounts for civil cases. That means a case could be filed in either court. Check both courts; never assume.

6. A Certain Truth

Just because records are maintained in a certain way in your state or county, do not assume that any other county or state does things the same way. Case document images are not generally available online because courts are still experimenting and developing electronic filing and imaging. Generally, copies of case documents are only on-site.

As your public record searching takes you from county-to-county or from state-to-state, always keep this truth in the back of your mind.

However, the National Center for State Courts reminds the investigator that court records are transitory and often unreliable and should not be the exclusive means or methods for determining the suitability of any subject. This is especially true of records in online formats since online "court records are not the official records of the court and are provided for informational purposes only— and may be subject to error or omission. Users of these court systems therefore have the responsibility to verify the accuracy, currency and completeness of the information retrieved from those systems."[21]

The employment form is a starting point for a background investigation; after the prospective employee fills it out, it is an investigator's job to then verify the information provided and potentially uncover information that was excluded. Therefore, it is important to determine the breadth of the background investigative request from the outset of the investigation. In Box 11.4, the client, referred to as subscriber, has placed an order regarding a certain applicant. The items in the lower section of the document, where the subscriber is asked to choose from a menu of services—credit, court, criminal, education, neighborhood, motor vehicle, present employment, previous employment, and industrial accident records—indicates the range of choices the investigator has in deciding the breadth of investigation.

BOX 11.4   PERSONNEL INVESTIGATION REQUEST TEMPLATE

PERSONNEL INVESTIGATION REQUEST

Client _____   Date _____

Address _____

Report to _____   Tel. # _____

Applicant's Name _____   Tel. # _____

Home Address _____

Previous Addresses _____

_____

DOB _____   Driver's License # _____

Sex _____   Nationality _____   Ht _____   Wt _____   SS# _____

Marital Status _____   Spouse _____   Maiden Name _____

Dependants _____

Education (High School, College, Trade School, etc.)

_____

_____

_____

Employment (past &present)

Name &Address	Position &Supervisor	Date
_____	_____	_____
_____	_____	_____

Services Ordered (please check)

☐ Credit   ☐ Education   ☐ Present Employment

☐ Court   ☐ Neighborhood   ☐ Previous

                            ☐ (present)   ☐ (previous)   Employment

☐ Criminal   ☐ Motor Vehicle Record   ☐ Industrial Accident

                                                     Record

Oral assertions about the applicant's reputation are hearsay (second- or third-hand remarks) and are therefore of little value. Quality and professionalism of a background investigation depend on written documentation. Information regarding the applicant's use of drugs, attendance records, and overall quality of labor can be requested from the applicant's previous employer (Box 11.5) and is a mandatory attachment to a finalized report on the applicant's employment background.

BOX 11.5   A SAMPLE LETTER TO AN APPLICANT'S PREVIOUS EMPLOYER

[cover letter for employment query for *peace officer* candidates who are not currently employed as peace officers]

[on agency letterhead]
[Date]

[Name]
[Mailing Address]
[City, ST Zip]

Dear Mr./Ms. _____.

_____[Name of Candidate]_____, who was employed by your firm from ____ to _____, is a candidate for the position of peace officer in this department. We are asking your assistance in helping to determine his/her qualifications for the position by supplying us with employment information regarding this individual.

Government Code Section 1031.1 requires employers to disclose written employment information when a person is applying for a peace officer position. A copy of the law is attached for you. An employer has an obligation to disclose written employment information, which includes information in connection with job applications, performance evaluations, attendance records, disciplinary actions, eligibility for rehire, and other information relevant to peace officer performance (except information prohibited from disclosure by any other state or federal law or regulation).

We would appreciate your cooperation in providing the above employment information regarding _____[Name of Candidate]_____. We are accompanying this request with a notarized authorization releasing you from civil liability. We would be glad to cover any costs you incur in copying and furnishing these documents to us. Of course, your responses are absolutely privileged under the law.

Very truly yours,

[Name]
[Title]

[Contact Number – *optional*]
[Email – *optional*]

Attachments: Government Code Section 1031.1
                      Authorization/Advisement Form

11.3.3 CREDIT HISTORY

Some security professionals hold that a subject's credit history, whether good or bad, provides a meaningful measure for character. Individuals who properly handle financial affairs, who intelligently weigh assets and liabilities, who do not take undue risk, or who do not show a history of impulsive buying, are usually considered reliable characters. Regulatory acts, such as the Fair Credit Reporting Act, limit inspection.[22] However, documents such as the authorization permit shown in Box 11.6 allow access.

BOX 11.6   A SAMPLE AUTHORIZATION REGARDING BACKGROUND INVESTIGATIONS

Authorization Regarding Background Investigation

By signing below, I acknowledge receipt of the following separate documents (and certify that I have read and understood them):

* DISCLOSURE REGARDING BACKGROUND INVESTIGATION;
* A SUMMARY OF YOUR RIGHTS UNDER THE FAIR CREDIT REPORTING ACT; and
* ADDITIONAL STATE LAW NOTICES.

By signing below, I also authorize _____ to obtain "consumer reports" (deemed "investigative consumer reports" under California law) about me at any time during the hiring process and throughout my employment, if applicable.

Signature: _____   Date: _____

Printed Name: _____

PERSONAL INFORMATION NEEDED FOR BACKGROUND CHECK

Please supply the following information to facilitate a background check on you.

			___-___-___	____/____
Last Name	First Name	Middle	Social Security Number	Date of Birth mm/dd
Other Name(s) Maiden/Married		Driver's License Number		State
Email Address				

RESIDENCES (Starting with current)			
Street Address	City/State	Zip	How Long? _____
Street Address	City/State	Zip	How Long? _____
Street Address	City/State	Zip	How Long? _____
Street Address	City/State	Zip	How Long? _____
Street Address	City/State	Zip	How Long? _____

Date of Birth ____/____/_____   Telephone (_____)_____

Unless consent is given or there are statutory exemptions in federal and state law, investigators have restricted access to credit reports.[23]

Web Exercise: See the Consumer Financial Protection Bureau's general advice on consumer credits and reports at: https://files.consumerfinance.gov/f/201504_cfpb_summary_your-rights-under-fcra.pdf.

Typically, the reverse side of a credit report explains the terms, conditions, and rules of construction for the interpretation of the credit report. The investigator should check directories for address and phone numbers of companies that specialize in tracking and reporting credit histories. Some of the more prominent companies engaged in the business are:

- Equifax
- Experian
- Trans Union Credit Information Co.
- Dun & Bradstreet
- National Association of Credit Management

At a minimum, a credit report makes an honest, though not perfect, attempt to reflect the overall credit history of an individual. Although the report deals mostly with forms of public credit, such as that reported by banks, investment companies, credit card companies, or other personal grant of credit, the results are not all-encompassing. Investigators should realize some of the more obvious omissions:

- Credit acquired under an assumed or changed name
- Credit not publicly reported, such as a loan between parent and child
- Mortgages/personal loans provided by owners of property in a land transaction
- Temporary lines of credit or corporate loans for key executives

Weighing creditworthiness calls for an examination of many other sources and documents. Access to a courthouse is essential for an investigator reviewing an individual's credit background and financial stability. "Online civil court records are not the official records of the court and may not reflect the official court file available at the court itself. There are a variety of reasons for this:

- some records are sealed,
- others are in paper-accessible files only,
- others are so old they are only available in the court's archive, not online.
- As with attempts to use criminal court records, the use of civil court records against a person may be prohibited by law."[24]

Direct or inferential evidence regarding financial data and creditworthiness can be collected from numerous sources, including:

- Credit bureaus
- Banks and financial institutions
- Employment records
- Local sources
- Public records
- Collection agencies
- Directories
- Key informants
- Newspapers
- Investment manuals
- Landlords
- State authorities
- Collection services
- Federal government
- Post offices
- Stock exchanges
- Company or person being investigated
- Investment firms
- Creditors
- Insurance companies
- Trade references[25]

To determine the exact scope of the financial investigation, the investigator should rely upon a document such as that shown in Box 11.7. The assignment form has a "confirm/verify" section and a courthouse record search section to pinpoint the types of activities the client wishes to undertake.

BOX 11.7 A SAMPLE ASSIGNMENT FORM

ASSIGNMENT FORM

To _____ From _____ Date Assigned _____

Assigned to _____ Requested by _____

Cost Limitation _____ Completion date _____

Request is made for your office to conduct an asset search, or other specified investigation on the following individuals and/or businesses

Name	Address

Please search the following areas covering a period of at least five years unless requested otherwise. Provide telephone numbers for each subject and/or business assigned and verify all possible information through pretext calling. Obtain copies of all complete documents pertinent to this investigation.

Please direct your research to the following counties and include the following search areas for each of the subjects and/or businesses assigned.

Counties: _____

_____

CONFIRM/VERIFY

Resident address – resident telephone number – present ownership of residence –
Market value – marital status – business status – business telephone number

COURTHOUSE RECORDS SEARCH

Deed records – UCC filings – assumed names – tax assessor – tax liens –
Criminal and civil records – bankruptcy – divorce – probate – voter registration – motor vehicles

Other _____

Special instructions _____

Often, the search for creditworthiness deals with the subject's assets and overall net worth. The investigator requests a review of the applicant's credit, businesses or corporations owned, real property, security interests, and other personal information. The hours, expenditures, and authorization rates for fees and expenses are also calculated. See Box 11.8 for a sample form.

BOX 11.8 A SAMPLE ASSET INVESTIGATION AUTHORIZATION TEMPLATE

ASSET INVESTIGATION AUTHORIZATION

Date Rec'd _____ Due Date _____

Subject _____ Investigator _____

Address _____ Completed _____

_____ Date Mailed _____

SS# _____   Auth. Hrs. _____

SS# _____   Auth. Rate _____

Employer _____   Mileage _____

_____   County _____   State _____

Summary of report _____

_____

_____

_____

Daily Progress of investigation

Date	Description	Hrs	Exp
	Credit		
	Corp.		
	CPF		
	Real Property		
	UCC		
	SS# Trace		
	Address Update		
	Neighborhood Search		

Information on real property can be found in a courthouse at the Recorder of Deeds or similar office. The review of real property can also determine the liens and liabilities currently attached against a property, such as mortgages, promissory notes, judgments, and other secured or liened interests.[26] Box 11.9 has the necessary language and clauses to thoroughly document the current state of liabilities against specific real property.

BOX 11.9   DOCUMENTING ANY LIENS AND LIABILITIES OF REAL PROPERTY

_____   _____   _____

Date Searched   Subject   County, State

                                     Real Property

Our investigation in _____   County,_____   (State) revealed

The following information pertaining to_____

Type of Deed:_____

Date Filed:_____

Volume &Page No._____

Grantor: _____

Grantee: _____

Property Location: _____

Property Description: _____

_____

A promissory note dated _____   in the amount of _____

is payable to _____   (Lender &City).

The current assessed value of property if _____

Type of Deed: _____

Date Filed: _____

Volume & page No. _____

Grantor: _____

Grantee: _____

Property Location: _____

Property Description: _____

_____

A promissory note dated_____ in the amount of _____

is payable to _____ (Lender &City).

The current assessed value of the property is _____

_____

Initials

The investigator must also be aware of personal property information recorded at the offices of tax assessors, Recorder of Deeds, or Register of Wills. In some jurisdictions, personal property tax forms listing stocks, bonds, other negotiable instruments, and even jewelry and other delineated personal property, must be filed annually. An excellent worksheet for recording this information is included at Box 11.10.

BOX 11.10   A WORKSHEET TO RECORD PERSONAL PROPERTY RECORDED AT OFFICES OF TAX ASSESSORS

_____   _____   _____

Date Searched   Subject   County, State

Personal Property

Year of Tax Roll: _____

Obtained from: _____   Tax Assessor's Office

                                                                                  Tax Appraisal District

Owner _____

Property Location: _____

Property Description: _____

_____

Valuation _____

Volume &page No. _____

_____

Owner _____

Property Location: _____

Property Description: _____

_____

Valuation _____

Volume &page No. _____

_____

Owner _____

Property Location: _____

Property Description: _____

_____

Valuation _____

Volume &page No. _____

_____

Initials

Web Exercise: Visit the website of your county and determine what property records are available online in your area.

A search of motor vehicle records through the Division of Motor Vehicles and Public Safety or other governmental authority provides another insight into the asset and liability quotient of a subject. Primary and secondary liens on the title of a vehicle suggest overextended credit or larger-than-normal liabilities. Boats and aircraft are also reportable in a central registry such as the Department of Marine Resources or the Federal Aviation Administration. This type of information can be recorded on a form such as Box 11.11.

BOX 11.11   DOCUMENTING VEHICLE RECORDS AND ANY POTENTIAL LIABILITY OR LIENS

_____   _____   _____

Date Searched   Subject   County, State

Vehicles

Owner _____

Year, Model, Make: _____

License #, State: _____

Vehicle ID Number: _____

Lien Date: _____

Lien Holder & Address: _____

_____

Value (Approx): _____

Remarks: _____

_____

Owner _____

Year, Model, Make: _____

License #, State: _____

Vehicle ID Number: _____

Lien Date: _____

Lien Holder & Address: _____

_____

Value (Approx): _____

Remarks: _____

_____

Initials

At the Secretary of State's office or other office of corporate and consumer business filings, Uniform Commercial Code filings or financing statements, evidencing a secured interest in another person's property, are centrally stored. Owners who have property and tangible assets that have sizable or inordinate financing statements on record often evidence a troubled financial situation. According to O'Block:

Serious indications of financial instability, which could lead to employee dishonesty, include a history of declared bankruptcies, defaults, and repossessions. Financial strains of this type may induce an employee to steal from the employer as a means of getting additional income or could force the employee to take a second job, which could cause decreased proficiency in the first job.[27]

The party who owes money is the debtor and the party who has extended credit is the secured party. Collateral is the property pledged as security during the life of the loan.[28] Box 11.12 is a sample of a form that can be used to record UCC filings.

BOX 11.12 UNIFORM COMMERCIAL CODE FILINGS SAMPLE FORM

Date Searched _____ Subject _____ County, State _____

Uniform Commercial Code Filings
(Financing Statement)

Instrument Number: _____

Date Filed: _____

Debtor: _____

Secured Party: _____

Collateral: _____
_____
_____

This UCC is also filed with the: _____
(Secretary of State/County)

under number _____ dated _____

Instrument Number: _____

Date Filed: _____

Debtor: _____

Secured Party: _____

Collateral: _____
_____

This UCC is also filed with the: _____
(Secretary of State/County)

under number _____ dated _____

Initials _____

Although documents to record information related to judgments, liens, and bankruptcies were reviewed in Chapter 5, the forms shown in Boxes 11.13–11.15 are provided for added insight.

BOX 11.13   FORM TO RECORD JUDGMENT RECORDS

Date Searched   Subject   County, State

Judgments

Case Number: _____

Court of Record: _____

Volume &Page Number: _____

Date Filed: _____

Petitioner vs. Defendant: _____

Amount of Judgment: _____

Case Number: _____

Court of Record: _____

Volume &Page Number: _____

Date Filed: _____

Petitioner vs. Defendant: _____

Amount of Judgment: _____

_____

Initials

BOX 11.14   FORM TO RECORD LIENS

Date Searched   Subject   County, State

Liens

(Tax, Mechanics, or Materialman's)

Document Number: _____

Date Filed: _____

Amount of Lien: _____

Petitioner vs. Defendant: _____

Document Number: _____

Date Filed: _____

Amount of Lien: _____

Petitioner vs. Defendant: _____

Document Number: _____

Date Filed: _____

Amount of Lien: _____

Petitioner vs. Defendant:

_____

Initials

BOX 11.15   FORM TO RECORD INSTANCES OF BANKRUPTCY

Date Searched	Subject	County, State

Bankruptcy
(Financing Statement)

Name of Bankrupt: _____

Case Number: _____

Date Filed: _____

Type of Bankruptcy: _____

(Voluntary/Involuntary – Chapter 7, 11, or 13) _____

U.S. Bankruptcy Court: _____   _____
                                     (District)   (Location)

Status (Choose One):   ☐ Pending   ☐ Closed

If closed, disposition: _____

List or provide copies of assets, debts and creditors.

                                                                            _____
                                                                            Initials

A variety of security enterprises exclusively emphasize these types of service. See Figure 11.4.[29]

Because private individuals often funnel assets through corporate and partnership enterprises, the investigator cannot acquire a true and accurate representation of overall net worth or creditworthiness without consideration of other business entities. Through various legal maneuverings and other corporate machinations, a subject may have transferred personal assets into corporate entities to render them untouchable. With this in mind, the investigator must always undertake an assessment of the subject's companies or corporate interests. The information regarding a company's

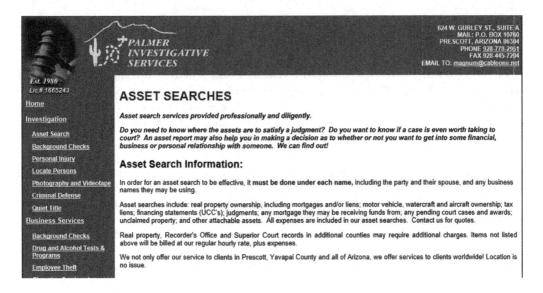

FIGURE 11.4 Numerous firms provide a wide variety of services in this regard. (Used with Permission, Palmer Investigative Services.)

officers, shareholders, and the like are accessible through the Secretary of State or other delegated agency. A sample of a form to record this type of data is shown in Box 11.16.

BOX 11.16   A FORM TO RECORD A SUBJECT'S COMPANIES OR CORPORATE INTERESTS

Date Searched _____   Subject _____   County, State _____

Companies/Corporations Incorporation

Our search of the records of the _____ Secretary of State Office revealed the following
                              (State)

information pertaining to _____

Corporation Name: _____

Address: _____

Charter Number: _____

Date of Incorporation: _____

Registered agent: _____

Officers: _____   Title: _____

Officers: _____   Title: _____

Officers: _____   Title: _____

Status: _____

Corporation Name: _____

Address: _____

Charter Number: _____

Date of Incorporation: _____

Registered agent: _____

Officers: _____   Title: _____

Officers: _____   Title: _____

Officers: _____   Title: _____

Status: _____

Initials _____

Various companies have created software systems to assist in asset investigations. Thompson Reuters has created CLEAR, which uses mapping technology to locate assets. See Figure 11.5.[30]

LexisNexis has created Accurint® for Private Investigators, which provides corporate security and private investigative professionals with critical information and insights to solve complex cases and minimize security risks. See Figure 11.6.[31]

General background investigation software is also a great advantage in today's technology driven society. Micropact has developed a program to assist tracking all elements in an investigation to ensure a potential employment candidate has been properly vetted. See Figure 11.7.[32]

IRBsearch provides more than forty searches that investigative professionals need for skip tracing and background verification. Each search fits under six main categories: People, Assets, Businesses, Courts, Licenses, and Phones. All search and report results are saved for seven days and are exportable as a PDF, Word document, or Excel spreadsheet. See Figure 11.8.[33]

Web Exercise: Conduct your own pre-employment background check at GoodHire.com.

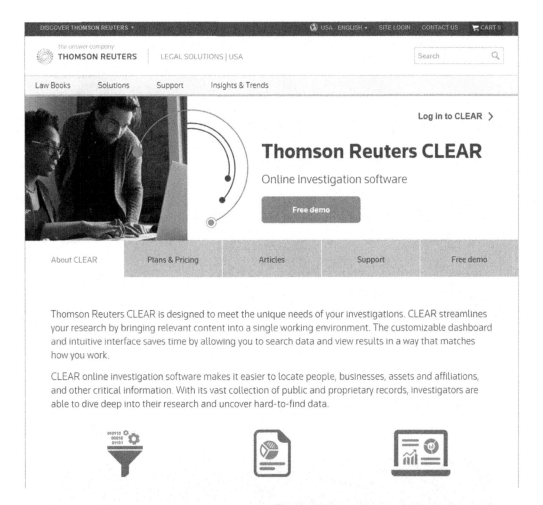

FIGURE 11.5 Companies now can provide unique search capabilities and services to locate assets and other critical pieces of information. (Reprinted with permission, Thomson Reuters.)

11.4 ALTERNATIVE METHODS OF BACKGROUND REVIEW

11.4.1 REFERENCES

References were once the chief means of personal evaluation and assessment, but as a result of the rise of technology, information sharing, and the polygraph machine, references have unfortunately lost their luster.[34] For most of the last century, the reliance on the personal reference made exquisite sense since the author of said reference personally invested time and energy in the assessment and, in a way, made the judgments about the subject very personal. Put another way, the reference writer invested the energy and time to paint the picture of the person that so many modern, technological techniques fail to do. Nevertheless, reference documents, like Box 11.17, can and still should be utilized due to their reliability and unrivaled insights.

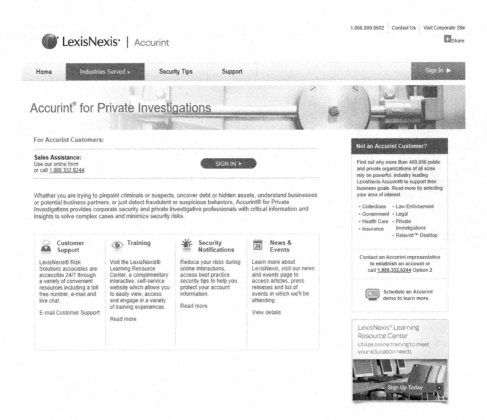

FIGURE 11.6 LexisNexis offers a variety of services to investigators. (Used with permission, LexisNexis.)

FIGURE 11.7 Background investigations are one of a number of solutions that MicroPact provides. (Reprinted with permission from MicroPact 2018. All rights reserved.)

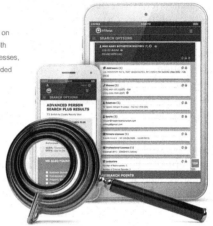

FIGURE 11.8   IRB puts it succinctly: "No more standing in long lines at the courthouse. With RetrieveALL the courthouse comes to you!" (Used with permission, IRBResearch, LLC.)

BOX 11.17   A SAMPLE REFERENCE LETTER

To Whom It May Concern:

I have known _____ for approximately two years. As the Director of the Criminal Justice Program, I am responsible for the evaluation of all faculty teaching within the program. In fulfilling this responsibility I am able to develop an awareness of the abilities demonstrated with the classroom. I have found _____ to be a mentally mature, emotionally intelligent, and highly sensitive professional person who works very well with people. He represents his ideas articulately and with enthusiasm. He certainly has had a profound effect upon my perception of the role of educator; he is able to combine research, intellectual concern, and communication arts into a very practical and understandable reality for the student.

Over the past year _____ has developed a sustained record of academic excellence in teaching, professional development, and service to the college. His consistently positive student evaluations reflect a unique ability to relate complex abstract material to the daily experiences of students' lives and a capacity to maximize the motivation of the students with diverse needs and varying histories of academic anxiety. As such, _____ has scheduled classes at times inconvenient to himself so as to accommodate the needs of shift workers who must change schedules from day to evening classes over the course of a semester. He has successfully instilled a love for learning in housewives, police officers, plant workers, and younger students with a history of academic failure.

_____ has an excellent basic understanding of the nuances of everyday living which gives him a rather remarkable ability to work effectively with the more difficult pragmatic realities of life. In addition, he works well within our social system and confronts issues and problems rationally and intelligently within a professional framework.

_____ is a superior member of the teaching profession and a dedicated force to the professionalism of our criminal justice system. I recommend him with the highest respect I can hold for an individual.

The reference letter fell out of favor for being cumbersome, difficult to manage, and sometimes of unreliable authorship. Other issues wore negatively on the historic methods such as:

(1) The investigator had to track down the author of the reference to assess the integrity of the information.
(2) The content and quality of the references lacked uniformity.
(3) The fear of lawsuits for falsehoods, misstatements, or misinformation, even when innocently made.

"Consequently, employers have come to put little faith in the traditional reference letters because they themselves refuse to be candid in responding when such questionnaires reach their own desks."[35]

Investigators who have read enough of these documents to understand their language and the implications that come forth recognize a good evaluation at once—the author is unequivocal in commendation. Mediocre or even negative assessments often are presented in a bland or neutral commendation, such as: "The applicant really tries hard," or "It's a shame the applicant has to leave, but he feels there are better opportunities elsewhere." Experienced investigators can differentiate the language of commendation versus the language of reservation.

11.4.2 Consultative Services

Social and behavioral scientists are increasing their visibility in background investigations by creating tests and other evaluative methodologies for the workplace. An extensive list of areas these tests cover includes:

- Personality
- Minnesota Multiphasic Personality Inventory
- The Glueck Predictability Table
- The Kvaraceus Delinquency Scale and Checklist
- The Rorschach Test
- Honesty or integrity
- Drug or alcohol usage
- Productivity and efficiency
- Work history
- Service capacity and relations
- Conduct and personal habits

Web Exercise: Take the 16-Type Jungian Personality Test at https://psychcentral.com/quizzes/personality/start.php.

Through a series of surveys and testing instruments—mainly in a yes-and-no format—multiple areas of character and personality development can be measured, like integrity or honesty. In the service test, a party's desire to establish effective and helpful relationships with customers, peers, and supervisors are the measurable factors. The Reid Report Assessment helps identify job applicants with high levels of integrity who are likely to become productive employees by assessing and measuring integrity, social behavior, substance use, and work background.[36,37,38]

11.4.3 THE POLYGRAPH TEST

Before the passage of the Employee Polygraph Protection Act of 1988,[39] the provisions of which became effective in the latter part of 1988,[40] the polygraph was considered by many American businesses as an instrumental and highly effective means of background investigation and review. Thus, before 1989, there were "tens of thousands of companies ... that utilize[d] polygraph screening for job applicants."[41] State and federal laws have placed extensive limitations on pre-employment screening. As a result, individual internal investigations are encumbered, which causes employers and security vendors to be uncertain about the future role of the polygraph.[42] Even so, public employees still engage security firms to conduct such tests. For example, the polygraph is still regularly utilized in police applicant screening since consent must be given by that applicant.[43]

In addition, the polygraph is a tool for the prosecutor's office as it seeks to screen and test the veracity of a defendant's claim of innocence. Here too, the defendant must consent. The admissibility of the polygraph results, except in the restrictive case of stipulation of the parties, has yet to be witnessed in the American legal system. See Figure 11.9[44] for an example of a poster outlining employee rights as they relate to the Employee Polygraph Protection Act.

Web Exercise: Visit www.dol.gov/whd/polygraph/ to become familiar with the many nuances of polygraph usage as described by the U.S. Department of Labor.

Surely, these suggestions represent a fraction of the approaches to discern the background of any subject. Other avenues for background assessment could be tackled as well, including:

1. Driving records
2. Student transcripts
3. Military service records
4. State licensing records
5. Professional license records
6. Workers' compensation[45]

11.5 COMPREHENSIVE BACKGROUND REPORT

The investigator's ultimate goal is to provide the client with a full, comprehensive picture of what is the subject's character. As the investigator moves through the various processes covered throughout this chapter, the results should be formally catalogued and composed. At this final and very crucial step, the investigator authors the Comprehensive Background Report.[46] The report should include the following:

- Identification information
- Records of convictions
- Proof of civil actions and other litigation
- Credit and financial history
- Educational records
- Neighborhood information
- Personal and business references
- Previous and current employment
- Opinions of previous and current employers
- Other financial data

EMPLOYEE RIGHTS

EMPLOYEE POLYGRAPH PROTECTION ACT

The Employee Polygraph Protection Act prohibits most private employers from using lie detector tests either for pre-employment screening or during the course of employment.

PROHIBITIONS

Employers are generally prohibited from requiring or requesting any employee or job applicant to take a lie detector test, and from discharging, disciplining, or discriminating against an employee or prospective employee for refusing to take a test or for exercising other rights under the Act.

EXEMPTIONS

Federal, State and local governments are not affected by the law. Also, the law does not apply to tests given by the Federal Government to certain private individuals engaged in national security-related activities.

The Act permits polygraph (a kind of lie detector) tests to be administered in the private sector, subject to restrictions, to certain prospective employees of security service firms (armored car, alarm, and guard), and of pharmaceutical manufacturers, distributors and dispensers.

The Act also permits polygraph testing, subject to restrictions, of certain employees of private firms who are reasonably suspected of involvement in a workplace incident (theft, embezzlement, etc.) that resulted in economic loss to the employer.

The law does not preempt any provision of any State or local law or any collective bargaining agreement which is more restrictive with respect to lie detector tests.

EXAMINEE RIGHTS

Where polygraph tests are permitted, they are subject to numerous strict standards concerning the conduct and length of the test. Examinees have a number of specific rights, including the right to a written notice before testing, the right to refuse or discontinue a test, and the right not to have test results disclosed to unauthorized persons.

ENFORCEMENT

The Secretary of Labor may bring court actions to restrain violations and assess civil penalties against violators. Employees or job applicants may also bring their own court actions.

THE LAW REQUIRES EMPLOYERS TO DISPLAY THIS POSTER WHERE EMPLOYEES AND JOB APPLICANTS CAN READILY SEE IT.

WAGE AND HOUR DIVISION
UNITED STATES DEPARTMENT OF LABOR

1-866-487-9243
TTY: 1-877-889-5627
www.dol.gov/whd

WH1462 REV 07/16

FIGURE 11.9 Employees' rights as they pertain to the Employee Polygraph Protection Act.

For a sample background investigation report see: Box 11.18.

BOX 11.18   A COMPREHENSIVE BACKGROUND INVESTIGATION REPORT

1. CRIMINAL INVESTIGATION:
   Search Type: Tennessee Statewide
   Status: Criminal Record Found
   CASE NUMBER: 99-CR5500403
   COUNTY: Davidson
   OFFENSE: Bad Checks
   LEVEL: Misdemeanor
   SENTENCE DATE: 9/13/1999
   DISPOSITION: Guilty on single count
   COMMENTS: Wrote a check for $404.45 to Wal-Mart which was returned. Did not pay the amount within 30 days as directed. Sentenced to pay restitution plus $65 fines, and placed on 1-year probation, which was completed without violations.
2. EDUCATION VERIFICATION: Davidson County Community College
   GRADUATION CLAIMED: 6/76
   GRADUATION VERIFIED: None
   DEGREE CLAIMED: A.A.
   DEGREE VERIFIED: None
3. EMPLOYMENT VERIFICATION: Fast and Speedy TruckingACCIDENTS

DATE	TYPE	COST	CHARGEABLE	FATALITIES	INJURIES
06/23/00	Backing	$3,400	Yes	No	Yes

4. MOTOR VEHICLE RECORD:
   SEARCH TYPE: Tennessee
   STATUS: Results Received
   RESULTS:
   LIC NUMBER: 888-11-8888
   ISSUED DATE: 7/24/99
   EXPIRES: 7/24/05LIC STATUS: Valid
   TYPE/CLASS: Operator
   RESTRICTIONS: None

VIOLATIONS

1. Speeding 83/55	6/12/01	Lowndes County SO, MS
2. Ignore Traffic Signal	1/3/03	Nashville PD, TN

ADDRESS SEARCH

RESULTS:

```
1. 11/2003 - 03/2004     APPLICANT, SAMPLE SSN: 888-11-8888
DOB: 03/1956  AGE:  47
   231 Peachtree Rd. SW
```

```
      ATLANTA, GA, 30303
      COUNTY: Fulton
      SSN VALID: yes ISSUED: TN


2. 09/1997 - 10/2003        APPLICANT, SAMPLE SSN: 888-11-8888
DOB: 03/1956  AGE:   47
      1641 Apple Orchard Dr.
      NAShVILLE, TN 37201
      COUNTY: DAVIDSON
      SSN VALID: yes ISSUED: TN
3. 01/1989 - 06/1997 APPLICANT, SAMPLE SSN: 888-11-8888  DOB: 03/1956
AGE:   47
      32B SUMMIT AVENUE
      CORAL GABLES, FL 33133
      COUNTY: DADE
      SSN VALID: yes ISSUED: TN


4. 08/1991 - 01/1989 APPLICANT, SAMPLE SSN: 888-11-8888  DOB: 03/1956
AGE:   47
      PO BOX 13A
      PICKENS, MS 39146 00879
      COUNTY: HOLMES
      SSN VALID: yes ISSUED: TN


5. 01/1980 - 01/1989 APPLICANT, SAMPLE SSN: 888-11-8888 DOB: 00/1957
AGE:   47
      347 PINE STREET
      NASHVILLE, TN 39095 98039
      COUNTY: DAVIDSON
      SSN VALID: yes ISSUED: TN
```

CRIMINAL INVESTIGATION

Search Type: Florida DOC
Status: No Records Found
Search Type: GA Statewide
Status: No Records Found

EDUCATION VERIFICATION

INSTITUTION
Davidson County Community College
100 Education Way
Nashville, TN 37201
PHONE: 615-444-3333 FAX: 615-555-6666
STATUS: Research Complete

	DATA SUPPLIED	DATA CONFIRMED	ALERT
Dates Attended	9/74 - 6/76	9/3/74- 6/15/76	No
Graduated Date	6/72	None	Yes
Degree	A.A.	None	Yes
Major	Liberal Arts	Liberal Arts	No

Minor	n/a	n/a	No
G.P.A.	3.0	3.0	No
Curr. Attend.	No	No	No

COMMENTS: Did not graduate or earn a degree of any kind.

VERIFIED BY: S. Kann
DATE VERIFIED: 2/19/04

EMPLOYMENT VERIFICATION

EMPLOYER
ABC Manufacturing
200 Metal Gear Avenue
Bigtown, GA 30303
STATUS: Research Complete

	DATA SUPPLIED	DATA CONFIRMED	DISCR.
Dates Of Employment	1/97 - 4/98	1/4/97 - 4/30/98	No
Supervisor / Title	Mr. Smith/Warehouse Manager	Mr. Smith (no longer there)	No
Job Title	Forklift driver	Forklift driver	No
Job Description	Drove forklift and kept stock neat	Forklift operations and stocker	No
Salary	$7.65/hr	$7.65/hr final	No
Currently Employed	No	No	No
Reason For Leaving	Learned to drive a truck	Left to drive a truck	No

CUSTOMIZED QUESTIONS

QUESTION	INFORMATION VERIFIED
Did this person get along well with coworkers?	"Always. Very friendly and helpful."
Was this person's attendance satisfactory?	"Missed time like others. Nothing unusual or problematic."

ELIGIBLE FOR REHIRE: Yes
EXPLANATION: "He was a fine worker. We were sorry to see him go."
COMMENTS: NO ADDITIONAL COMMENTS PROVIDED.
VERIFIED BY: D. Lewis
DATE VERIFIED: 03/11/04

EMPLOYER
Fast and Speedy Trucking
123 East Main St.
Nashville, TN 37201
STATUS: Research Complete

	DATA SUPPLIED	DATA CONFIRMED	DISCR.
Dates Of Employment	2/97 - 2/02	2/1/97 - 2/14/02	No
Supervisor / Title	Ms. Adams/Safety Director	Ms. Adams/Safety Director	No
Job Title	Trcuk driver	Truck driver	No
Job Description	Drove 18-wheeler	Drove OTR	No
Salary	32 cents/per mile	n/a	No
Currently Employed	No	No	No
Reason For Leaving	Sought new position with city	Left with appropriate notice	No

CUSTOMIZED QUESTIONS	
QUESTION	INFORMATION VERIFIED
Did this person get along well with coworkers?	"Yes."
Was this person's attendance satisfactory?	"He rated very well in this category."
ELIGIBLE FOR REHIRE: Yes EXPLANATION: "Would need to be retested for drug and alcohol." COMMENTS: NO ADDITIONAL COMMENTS PROVIDED. VERIFIED BY: Ms. Adams DATE VERIFIED: 03/12/04	

DOT EMPLOYMENT VERIFICATION

STATUS: Research Complete

CAUSE FOR SEPARATION: Voluntary
TYPE OF COMPANY: Small Trucking
EQUIPMENT TYPE: Tractor-semi
TRAILER TYPE: Dry Van
TYPE OF FREIGHT HAULED: Appliances and auto parts
GEOGRAPHIC AREA: 48 states
FULL OR PART TIME: Full Time
OVER THE ROAD OR LOCAL: Over The Road
QUALIFIED FOR SINGLE OPERATION: Yes
QUALIFIED FOR TEAM OPERATION: No
HAZARDOUS MATERIALS: Yes

ELIGIBLE FOR REHIRE: Yes
DETAILS: Would need to be retested for drug and alcohol.

TESTED POSITIVE FOR A CONTROLLED SUBSTANCE IN THE LAST 3 YEARS:
No
DETAILS: N/A

ALCOHOL TEST WITH A BREATH ALCOHOL CONCENTRATION OF 0.04 OR GREATER IN THE LAST 3 YEARS: No
DETAILS: N/A

REFUSED A REQUIRED TEST FOR DRUGS OR ALCOHOL IN THE LAST 3 YEARS: No
DETAILS: N/A

VIOLATED OTHER D.O.T. DRUG/ALCOHOL REGULATIONS: NO

IF SO, IS THERE DOCUMENTATION OF SUCCESSFUL COMPLETION OF D.O.T. RETURN-TO-DUTY REQUIREMENTS, INCLUDING FOLLOW-UP TESTS: N/A

SUBSTANCE ABUSE PROFESSIONAL:N/A
LOCATION: N/A

NUMBER OF ACCIDENTS: 1

ACCIDENTS

DATE	TYPE	COST	CHARGEABLE	FATALITIES	INJURIES
06/23/00	Backing	$18,000	Yes	No	Yes

Practical Exercise: Carefully review the document in Box 11.18 and respond to these questions.

1. How many children does the subject have?
2. Where has the subject worked?
3. Has the Better Business Bureau received complaints about AC&T?
4. What is the subject's name?
5. What is the subject's credit record?
6. Has the subject ever been convicted of a crime?
7. What is the subject's address?
8. What is Jack Gray's relationship to the subject?
9. Has the subject attended any colleges or universities? If so, did he graduate?
10. Who is the investigator's client?

11.6 CONCLUSION

The role of the investigator in background investigations is quite formidable, whether internally as the designated party to review people and persons or in a consultative capacity where agencies and entities hire this specific expertise. The chapter provides detailed information on the various background categories in need of review, from employment to educational records, from residential history to civil and criminal litigation histories. Forms and checklists to carry out these functions are included as well as recommendations on how new technological products and services can assist in the background review. At the end of the chapter, the reader is exposed to the Comprehensive Background Report which gathers all relevant information about the subject and memorializes the information in documentary form.

NOTES

1. S. Young, "Slipping Through the Cracks," *Surveillance &Society* 15, no. 1 (2017): 125–136.
2. William C. Cunningham and Todd H. Taylor, *The Hallcrest Report: Private Security and Police in America* (1985): 43; see also Peter Psarouthakis, "Business Background Investigations: Tools and Techniques for Solution Driven Due Diligence," *Security Management* (June 2008): 120; Kris Frieswick, "Background checks: worries about personnel integrity are creating a few worries of their own," *CFO, The Magazine for Senior Financial Executives*, August 2005: 63.
3. See Charles P. Nemeth, *Private Security and the Law*, 5th ed. (Boca Raton, FL: CRC Press, 2018); D. Showmaker, "Improving Security with Global Background Checks," *Security* 50, no. 10 (2013): 38–38, 41; Lessing E. Gold, "Better Check the Background," *Security Distributing &Marketing* (October 2009): 34.
4. J. Brennan and L. Mattice, "Pre-Employment Vetting: Value or Liability," *Security* 52, no. 4 (2015): 40.
5. J. Kirk Barefoot, *Employee Theft Investigation* (1979): 190.

6. Lester Rosen, "International Hiring 101: Background Checks, Due Diligence &Legal Compliance," *Security* 49, no. 11 (November 2012): 126–127.

7. See Kenneth Springer, "The Case for Extra Due Diligence; Private eyes are not just for film noir—they can be useful to conduct a background check for investors who want to protect themselves," *Investment Dealers' Digest*, January 21, 2011: 22.

8. W. B. Nixon, "The Emergence of Infinity Screening to Mitigate Risk," *Security* 53, no. 9 (September 2016): 81–82.

9. Jerry Brennan and Lynn Mattice, "Pre-Employment Vetting: Value or Liability," *Security* 52, no. 4 (April 2015): 40.

10. "Background Checks: What Employers Need to know," U.S. Equal Employment Opportunity Commission, accessed July 21, 2018, www.eeoc.gov/eeoc/publications/background_checks_employers. cfm.

11. Robert O'Block, *Security and Crime Prevention* (1981): 191; Linda B. Dwoskin et al. "Welcome Aboard! How to Hire the Right Way," *Employee Relations Law Journal* (Spring 2013): 28; see also Sue Stott and Jonathan Longino, "The Law on Screening Employees in the Information Age," *Security* 53, no. 3 (March 2016): 40–40, 42.

12. For an excellent series of suggestions for background protocol, see Dwoskin et al. "Welcome aboard!"

13. "Investigations &Intelligence," Critical Intervention Services, accessed July 21, 2018, www.cisworld-services.org/services/investigations.html.

14. See Lessing E. Gold, "Better Check the Background," *Security Distributing &Marketing* (October 2009): 34; see also Suzanne Lucas, "What happens on a pre-employment background check?" *MoneyWatch*, December 9, 2013, www.cbsnews.com/news/what-happens-on-a-pre-employment-background-check.

15. See D. Showmaker, "Improving Security with Global Background Checks," *Security* 50, no. 10 (2013): 38–41.

16. N. Bottom and J. Kostanoski, *Introduction to Security and Loss Control* (1990): 158; see also National Employment Screening Services, *The Guide to Background Investigations* (1990); "Employee Background Checks How to Do Employee Background Checks: The Complete Guide," BetterTeam. com, www.betterteam.com/employee-background-checks; "Background Checks: What Employers Need to know," U.S. Equal Employment Opportunity Commission, www.eeoc.gov/eeoc/publications/background_checks_employers.cfm; Stott and Longino, "Screening Employees."

17. T. Ricks, B. Tillett, and C. Van Meter, *Principles of Security*, 2nd ed. (1988): 204–205; U.S. EEOC, "Background Checks"; Stott and Longino, "Screening Employees."

18. Ibid.: 205–206; U.S. EEOC, "Background Checks"; Stott and Longino, "Screening Employees."

19. Ibid.: 206; U.S. EEOC, "Background Checks"; BetterTeam.com, "Background Checks"; see also Michael Sankey, "A Primer on Searching Recorded Documents, Judgments, and Liens," Public Record Retriever Network, www.prrn.us/documents/Searching.pdf.

20. "Tip Sheet for Searching Court Records," Public Record Retriever Network, www.prrn.us/documents/CourtTipsheet.pdf.

21. National Center for State Courts, "Online court records are not the same as background checks," www.ncsc.org/Topics/Technology/Records-Document-Management/Background-Checks.aspx.

22. See Tony Rodriguez and Jessica Lyon, "Background screening reports and the FCRA: Just saying you're not a consumer reporting agency isn't enough," January 10, 2013, www.ftc.gov/industry/human-resources.

23. Federal Trade Commission, "Using Consumer Reports: What Employers Need to Know," www.ftc.gov/tips-advice/business-center/guidance/using-consumer-reports-what-employers-need-know; Rodriguez and Jessica Lyon, "Background screening reports"; see the guidance of the Federal Trade Commission regarding credit background checks at www.ftc.gov/industry/human-resources.

24. National Center for State Courts, "Online court records are not the same as background checks," www.ncsc.org/Topics/Technology/Records-Document-Management/Background-Checks.aspx.

25. Pinkerton's Inc., *Investigations Department Training Manual* (1990): 97.

26. See Charles P. Nemeth, *The Reality of Real Estate* (Prentice Hall, 2015). Sankey, "A Primer"; Public Record Retriever Network, "Tip Sheet."

27. R. O'Block, "Security": 193; Springer, "Due Diligence"; "Using Consumer Reports: What Employers Need to Know," Federal Trade Commission, www.ftc.gov/tips-advice/business-center/guidance/using-consumer-reports-what-employers-need-know.

28. See Nemeth, "Resource Manual": 226; Wells Fargo, "Types of Secured Loans and Lines of Credit," www.wellsfargo.com/goals-credit/large-expenses/secured-loan-types.

29. Palmer Investigative Services, 624 W. Gurley St., Suite A, Mail: P.O. Box 10760, Prescott, Arizona 86304, http://www.palmerinvestigative.com/asset.htm.

30. Clear: Online Investigation Software, Thomson Reuters, https://legalsolutions.thomsonreuters.com/law-products/solutions/clear-investigation-software.

31. "Accurint® for Private Investigations," LexisNexis, www.accurint.com/privateinvestigations.html.

32. "Background Investigation," MicroPact, www.micropact.com/solutions/background-investigation.

33. "Advanced Person Search PLUS," IRBsearch, http://irbsearch.com/irbfocus-avp-plus.html.

34. Peter Mirfield, "Character and Credibility," *Criminal Law Review*, March 2009: 135; Dwoskin et al., "Welcome aboard!"

35. Barefoot, "Investigation": 191; Dwoskin et al., "Welcome aboard!"

36. Lester Rosen, "International Hiring 101: Background Checks, Due Diligence &Legal Compliance," *Security* 49, no. 11 (November 2012): 126–127; Springer, "Due Diligence"; Stott and Longino, "Screening Employees."

37. "The Reid Report Risk Assessment," Fraud &Forensic Services, www.arastl.com/reid-risk-assesment/.

38. "Reid Report 30th Ed.," PSI Services, www.psionline.com/assessments/reid-report-29th-ed/.

39. 29 USC 2001; 29 CFR Part 801; "Employee Polygraph Protections Act (EPPA)," U.S. Department of Labor, Wage and Hour Division, www.dol.gov/whd/polygraph; "Other Workplace Standards: Lie Detector Tests," U.S. Department of Labor, Employment Law Guide, https://webapps.dol.gov/elaws/elg/eppa.htm.

40. See *Congressional Record*, Vol. 131, No. 148, S. 1815 (1988).

41. Barefoot, "Investigation": 192.

42. Charles P. Nemeth, "Erosion of Privacy Right and Polygraphs," *Forensic Science International* 21 (1984): 103.

43. Mark Handler et al., "A Focused Polygraph Technique for PCSOT and Law Enforcement Screening Programs," *Polygraph* 38 (2009): 77; Amy-May Leach et al., "The Reliability of Lie Detection Performance," *Law &Human Behavior* (February 2009): 96; "Other Workplace Standards: Lie Detector Tests—Who is Covered," U.S. Department of Labor, Employment Law Guide, https://webapps.dol.gov/elaws/elg/eppa.htm#who.

44. U.S. Department of Labor, "Employee Rights: Employee Polygraph Protection Act," www.dol.gov/whd/regs/compliance/posters/eppac.pdf.

45. "Employee Background Checks," Betterteam, www.betterteam.com/employee-background-checks.

46. Laura P. Worsinger, "Tips for Background Checks," *Security Management* (October 2006): 85; BetterTeam, "Employee Background Checks."

12 The Security Office: Administrative Issues

12.1 SOME GENERAL PRINCIPLES OF OFFICE ADMINISTRATION

Security investigators will quickly discover that an organized method of investigation will make life easier and more productive for themselves and their supervisors. Being organized is a very enviable trait for the security professional. At its base, the security industry is a business which seeks a profit, which engages its clients in order that a cost will not exceed a benefit and that the security operative and his or her business will be fruitful. Hence, there is an ongoing need for internal processes which track and trace the business. One security expert referred to the security business and operation as a sort of "ecosystem" that needs to be tracked at every level including "applicant tracking, onboarding, security operations, scheduling, payroll, invoicing, accounting, and other business operations."[1]

Learn, early on, to organize and document. When in doubt, create a form, an exhibit, a checklist, a document, a chart, a graph—some system for controlling the ebb and flow of the investigative process. A failure to be administratively efficient is one of the chief causes of a loss in corporate profits. A lack of organization has economic consequences for any commercial operation, from lost property to pilfered goods and, just as critically, employees that will remain unchecked if not tracked by internal documentation relating to performance and task.[2]

The security business is no different; without a routine, standardized operational procedure, the company for which the security operative works will suffer. Robert Half, president of Robert Half International (a personnel service center with 86 offices worldwide), refers to this phenomenon as "time theft," a sort of unintentional, even normative behavior that regularly occurs at offices in the business and industrial sector and results in an inefficient administrative operation.[3] Currently, the ten most common methods for wasting time include:

- Cellphone/texting
- Gossip
- The Internet
- Social media
- Snack breaks or smoke breaks
- Noisy coworkers
- Meetings
- Email
- Coworkers dropping by
- Coworkers putting calls on speakerphone[4]

Security firms are just like any other business: Time wasted is money evaporating. Dominic Deeson describes time wasting as a form of theft and surely bad management practice that must be controlled.[5] The following seven "normal" workday tasks can also cut into an employee's productivity:

1. Unnecessary meetings
2. Unnecessary reports
3. Outdated processes

4. Too much communication
5. Unimportant data
6. Responding to distractions
7. Complaining and gossiping[6]

See Box 12.1 for a list of the "Top 40 Time Wasters Worldwide."

BOX 12.1   IN THE SPIRIT OF "TIME IS MONEY," A LIST OF THE TOP 40 TIME WASTERS

Top 40 Time Wasters Worldwide

PLANNING

1. Lack objectives/priorities/planning
2. Crisis management, shifting priorities
3. Attempting too much at once/unrealistic time estimates
4. Waiting for planes/appointments
5. Travel
6. Haste/impatience

ORGANIZING

7. Personal disorganization/cluttered desk
8. Confused responsibility and authority
9. Duplication of effort
10. Multiple bosses
11. Paperwork/red tape/reading
12. Poor filing system
13. Inadequate equipment/facilities

STAFFING

14. Untrained/inadequate staff
15. Under-/overstaffed
16. Absenteeism/tardiness/turnover
17. Personnel with problems
18. Overdependent staff

DIRECTING

19. Ineffective delegation/involved in routine details
20. Lack motivation/indifference
21. Lack coordination/teamwork

CONTROLLING

22. Telephone interruptions
23. Drop-in visitors
24. Inability to say "No"
25. Incomplete/delayed information

26. Lack self-discipline
27. Leaving tasks unfinished
28. Lack standards/controls/progress reports
29. Visual distractions/noise
30. Overcontrol
31. Not being informed
32. People not available for discussion

COMMUNICATING

33. Meetings
34. Lack/unclear communication, instructions
35. Socializing/idle conversation
36. "Memo-itis"/overcommunication
37. Failure to listen

DECISION MAKING

38. Procrastination/indecision
39. Wanting all the facts
40. Snap decisions

Aside from the economic disadvantages of inefficiency, any professional approach insists upon high-level organizational and administrative skills. Intelligent management dictates enlightened administrative practice.

12.2   TIMEKEEPING METHODS

From the outset of any security service, the tracking of time becomes a crucial step for the security professional. Clients are rightfully impressed with a well-organized security professional and just as rightfully distressed over the inefficient and bungling operative. As an example, missed, confused, or conflicting appointments cause a poor impression from the outset for any security firm. Track and memorialize appointment dates by using either appropriate systems, either manual or electronic, to monitor the calendar. Numerous companies worldwide deliver software programs that address appointment tracking and time and task management for the busy security professional. See Figure 12.1[7] outlining InTime Software Scheduling Software.

Insert Web Exercise: Check out software for timekeeping expressly developed for the security industry at: www.guard1.com/en/home.htm.

To avoid overlapping appointments, the investigator should make certain that he/she has some understanding or awareness of the depth and breadth of the case to be investigated. Fifteen minutes is not long enough for a case at first visitation. On the other hand, a relatively easy case, for which a portion can be handled by secondary personnel, such as the office secretary, should not be scheduled for a long period of time.

One method of assuring client awareness as to date and time of an appointment is the use of a reminder card or phone call. Historically, lawyers, doctors, and other professionals have used this method to jog a client's memory. Private security offices should give this practice consideration, particularly when the volume of appointments is steadily increasing.

Scheduling both personnel and assignments clearly produces internal office efficiency. It is a good idea to use schedule systems to keep track of upcoming appointments and field assignments.

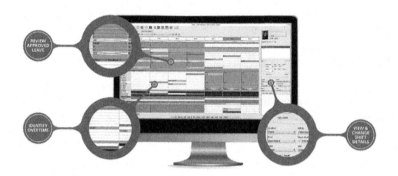

BUILD

InTime gives you the ability to easily build and view schedules weeks, months, even years in advance. Create a template, apply it to as many employees as applicable.

MAINTAIN

Once the heavy lifting is done, day-to-day maintenance of your schedule is a piece of cake. Daily operations like swapping shifts, temporary unit changes and putting employees on leave can be done in a matter of seconds

CONTROL

Bringing it full circle, InTime equips you with powerful oversight tools and reporting to help you stay within budget and measure the impact of your scheduling decisions.

FIGURE 12.1   Scheduling software can help in organization, time, and task management. (Used with Permission, InTime Solutions, Inc.)

(See Figure 12.2.) For those clients who fail to keep appointments, a memo, usually in the form of a postcard or letter, can be a courteous reminder, but this type of memo should have a positive personal flavor to maintain goodwill.

12.3   THE VALUE OF ADMINISTRATIVE DOCUMENTS

The initial client interview, claim evaluation, and maintenance of client contact have been covered in other portions of this text. As a case progresses, assuming that fee and contract agreements and other preliminary matters have been cleared up, some type of memory notation system should be adopted by the investigator and his or her employing firm. Forms for an insurance investigation request and for reporting the facts of an interview are presented in Table 12.1 and Box 12.2. By using forms of these types, the security investigator has convenient, though admittedly abbreviated information that can be inserted in the beginning of the file.

SCHEDULE				Effective Date:		
Client Name:				Subject:		Page of
SUNDAY	MONDAY	TUESDAY	WEDNESDAY	THURSDAY	FRIDAY	SATURDAY
Shift 1:	Shift 1:	Shift 1:	Shift 1:	Shift 1:	Shift 1:	Shift 1:
Shift 2:	Shift 2:	Shift 2:	Shift 2:	Shift 2:	Shift 2:	Shift 2:
Shift 3:	Shift 3:	Shift 3:	Shift 3:	Shift 3:	Shift 3:	Shift 3:

Officer:	Rank:	Badge:	Assignment:	Hours:
			Total Scheduled Hours	

FIGURE 12.2 Employee work schedule.

TABLE 12.1

An Insurance Investigation Request

INSURANCE INVESTIGATION REQUEST   File No:

Subject's Name _____ Date of request _____

Current Address _____ Phone Number _____

Previous Address _____

Employer _____ Job title _____ Phone Number _____

Client _____ Client file number _____

Address _____ Phone number _____

Requested by   Letter ☐   Phone ☐   Email ☐   New Case ☐   Rework ☐

Type of Case   ☐ Worker Compensation   ☐ Accident
                                ☐ No-fault   ☐ Uninsured motorist
                                ☐ Liability   ☐ Location
                                ☐ Medical Malpractice
                                ☐ Other _____

Budget/Time allocation _____

Nature of investigation _____

Subject description   DOB _____ Race _____ Sex _____

Height   Weight_____Hair_____ Eyes_____

Glasses_____ Mustache/Beard _____ Build _____

SSN _____ Other comments _____

Attorney _____

Spouse/dependents _____

Other parties involved _____

Vehicle information _____

Client special requests _____

BOX 12.2   AN INTERVIEW REPORT

INTERVIEW REPORT

Case Name: _____ Interview Date: _____

Case Number: _____ Interview Duration: _____ To _____

Interviewer: _____

Name of Person Interviewed: _____

Location of interview: _____

Relationship to subject: _____

Detailed summary of interview: _____

_____
_____
_____
_____
_____
_____
_____
_____
_____
_____
_____
_____
_____

The investigator should not merely collect information, but adopt methods which make the information meaningful and understandable at a later date. One of the recurring flaws in security practice and procedure is the duplicity and haphazard maintenance of the information collected. In order for information gathering to be a profitable exercise, the investigator must pare down information and employ language that is universally understood by all parties that may be granted access to the file. While forms, checklists, and other exhibits focus and cohesively preserve a wealth of information, the content of these documents must be prepared in such a way that benefits the investigative team. The clientele the security firm serves has better things to do than to wade through pages of redundant material or decipher long-winded reports. The importance of selecting the correct facts to include in a report cannot be emphasized enough:

> There was a time when investigators were encouraged to write as much as possible; that time has passed. Our clients today do not have the time to wade through pages and pages of chitchat prepared by an investigator on a daily basis. Our clients are paying good money for cold, hard fact. They have learned to expect it, and they are determined to get it. This does not mean investigators should be told to use their own initiative as to what should and what should not go into a report. Quite often, neither you nor the investigator can evaluate the importance of a piece of information to your client. The facts should be in, but the report need not finish off like the great American novel![8]

At the conference or personal visitation level, some formal notation should be made regarding results. The security officer should be allowed to write out impressions and obligations resulting from those discussions on a conference note form. As the investigation progresses, the security officer may wish to use the same form for jotting down specific factual or legal issues as well as mental impressions that may become a part of the greater picture.

Aside from documenting the facts, circumstances, and conditions in the investigation, these forms and documents serve another critical purpose: protecting the security firm and operative from the accusations of professional malpractice and negligence. The problem of malpractice is substantial in private security, so thorough, accurate record keeping is an intelligent defense mechanism. For instance, private security firms and individuals are coming under threats of litigation for their failure to perform their jobs in a professional manner. Correspondence and solid, written documentation, if adopted and routinely employed, can refute allegation and innuendo. The forms and documents become part of the case's permanent record and adequately defend an accusation of professional incompetence.

12.3.1 SOFTWARE CONSIDERATIONS

Software systems are now normal for the security office. Software packages are readily available to the industry although there are a bevy of consultants and companies. A variety of companies have set out to assist businesses in the coordination of all activities related to the complexities of file and case management. Some of these software products have been examined previously in this text. If the software system accomplishes the following ends, it is worth consideration:

1. Generates form letters for contact with clients, witnesses, and experts with corresponding authorizations
2. Provides either a chronological or sequential review of documents, witnesses or events, and conditions involving the case at hand
3. Has document indexing capacity
4. Is a compatible system with a run-of-the-mill PC rather than some sophisticated, avant-garde system that is not interchangeable
5. Is easy to edit
6. Produces a simple display screen
7. Can search simple to complex ideas and issues
8. Can provide document coding
9. Has data files which are flexible in that titles can be changed easily
10. Provides information that is relevant to the firm's most usual form of investigation
11. Is easily learned

Of course, as the firm's investigative practice becomes more sophisticated and the experiential base of all participating investigators expands, the software should have the capacity to archive information. One of the beauties behind technology is its ability to store repetitive information and to compare and contrast cases with similar or different fact patterns. It pays to have software that creates a database that is easily accessible, not only for use in the present case, but also cases which will occur in the future. Tracking of documents, witnesses, and fact analysis is most helpful. See Figures 12.3[9] and 12.4[10] for a few sample advertisements.

Home   ITrac   Services   Client Tools   Links   Contact Us   Admin

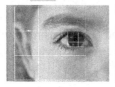

ITrac - Case Management System

ITrac is a Case Management Software customized to serve Private Investigation firms and individual investigators. ITrac is a Relational Database that keeps track of all your case information. Try our Free Demo to see how easy it is to enter and retrieve your case details. ITrac stores all of the information related to each case. Your case reports, which can be merged from case information, media (video and audio that can be streamed online), invoices, expenses, and more! Your investigators can use ITrac to update case information and create case reports directly. You won't need to flip through paper files any more, everything related to a case is right where you need it, when you need it!

* Detailed Information
* Pricing and Services
* Sign Up!

ITrac is web based. Your data is always available from anywhere, and it is always backed up. You can access and work with your files using any computer with a web browser and Internet connection.

* Store and deliver surveillance video and audio statements to your clients.
* Securely deliver case reports, documents, images, and files to your clients.
* Clients can request new case assignments securely online.
* Investigators can upload video, audio, generate reports, and update case notes for assigned cases.
* Create professional invoices with your logo.
* Reminders & notifications for cases that have items coming due.

Highlights

* Stores All Related Case Information
* Streaming Media (Video / Audio) for case content
* Easy to Use
* Includes free Unlimited Access for your clients!
* Your logo and custom report templates on all versions

Detailed Information Online Video Demo

* Case Entry
* General Navigation
* Media Upload

FIGURE 12.3   Digital Aerospace Solutions website. (Used with permission, Digital Aerospace Solutions.)

FIGURE 12.4 Trackops investigation management software website. (Used with permission, Trackops, LLC.)

Built for security professionals, Trackforce helps track your employees, manage visitors, and produce incident reports to improve accountability and operations. The software provides the capability to customize client and activity reports, with desktop (Post) and two mobile products (m-Post and Patrol) available. See Figure 12.5.[11]

Silvertrac is another popular guard management software program that provides automated reports, officer performance tracking, client and officer communication. The software also features advanced reporting and management capabilities to improve organizational efficiency. See Figure 12.6.[12]

OfficerReports.com has an easy to use platform for officers, which includes daily activity and incident reports and checklists, post orders, and policy manuals.[13] For smaller companies electronic report templates may be an excellent option. Investigator Marketing.com provides an "Investigator's Bundle" of electronic templates at an affordable price. The package includes a retainer agreement, surveillance report, and an investigation invoice, among others.[14]

Web Exercise: Visit Capterra's website to explore many software vendors in the investigations field at: www.capterra.com/investigation-management-software/.

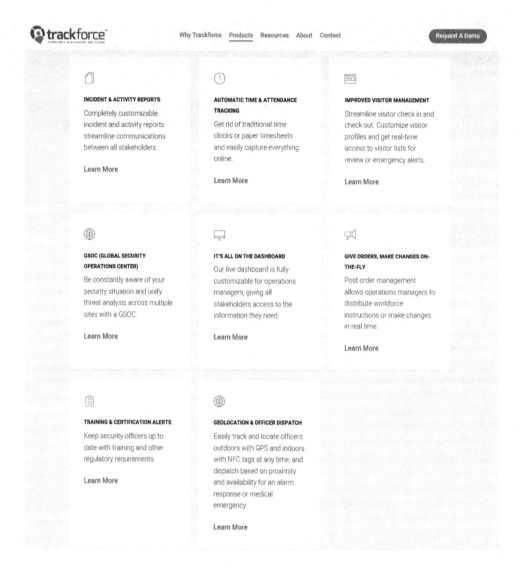

FIGURE 12.5 Trackforce's website. (Used with permission, Trackforce.)

12.4   FILING SYSTEMS

12.4.1   Setup and Maintenance

An effective filing system is mandatory to promote a competent investigation. Just imagine the security professional, operating under a deadline, who cannot locate the necessary information regarding parties, places, and conditions. Envision the security investigator who receives a call from a client inquiring about case status, and the file is buried deeply beneath a stack of papers or other documents arranged without rhyme or reason. In any office, time spent searching is time wasted.

First, the filing system should be centralized—that is, in one location, with one person appointed to assure the integrity and organization of the system. When a file has been removed, it should be returned to that location for refiling.

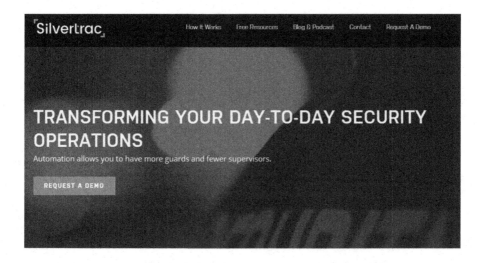

Meet with your client and identify responsibilities

Tell Silvertrac what's expected from your officers

Take appropriate action

Silvertrac notifies you of any problems

Run a Tighter Operation

Are your security operations running as smoothly as possible? Are your personnel completing all of their work? Are you aware of any flaws in your system? Unfortunately, identifying gaps in operations is a time-consuming process that pulls your attention away from important tasks.

Silvertrac is a secret weapon for automatically identifying inefficiencies in your organization. With a variety of automated reports, you and your supervisors can stay constantly aware of urgent issues, underperforming personnel, and more. Let us arm you with information so you can take action.

FIGURE 12.6 Silvertrac's website. (Used with permission, Silvertrac Software.)

The filing classifications depend upon the scope, type, and style of investigation but should follow these guidelines:

- Current matters
- Correspondence
- Billing
- Drafts
- Extra copies
- Invoices/receipts
  - Paid
  - Unpaid
- Memoranda (internal)
- Research
- Telephone calls
- Work papers
- Photographs/videos
- Investigative reports
- Witness statements

If correspondence with several parties is anticipated, individual folders are suggested. Various techniques for filing systems exist. An example of a subject matter filing system is reproduced at Figure 12.7.

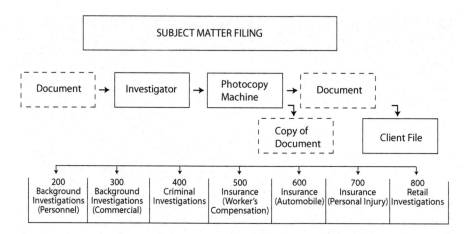

FIGURE 12.7   A suggested subject matter filing system.

As the form indicates, subjects have been designated by numerical code. A numerical coding system saves space, offers quick reference, and can be easily integrated in a computerized filing system. The numerical system can be further enhanced by the use of color coding. The numerical filing system should also be as informative as possible to help persons unfamiliar with the case to know its dynamics at a glance. A numerical system provides a quick reference guide for storage and disposal techniques. The system should indicate the name of the client; the year the file was opened; the number of the case for that year; and the number code assigned to the type of investigation. As an example:

New client Sam Brown meets with investigator John Lee in January 2018 desiring surveillance of employees suspected of theft activities. The file then could be identified in this manner:

Brown, Sam 18-0005.200

The coding indicates Brown, Sam (client); 18 (year file opened); 0005 (case number for year opened); 200 (number code for theft).

The folders should have tabs extending a little above the expanding files so that they are quickly visible, and documents should be contained within the folders with the use of some form of clip to prevent loss. Generally, insertion should be chronological with the latest information on top. Insertion arrangements depend on the particular documents being filed and should be mutually agreed upon by security personnel and the file maintainer.

12.4.2   TICKLER FILES

The security profession is regulated by both clock and calendar. Clients have a natural expectation for their time to be used wisely regarding both the end result and related costs. Therefore, it is essential to have a tracking system which comprehensively outlines upcoming events in each case. One such system is a tickler system, which is very effective and consists of:

- $3'' \times 5'' \times 12''$ cardboard index card box
- Several sets of 1-31 daily index card dividers
- One set of January-December monthly index card dividers
- Yearly index card dividers
- Supply of index cards in several colors

The dividers and cards should be arranged as follows, from the front of the index card box to the back:

- Current year
- Current month
- Set of daily dividers
- Next several months with daily dividers
- Remaining months to December
- Next year
- January to prior month divider
- Remaining years
- Blank cards

The cards may also be color-coded, for example:

White: Client billable matters
Green: Non-billable matters
Yellow: Personal
Blue: Names of people you meet, per occasion, by date
Orange: Quotations
Red: Important deadlines[15]

A simple reminder method is to use a special memo form such as that shown in Box 12.3. The security operative needs only to check the matter to be performed and to place it in numbered files, which should be checked on a daily basis.

BOX 12.3   A TICKLER MEMO USED AS A REMINDER

TICKLER MEMO

Client Name: _____Client No.:

Investigator: _____Date: _____

Reminder:

Appointment with:
Meeting scheduled with:
Place:
Date:_____Time: _____, Confirmed (Y/N)
Interview with (witness name):
Statute of Limitations expires:
File Report.
Bill Client.
Close file.
Follow-up.

Notes:

Other types of reminder systems such as a large calendar or a desk date book can also be used. The choice of systems generally depends on the size of the security firm and corresponding work-load of its personnel.

12.4.3 SOFTWARE CONSIDERATIONS

Report Exec provides a wide range of reporting, operational, and analysis modules, including a mobile platform, in its software suite to cover all documentation needs. See Figure 12.8.[16]

i-Sight is an intuitive case management software designed by investigators, for investigators. The software has been developed to grow with an investigator's expanding needs, from intake to investigation reports and case history tracking. See Figure 12.9[17] for a representation of available features.

PI Direct is another all-encompassing program for companies ranging in size from a solo PI to companies with 15 or more investigators. System features include case management tasks, social media investigations, form and report generation, and evidence and document storage.

12.5 BILLING

Of all the administrative tasks a security professional performs, calculation of expenses and recording of billable time is decidedly a priority. The security professional must be diligent in this endeavor because clients, no matter how friendly or well intentioned, may be slow to pay their bills. Figure 12.10[18] charts the progression of a legal case. The diagram show that all billings must be completely calculated and sent to the client expeditiously because there is a natural decrease in a client's willingness to pay bills as time passes. A comparable pattern is applicable in the private security setting.

Financial responsibility and bill collection are certainly not favored activities in the security office. However, without sound economic practices and client fiscal responsibility, the office is placed in jeopardy. Pinkerton's, Inc. urges its employees to act with sound business judgment.

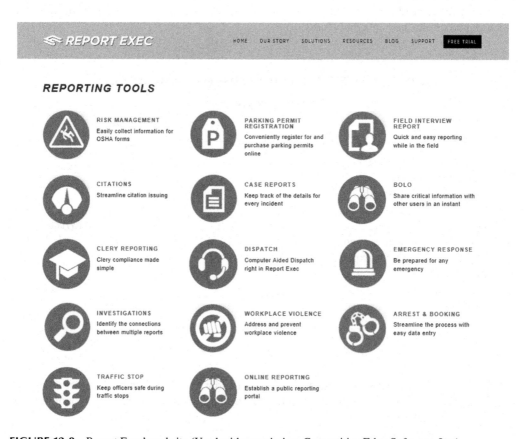

FIGURE 12.8   Report Exec's website (Used with permission, Competitive Edge Software, Inc.)

INVESTIGATION DASHBOARD

DASHBOARD

Dashboards display complex information about investigations in an easy-to-understand graphical format. Read More

REPORTING FOR BUSINESS INTELLIGENCE

REPORTS

With all investigation data stored in a central repository, powerful data reporting and analysis are fast and easy. Read More

ONE-CLICK INVESTIGATION REPORTS

INVESTIGATION REPORTS

Create final case reports in seconds, with the click of a mouse, saving hours of administrative time and effort. Read More

SMART WORKFLOWS

WORKFLOW

i-Sight is structured to ensure all information is collected, steps are never missed, and there's a complete record of every action taken during an investigation. Read More

CASE ASSIGNMENT

INTAKE

Assign cases manually or automatically, based on defined criteria. i-Sight streamlines case assignment so that nothing falls through the cracks. Read More

ANONYMOUS ETHICS HOTLINE

HOTLINE

Capture every report with an ethics hotline. Uncover problems early, address them quickly and maintain a safe and ethical workplace. Read More

AUDITABLE CASE HISTORY

TRACKING

Each case file contains the entire history of the investigation and provides a complete audit trail, which can be exported as a comprehensive investigation report. Read More

INTEGRATE WITH EXISTING SYSTEMS

INTEGRATION

Integrate i-Sight with your existing databases to eliminate time consuming data entry tasks or to ensure that other internal systems have up-to-date investigation information. Read More

WEB-ENABLED AND MOBILE-OPTIMIZED

MOBILE FRIENDLY

i-Sight delivers the tools you need to manage your investigations remotely and effectively through a simple, intuitive web interface. Read More

COLLABORATION AND ACCESS ROLES

ACCESS ROLES

Collaborate on cases and communicate with others in real time with secure, role-based access from anywhere at any time. Read More

EMAIL TO CASE

EMAIL

Send emails, files and attachments of any type directly and securely into case files from inside or outside i-Sight. Read More

QUICK NOTES

NOTES

You can quickly add notes from inside a case file or simply by clicking on the + button from anywhere in i-Sight. Read More

ATTACHMENTS AND EVIDENCE

EVIDENCE

Add attachments and digital evidence to the centralized case file by emailing files, attaching a file to a note or simply saving the evidence directly to the case file. Read More

QUICK AND EASY SEARCH

SEARCH

Search across the entire investigation database or within a specific field to find the information you need by entering your keyword into i-Sight's powerful search function. Read More

MANAGEMENT OVERSIGHT

OVERSIGHT

Ensure real-time oversight of cases, timely case review, and track time, expenses, restitution and recoveries with ease. Read More

CUSTOMIZED

BRANDABLE

Customizing i-Sight with your logo, colors and company branding has been shown to improve adoption and user comfort. Read More

FIGURE 12.9   i-Sight's website (Used with permission, i-Sight.)

You have all been called to the office of a prospective client with whom you are unfamiliar. You do not know the man, you are not fully acquainted with his business, and common sense tells you that you must take precautions. Are you really embarrassed when you ask this man to prove his financial stability? Do you really think that he is going to be embarrassed when you put the question to him? The answer to both questions, gentlemen, is negative. If your client is a businessman, he will respect your concern. If you are tactful and polite, no harm is done, and you will have safeguarded your position. At this particular point, you must make a decision. Is this man going to pay his bill when you want him to pay it? If you believe the answer is "No," you must ask for a retainer.

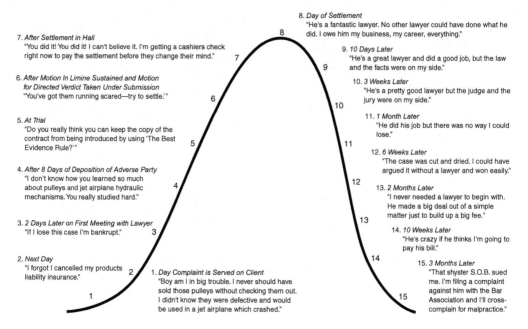

8. Day of Settlement
"He's a fantastic lawyer. No other lawyer could have done what he did. I owe him my business, my career, everything."

7. After Settlement in Hall
"You did it! You did it! I can't believe it. I'm getting a cashiers check right now to pay the settlement before they change their mind."

9. 10 Days Later
"He's a great lawyer and did a good job, but the law and the facts were on my side."

6. After Motion In Limine Sustained and Motion for Directed Verdict Taken Under Submission
"You've got them running scared—try to settle.'"

10. 3 Weeks Later
"He's a pretty good lawyer but the judge and the jury were on my side."

5. At Trial
"Do you really think you can keep the copy of the contract from being introduced by using 'The Best Evidence Rule?'"

11. 1 Month Later
"He did his job but there was no way I could lose."

4. After 8 Days of Deposition of Adverse Party
"I don't know how you learned so much about pulleys and jet airplane hydraulic mechanisms. You really studied hard."

12. 6 Weeks Later
"The case was cut and dried. I could have argued it without a lawyer and won easily."

3. 2 Days Later on First Meeting with Lawyer
"If I lose this case I'm bankrupt."

13. 2 Months Later
"I never needed a lawyer to begin with. He made a big deal out of a simple matter just to build up a big fee."

2. Next Day
"I forgot I cancelled my products liability insurance."

1. Day Complaint is Served on Client
"Boy am I in big trouble. I never should have sold those pulleys without checking them out. I didn't know they were defective and would be used in a jet airplane which crashed."

14. 10 Weeks Later
"He's crazy if he thinks I'm going to pay his bill."

15. 3 Months Later
"That shyster S.O.B. sued me. I'm filing a complaint against him with the Bar Association and I'll cross-complain for malpractice."

FIGURE 12.10   The Client's Curve of Gratitude from *How to Start and Build a Law Practice*, 5th Ed. (Used with permission, Jay G. Foonberg and the American Bar Association.)

A retainer in full, covering all possible time and all possible expenses. If you believe the answer to be "Yes," may I advise you still to take certain elementary precautions. Ask with whom your client's business does its banking. You will have no problem; he'll willingly tell you, and from then on it is a simple matter to have your own bank make a credit check for you, to ascertain if your client is good for the amount estimated by you as being the final bill.[19]

The security guard or investigator should adhere to company directives and policies in setting fees. The costs of undertaking any security activity should be planned, weighed in advance of performance, and calculated for costs. Figures 12.11 and Figure 12.12 are good models to follow in recording preliminary and ongoing facts.

Of greater relevance is the investigator's responsibility to keep track of the time spent on billable tasks. Oftentimes this is tracked to the payroll function and role of the company. Even so, payroll in the "security service business is not rocket science, but that does not mean it is easy. Paying people for the hours that they work ties into scheduling, time and attendance, industrial relations, human resource management, and billing."[20] The investigator may use a time and expense report to fully track dates of service, correspondence, and related expenses, such as transportation fares, telephone, meals, lodging, and other miscellaneous expenses (Figure 12.13), or a general expenses form such as that shown in Figure 12.14. Another way is to use a credit card for expenses and record them on a verification form (Figure 12.15).

Out-of-pocket expenses for travel and travel-related matters such as client entertainment, tolls, parking, etc., may be recorded on forms such as those presented in Figures 12.16 and 12.17. These expenses noticeably influence the profit and loss statement of any investigative practice. Some firms track both the traveler's expenditures and original acquisition costs. (With the differences in the fees charged by airlines and other transportation carriers, proper preliminary planning and selection should be substantial considerations.) Other security firms often make available to their agents and investigators an advance of funds or an expense account from which they may draw funds. The security professional should realize that the advance is neither salary nor wages but is a loan of the company's money to cover expenses. Any amount beyond ordinary and reasonable expenditures should be returned to the firm.

Preliminary Fact Investigation	
Timekeeper	Hours

Task Assumptions

State Date _____ End Date _____ Approximate Duration _____

Tasks to consider:
* Conduct client interviews
* Conduct witness interviews
* Prepare memos to file
* Review public documents
* Analyze documents

Assumptions:

Cost Assumptions

Costs to consider:
* Copying
* Document processing
* Online research
* Investigator fees
* Travel

Assumptions:

FIGURE 12.11 Report form used to file results of preliminary investigation.

Another type of form is a general time slip to track various types of services. An ongoing record can outline for a client the bills that might otherwise result in a form of "sticker shock." This type of form is shown in Figure 12.18. Regular completion of such documents creates a record upon which the investigator and client can rely. It also increases dramatically one's ability to collect such expenses.

After all billable hours have been calculated, expenditures have been surveyed and accounted for, and expenses related to travel, telephone, and other ordinary and reasonably related matters have

On-Going Fact Investigation	
Timekeeper	Hours

Task Assumptions

State Date _____ End Date _____ Approximate Duration _____

Tasks to consider:

* Conduct client interviews
* Conduct witness interviews
* Review selected client documents
* Review publicly available documents
* Analyze and organize documents

Assumptions:

Cost Assumptions

Costs to consider:
* Copying
* Document processing
* Online research
* Investigator fees
* Travel

Assumptions:

FIGURE 12.12 Ongoing fact investigation report.

TIME AND EXPENSE REPORT

Client _____   Operation _____

Billing address _____   Client Account No. _____

_____   Phone _____

Services				Amount	Total amount
Inv.	Dates	Hours/day	Rate		
				Total➜	

Expenses:

Local & Bus fares
Telephone
Auto expense
Meals
Other travel expense
Lodging

Miscellaneous: _____
(Itemize) _____
_____

Total➜

Grand total _____

Attach all items to support expenses

FIGURE 12.13 Sample form used to list expenses and track time on each individual investigation.

OFFICE EXPENSE MEMORANDUM

Client _____   Client Account No. _____

Operation _____   For the month of _____ 20 _____

Investigator _____   Date submitted _____

Date	Description	Expense		Surcharge		Total billable	
	Totals						

_____
       Investigator

FIGURE 12.14   Form on which expenses are listed.

VERIFICATION OF CHARGE CARD PURCHASES				
Employee _____		For month of _____		
Date	Description	Amount	Billed to	Client No.
	Total			

Employee

FIGURE 12.15 Verification of charge card purchase form.

EXPENSE REPORT

Name _____

Period Ending _____

Day/Date	Case #	Mileage	Lodging	Per Diem	Entertainment	Tolls/Parking	Miscellaneous	Daily Totals
Sunday								
Monday								
Tuesday								
Wednesday								
Thursday								
Friday								
Saturday								
Sub-Total								
Other								
Total Expenses Reported								
Total Expenses Due								

PURPOSE OF TRIP

SUMMARY

Total Expenses	
Less Cash Advance	
Less Company Charges	
Amount Due Employee	
Amount Due Company	

Prepared by _____ Date _____

Approved by _____ Date _____

FIGURE 12.16 Sample of expense report form.

EXPENSE STATEMENT

Client Name	Case Number	File Number

Date	Expense Total	

☐ **Travel**

From	To	

Starting Mileage	Ending Mileage	Total Mileage

☐ Personal Auto　　　　　　　☐ Business Auto

☐ Air　☐ Taxi　☐ Bus　☐ Train　☐ Subway　Total:

☐ **Phone Calls**

To:

City:	State:	Phone Number:

Made by:

☐ Personal Phone Bill　　　☐ Credit Card　　　☐ Collect

☐ **Entertainment**

Where

Client Name

Purpose

☐ **Other**

☐ Postage　　　☐ Parking　　　☐ Photocopies: Number _____　　　☐ Other

Signature:　　　　　　　　　　　Date:

FIGURE 12.17　Sample expense statement.

TIME SLIP

Client Name: Case Number:

Concerning

_____

Type of Activity   Total Time Charged:

Notes:

_____

_____

_____

_____

_____

Signature: Date:

FIGURE 12.18 Sample time slip.

been tabulated, an invoice should be submitted to the client. A basic billing format is at Box 12.4. Box 12.5, Figure 12.19, and Table 12.2 present other pertinent forms that aid in the billing process.

BOX 12.4

NAME OF SECURITY COMPANY
123 ABC Street
Anytown, USA 00000

TO:

FOR SERVICES RENDERED:

BOX 12.5   SAMPLE DAILY TIME AND EXPENSE SUMMARY

DAILY TIME RECORD AND EXPENSE SUMMARY

Subject _____
Case Number _____ Date _____
Investigator _____
Travel time _____ Surveillance Time _____
Mileage _____
Expenses: Please list and attach receipts.

Vehicle Driven _____

Cell Phone Charges. Please attach phone log and list of charges

Report Time _____

SUMMARY OF ACTIVITIES

Cash Statement

Date Submitted		Office		Name (Print)		Period Ending	

Date		Supervisor's	Amount		Date		Supervisor's	Amount	
Month	Day	Initials	Advances	Expenses	Month	Day	Initials	Advances	Expenses
						Totals Forwarded			
		Totals Forward					Grand Totals		

FIGURE 12.19 Sample record of advances and cash expenditures.

TABLE 12.2
Sample Weekly Time Sheet

Weekly Time Sheet						
Employee Name		Employee Number		From		To
Date	Case#	Office	Travel	Surveillance	U/C	Total Hours
Total by Activity Type						
					Grand Total	
Employee Signature:				Date:		
Supervisor Signature:				Date:		

Finally, legitimate office procedure can be careless about documenting incidents and/or injuries at the work location. A formal report should recount how the injury occurred, what the function or task of the employee was, and what level of benefits exist.

12.5.1 SOFTWARE CONSIDERATIONS

CROSStrax Investigation billing software tracks and facilitates billing and expenses as well as client invoicing. CROSStrax provides a simple interface for investigators to track time and/or activity. In addition, the software includes report templates, case histories, case notes, and integrated email. See Figure 12.20.[21] Officer Reports.com has time and attendance software to help take care of scheduling, payroll, and client billing. See Figure 12.21.[22]

Virtual Case Management software for private investigators provides a customizable system to help you manage your cases, contacts, documents, communication, and accounting. The system features seamless email integration, online payment processing, and invoice creation. See Figure 12.22.[23]

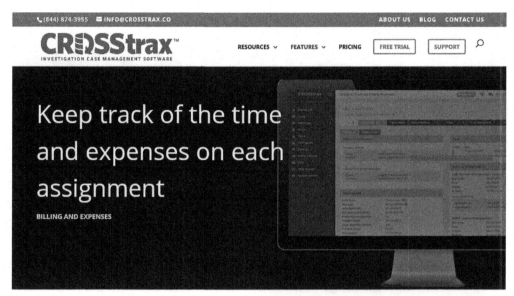

Investigation Billing Software

Investigation billing software that tracks and facilitates billing and expenses as well as client invoicing. CROSStrax has the financial tracking integration you need to make informed business decisions.

CROSStrax provides a simple interface for investigators to track time and/or activity. Each activity is recorded with a description of the activity, the person who performed the activity and the amount of time spent, acting as an online timesheet.

Your investigative staff can easily input and track their case related time and expenses through CROSStrax. When it comes time to invoice your customer, you'll be able to convert all billable time and expenses into an invoice with a click of a mouse!

FIGURE 12.20 CROSStrax website. (Used with permission, CROSStrax, LLC.)

Security Guard Time and Attendance Software

Save time
scheduling officers

Schedule officers online in minutes. Get alerts for
open posts to help eliminate liability. Officers can
view their schedules anywhere, anytime, from
any device.

Control clock-in
and clock-out
activity

Control when and where officers clock-in and
clock-out with GPS based time clock tools.
Monitor activity and receive alerts when
officers are not clocked-in on time.

Simplify Client
Billing

Create and export time clock summary
reports with just a few simple clicks to
verify billable hours by officer, site, or
client for hassle-free invoicing.

Streamline
Officer Payroll

Eliminate data entry and streamline payroll.
Customize your payroll settings and export
data straight to payroll processors, such as
ADP PayForce or PayChoice.

FIGURE 12.21 OfficerReports.com website. (Used with permission, OfficerReports.com.)

FIGURE 12.22 Virtual Case Management's website. (Reprinted with permission of VirtualCaseManagement.com. All rights reserved.)

12.6 CONCLUSION

This completes our examination of the investigative process in the security industry. The final topic dwells on the administrative tasks so crucial for effective delivery of privatized investigative services, from tracking employee performance to office tools, both soft and documentary, which trace activity, from mechanisms to calculate bills and billable activities to programs that compute travel and other reimbursement. An office that does not function correctly is an operation that will not be able to meet its promised services. In addition, the industry needs tracking tools which monitor not only the work and outcomes of the services provided but also provide a means and method to keep employees on the straight and narrow. And in the end, a well-managed office minimizes potential legal liabilities. "Employers have a duty to keep their people safe. Whether your employees are on-site or travelling, in a cubicle or on a construction site, in the States or abroad, that duty remains—to protect your employees from unnecessary risk of harm. But an increasingly mobile and global workforce has brought new challenges to fulfilling these obligations."[24]

Private security plays an integral role in the legal, economic, and social fabric of this nation. From insurance investigations to asset protection, private security personnel involve themselves in most major institutions, including schools, universities, museums, entertainment complexes, Fortune 500 companies, and the majority of the retail and commercial marketplaces. It is hoped that this work leaves the reader an eclectic impression of the functions of private security and, perhaps, a sense of awe for the future of this great undertaking.

NOTES

1. See Mark Folmer, "The Guard Scheduling Conundrum," *Security Management*, August 2017, https://sm.asisonline.org/Pages/The-Guard-Scheduling-Conundrum.aspx.
2. See Mark Tarallo, "The Fraudster Down the Hall," *Security Management*, August 2018, https://sm.asisonline.org/Pages/The-Fraudster-Down-the-Hall.aspx.
3. R. Half, "Time Death: How Bosses Can Reduce Ranks of Goof-Offs," *USA Today*, January 3, 1985; see also Jack Gordon, "Wasting Time on the Company Dime," *Training*, May 2006: 6; George M. Naimark, "Stop Wasting Valuable Time," *Harvard Business Review*, December 2004: 143; M. E. Brock, L. E. Martin, and M. R. Buckley, "Time Banditry," *International Journal of Selection and Assessment* 21 (2013): 309–321, https://onlinelibrary-wiley-com.ez.lib.jjay.cuny.edu/doi/full/10.1111/ijsa.12040; Y. Liu and C. M. Berry, "Identity, Moral, and Equity Perspectives on the Relationship between Experienced Injustice and Time Theft," *Journal of Business Ethics* 118, no. 1 (2013): 73–83, doi:http://dx.doi.org.ez.lib.jjay.cuny.edu/10.1007/s10551-012-1554-5.
4. V. Fludd, "Workplace Productivity Drains," *Talent Development* 6, no. 9 (2014): 20.
5. Dominic Deeson, "Time Wasting Is Theft and Bad Management," *Management Services*, Spring 2005: 3; Brock, Martin, and Buckley, "Time Banditry"; Liu and Berry, "Equity Perspectives."
6. John Boitnott, "7 Tasks You Do Every Day that Waste Time and Cost Your Business Money," October 4, 2016, *Entrepreneur*, www.entrepreneur.com/article/283205.
7. "Scheduling Software," inTime Software, https://intime.com/solutions/scheduling-software.
8. Pinkerton's Inc., *Administration of the Investigations Department* (1990): 4.
9. "Itrac Case Management System," Digital Aerospace Solutions, accessed September 12, 2018, www.1das.com/main.aspx.
10. "Home page," Trackops, accessed September 12, 2018, https://trackops.com/.
11. "POST Security Operation Apps," Trackforce, accessed September 3, 2018, https://trackforce.com/post-security-operation-app/#post_features; for a flowchart which tracks client and case, see Charles P. Nemeth, *The Paralegal Resource Manual*, 3rd ed. (Anderson Publishing, 2008): 319.
12. "Automated Security Guard Management," Silvertrac, accessed September 12, 2018, www.silvertracsoftware.com/automated-security-guard-management.
13. Officer Reports.com, http://officerreports.com/products.html.
14. "Investigators Bundle," Investigator marketing.com, https://investigatormarketing.com/shop/#included.
15. Pennsylvania Bar Institute, *The Pennsylvania Young Lawyer's Handbook* (1984): 28.
16. "Solutions," ReportExec, http://reportexec.com/solutions.
17. "Software," i-Sight, https://i-sight.com/features/.

18. Jay G. Foonberg, *How to Start and Build a Law Practice*, 5th ed. (American Bar Association, 2004): 309.
19. Pinkerton's, "Administration": 12.
20. See Mark Folmer, "Speak the Language of Payroll," *Security Management*, January 2018, https://sm.asisonline.org/Pages/Speak-the-Language-of-Payroll.aspx.
21. "Billing and Expenses," Crosstrax, www.crosstrax.co/crosstrax-features/billing-and-expenses.
22. "Time and Attendance Software," Officer Reports.com, http://officerreports.com/time-and-attendance-software.html.
23. "Private Investigators &Process Servers," Virtual Case Management, www.virtualcasemanagement.com/private.aspx.
24. See Brett Andrew, "How to Use Technology to Improve Duty of Care Obligations," *Security Management*, August 14, 2018, www.securitymagazine.com/articles/89335-how-to-use-technology-to-improve-duty-of-care-obligations.

Index

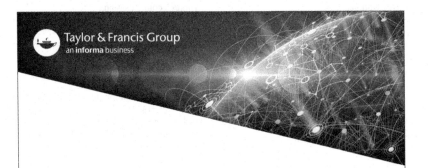

Printed in the United States
by Baker & Taylor Publisher Services